MARTIN & MALCOLM & AMERICA

Martin Luther King, Jr., and Malcolm X, at the U.S. Capitol, March 26, 1964.

MARTIN & MALCOLM & AMERICA

A Dream or a Nightmare

JAMES H. CONE

ORBIS BOOKS

Maryknoll, New York 10545

Tenth Printing, April 2022

Founded in 1970, Orbis Books endeavors to publish works that enlighten the mind, nourish the spirit, and challenge the conscience. The publishing arm of the Maryknoll Fathers and Brothers, Orbis seeks to explore the global dimensions of the Christian faith and mission, to invite dialogue with diverse cultures and religious traditions, and to serve the cause of reconciliation and peace. The books published reflect the views of their authors and do not represent the official position of the Maryknoll Society. To learn more about Maryknoll and Orbis Books, please visit our website at www.maryknollsociety.org.

Copyright © 1991, 2012 by James H. Cone
First paperback edition July, 1992
Published by Orbis Books, Maryknoll, NY 10545
Manufactured in the United States of America

Library of Congress Cataloging-in-Publication Data

Cone, James H.
    Martin & Malcolm & America: a dream or a nightmare / James H. Cone.
      p. cm.
    Includes bibliographical references and index.
    ISBN 0-88344-721-5 (cloth)   0-88344-824-6 (pbk.)
    1. King, Martin, Jr., 1929-1968 — Philosophy 2. X, Malcolm, 1925-1965 — Philosophy 3. King, Martin Luther, Jr., 1929-1968 — Religion. 4. X, Malcolm, 1925-1965 — Religion. 5. Afro-Americans — Intellectual life. 6. Afro-Americans — Religion. 7. United States — Race relations. 8. Black nationalism — United States. I. Title.
II. Title: Martin and Malcolm and America.
E185.97.K5C66 1991
973'.0496073022 — dc20
                                     90-14159
                                       CIP

To C. Eric Lincoln
Beloved Friend,
Scholar, and Teacher

CONTENTS

PREFACE TO THE TWENTIETH ANNIVERSARY EDITION

I had no choice but to write *Martin & Malcolm & America* when I did. Martin Luther King Jr. and Malcolm X were like two hot flames burning inside me that would not go out. They were burning when I sat down to write my first book, *Black Theology and Black Power* (1969), in the wake of the fires burning in Newark and Detroit during July 1967. Malcolm represented the flame of blackness in black theology and Martin the flame of faith in its Christian theological expression.

In the 1960s however, Malcolm and Martin, blackness and Christianity, were widely considered opposites. There was a war going on in black and white America between Martin and Malcolm. Everyone was forced to choose sides but I could not. They were like my left and right hands, both necessary for the full expression of my humanity and for my struggle to find my voice in the black freedom movement. I needed both Martin and Malcolm to defend black humanity under assault by white supremacy in America, and I understood why they talked differently about Christianity and blackness, nonviolence and violence, love and hate. I tried to demonstrate that in my writings about black liberation theology.

I thought about Martin and Malcolm as I developed the central themes *A Black Theology of Liberation* (1970), *The Spirituals and the Blues* (1972), and *God of the Oppressed* (1975), but their flames still burned hot within me. I continued to wrestle with both of them at a deeper level in order to understand more fully their political and cultural meaning. For nearly ten years before writing this text I immersed myself in their world, as they overshadowed nearly everything I thought, read, debated, and wrote. The Ronald Reagan and George Herbert Walker Bush years of the 1980s and early 1990s clearly showed how much America needed Martin and Malcolm, especially in light of the criminalization of black America expressed in the Willie Horton ad and the elevation of

Clarence Thomas to the Supreme Court. Rethinking *Martin & Malcolm & America* twenty years later, I realize that this book expresses what I wanted to say about these two great flames of freedom, and there is nothing to add or subtract.

Are Martin and Malcolm still needed in the twenty-first century—this so-called post-racial age? Have we moved beyond the need to talk about blackness? Are we not just Americans, no longer defined by the color of our skin? Perhaps. But I would not bet on it.

We need Martin and Malcolm today precisely because many people think we have moved beyond the need to talk about race. Nothing could be further from the truth. The rising dominance of conservative, right-wing religious and political discourse in our national life shows the enduring significance of race. The election of Barack Obama as the first black president has in many ways served to heighten racial awareness among white people, inciting some to defend their privilege, with many taking up the Tea Party's popular slogan, "Take back America." White supremacy has not gone away. It lurks behind the persistent doubt that Obama is a "real American," in the racial profiling/criminalization of young black males, in the stigmatizing of welfare and food stamp recipients, and in systematic efforts to disenfranchise black voters. It has merely changed its form of expression, making it difficult for some people to see it and to name it. In a persuasive analysis, Michelle Alexander calls it the "New Jim Crow." It is different from the Old Jim Crow, which was open and often legalized, defined by segregation and lynching. The New Jim Crow is less visible but it accomplishes the same thing—the subordination of blacks and the elevation of whites.

No one could name white supremacy like Martin and Malcolm. That is why we still need them. If we do not name white supremacy, we cannot destroy it. If we do not name it, we cannot get beyond it to what Martin called the "beloved community" and Malcolm called freedom for all human beings. We still need both of them to remind us as Americans that we are fighting against injustice in all its forms and fighting for the liberation of all people. As Martin put it: "Injustice anywhere is a threat to justice everywhere."

James H. Cone
June 2012

PREFACE

This book is about Martin Luther King, Jr., and Malcolm X—their relationship to each other and their meanings for America. The "dream" and "nightmare" images are used to focus their perspectives on America and to reveal something about the audiences to whom and for whom they spoke.

In memory as in life Martin King and Malcolm X are still highly controversial African-American leaders. More than twenty years after their assassinations, their names arouse passionate acceptance or rejection, and few people, black or white, have unbiased opinions about them. Thus it is important for any interpreter to beware of misleading notions about them that are promoted by both their admirers and detractors. The best way to gain reliable knowledge about Martin and Malcolm is through a careful examination of the life and thought of each figure in relation to the other and in the light of the two main resistance traditions in African-American history and culture—integrationism and nationalism.

In the introduction, the meaning of integrationism and nationalism for African-American intellectual history is briefly described, and a plea is made to freedom-loving Americans to turn to Martin and Malcolm for resources in the struggle for justice.

Chapters 1 and 2 analyze the social origins of Martin's dream and Malcolm's nightmare by examining the family contexts which shaped their perspectives on America.

In chapters 3 and 4, I examine the first stage of their thinking on the dream and nightmare—from the beginning of their public ministries in the 1950s through 1963 (Malcolm) and 1964 (Martin). This was the period when their differences were most pronounced, especially regarding their understanding of freedom and the means by which it could be achieved.

Martin and Malcolm were, respectively, Christian and Muslim ministers. Chapters 5 and 6 show how their views of America were influenced by their religious beliefs.

Popular images of Martin and Malcolm seldom acknowledge their movement toward each other and their break with earlier deeply held convictions about America. Malcolm's "chickens came home to roost" in 1963–65 (chapter 7). His heart-wrenching break with Elijah Muhammad, his spiritual father, initiated a new stage in his thinking. Malcolm began to acknowledge the value of Martin King's contribution to the black freedom movement. He began to advocate "hope," that is, the participation of African-Americans in the American political process.

Martin King's dream was shattered in 1965–68 (chapter 8) as he observed the nightmare in America's cities and on the battlefields of Vietnam. He began to talk like Malcolm X. In Martin's and Malcolm's radical shifts in perspective, they came to appreciate each other's views about America.

Martin and Malcolm illuminate the two roads to freedom that meet in the African-Americans' search for identity in the land of their birth. These roads are traveled in chapter 9.

Martin and Malcolm were nothing but men, with all the strengths and weaknesses pertaining to their gender. Only as we consider their weaknesses (chapter 10) can we really appreciate their strengths (chapter 11).

I hope that we have the imagination and the insight to appreciate their great legacies. God knows the African-American community needs Martin and Malcolm. America needs them too. Together Martin and Malcolm can help this nation to move closer to the goal of justice for all.

A word should be said about the uses of the terms "Negro," "African," "black," and "Afro-American." Because Martin King used the term "Negro" when he referred to the African-American community, I have frequently used it when articulating his views. Malcolm X despised the term "Negro" as a self-designation. He preferred "African," "black," and "Afro-American." These terms are employed to express his perspective.

The reader is entitled to know the perspective which has shaped my interpretation of Martin and Malcolm and the audience to which this book is primarily directed. I am an African-American theologian whose perspective on the Christian religion was shaped by Martin King and whose black consciousness was defined by Malcolm X. In more than twenty years of writing and teaching black liberation theology, I have been attempting to relate Malcolm X and Martin King to Christian living in America, seeking to show that *justice* and *blackness* are essential ingredients in the identity of the Christian faith for African-Americans. This book is an examination of the meaning of justice and blackness in America in the context of the lives and thought of Martin King and Malcolm X. While it focuses on the African-American struggle for justice and identity, I hope that other people will find something useful for their struggles as well. I do not expect all persons to agree with what Martin, Malcolm, and I say about justice and blackness in America. I only hope that they will recognize that our proclamations for and against America are in fact expressions of our love for humanity. Unless America recognizes the rights of human beings, its future is doomed. I write because I believe in human beings. "We shall overcome!"

ACKNOWLEDGMENTS

I have enjoyed researching and writing this book. Daily for ten years I have been listening to audiotapes and watching videotapes of Martin's and Malcolm's speeches, reading their published and unpublished writings, as well as what others have written about them, and talking to people who knew them personally. I am deeply grateful to the many people who were generous with their time, challenging with sharp and insightful criticism, and very supportive with personal encouragement. There are, of course, too many to name, but some persons must be mentioned.

I am especially grateful for the support of the Union Seminary community — its board, administration, faculty, students, and staff. President Donald Shriver, former dean Milton Gatch, and my colleagues in the Theological Field deserve a special word of thanks for their support and encouragement. The faculty also read a selection of my research and devoted several sessions to a critical discussion of it. In my class on Martin and Malcolm, Union students told me what they thought about what I was writing. I love teaching at Union chiefly because of the quality of the commitment and intellect of its students. They have challenged and nurtured me during twenty-one years of teaching and particularly during the writing of this book.

Four excellent secretaries made the writing of this book much easier and more delightful than it would have been without them. Elizabeth Launer, my first secretary, set a high standard that was continued by Fredricka Harlow, Betty Thomas, and Donna Zanolla. Each one let me know in her own special way that she cared about Martin and Malcolm and me. Dwight Hopkins, Mark Chapman, and JoAnne Terrell served as my research assistants. They not only tracked down many hard to find news items, tapes, and other documents but also read my manuscript and offered many helpful insights.

Several of my former and current graduate students read all or parts of my manuscript and offered helpful comments. They include: Kelly D. Brown, Josiah Young, Dennis Wiley, Ben Ramsey, Chung Hyun Kyung, Howard Wiley, and Jackie Grant. Mary Marshall Clark was very helpful by making available many items about Martin and Malcolm in the *New York Times*.

I spent a lot of time at the Martin Luther King, Jr., Library and Archives in Atlanta. My special thanks to D. Louis Cook, the former director, who was helpful in too many ways to name. I know of no library which operates more efficiently. Diane Ware, then reference archivist, was also quite helpful. I also wish to express my thanks to Howard Dodson and James Murray at the Schomburg Center for Research in Black Culture; Esme Bhan at the Moorland-Spingarn Research Center of Howard University; Charles Niles and Howard Gotlieb of Boston University's Mugar Library; and Minnie Clayton of Atlanta University's Woodruff Library.

A special word of thanks is due to Betty Bolden and Kirk Moll of Union Seminary. Everyone, however, went out of their way to help my research assistants and me. There was hardly anything we requested which they did not find a way to make available to me.

I also owe a special thanks to Wyatt Tee Walker and Gayraud S. Wilmore for their critical evaluation of my manuscript. Both are friends of many years but also tough critics. While I did not agree with all of their suggestions, I accepted most and listened attentively to all of them. Others who assisted me in my research and read all or parts of my manuscript were Makada Coasten, Lydia Hernandez, William Sales, Abdul Alkalimat, Omar Farooq, Lewis V. Baldwin, Edith Campbell, and Bobby Joe Saucer.

Two Martin King researchers have been a special source of inspiration to me. I know that I could not have written this book without the monumental research of my friend David Garrow. We not only spent many hours talking about Martin and the civil rights movement, but he also made available to me many interviews and FBI files on both Martin and Malcolm. Whenever I needed to discuss a point of research, he was always ready to share what he knew. Serge Molla and I first met in Geneva, Switzerland, and later we became better acquainted as we both started our research at the King Center Archives. As friends and fellow researchers, we talked many hours about Martin, Malcolm, James Baldwin, and black theology.

The Scherer family (Lester and Patricia, along with their daughters, Diane and Carol, their sons, Steve and Tom, and their children's spouses) provided a place for me to think, write, and retreat. All have been supportive. Lester, my beloved friend of many years and former colleague, has been not only a source of inspiration but my best critic. He has spent many hours discussing and reading the manuscript at every stage of its development and offered his critical evaluation.

My mother, Lucy Cone, and my brothers, Cecil and Charles, have been the best family one could ever expect. They have always believed in me, providing me with a captive audience whenever and wherever I wanted to talk about Martin and Malcolm.

Anyone who has been around me in the last ten years knows that with only the slightest encouragement, I would talk for hours about Martin and Malcolm. Fortunately, much of this need was met with invitations to lecture at many colleges, universities, seminaries, churches, and conferences in many parts of the world—including Asia, Africa, and Latin America. I do wish to express my thanks to everyone for listening to me talk about my favorite topics: Martin Luther King, Jr., and Malcolm X—their meaning for blacks, America, and the world. I hope that this book makes the waiting for it worthwhile.

Introduction

AMERICA: A DREAM OR A NIGHTMARE?

I have a dream that one day this nation will rise up and live out the true meaning of its creed, "We hold these truths to be self-evident, that all men are created equal." I have a dream that one day . . . sons of former slaves and the sons of former slave owners will be able to sit down together at the table of brotherhood. . . . This is our hope. . . . With this faith we will be able to work together, to pray together, to struggle together, to go to jail together, to stand up for freedom together, knowing that we will be free one day. . . . This will be the day when all God's children will be able to sing with new meaning, "My country 'tis of thee, sweet land of liberty, of thee I sing."

Martin Luther King, Jr.
March on Washington
Washington, D.C.
28 August 1963

No, I'm not an American. I'm one of the 22 million black people who are the victims of Americanism. One of the . . . victims of democracy, nothing but disguised hypocrisy. So, I'm not standing here speaking to you as an American, or a patriot, or a flag-saluter, or a flag-waver— no, not I! I'm speaking as a victim of this American system. And I see America through the eyes of the victim. I don't see any American dream; I see an American nightmare!

Malcolm X
Cory Methodist Church
Cleveland, Ohio
3 April 1964

1

THE MEETING OF MALCOLM AND MARTIN

"Well Malcolm, good to see you," Martin said. "Good to see *you,*" Malcolm replied.

After nearly eight years of verbal sparring through the media, two great African-American leaders, Martin Luther King, Jr., and Malcolm X, finally met for the first and only time in Washington, D.C., 26 March 1964. Both were attending the U.S. Senate's debate of the Civil Rights Bill. Initiated by Malcolm following Martin's press conference, the meeting was coincidental and brief. There was no time for substantive discussions between the two. They were photographed greeting each other warmly, smiling and shaking hands. The slim, six-foot three-inch Malcolm towered over the stocky, five-foot eight-inch Martin. They walked together a few paces through the corridor, whispering to each other, as their followers and the media looked on with great interest. As they departed, Malcolm teasingly said, "Now you're going to get investigated."

Although the media portrayed them as adversaries, Martin and Malcolm were actually fond of each other. There was no animosity between them. They saw each other as a fellow justice-fighter, struggling against the same evil—racism—and for the same goal—freedom for African-Americans.

"I'm throwing myself into the heart of the civil rights struggle and will be in it from now on," Malcolm told James Booker of the *Amsterdam News* the day before he departed for the nation's capital. Recently expelled from the Black Muslim movement, he was trying to develop a new image of himself so he could join the mainstream of the civil rights movement. In Washington, Malcolm observed the debate from the Senate gallery and held impromptu press conferences during much of the day. He was pleased that the Senate voted against sending the bill to the Judiciary Committee and then voted to start debate on the bill in the full Senate. He told the media that the Senate should pass the House-passed bill "exactly as it is, with no changes." But he predicted glumly, "If passed, it will never be enforced." "You can't legislate good will—that comes through education."[1]

In another section of the Senate gallery, Martin King was observing the same debate. Like Malcolm, he also held several press conferences and cheered the Senate's decision to take up the bill. But he expressed concern about the southern filibuster which threatened to weaken it. Martin told the media that a month of "legitimate debate" was acceptable. But he vowed that "if the Senate is still talking about the bill after the first week of May," he would initiate a creative direct-action program in Washington and throughout the country "to dramatize the abuse of the legislative process." He did not rule out civil disobedience. "At first we would seek to persuade with our words and then with our deeds." Martin also promised that he would fight for more civil rights legislation the following year. "We cannot stop till Negroes have absolute and complete freedom."[2]

The meeting of Martin and Malcolm has profound, symbolic meaning for the black freedom movement. It was more than a meeting of two prominent leaders in the African-American community. It was a meeting of two great resistance traditions in African-American history — integrationism and nationalism. Together Martin, a Christian integrationist, and Malcolm, a Muslim nationalist, would have been a powerful force against racial injustice. When they were separated, their enemies were successful in pitting them against each other and thereby diluting the effectiveness of the black freedom movement. Both Martin and Malcolm were acutely aware of the dangers of disunity among African-Americans. They frequently spoke out against it and urged African-Americans to forget their differences and to unite in a common struggle for justice and freedom. Why then did Martin and Malcolm not set an example by joining their forces together into a black united front against racism? The answer to this question is found partly in the interrelationship of integrationism and nationalism in African-American history. These two resistance traditions also provide the historical context for a deeper understanding of Martin's dream and Malcolm's nightmare.

INTEGRATIONISM AND NATIONALISM IN AFRICAN-AMERICAN INTELLECTUAL HISTORY

No one stated the dilemma that slavery and segregation created for Africans in the United States as sharply and poignantly as W. E. B. Du Bois. In his classic statement of the problem, he spoke of it as a "peculiar sensation," a "double-consciousness," "two souls, two thoughts, two unreconciled strivings; two warring ideals in one dark body, whose dogged strength alone keeps it from being torn asunder." The "twoness" that Du Bois was describing stemmed from being an African *in* America. "Here, then, is the dilemma," he wrote in "The Conservation of Races." "What, after all, am I? Am I an American or am I a Negro? Can I be both?"[3]

Integrationist thinkers may be defined as those who answer "Yes" to the question, "Can I be both?" They believe it is possible to achieve justice in the United States and to create wholesome relations with the white community. This optimism has been based upon the "American creed," the tradition of freedom and democracy as articulated in the

Declaration of Independence and the Constitution, and is supported, they believe, by the Jewish and Christian Scriptures. The integrationist line of thought goes something like this: If whites really believe their political and religious documents, then they know that black people should not be enslaved and segregated but rather integrated into the mainstream of the society. After all, blacks are Americans, having arrived even before the Pilgrims. They have worked the land, obeyed the laws, paid their taxes, and defended America in every war. They built the nation as much as white people did. Therefore, the integrationists argue, it is the task of African-American leaders to prick the conscience of whites, showing the contradictions between their professed values and their actual treatment of blacks. Then whites will be embarrassed by their hypocrisy and will grant blacks the same freedom that they themselves enjoy.

On the other hand, nationalist thinkers have rejected the American side of their identity and affirmed the African side, saying "No, we can't be both." They have contended that 244 years of slavery, followed by legal segregation, social degradation, political disfranchisement, and economic exploitation means that blacks will never be recognized as human beings in white society. America isn't for blacks; blacks can't be for America. The nationalists argue that blacks don't belong with whites, that whites are killing blacks, generation after generation. Blacks should, therefore, separate from America, either by returning to Africa or by going to some other place where they can create sociopolitical structures that are derived from their own history and culture.

Integrationism and nationalism represent the two broad streams of black thought in response to the problem of slavery and segregation in America. Of course, no black thinker has been a pure integrationist or a pure nationalist, but rather all black intellectuals have represented aspects of each, with emphasis moving in one direction or the other, usually at different periods of their lives. What emphasis any black thinker made was usually determined by his or her perspective on America, that is, whether he or she believed that blacks would soon be included in the mainstream of American life on a par with whites. When blacks have been optimistic about America—believing that they could achieve full equality through moral suasion and legal argument—they have been integrationists and have minimized their nationalist tendencies. On the other hand, despair about America—believing that genuine equality is impossible because whites have no moral conscience or any intention to apply the laws fairly—has always been the seedbed of nationalism. To understand Martin King's and Malcolm X's perspectives on America and their relation to each other, it is important to see them in the light of these two different but interdependent streams of black thought.

INTEGRATIONISM BEFORE MARTIN KING

Integrationists have had many able advocates since the founding of the republic. Among them were the great abolitionist Frederick Douglass, many prominent black preachers, and representatives of the National Association for the Advancement of Colored People (NAACP), the National Urban League, and the Congress of Racial Equality (CORE).

Frederick Douglass was the outstanding advocate of integrationism during the nineteenth century. Born a slave, Douglass escaped from slavery and became an international figure with his powerful speeches and writings in defense of the full citizenship rights of blacks. For him the existence of slavery was a staggering contradiction of the principles of the Constitution and the concept of humanity.

Unlike the white abolitionist William Lloyd Garrison, who denied his allegiance to a Constitution ratified by slaveholders, Douglass embraced it as an "anti-slavery document" and then proceeded to quote it as supporting evidence for the abolition of slavery. The Constitution reads, " 'We the people'; not we the white people," Douglass proclaimed; "and if Negroes are people, they are included in the benefits for which the Constitution of America was ordained and established."[4]

No one was as persuasive as Frederick Douglass in pointing out to whites the hypocrisy of extolling the "principles of political freedom and of natural justice" articulated in the Declaration of Independence while holding blacks as slaves. His well-known Independence Day speech in Rochester, New York, on the topic "What to the Slave Is the Fourth of July?" was calculated to cut deeply into the conscience of whites who thought of themselves as civilized. "To [the slave], your celebration is a sham," he proclaimed to a stunned white audience. "Your denunciation of tyrants, brass-fronted impudence; your shouts of liberty and equality, hollow mockery. . . . There is not a nation on the earth guilty of practices more shocking and bloody than are the people of the United States."[5]

Douglass's scathing words did not mean that he had given up on America and would accordingly seek separation from the land of his birth. He was offered an opportunity to stay in England where he was given many honors, but he rejected the idea. Douglass believed that blacks could find justice in the United States and safely intertwine their future with that of the white majority. He was severely critical of blacks and whites who proposed the colonization of blacks in Africa or some other place. "It's all nonsense to talk about the removal of eight million of the American people from their homes in America to Africa," he said. "The destiny of the colored Americans . . . is the destiny of America. We shall never leave you. . . . We are here. . . . To imagine that we should ever be eradicated is absurd and ridiculous. We can be modified, changed, assimilated, but never extinguished. . . . This is our country; and the question for the philosophers and statesmen of the land ought to be, What principle should dictate the policy of the nation toward us?"[6]

Although Douglass experienced many disappointments in his fight for justice, he never lost his love for America or his belief that blacks would soon achieve full freedom in the land of their birth. "I expect to see the colored people of this country enjoying the same freedom [as whites]," he said in 1865, "voting at the same ballot-box . . ., going to the same schools, attending the same churches, traveling the same street cars, in the same railroad cars, . . . proud of the same country, fighting the same foe, and enjoying the same peace, and all its advantages."[7]

Optimism about blacks achieving full citizenship rights in America has always been the hallmark of integrationism. This optimism has been based not only on the political ideals of America but also upon its claim to be founded on Christian principles. Blacks have believed that the Christian faith requires that whites treat them as equals before God. No group articulated this point with more religious conviction and fervor than black preachers.

According to black preachers, Christianity is a gospel of justice and love. Believers, therefore, must treat all people justly and lovingly—that is, as brothers and sisters. Why? Because God, the creator of all, is no respecter of persons. Out of one blood God has created all people. On the cross Jesus Christ died for all—whites and blacks alike. Our oneness in creation and redemption means that no Christian can condone slavery or segregation in the churches or the society. The integration of whites and blacks into one community, therefore, is the only option open for Christians.

As early as 1787, Richard Allen (an ex-slave and a Methodist minister) led a group of blacks out of St. George Methodist Church in Philadelphia, and in 1816 he founded the African Methodist Episcopal (AME) Church. He did this because he and his followers refused to accept segregation in the "Lord's house." A few years later, James Varick and other blacks in New York took similar action and organized the African Methodist Episcopal Zion (AMEZ) Church. Black Baptists also formed separate congregations.

Independent black churches were not separatist in the strict sense. They were not separating themselves from whites because they held a different doctrinal view of Christianity. Without exception, blacks used the same articles of faith and polity for their churches as the white denominations from which they separated. Separation, for blacks, meant that they were rejecting the *ethical* behavior of whites—they were rejecting racism that was based on the assumption that God created blacks inferior to whites. Blacks also wanted to prove that they had the capability to organize and to operate a denomination just like whites. In short, black Christians were bearing witness to their humanity, which they believed God created equal to that of whites. The motto of the AME Church reflected that conviction: "God our Father, Christ our Redeemer, Man our Brother." "When these sentiments are universal in theory and practice," the AME bishops said in 1896, "then the mission of the distinctive colored organization will cease."[8]

Not all black Christians chose the strategy of separation. Instead, some decided to stay in white denominations and use them as platforms from which to prick the conscience of whites regarding the demands of the gospel and to encourage blacks to strike a blow for freedom. "Liberty is a spirit sent out from God," proclaimed Henry Highland Garnet, a Presbyterian minister, "and like its great Author, is no respector of persons."[9]

Following the Civil War, the great majority of black Christians joined black-led churches among the Methodists and Baptists. The independence of these churches enabled their pastors to become prominent leaders in the black struggle for integration in the society. Prominent Baptists included Adam Clayton Powell, Sr., and Jr., of the Abyssinian Baptist Church (New York), Martin Luther King, Sr., of Ebenezer Baptist Church (Atlanta), William Holmes Borders of the Wheat Street Baptist Church (Atlanta), and Vernon Johns of the Dexter Avenue Baptist Church (Montgomery). Reverdy C. Ransom, an AME minister, was a "pioneer black social gospeler." Other significant voices included Benjamin E. Mays, president of Morehouse College, and Howard Thurman, dean of Rankin Chapel and professor of theology at Howard University. All spoke out against segregation and racism in the white churches and the society, insisting that the integration of blacks and whites into one community was the demand of the Christian faith. In his book *Marching Blacks,* Adam Powell, Jr., accused white churches of turning Christianity into "churchianity," thereby distorting its essential message of "equality" and "brotherhood." "No one can say that Christianity has failed," he said. "It has never been tried."[10]

How can whites claim to be Christians and still hold blacks as slaves or segregate them in their churches and the society? That has been the great paradox for black Christians. Since whites attended their churches regularly, with an air of reverence for God, and studied the Bible conscientiously, blacks expected them to see the truth of the gospel and thereby accept them into their churches and the society as brothers and sisters. Many black Christians believed that it was only a matter of a little time before Jesus would reveal the gospel truth to whites and slavery and segregation would come tumbling down like the walls of Jericho. That was the basis of the optimism among black Christians.

Too much confidence in what God is going to do often creates an otherworldly perspective which encourages passivity in the face of injustice and suffering. That happened to the great majority of blacks from the time of the Civil War to the coming of Martin Luther King, Jr. The organized fight for justice was transferred from the churches to secular groups, commonly known as civil rights organizations, especially the NAACP, the National Urban League, and CORE. Each came into existence for the sole purpose of achieving full citizenship rights for African-Americans in every aspect of American society. They often have used different tactics and have worked in different areas, but the goal has been the same — the integration of blacks into the mainstream of American society so that color will no longer be a determining factor for success or failure in any human endeavor.

Founded by prominent whites and blacks in 1909, the NAACP was the first and has been the most influential civil rights organization. Branded as radical before the 1960s, it has been a strong advocate of integration, using the courts as the primary arena in which to protest segregation. The NAACP is best known for its successful argument before the United States Supreme Court against the doctrine of "separate but equal" schools for blacks and whites, claiming that such schools are inherently unequal and therefore unconstitutional. The 17 May 1954 school desegregation decision has often been called the beginning of the black freedom movement of the 1950s and 1960s.

One year after the founding of the NAACP, the National Urban League was organized. Less aggressive than the NAACP, the Urban League was founded "for the specific purpose of easing the transition of the Southern rural Negro into an urban way of life. It stated clearly that its role was to help these people, who were essentially rural agrarian serf-peasants, adjust to Northern city life." Using the techniques of persuasion and conciliation, the Urban League appealed to the "enlightened self-interest" of white business leaders "to ease the movement of Negroes into middle class status."[11]

A generation later, in 1942, the Congress of Racial Equality was founded in Chicago. The smallest and most radical of the three groups, CORE is best known for introducing the method of nonviolent direct action, staging sit-ins in restaurants and freedom rides on buses. This new dimension of the black struggle for equality had a profound effect on the civil rights movement in the 1950s and 1960s and particularly on Martin King.

Unlike the black churches, which had few white members and no white leaders, the civil rights organizations included whites in every level of their operations. For example, a white person has often served as the president of the NAACP, and each of the three organizations has had a significant number of whites serve on its board of directors. They claimed that the implementation of integration must apply to every aspect of the society, including their own organizations. The inclusion of whites also limited their independence and made them vulnerable to the nationalist critique that no black revolution can be successful as long as its leadership is dependent upon white support.

BLACK NATIONALISM BEFORE MALCOLM X

The roots of black nationalism go back to the seventeenth-century slave conspiracies, when Africans, longing for their homeland, banded together in a common struggle against slavery, because they knew that they were not created for servitude. In the absence of historical data, it is not possible to describe the precise ideology behind the early slave revolts. What we know for sure is that the Africans deeply abhorred slavery and were willing to take great risks to gain their freedom.

This nationalist spirit was given high visibility in the slave revolts led by Gabriel Prosser, Denmark Vesey, and Nat Turner during the first third of the nineteenth century. But it was also found in the rise of mutual-aid societies, in the birth and growth of black-led churches and conventions, and in black-led emigration schemes. Unity as a people, pride in African heritage, the creation of autonomous institutions, and the search for a territory to build a nation were the central ingredients which shaped the early development of the nationalist consciousness.

There have been many articulate voices and important movements of black nationalism throughout African-American history. Among them were David Walker and Martin Delany during the antebellum period and Henry McNeal Turner, Marcus Garvey, Noble Drew Ali, and Elijah Muhammad during the late nineteenth and early twentieth centuries.

The central claim of all black nationalists, past and present, is that black people are primarily Africans and not Americans. Unlike integrationists, nationalists do not define their significance and purpose as a people by appealing to the Declaration of Independence, the Constitution, Lincoln's Emancipation Proclamation, or even the white man's religion of Christianity. On the contrary, nationalists define their identity by their resistance to America and their determination to create a society based on their own African history and culture. The posture of rejecting America and accepting Africa is sometimes symbolized with such words as "African," "black," and "blackness." For example, Martin Delany, often called the father of black nationalism, boasted that there lived "none blacker" than himself. While Douglass, in typical integrationist style, said, "I thank God for making me a man simply," he reported that "Delany always thanks Him for making him a black man."[12]

The issue for nationalists was not only human slavery or oppression. It was also the oppression of *black* people by *white* people. Nothing aroused the fury of nationalists more than the racial factor in human exploitation. Their identity as black touched the very core of their being and affected their thoughts and feelings regarding everything, especially their relations with white people. Nationalists, unlike integrationists, could not separate their resentment of servitude from the racial identity of the people responsible for it. "White Americans [are] our *natural enemies,*" wrote David Walker in his *Appeal* in 1829. "By treating us so cruel," we "see them acting more like devils than accountable men." According to Walker, "whites have always been an unjust, jealous, unmerciful, avaricious and blood-thirsty set of beings, always seeking after power and authority."[13]

Black nationalism was defined by a loss of hope in America. Its advocates did not believe that white people could ever imagine humanity in a way that would place black people on a par with them. "I am not in favor of caste, nor a separation of the brotherhood of mankind, and would as willingly live among white men as black, if I had an *equal possession and enjoyment* of privileges," Delany wrote in 1852 to the white abolitionist William Lloyd Garrison; he went on: "but [I] shall never be reconciled to live among them, subservient to their will—existing by mere *sufferance,* as we, the colored people, do, in this country. . . . I have no hopes in this country—no confidence in the American people."[14]

This difference in emotional orientation between nationalists and integrationists led to disagreement in their definition of freedom and their strategies for achieving it. For nationalists, freedom was not black people pleading for integration into white society; rather it was separation from white people so that blacks could govern themselves. For many nationalists, separation meant emigration from the United States to some place in Africa or Latin America. "Every people should be the originators of their own designs, the projector of their own schemes, and creators of the events that lead to their destiny—the consummation of their own desires," Delany wrote in his best-known work, *The Condition, Elevation, Emigration, and Destiny of the Colored People of the United States* (1852). "No people can be free who themselves do not constitute an essential part of the *ruling element* of the country in which they live," said Delany. "The liberty of no man is secure, who controls not his political destiny. . . . To suppose otherwise, is that delusion which at once induces its victim, through a period of long suffering, patiently to submit to every species of wrong; trusting against probability, and hoping against all reasonable grounds of expectation, for the granting of privileges and enjoyment of rights, that will never be attained."[15]

The ebb and flow of black nationalism, during the nineteenth century and thereafter, was influenced by the decline and rise of black expectations of equality in the United States. When blacks felt that the achievement of equality was impossible, the nationalist sentiment among them always increased. Such was the case during the 1840s and 1850s, largely due to the Fugitive Slave Act (1850) and the Dred Scott Decision (1857).

During the Civil War and the Reconstruction that followed it, black hopes soared and even Delany stopped talking about the emigration of blacks and began to participate in the political process in South Carolina, running for the office of lieutenant-governor.

Black expectations of achieving full citizenship rights, however, were short-lived. The infamous Hayes Compromise of 1877 led to the withdrawal of federal troops from the South, thereby allowing former white slaveholders to deal with their former slaves in any manner they chose. The destructive consequences for blacks were severe politically, economically, and psychologically. Accommodationism emerged as the dominant black philosophy, and Booker T. Washington became its most prominent advocate. Washington replaced Frederick Douglass as the chief spokesperson for blacks, and ministers were his most ardent supporters.

During the period of the "nadir" and the "long dark night" of black people's struggle for justice in America, Henry McNeal Turner, a bishop in the AME Church, and Marcus Garvey of the Universal Negro Improvement Association (UNIA) articulated nationalist perspectives that were more directly linked with the subsequent philosophy of Malcolm X. Like Malcolm's, their perspectives on America were derived from the bottom of the black experience. They spoke a language that was full of racial pride and denunciation of white America. It was intended to elevate the cultural and psychological well-being of downtrodden blacks burdened with low self-esteem in a society dominated by the violence of white hate groups and the sophisticated racism of the Social Darwinists.

A native of South Carolina, Turner grew up on the cotton fields with slaves and learned to read by his own efforts. He was a proud and fearless man, and his nationalism was deepened as he observed the continued exploitation of blacks by whites, North and South, during and following Reconstruction. When the Supreme Court ruled in 1883 that the Civil Rights Act of 1875 was unconstitutional, Turner felt that that "barbarous decision" dissolved the allegiance of black people to the United States. "If the decision is correct," he wrote, "the United States Constitution is a dirty rag, a cheat, a libel, and ought to be spit upon by every negro in the land."[16]

The betrayal of Reconstruction, the "enactment of cruel and revolting laws," lynching and other atrocities, reenslavement through peonage, and political disfranchisement encouraged Turner to conclude that blacks would never achieve equality in the United States. He became an ardent advocate of emigration to Africa. "There is no more doubt in my mind," Turner said, "that we have ultimately to return to Africa than there is of the existence of God."[17]

Although Turner was elected a bishop in the AME Church, he was not the typical holder of that office. The more whites demeaned blackness as a mark of inferiority, the more Turner glorified it. At a time when black and white Christians identified God with European images and the AME Church leaders were debating whether to replace the word "African" in their name with "American," Turner shocked everyone with his declaration that "God is a Negro."[18]

Although Turner addressed his message to the sociopolitical problems of the black masses in the rural South, he did not create an organization to implement his African dream. That distinction fell to Marcus Garvey.

On 23 March 1916, one year after Turner's death, Marcus Garvey came to the United States from his native Jamaica. While Turner's base was the rural South, Garvey worked in the urban North, mainly in Harlem. While the geography was different, the people were essentially the same, being mostly immigrants from the South in search of the American dream of economic security, social advancement, and political justice. Instead they entered a nightmare of racism and poverty which they thought they had left behind in the South.

Garvey understood the pain of color discrimination because he experienced it personally and observed it in the lives of other blacks in Jamaica and also during his travels in Central America, Europe, and the United States. It seemed that everywhere he traveled blacks were being dominated by others. "Where is the black man's Government?" he asked. "Where is his King and his kingdom? Where is his President, his country, and his ambassador, his army, his navy, his men of big affairs?" Unable to find them, Garvey, with the self-assurance of a proud black man, then declared: "I will help to make them."[19]

Garvey knew that without racial pride no people could make leaders and build a nation that would command the respect of the world. This was particularly true of blacks who had been enslaved and segregated for three hundred years. In a world where blackness was a badge of degradation and shame, Garvey transformed it into a symbol of honor and distinction. "To be a Negro is no disgrace, but an honor, and we of the Universal Negro Improvement Association do not want to become white."[20] He made blacks feel that they were somebody and that they could do great things as a people. "Up, you mighty race," Garvey proclaimed, "you can accomplish what you will," and black people believed him.

As whites ruled Europe and America, Garvey was certain blacks should and would rule Africa. To implement his African dream, he organized the UNIA, first in Kingston, Jamaica, and later in New York. "Africa for the Africans" was the heart of his message. In 1920 Garvey called the first International Convention of Negro Peoples of the World, and 25,000 delegates from twenty-five countries met in New York City. A redeemed Africa, governed by a united black race proud of its history, was the theme which dominated Garvey's speeches. "Wake up Ethiopia! Wake up Africa!" he proclaimed. "Let us work towards the one glorious end of a free, redeemed and mighty nation. Let Africa be a bright star among the constellation of nations." "A race without authority and power is a race without respect."[21]

No one exceeded Garvey in his criticisms of the philosophy of integration, as represented by the members of the NAACP and other middle-class black leaders and intellectuals. He believed that any black organization that depended upon white philanthropy was detrimental to the cause of Africa's redemption and the uplifting of the black race. "No man will do as much for you as you will do for yourself."[22] By depending on whites, blacks were saying that they could not do it alone, thereby creating a sense of inferiority in themselves.

According to Garvey, integration is a self-defeating philosophy that is promoted by pseudo-black intellectuals and leaders. He accused integrationists of wanting to be white and completely ignoring the socio-economic well-being of poor blacks at the bottom. W. E. B. Du Bois, then the editor of the NAACP's *Crisis* magazine, was one of Garvey's favorite targets of criticism. Garvey urged his followers that "we must never, even under the severest pressure, hate or dislike ourselves."[23] His criticism of the NAACP and Du Bois was very similar to Malcolm X's attack upon the same organization and its executive director, Roy Wilkins, during the 1960s. Black nationalists are defined by race confidence and solidarity, and they are often intemperate in their criticisms of black integrationists, for they believe integrationists compromise the self-respect and dignity of the race by wanting to mingle and marry white people—the enemy.

In 1920, Garvey's UNIA claimed a membership of four million and a year later six million, with nine hundred branches. While most scholars insist that the numbers were inflated, no one denies that Garvey organized the largest and most successful mass movement of blacks in the history of the United States. Garvey did what all black nationalists after him have merely dreamed of doing, and that is why they continue to study his life and message for direction and inspiration.

Concerned about Garvey's popularity, the government, with the help of black integrationist leaders, convicted him of mail fraud. Upon his imprisonment and deportation, black nationalism entered a period of decline. But the problems of oppression and identity which gave rise to it did not disappear.

In addition to Marcus Garvey's UNIA, two movements were important in defining the nationalism that influenced Malcolm X: the Moorish Science Temple founded by Noble Drew Ali in Newark, New Jersey, and the Nation of Islam — the "Black Muslims" — founded in Detroit in 1930 by the mysterious Wallace D. Fard and later headed by his disciple, Elijah Poole, a former Baptist minister from Sandersville, Georgia. Elijah Poole as Elijah Muhammad achieved his authority in the Black Muslim religion because he convinced Black Muslim believers, including Malcolm, that Allah came to North America "in the person of Wallace D. Fard," taught him for three and a half years, and then chose him as his Messenger.

Both movements rejected Christianity and white people and affirmed the religion of Islam and an African-Asian identity. Both movements were primarily religious, having less political emphasis than Garvey's UNIA. Although the Moorish Science Temple is still in existence, it was important mainly as a forerunner of the Nation of Islam. The Nation of Islam received many members from the Moorish Science Temple following the assassination of Noble Drew Ali.

The Nation of Islam was the most important influence on the life and thought of Malcolm X. Its importance for Malcolm was similar to the role of the black church in the life of Martin King. While Garvey influenced Malcolm's political consciousness, Elijah Muhammad defined his religious commitment. Elijah Muhammad was the sole and absolute authority in defining the doctrine and practice of the Nation of Islam. While affirming solidarity with worldwide Islam, he proclaimed distinctive doctrines. The most important and controversial one was his contention that whites were by nature evil. They were snakes who were incapable of doing right, devils who would soon be destroyed by God's righteous judgment. White people, therefore, were identified as the sole cause of black oppression.

In Black Muslim theology the almighty black God is the source of all good and power. To explain the origin of the evil of black oppression,

Muhammad rejected the Christian recourse to divine mystery or God's permissive will, instead setting forth his own distinctive explanation, which focused on the myth of Yacob. Out of the weak individuals of the black race, Yacob, a renegade black scientist, created the white race, thereby causing all of the evil which has flowed from their hands: "The human beast — the serpent, the dragon, the devil, and Satan — all mean one and the same: the people or race known as the white or Caucasian race, sometimes called the European race. Since by nature they were created liars and murderers, they are the enemies of truth and right-eousness, and the enemies of those who seek the truth."[24] This myth was important for Malcolm's view that the whites are evil by nature. The myth and its doctrinal development came exclusively from Elijah Muhammad.

The logical extension of this doctrine is that since black people are by nature good and divine, they must be separated from whites so they can avoid the latter's hour of total destruction. The solution to the problem of black oppression in America, therefore, is territorial sepa-ration, either by whites financing black people's return to Africa or by providing separate states in America.

Although the Nation of Islam and other nationalist movements (espe-cially Garvey's) were the dominant influence in shaping Malcolm's life and thought, he was also indebted to the integrationist protest tradition. The same kind of cross current of nationalist and integrationist influ-ences bore upon the career of Martin King, though he was indebted far less to the nationalist tradition. No sharp distinction can be drawn between the traditions, because representatives of both were fighting the same problems — the power of "white over black" and its psycho-logical impact upon the self-esteem of its victims. Nationalists and inte-grationists were aware of the truth of each other's viewpoint, even though they did not always acknowledge it. Integrationists realized the danger of complete assimilation into American society. Like national-ists, they did not want to destroy the cultural and spiritual identity of blacks. That was perhaps the major reason why black churches and fraternal and sororal organizations remained separate from whites. Despite their repeated claim about 11:00 A.M. on Sunday morning being the most segregated hour of the week, black ministers in black denom-inations made no real efforts to integrate their churches. They knew that if they did, their power as blacks would have been greatly curtailed and their own cultural and spiritual identity destroyed. The advocates of integration, therefore, focused their energies primarily on the polit-ical and economic life of America. They believed that justice was pos-sible if whites treated blacks as equals under the law.

Likewise, black nationalists realized the danger of complete isolation from the political and economic life of America. That was perhaps the major reason for the frequent shifts in their philosophy. Black nationalism was not primarily a Western, "rational" philosophy, but rather a black philosophy in search of its African roots. It was a cry for self-esteem, for the right to be recognized and accepted as human beings. Its advocates knew that blacks could not survive politically or economically in complete separation from others, especially whites in the United States. Neither could any other people (including whites) survive in isolation from the rest of the world. Everyone was interdependent. The black masses, therefore, did not follow nationalists because of their call for separation from America. Rather it was because of the nationalists' ability to speak to their "gut level" experience, that is, to express what it *felt* like to be black in white America.

Integrationists and nationalists complemented each other. Both philosophies were needed if America was going to come to terms with the truth of the black experience. Either philosophy alone was a half-truth and thus a distortion of the black reality in America. Integrationists were *practical*. They advocated what they thought could be achieved at a given time. They knew that justice demanded more. But why demand it if you can't get it? Why demand it if the demand itself blocks the achievement of other desirable and achievable goals? In their struggle for justice, they were careful not to arouse the genocidal instincts inherent in racism. Thus they chose goals and methods which many whites accepted as reasonable and just. The strengths and weaknesses of the integrationist view are reflected in the life and ministry of Martin King.

Nationalists were *desperate*. They spoke for that segment of the African-American community which was hurting the most. Thus, they often did not consider carefully the consequences of their words and actions. The suffering of the black poor was so great that practical or rational philosophies did not arouse their allegiance. They needed a philosophy that could speak to their existence as black people, living in a white society that did not recognize their humanity. They needed a philosophy that empowered them to "respect black" by being prepared to die for it. Overwhelmed by misery, the black poor cried out for relief, for a word or an act that would lift them to another realm of existence where they would be treated as human beings. In place of an American dream, nationalists gave the black poor an African dream. The strengths and the weaknesses of this perspective were reflected in the life and ministry of Malcolm X.

Martin King and Malcolm X were shaped by what Vincent Harding has called the "Great Tradition of Black Protest,"[25] a tradition that comprised many variations of nationalism and integrationism. Their perspectives on America were influenced by both, even though they placed primary emphasis on only one of them. Both integrationism and nationalism readied Martin and Malcolm for leadership in the black freedom movement of the 1950s and 1960s—with Martin proclaiming an American dream from the steps of the Lincoln Memorial and Malcolm reminding him of an American nightmare in the streets of Harlem.

1

THE MAKING OF A DREAMER
(1929–55)

It is quite easy for me to think of a God of love mainly because I grew up in a family where love was central and where lovely relationships were ever present. It is quite easy for me to think of the universe as basically friendly mainly because of my uplifting hereditary and environmental circumstances. It is quite easy for me to lean more toward optimism than pessimism about human nature mainly because of my childhood experiences. It is impossible to get at the roots of one's religious attitudes without taking in account the psychological and historical factors that play upon the individual.

Martin Luther King, Jr.
"Autobiography of Religious Development"
Crozer Theological Seminary
1949

No one has communicated the idea of the American dream with greater moral and oratorical power, with greater political and religious imagination, than Martin Luther King, Jr. His expression of black people's struggle for freedom in the "I Have a Dream" address (March on Washington, 28 August 1963) captured the imagination of America and established him among the pantheon of America's leaders. He became the symbol not only of the civil rights movement but of America itself: a symbol of a land of freedom where people of all races, creeds, and nationalities could live together as a "beloved community."

The idea of the American dream dominated the speeches and writings of Martin King and the comments about him. No metaphor of his life and message is more widely known and more often repeated. King's admirers frequently refer to him as the "dreamer." On most occasions celebrating his life and message, this image is placed at the forefront, in such expressions as "living the dream," "keeping the dream," and "we still have a dream." Even corporations advertise their products with his dream. Coca-Cola says, "When we share the dream, the dream comes true"; Delta Air Lines salutes his memory with the statement: "May his dream live on." And the *Atlanta Journal-Constitution* says: "On January 15, 1929, a dream was born."

With so many references to Martin King's dream, it is not only easy to distort what he meant but also to trivialize it. As I pointed out in the introduction, the meaning of King's dream has deep historical roots in the African-American struggle for justice in the United States. Equally important was the influence of his social development in Atlanta, Georgia. To understand the "dreamer," if that is how we wish to refer to him, we must know something not only about the dreams he inherited from his slave grandparents but also something about the ones that were instilled in him as a child by his parents and other African-Americans who loved him.

Martin King *made* history, but he was also *made by* history. Karl Marx was right: "Men make their own history but they do not make it under circumstances chosen by themselves, but under circumstances directly encountered, given and transformed from the past." To understand the history that Martin King made, it is necessary to know something about the circumstances that made him. Only through an investigation of his social, educational, and religious development, from birth to early adulthood, will we be able to understand the nature of his dream and the dimensions of his accomplishment.

●

On 15 January 1929, Martin Luther King, Jr., was born in Atlanta, Georgia, into a middle-class family, the second child and first son of Alberta Christine Williams and Martin Luther King, Sr. Alfred Daniel Williams, young Martin's maternal grandfather, and Martin King, Sr., were prominent Baptist preachers in Atlanta. The church was the dominant institution in the social life of Atlanta's African-American community, serving as the source for leadership development and also providing the moral values which leaders used to achieve justice for blacks. It also erected a protective shelter against the hostile white world.

Most civil rights leaders were members of the church, and many were ministers as were Martin King's grandfather and father. Both served as pastors of the influential Ebenezer Baptist Church and actively participated as community leaders in fighting for equality and justice in a southern city where segregation was a way of life. They combined the self-help, accommodationist philosophy of Booker T. Washington and the protest, integrationist philosophy of Frederick Douglass and the NAACP with the religious values of the black community. The leadership style of combining "protest," "accommodation," and "self-help" was particularly suited for the South and consistent with the spirituality of the black church. Protest emphasized the right of black people to share in the benefits of America on an equal level with whites; accommodation meant that the black fight for equality would always be nonviolent, using the American democratic and Christian traditions of freedom as a way of appealing to the conscience of whites; and self-help stressed the economic, educational, and moral development of the black community, thereby accenting blacks' self-worth and self-confidence as a people. The black middle class believed that success in education, morality, and business would eventually cause whites to accept them as human beings and thus as equal partners in the social and political life of America. The perceived powerlessness of blacks meant that the approach toward social change had to be cautious, realistic, and sensitive to the mores of the white community. Black leaders believed that the movement toward equality depended upon the support, good will, and generosity of the ruling white elite. This is the leadership tradition that Martin Luther King, Jr., inherited.

Although the ideas of protest, accommodation, and self-help were found in the traditions of both nationalism and integrationism, it was the latter, combined with the spirituality of the black church, that had the greater influence upon the black leadership of Atlanta. Political protest was associated with the Old Testament theme of justice, a theme that is found especially in the prophets and that is dominant in songs and sermons of the black church. Accommodation was closely related to the New Testament idea of love, particularly emphasized in the Sermon on the Mount, and, like justice, a major theme in black religion. Self-help emphasized Christian obedience, which was interpreted by the black church to mean that "God helps those who help themselves." The black leadership tradition of Martin King, so clearly defined by his grandfather and father, represented a black middle class, a ruling black elite of Atlanta. Black leaders were strongly influenced by the spiritual values of justice, love, and obedience, and most believed that if members of the black community practiced those values, they would gain political and economic benefits. Faith in the American political and religious traditions and the perceived progress of the black middle class instilled an optimism that blacks would eventually achieve full citizenship. According to the values of the "black bourgeoisie," as E. Franklin Frazier called them, black people could "make it" if they studied hard, worked hard, saved their money, and stayed out of trouble.

Martin Luther King, Sr., the son of a sharecropper, was a classic example of a person who pulled himself up by his own boot straps, thereby becoming a persuasive symbol of the merits of thrift, service, responsibility, and sacrifice. As a youth "with his only pair of shoes slung over his shoulder," he left rural Stockbridge, Georgia, for Atlanta. There against enormous odds he worked and studied hard to fulfill a promise he made to himself after being denied entrance through the front door of his white friend's house. "Someday," he said, shaking his fist at the white banker's house, "I'm going to have a brick house as big as that—bigger. Someday I'm going to be a director of a bank like that man."[1] "Daddy King," as King, Sr., came to be known, more than fulfilled that promise.

Martin King, Sr., became "a major force" in Atlanta's black community, thereby serving as a powerful example for M. L., as Martin, Jr., was affectionately called. King, Sr., not only succeeded his father-in-law, A. D. Williams, as pastor of Ebenezer, increasing the membership to four thousand; he also became an influential businessman, served on the executive board of the local NAACP and on the board of Morehouse College, and was an active participant in the Negro Voters League. He led the fight to equalize black and white teachers' salaries in Atlanta's public schools. King, Sr., was so militant in his fight for the equality of blacks that he received threats from the Ku Klux Klan. He was so prominent that he became a participant in a small group of black and white elite who eased the tensions between their communities.

Home and church were the most important influences upon the early life of Martin King, Jr. In both contexts he was introduced to the integrationist values of protest, accommodation, self-help, and optimism as they were related to the religious themes of justice, love, obedience, and hope. He was introduced to the value of education as a potent way of helping himself: the way to assert his self-worth, to become a church and community leader, and to fight racism in the larger society. Young King not only adopted many of these values for his personal life style but also incorporated them into his definition of freedom and into his strategy for achieving it.

As one who knew existentially the depth of poverty, King, Sr. (with the support of his wife), taught his children (the others included Christine, Martin's older sister, and A. D., his younger brother) early the value of self-help, that is, the need to take the initiative to make something of oneself, despite the disadvantages of being born a "Negro"—as African-Americans called themselves—in a white, racist society. According to King, Sr., among the principles of the King home were three S's: "Spending, Saving, and Sharing." Young Martin grew up in a community during the 1930s in which nearly 65 percent of African-

Americans were on public relief, but not the King family. They always had plenty of food and suitable attire. Daddy King said the family had "never lived in a rented house" and had "never ridden too long in a car on which payment was due."[2]

Although Daddy King provided for young Martin's material, educational, and religious needs during childhood, he could not provide an environment free of racism. He could not protect him from the ugly manifestations of segregation in every segment of black-white life in Atlanta. At the age of six, young Martin had his first significant experience with the "color bar," and he never forgot it. The father of a white friend told him that they could no longer play together because he was "colored." ("Colored" was the polite term whites used to refer to African-Americans.) The news stunned young Martin because he was unaware of the "racial differences—of the race problem." He did not know quite what to do or say, except to run home and tell his parents about this strange, heartbreaking incident. His parents sat him down and calmly informed him of the "facts of life" about the "color problem" in America. They told him what many African-American parents told their children, namely, about the history of slavery and segregation, and how cruel whites have been and continue to be in their behavior toward blacks. Martin's parents told him that although whites act as if blacks were inferior, nothing could be further from the truth. They assured him of his essential worth. "Don't you let this thing impress you," they said emphatically to him. "Don't let it make you feel you are not as good as white people. You are as good as anyone else, and don't you forget it."[3]

Young Martin's initial responses to his encounter with racism were resentment and reaffirmation of his self-worth. "As my parents discussed some of the tragedies that had resulted from this problem and some of the insults they themselves had confronted on account of it," Martin later recalled, "I was greatly shocked, and from that moment on I was determined to hate every white person." Martin's parents, however, reminded him continually that he "should not hate the white man," because "it was my duty as a Christian to love him." As young Martin struggled with the Christian command to love and the brutal reality of racism, he asked himself, "How can I love a race of people who hate me?" "This was," he said, "a great question in my mind for a number of years."[4]

Martin observed that his father did not "turn the other cheek" to the brutalities of the white man but "had begun to strike back." Daddy King did not "bow and smile" when he was insulted, but was always "straightening out the white folks." "When I stand up," he often proclaimed, "I want everyone to know that a *man* is standing there." On one occasion when Martin was riding in the car with his father, a police-man stopped him and said, "Boy, show me your license." Daddy King shot back, "That's a *boy* there," pointing to young Martin. "I'm a *man*. I'm Reverend King."[5]

Martin observed another racial incident between his father and a clerk in a shoe store. When he and Daddy King sat down in the front seats reserved for whites, the clerk said, "If you will move to the back, I'll be glad to help you." Daddy King snapped angrily, "You will wait on us here or we won't buy any shoes." When the clerk refused to serve them, Daddy King took Martin by the hand and marched out mumbling, "I don't care how long I have to live with this thing, I'll never accept it. I'll fight it till I die. Nobody can make a slave out of you if you don't think like a slave."[6]

Thinking like a free person was not easy for a black child growing up in the South during the 1930s and 1940s. Although young Martin's parents assured him that he was somebody, inferior to no one, the "strict system of segregation" created "something of an inner tension." That system told him: " 'You are less than,' 'You are not equal to.' " It was hard for Martin to believe that he was somebody when America treated him like he was a nigger. Seeing "WHITE ONLY" signs for waiting rooms, restrooms, water fountains, and eating places constantly remind-ed young Martin what it meant to be a nigger in a white man's society. "I could not use the swimming pools," Martin said, as he reflected on his childhood in Atlanta. "Certainly a negro child in Atlanta could not go to any public park. I could not go to the so-called white schools. . . . In many of the stores downtown, . . . I could not go to a lunch counter, to buy a hamburger or a cup of coffee. . . . I could not attend any of the theaters." He also saw the police and the Ku Klux Klan "beating negroes on some of the streets in Atlanta."[7]

Young Martin's daily reminders of whites' rule over blacks seemed to contradict what his parents taught him about human dignity. "You're the little nigger who stepped on my foot," a white woman shouted as she slapped him. Only eight years old at the time, Martin stood there ("in one of the downtown stores of Atlanta") in stunned silence, and then he ran to his mother.[8] He also heard whites addressing blacks as "boy" and "girl," "uncle" and "auntie," and by any other insulting names they cared to use, and blacks had no power to stop them. For blacks to return the insults meant risking not only their livelihood but often their lives. Even among the best relationships, blacks were required to address whites as "Mr." and "Mrs." Whites, however, except in exceptional circumstances, did not return the respect. They called blacks by their first names—"Lucy," "Charlie," and "Pearl."

A deeply painful racial incident occurred when young Martin was in high school. He and his teacher were returning one night from an oratorical contest in Valdosta, Georgia, and the bus driver demanded that both give up their seats near the front for the newly boarding whites. "When we didn't move right away," Martin recalled, "the driver started cursing us out and calling us black sons of bitches. I decided not to move at all, but my teacher pointed out that we must obey that law. So we got up and stood in the aisle the whole 90 miles to Atlanta. It was a night I'll never forget. I don't think I have ever been so deeply angry in my life."[9]

If blacks were going to believe that they were somebody in spite of what whites did to them, from what sources could they derive that belief? One source was the faith of the church. The church was like a "second home" for Martin. It was not only the place where he developed many of his early friendships; it also reinforced the values he learned at home. At Ebenezer Baptist Church, Martin experienced a community at worship—singing, praying, testifying, preaching, and shouting—as they celebrated and praised "the Lord who has been better to us than we have been to ourselves." No reality was more important than God, in this life and the next. God, African-American Christians claimed, could make the "crooked roads straight" and the "rough places plain." They believed that God "builds you up when you are torn down" and "props you up on every leaning side." No matter what whites said about blacks or what wicked laws they enacted against their humanity, the people of Ebenezer believed that God had bestowed upon them a somebodyness which had been signed and sealed by Jesus' death and resurrection. That was why they sang with great enthusiasm and prayed with much thankfulness for what the Lord had done for them. Their activity in worship reflected a fervor commensurate with the gladness they felt in their hearts. They wanted to let the whole world know that God was real and present at Ebenezer. Daddy King and other ministers showed a similar excitement in their preaching, causing the people to respond with shouts of praise, saying "amen" and "thank you, Lord." The church was a haven, a place where blacks could be free of white folks, free of Jim Crow, free of everything that demeaned and humiliated them. They could "sing and shout" and "there'd be nobody there to turn them out." At the age of five Martin joined the church, as he later said, "not out of any dynamic conviction, but out of a childhood desire to keep up with my sister."[10] Yet at Ebenezer the spirituality of the black church was planted deeply in his being, and it grew to become the sustaining force of his life.

In addition to religion, education also played an important role in helping Martin to overcome the disadvantages of being born black in a white, racist society. At an early age, he became fascinated by language, by the sound and power of words to arouse an audience. "You just wait and see," he told his parents, "I'm going to get me some big words."[11] He liked having books around him even before he could read and also tried to go to school before he reached the eligible age. He skipped grades twice and found himself at Morehouse College at the age of fifteen.[12]

Although the spirituality of the black church bestowed upon Martin a somebodyness that racism could not destroy, it did not at first change his mind about hating white people. Education and exposure beyond the church did that. "I did not conquer this antiwhite feeling until I entered college and came in contact with the white students through working in interracial organizations." Through the study of sociology under the direction of Walter Chivers and other professors at Morehouse, Martin came to see that racism was not primarily personal but structural and thus linked to the political economy of capitalism. He also observed that some whites were working, albeit gradually, to eliminate racism. His resentment slowly began to disappear as he associated with more whites of goodwill, especially in an interracial Intercollegiate Council. "The wholesome relations we had in this group convinced me that we have many white persons as allies, particularly among the younger generation," Martin recalled. "I had been ready to resent the whole white race, but as I got to see more whites, my resentment softened and a spirit of cooperation took its place."[13]

Martin also came in contact with whites in Connecticut during his summer employment on a tobacco farm. It had a significant impact on his evolving perspective on race. In Hartford, unlike Atlanta and other places in the South, Martin was free of overt, legal segregation. He and his friends went to restaurants and movies with whites. To the young African-American who had never been exposed to that sort of "equality," these experiences gave an "exhilarating sense of freedom." When he returned South, however, he had to renew his acquaintance with Jim Crow, as he was forced to sit behind a curtain on a train. "I felt as though that curtain had dropped on my selfhood," Martin said. "It was a bitter feeling going back to segregation. It was hard to understand why I could ride wherever I pleased on the train from New York to Washington and then had to change to a Jim Crow car at the nation's capital in order to continue the trip to Atlanta."[14] But instead of segregation making him hate all white people, as he had done earlier, this incident, and others like it, only made him more determined to join with others of both races to fight for the integration of Negroes into the mainstream of American society.

As Martin became less antagonistic toward whites during college, he became more antagonistic toward religion. The relationship between religion and education was not always clear to Martin. Although he grew up in the church and had an inner urge to enter the ministry during high school, his exposure to modern thinking at Morehouse created many doubts in his mind about the truth-value of religion in a scientific world. The critical discourse of the secular disciplines seemed to conflict with the claims of religion. He was especially repelled by the emotionalism he observed at Ebenezer and other black churches. "I had doubts that religion was intellectually respectable," he recalled later. "I revolted against the emotionalism of Negro religion, the shouting and the stamping. I didn't understand it and it embarrassed me."[15] That was why he initially rejected the ministry as a vocation and wanted to become a doctor and later a lawyer. However, Benjamin Mays, president of Morehouse and a well-known advocate of civil rights, and Morehouse professor of religion, George Kelsey, demonstrated to Martin that the ministry could be socially relevant and intellectually stimulating.

In the summer of 1947, at the end of his junior year of college, Martin decided to enter the ministry. He was eighteen. A year later he was ordained. Unlike most Baptist ministers' "call," Martin's, as he later said, "was not a miraculous or supernatural something" but "an inner urge calling me to serve humanity."[16] Like his father and grandfather before him and like Benjamin Mays and George Kelsey, Martin concluded that the ministry was the most appropriate vocation for fighting for the integration of Negroes into the mainstream of American society.

Religion and education gave the black middle class a sense of self-worth and a belief that through devotion to God, industry, intelligence, and peaceful protest, equality in America would soon be realized. Among blacks during the 1940s and early 1950s, only the middle class valued education enough to accept the social isolation and mental discipline required to succeed academically and professionally in white northern universities and seminaries. "Exaggerated Americans" is the phrase Gunnar Myrdal used to describe them in *An American Dilemma*. E. Franklin Frazier, with the same thought in mind, called them "Super Americans." They were always trying to prove that they were as good as whites and thus capable of performing any task with the same degree of excellence. When Martin left Atlanta's Morehouse and went to Crozer Seminary in Chester, Pennsylvania, in 1948, he was determined to prove that "he was as good as the next man."[17]

I was well aware of the typical white stereotype of the Negro — that he is always late, that he's loud and always laughing, that he's dirty and messy — and for a while I was terribly conscious of trying to avoid identification with it. If I was a minute late to class, I was almost morbidly conscious of it and sure that everyone else noticed it. Rather than be thought of as always laughing, I'm afraid I was grimly serious for a time. I had a tendency to overdress, to keep my room spotless, my shoes perfectly shined and my clothes immaculately pressed.

Martin also recalled his feelings at an outing when he discovered that watermelon was being served. He remembered: "I didn't want to be seen eating it because of the association in many people's minds between Negroes and watermelon. It was silly, I know, but it shows how white prejudices can affect a Negro."[18]

Martin King's rejection of the "white stereotype of the Negro" motivated him to finish first in his class, learning how to analyze European theologians and philosophers better than his white student colleagues. He was successful not only in the classroom but in other aspects of the seminary life as well. Martin was well-liked by both teachers and students. His acceptance by whites and assimilation into their value-system were so thorough that he developed a serious personal relationship with a white woman and discussed marriage.

Nevertheless, King had some unpleasant racial incidents at Crozer. The best known was when a North Carolina white student drew a pistol and threatened to shoot him. He accused Martin of messing up his room, a prank students often played on each other. Martin remained remarkably calm during the incident, firmly denying the accusation, as other students persuaded the North Carolinean to put the gun away. He also refused to make charges against the white student, even though he was well-known for his racist views, often calling blacks "darkies." Following the incident, Martin became quite popular in the Crozer community and was elected president of the student body. His social and academic success at Crozer had a profound effect upon his civil rights philosophy in later years.

Another time Martin and his friends were refused service at a New Jersey restaurant. The owner forced them out at the point of a gun. Martin and his friends filed suit but none of the white witnesses to the incident would agree to testify in court.

Despite bitter experiences, the social and intellectual environment at Crozer and in the surrounding area reinforced King's optimism that justice could and would be achieved with intelligent blacks and whites working together to eliminate racism. King became convinced not only that integration was the most appropriate goal of the Negro struggle but also that nonviolence was the best method for achieving it. He decided that nonviolence was the only way Negroes could gain white support in their fight for equality. In several classes King heard about Mahatma Gandhi's successful nonviolent movement in India. But more important were lectures on Gandhi by the noted pacifist A. J. Muste and by Mordecai Johnson (then president of Howard University) following his visit to India. King was deeply moved by what he heard and immediately started to read more about Gandhi's life and teachings. He still rejected any ideological commitment to nonviolence (he agreed with Reinhold Niebuhr's critique of pacifism), yet, in regard to the Negro situation in America, nonviolence (again he followed Niebuhr) seemed to be the only practical method that promised success. Integration and nonviolence appeared to be interrelated in regard to the Negro fight for justice in the United States. However, the nonviolence issue remained academic until the Montgomery bus boycott.

When King went to Boston University for doctoral studies, his experience was much as it had been at Crozer. His social acceptance and success academically had a strong influence upon him. He liked the liberal theological thinking he encountered at both places. Liberalism delivered him from the "fundamentalism" he grew up with at Ebenezer and set him on the road toward "a serious intellectual quest for a method to eliminate social evil."[19] Martin also explored theological and philosophical treatises on the question of why evil exists. He was particularly impressed by his systematic theology teachers, George Davis of Crozer and L. Harold DeWolf of Boston, who were probably the chief reasons why he chose systematic theology for his major concentration in his Ph.D. studies. Both espoused similar points of view which King found congenial to his own emerging theological perspective. They were representatives of "evangelical liberalism," which rejected the neo-orthodoxy of Karl Barth by stressing an openness to modern culture and the possibilities of good in humanity. King's study of Walter Rauschenbusch's *Christianity and the Social Crisis* (1907) moved him deeply, especially Rauschenbusch's interpretation of the Hebrew prophets and "the social aims of Jesus."[20]

When King turned to philosophy, it was Edgar S. Brightman's personalism that captivated him, causing him to adopt it as his own. "Personalism's insistence that only personality—finite and infinite—is ultimately real strengthened me in two convictions," he wrote in his well-known essay "Pilgrimage to Nonviolence." "It gave me metaphysical and philosophical grounding for the idea of a personal God, and it gave me a metaphysical basis for the dignity and worth of all human personality."[21] Belief in a personal God and in the dignity and worth of the human person has always been a deeply held conviction in the African-American Christian community. Therefore, it was easy, almost natural, for King to embrace the philosophy of personalism. But he rejected Brightman's concept of the finite God as an explanation for the existence of evil. King's commitment to the faith of the Negro church was too strong to allow him to embrace a limited God. As long as he was in graduate school, the question "Is the universe friendly?" remained academic and was dealt with theoretically, that is, in the realm of ideas and not in life itself. It was a topic for intellectual debate in a seminar classroom or his philosophy club. The question did not acquire a practical and existential significance until he personally confronted the fear of death during the Montgomery bus boycott, and this question took on even greater significance when he had to preach the eulogies for many fallen black and white comrades in the civil rights movement.

Although King embraced Protestant liberalism as his theological perspective, he also acknowledged his debt to Reinhold Niebuhr. "Niebuhr's great contribution to contemporary theology is that he has refuted the false optimism characteristic of a great segment of Protestant liberalism." King was particularly challenged by Niebuhr's critique of pacifism and his "extraordinary insight into human nature, especially the behavior of nations and social groups." Niebuhr, King observed, "is keenly aware of the complexity of human motives and the relation between morality and power." King not only wrote several appreciative essays on Niebuhr in graduate school but continued to apply his thinking to his work in the civil rights movement. Niebuhr was unquestionably the theologian who shaped King's ideas regarding sin and its relations to group power.[22]

King's reading of the social gospel theologians and the personalist philosophers gave him the intellectual structure to express his concern about justice and his optimism that justice could be achieved. To be sure, Martin's early encounters with racism caused him to have deep resentment toward whites, and his reading of Niebuhr reminded him of "the reality of sin on every level of man's existence." But neither his early resentment of whites nor Niebuhr's doctrine of sin could eliminate his deeply felt belief in the possibilities of humanity to solve social problems, particularly racism in America. King's study of the philosopher Hegel, under the direction of Brightman (reading mainly the *Phenomenology of Mind*), as he said, "helped me to see that growth comes through struggle."[23] Hegel provided King with a dialectical method that enabled him to resolve conflicts in ideas by moving from two opposites (thesis and antithesis) to a higher synthesis.

But in regard to deepening King's optimism about the elimination of racism, the political philosophy of integrationism and the faith of the black church were much more important than Hegel or any other white thinker.[24] In graduate school, King deepened his conviction about the merits of integration, grounding it in academic ideas in theology and philosophy. It is important to note that he did not even mention racism in most of his graduate papers that dealt with justice, love, sin, and evil.

In six years of graduate study at Crozer and Boston, King never identified racism as a theological or philosophical problem or mentioned
whether he recognized it in the student body and faculty. His academic
success and popularity as a student seemed to blind him to the manifestations of sophisticated racism among liberal whites. Like most integrationists of his time, and in contrast to Malcolm and the nationalists,
Martin appeared to be glad merely to have the opportunity to prove
that Negroes could make it in the white man's world. That was no doubt
why he did not dwell on the subject of race inside or outside the classroom when doing theology or dealing with whites. Integrationists
believed that whites would change their views about Negroes when they
got to know each other. According to Major Jones — King's Boston class-
mate and friend who was to become president-dean of Gammon Theological Seminary in Atlanta — both of them decided together that they
would not write their dissertations on the "race problem" but instead
would focus on something "intellectually substantial" in theology, ethics,
and philosophy. King wrote his on "A Comparison of the Conceptions
of God in the Thinking of Paul Tillich and Henry Nelson Wieman."
Although he described the limitations of their views in relation to justice
and love, he did not relate that theme to the situation of black people
in America. It was as if the black experience in the white world had
nothing to contribute to King's critique of Tillich and Wieman or any
other thinker or idea in Euro-American history.

The faith of the Negro church also supported King's integrationist
views in that it too claimed to be nonracial, expounding a Christian
gospel that transcends color. In Christ, "there is no east or west," "no
north or south." "There is," as Paul said, "neither Jew nor Greek,"
"slave nor free," "male nor female." It follows, therefore, that there is
neither "Negro nor white." We are "all one in Christ Jesus" (Gal. 3:28).
This faith is deeply ingrained in the Negro church tradition and is
preached Sunday after Sunday. King knew it well, and he accepted it
as his own. By avoiding the issue of race in graduate school, he was
seeking to demonstrate its irrelevance, which was the goal of the integrationist. The more one could succeed in making race irrelevant the
more one could succeed in getting rid of racism. King had no desire to
become a "good Negro" theologian, writing essays on the theological
implications of racism in America. "If you're setting out to do a good
Negro's job," he would later proclaim many times to black audiences,
"you've already flunked your matriculation exam for entrance into the
university of integration."[25] He wanted instead to become a good theologian, capable of analyzing intelligently any problem in theology. King
was motivated by his desire to be *excellent*, which for him meant doing
a job so well that no one else could do it better. To particularize one's

vocational identity with race was to limit it to a certain group and thereby support segregation instead of the Christian goal of integration.

When King completed his residence requirements at Boston University and offered himself for employment, he could have stayed in the East. Churches in New York and Massachusetts sought him as a pastor. His wife, Coretta Scott, whom he married 18 June 1953, urged him to stay in the East so she could pursue a music career. Of course, his father wanted him to become his associate at Ebenezer and eventually succeed him. While not offending his father, King made it quite clear that he wanted to start out on his own. Several colleges offered him positions as well, including Morehouse, through his friend President Mays.

After soul-searching reflection and much discussion between them, Martin and Coretta, despite segregation, chose to return to "Dixie" because, as Martin wrote, "our greatest service could be rendered in our native South."[26] Service to the less fortunate of the race occupies a central place in the Negro church and in the integrationist tradition in African-American history. King placed that value at the center of his ministry, and thereby acquired the character of humility and self-sacrifice for others which set him apart from his peers. However, King's view of serving Negroes meant helping them to raise their moral and religious standards, educational level, and political consciousness.

Martin King believed deeply that he was a debtor, "eternally in the red," as he often said. He was in debt to the many seen and unseen people who had gone before him, making it possible for him to achieve excellence in education, culture, and social development. He felt in debt to the Negro leaders of the past, like Frederick Douglass and Booker T. Washington, who paved the way on the racial front, demonstrating that Negroes deserve an equal chance in America. King especially felt indebted to his mother and father, who sacrificed for his education, enabling him to stay in school, without having to work, until he had completed the residence requirements for his Ph.D. He was also in debt to the Negro church, founded by his slave ancestors. The church provided a spiritual center for his life, a faith that sustained him and let him know that there is a divine power at work in the world, "transforming dark yesterdays into bright tomorrows."

Although King had been successful in the white world of academia, he felt that he had to return and pay his debt to the Negro community that nurtured his social, educational, and religious development. Many successful Negroes before and during the civil rights era had similar feelings. King's vocational quandary had to do not only with going back South but also with whether he should become a pastor or a professor. Teaching was especially attractive to King since he had been such a successful graduate student, and many of his professors, especially his adviser, Harold DeWolf, urged him to become a scholar. DeWolf "rated him as one of the best five or six graduate students he had taught in his thirty-one years at Boston University."[27] King felt a great debt to his teachers at Crozer and Boston and wanted very much to fulfill the expectations they had of him. He decided that he would become a pastor for a few years and then become a professor and scholar of theology.

Among all the possibilities that King had, he chose to become the pastor of the Dexter Avenue Baptist Church, with about three hundred members, in the city of Montgomery, Alabama. Several factors were involved in his selection of Dexter, the most important of which was perhaps its class orientation. Dexter was a black, middle-class, educated congregation that was well-known for its sophistication and service to the black community of Montgomery. As King himself described it, "Dexter was a sort of silk-stocking church catering only to a certain class." Some people called it the "big folks church." Although King wanted to change the negative aspects of Dexter's middle-class image and make it a place where "people of all levels of life" could come "together to realize their oneness and unity under God," he liked the educational level of its membership, thereby enabling him to combine "emotion and intellect" in his preaching.[28] He was determined not to become a preacher who "whooped and hollered," playing on the emotions of the people, without saying anything. Since most of Dexter's members were college graduates, many of them professors and administrators at Alabama State College in the city, King could use the educational training that he had acquired in the North in his sermons. He was pleased to be following the controversial and legendary Vernon Johns, who was highly educated.

King's love for European culture and education can be seen in the way he described his first visit to Montgomery:

> On a cool Saturday afternoon in January 1954, I set out to drive from Atlanta, Georgia, to Montgomery, Alabama. It was a clear wintry day. The Metropolitan Opera was on the radio with a performance of one of my favorites operas—Donizetti's *Lucia di Lammermoor.* So with the beauty of the country-side, the inspiration of Donizetti's inimitable music, and the splendor of the skies, the usual monotony that accompanies a relatively long drive . . . was dispelled in pleasant diversions.[29]

This was the language of an educated Negro who had been deeply influenced by the values of European culture. According to his soon-to-be closest friend, Ralph Abernathy, King did not take that ride alone, as he reported, but was accompanied by Vernon Johns, who preached at First Baptist Church where Abernathy was pastoring at the time.[30] If that were the case, it shows that King altered a few facts in order to demonstrate to whites that Negroes, if given the chance for cultural and educational development, as he had received at Boston University, would become just as cultured as they.

When Martin King became the official pastor of Dexter in September 1954, he immediately set up a clearly defined organizational structure that reflected what he had learned in his church administration and theology courses at Crozer Seminary and Boston University. It included a cultural committee, "to lift the general cultural appreciation of our church and community"; a scholarship fund committee, to assist the church's high school graduates to attend college, thereby accenting the importance of education; and a social and political action committee. It is particularly revealing to note what King said about the latter committee: "Since the gospel of Jesus is a social gospel as well as a personal gospel seeking to save the whole man, a Social and Political Action Committee shall be established for the purpose of keeping the congregation intelligently informed concerning the social, political and economic situation."[31]

Although King was deeply influenced by his theological teachers at Crozer and Boston, the black church tradition was the most decisive influence in defining not only his faith but also the organizational structure in his church. In the black church, the absolute *authority* of the minister, derived from his divine calling, was unquestioned, particularly in matters related to the operation of the church. Since Dexter was known as a difficult church to pastor (the church had just dismissed Vernon Johns), Martin wanted the deacons and other members to know from the outset that he would not tolerate anything less than complete authority over the operation and worship life of the church. "When a minister is called to the pastorate of a church," King wrote in the "Recommendations to the Dexter Avenue Baptist Church for the Fiscal Year 1954–1955," "the main presupposition is that he is vested with a degree of authority. The source of this authority is twofold. First of all, his authority originates with God. Inherent in the call itself is the presupposition that God directed that such a call be made. This fact makes it crystal clear that the pastor's authority is not merely humanly conferred, but *divinely* sanctioned." Secondly, the authority of the pastor, he continued, "stems from the people themselves. Implied in the call is the unconditional willingness of the people to accept the pastor's leadership. This means that *the leadership never ascends from the pew to the pulpit, but it invariably descends from the pulpit to the pew.*"[32]

During his first year in Montgomery, King devoted most of his time to the activities of his church. He faithfully attended the meetings of all the new committees he had set up so that he could carefully monitor their effectiveness. He also devoted fifteen hours per week to his sermons, carefully preparing what he had to say each Sunday. King's first year as a pastor was quite successful in that he was pleased with his congregation's response to his leadership, and they were immensely satisfied with his attention to their needs and with his outstanding oratory each week. He became well-known to the community in Montgomery and throughout the South and North in Baptist church circles. "Every way I turn people are congratulating me for you," Daddy King told Martin. "You see young man you are becoming very popular."[33]

King also completed his dissertation during his first year in Montgomery, rising at 5:30 A.M. and working for three hours and also devoting the same number of hours late in the evening. His professors at Boston were quite pleased with his defense of it in the spring of 1955. King spoke at an interracial church during the weekend of his defense, and most of his teachers came to hear him. "He called them by name, one by one. He thanked them individually, told them how much he owed them, how he would never have been where he was without them, how grateful he was for their loving concern."[34]

Despite the work on his dissertation and in the church, King still found time to become involved in the political life of the Montgomery community. Montgomery was well-known as the "Cradle of the Confederacy," the place where Jefferson Davis was made president of the southern states that seceded from the Union. Segregation was alive and well in Montgomery and no African-American could escape it. Even taxis were segregated, a law required "white operators [to serve] white passengers exclusively and Negroes rode in a separate system confined to them." But nothing was more demeaning to the dignity of the great majority of African-Americans in Montgomery than the segregated bus service. While African-Americans made up 70 percent of the passengers, bus drivers were "abusive and vituperative," calling them " 'niggers,' 'black cows,' and 'black apes.' "[35] Other insults involved paying one's fare at the front door and being forced to enter at the rear, and even sometimes having the driver pull off before one could board the bus. The bus driver could command blacks to give up their seats to white passengers, even though they were not seated in the section reserved for whites. Most blacks who could do so avoided riding the buses.

Several bus incidents happened before the famous Rosa Parks event; the best-known incident involved Claudette Colvin, a fifteen-year-old high school student who "was pulled off a bus, handcuffed, and taken to jail because she refused to give up her seat to a white passenger." The incident nearly produced a boycott. It did produce a "citizens committee . . . to talk with the manager of the bus company and the City Commission."[36] Although King had not yet arrived in Montgomery as the full-time pastor of Dexter, he was asked to serve on the committee. The main concern of the committee was more courtesy from the bus drivers and clarification of the seating policy. Both the bus company officials and the members of the city commission seemed willing to cooperate. But according to the Negroes of Montgomery, nothing really changed.

The stage was being set for the Rosa Parks event and for the emergence of Martin Luther King, Jr., as the leader of the now-famous Montgomery bus boycott. Like his grandfather and father, King became a social activist pastor, speaking out against the injustice of segregation whenever the opportunity presented itself. He joined the NAACP, a radical organization when evaluated in the sociopolitical context of the South during the 1950s. He also urged the members of Dexter to do the same. In fact, Dexter became the largest NAACP contributor among the black churches of Montgomery. King also made several speeches for it locally and throughout the state, and became a member of the executive committee of the local Montgomery chapter. He was even urged to run for president but declined because he wanted to devote more time to the organization of his church.

King also joined the Alabama Council on Human Relations, the only interracial organization in Montgomery. As the NAACP used the courts to force change, the council sought to effect change through education. It was a small group because few whites risked their social standing by associating with blacks. The council often met in the basement of Dexter.

It seems that King's life from his birth into the middle-class King family in Atlanta to the beginning of his second year in Montgomery as the pastor of Dexter was socially, religiously, and educationally shaped so that his proclamation of the "American dream" was just about inevitable. It was quite easy for him to think of America as a dream and to be optimistic that it could be realized because he himself was a concrete embodiment of its realization. He was well-educated, culturally refined, and politically aware. King believed that if other Negroes were given the same opportunity as he had, they too would manifest a similar social and educational development. That was why integrationism became the major theme of his political philosophy. King believed that fear was the primary reason the majority of whites had not advocated the full integration of Negroes into their society. "Men often hate each other because they fear each other; they fear each other because they do not know each other; they do not know each other because they cannot communicate; they cannot communicate because they are separated."[37]

He repeated this statement during most of his career, for it represented the heart of his integrationist philosophy, which served as the foundation of his dream.

We will have an opportunity to explore more deeply the meaning of King's dream and its impact upon the white and Negro audiences to which he addressed it. But now we must move to an exploration of the development of a gifted African-American whose social, educational, and religious context was not as privileged as Martin King's. King's life represented only one side of the African-American experience, the *American* side. The *African* side was represented in the life of Malcolm X. As King's early life shows the bright (American), integrationist side of the African-American struggle, Malcolm X's early life shows its dark (African), nationalist side. We turn now to the early life of Malcolm, the "bad nigger," without losing sight of Martin, the dreamer.

2

THE MAKING OF A "BAD NIGGER" (1925–52)

People are always speculating—why am I as I am? To understand that of any person, his whole life, from birth, must be reviewed. All our experiences fuse into our personality. Everything that ever happened to us is an ingredient. . . . I think that an objective reader may see how in the society to which I was exposed as a black youth here in America, for me to wind up in a prison was really just about inevitable.

> Malcolm X
> *The Autobiography of Malcolm X*
> 1965

No one has pointed out the past and current injustices of American society in relation to its inhabitants of African descent as trenchantly and as truthfully as Malcolm X. Whether he was speaking to whites at Harvard University or to blacks on the streets of Harlem, the force and the integrity of his language compelled people to listen to him. Nothing was more important to Malcolm X than telling the truth about black-white relations in the United States and the world. His truth was not derived from a university education. He spoke a truth that he had lived, a truth that came from the bottom of the black experience and not from privileges of the black middle class. He rejected Martin King's idea of integration and defined his identity as an affirmation of blackness in opposition to America. "I'm black first," he said. "My sympathies are black, my allegiance is black, my whole objectives are black. . . . I am not interested in being American, because America has never been interested in me."[1]

In opposition to Martin King's middle-class, integrationist image of the American dream of Negroes and whites working together, Malcolm

X, looking at America from the viewpoint of the "black masses living at the bottom of the social heap," invoked the contrasting image of the nightmare to describe the sociopolitical reality of America for the vast majority of African-Americans. "While King was having a dream," he snapped about the March on Washington, "the rest of us Negroes are having a nightmare."[2]

Like Martin King's dream, Malcolm X's nightmare has suffered distortions, by friend and foe alike. In both cases most of the distortions are the work of people who regard themselves as admirers of Martin but not of Malcolm. As Martin is in danger of being romanticized as a saint, Malcolm is portrayed as a "messiah of hate" and a "violence-preaching Black Muslim racial agitator." No black person's philosophy has been more maligned than Malcolm X's. Largely because of fear and ignorance, significant segments of the media, government, church, and educational and civil rights establishments labeled Malcolm and his followers a "black Ku Klux Klan of racial extremists" and claimed that Malcolm was destroyed by the violence he spawned.[3] When he was assassinated, 21 February 1965, the media unleashed its venom against him. The *Washington Post* described him as "the spokesman of bitter racism."[4] *Newsweek* called him "an extravagant talker, a demagogue who titillated slum Negroes and frightened whites with his blazing racist attacks on the 'white devils' and his calls for an armed American Mau Mau."[5] *Time* said that he "was an unashamed demagogue" whose "gospel was hatred" and who "in life and in death—was a disaster to the civil rights movement."[6] The *New York Times* called him an "irresponsible demagogue," an "extraordinary and twisted man" who turned "true gifts to evil purpose."[7] The *New York Herald Tribune* said that "the cause of Negro equality" lost nothing "valuable by Malcolm X's passing" because "he was a destructive force."[8] Columnist Walter Winchell of the *Journal American* referred to him as "a petty punk who pictured himself as a heroic figure."[9] The *Nation* described him as "the highly intelligent, courageous leader of one segment of the Negro lunatic fringe."[10] Commenting on Malcolm's forthcoming autobiography, an excerpt of which it published, the *Saturday Evening Post* said of him: "If Malcolm were not a Negro, his autobiography would be little more than a journal of abnormal psychology, the story of a burglar, dope pusher, addict and jailbird—with a family history of insanity—who acquires messianic delusions and sets forth to preach an upside down religion of 'brotherly' hatred. . . . We shall be lucky if Malcolm X is not succeeded by even weirder and more virulent extremists."[11]

Malcolm's reputation in Canada and Europe was similar to his American image. Pierre Berton, a Canadian television interviewer, called Malcolm a "black vigilante."[12] Humphrey Berkley, a member of the

British Parliament, referred to him as "North America's leading exponent of Apartheid."[13] When Malcolm was killed, the *London Times* referred to him as a "black extremist" who advocated the "destruction of the whites." The West German media described Malcolm's assassination as if it were in the "Chicago gangster tradition."[14]

During Malcolm's life and immediately following his assassination, the black media were often as intemperate and uninformed as the white media in their evaluation of him. Columnist Ralph Matthews of the *Washington Afro-American* referred to him as a "professional race-baiter." *Muhammad Speaks,* the official organ of Nation of Islam, was well-known for its attacks upon Malcolm after his break with Elijah Muhammad. John Shabazz compared him to Judas and labeled him "the number one hypocrite of all time."[15] Minister Louis X of Boston (now known as Louis Farrakhan) called him a "cowardly hypocritical dog" who "is worthy of death."[16] *The Call* of Kansas City, Missouri, responded to Malcolm's assassination with an editorial entitled "Violence Begets Violence: 'Chickens Come Home To Roost.' "[17] A similar comment was made by the *Michigan Chronicle,* which said that Malcolm "reaped the harvest of his own philosophy."[18] Carl T. Rowan, then director of the United States Information Agency, was greatly disturbed about the high tributes that African and Asian countries paid to Malcolm when he was assassinated. He said that "he could not understand all the fuss about an ex-convict, ex-dope peddler who became a racial fanatic."[19] The *Indianapolis Recorder* contended that Malcolm made no contribution "to gains in social justice." He merely caused discord which was "contrary to . . . the Founding Fathers of Our Republic."[20]

Black civil rights leaders were especially unkind in their characterization of Malcolm. In a debate with him at Harvard, Walter C. Carrington of the NAACP described Malcolm's philosophy as "the best thing that happened to the KKK since the invention of the bedsheet." Ralph Bunche said that he was "mentally depraved." James Farmer of CORE called Malcolm a "talented demagogue." Bayard Rustin said that he was a "conservative force in the Negro community" whose "violent rhetoric" was a "cop-out."[21]

The negative assessment of Malcolm is not as widely promoted among African-Americans today. Twenty-five years after his assassination, there is a resurgence of interest in him, especially among the young who were not yet born when he died. Malcolm's name, words, and face appear on buttons, T-shirts, and the covers of rap records. His life has become the basis of films, plays, and even operas. He is now being quoted by mainstream black leaders, who once despised him. Some have compared him to Nelson Mandela of South Africa and Martin King, saying that Malcolm's image embodies the best in both. Malcolm's popularity has even inspired a new movement to declare his birthday, May 19, a "National African-American Day of Commemoration." Conferences, seminars, and parades are being held in his honor, and streets, schools, and organizations are being named after him. People are making annual pilgrimages to his birthplace and grave site.

Despite the rekindled interest in Malcolm, it has not led to a greater understanding of what he was all about. "He's getting attention, but I still think he's misunderstood," said Attallah Shabazz, Malcolm's oldest daughter. "[Young people are] inspired by pieces of him instead of the entire man."[22] The same is true of the people who knew him and walked by his side. Both the lingering effects of the earlier negative attacks and the current popular interest encourage people not to take Malcolm seriously as a complete thinker and a major actor in the African-American struggle for justice, instead allowing his true image to fade from memory. The memory of Malcolm is likely to be both false and dim. There are still many African-Americans who have never heard of him. Even college students, seeing public lecture notices on "Malcolm X," have been known to ask, "Who is this Malcolm Ten?" There are other African-Americans who know his name but do not know who he really was and what he really stood for. In such conditions a critical description of him, in his social context and in relation to Martin King, is much needed.

●

In contrast to Martin King's origin in the southern Negro middle class, Malcolm X was a product of the northern poor black masses. Born Malcolm Little in Omaha, Nebraska, 19 May 1925, he was the seventh child of J. Early Little (who had "three children by a previous marriage") and the fourth of M. Louise Norton, a West Indian from Grenada. Malcolm grew up in Lansing, Michigan, and worked as a hustler in Boston and New York until he was sentenced to Charlestown State Prison, 27 February 1946. Like Martin, Malcolm was the son of a Georgia Baptist preacher; but unlike the influential Martin King, Sr., Earl Little was a "jackleg" preacher who was never called to a permanent pastorate. Like Martin's father, Malcolm's father was deeply involved in black people's struggle for dignity and justice. But unlike the integrationist King, Sr., Earl Little was a nationalist and "a dedicated organizer" for Marcus Garvey's UNIA. As Martin was influenced by the integrationist activity of his father, Malcolm was affected by the nationalist work of his. The seeds of Malcolm's nationalist sentiments were sown by both his father and mother. His father served as the president of the Omaha branch of the UNIA, and his mother was the reporter. Malcolm remembered his mother as "an active worker in the Garvey Movement" who was proud of her African blood and heritage and who instilled that pride in her children. Malcolm's father, however, was the most potent symbol of blackness in the Little family. Malcolm remembered his father as the one who took him to Garveyite meetings in Lansing, Michigan:

> The image of him that made me proudest was his crusading and militant campaigning with the words of Marcus Garvey. . . . I can remember hearing . . . "Africa for the Africans," "Ethiopians, Awake!" And my father would talk about how it would not be much longer before Africa would be completely run by Negroes — "by black men," was the phrase he always used. "No one knows when the hour of Africa's redemption cometh. It is in the wind. It is coming. One day, like a storm, it will be here."[23]

Like Martin, Malcolm was a minister, a "man of the cloth," to use a phrase often heard in the black community. But Malcolm was a minister of the religion of Islam, initially as defined by Elijah Muhammad and later according to the teachings of the worldwide Sunni Islamic community. Like Martin, Malcolm spent many years preparing for his vocation as a minister and a public speaker. But unlike Martin, who earned his doctorate, Malcolm's formal education ended at the eighth grade, but continued informally in the ghettos of Boston and New York, in Charlestown Prison, and under his father in the ministry, Elijah Muhammad. Malcolm often introduced himself for public debates like this: "Gentlemen, I finished the eighth grade in Mason, Michigan. My high school was the black ghetto of Roxbury, Massachusetts. My college was in the streets of Harlem, and my master's was taken in prison."[24]

Although there were many similarities between Martin King's and Malcolm X's social, religious, and educational development, their *dissimilarities* stand out the most. In his autobiography, Malcolm spoke of his early childhood as a "nightmare." His family was driven out of Omaha by the Ku Klux Klan when he was a baby. Another white hate group, called the Black Legionnaires, burned down their house during his childhood in Lansing, an experience Malcolm called "the nightmare in 1929, my earliest vivid memory."

> I remember being suddenly snatched awake into a frightening confusion of pistol shots and shouting and smoke and flames. My father had shouted and shot at the two white men who had set the fire and were running away. Our home was burning down around us. We were lunging and bumping and tumbling all over

each other trying to escape. My mother, with the baby in her arms, just made it into the yard before the house crashed in, showering sparks. I remember we were outside in the night in our underwear, crying and yelling our heads off. The white police and firemen came and stood around watching as the house burned down to the ground.[25]

As a child, Malcolm experienced not only the violence of whites but also the violence of his father and mother against each other and of both against his seven brothers and sisters and himself. While Martin King could "hardly remember" his mother and father arguing, Malcolm's parents "seemed to be nearly always at odds. Sometimes my father would beat her." Both beat the children, with Malcolm's mother meting out most of his punishments and his father being "belligerent toward" the others. Malcolm believed that his father, who was "jet-black," exempted him from whippings because he was the "lightest child." "As antiwhite as my father was," Malcolm said, reflecting back, "he was subconsciously so afflicted with the white man's brainwashing of Negroes that he inclined to favor the light ones." Malcolm's mother, who was a "near-white" (her mother was raped by a white man), was prejudiced in the opposite direction. "Just as my father favored me for being lighter than the other children, my mother gave me more hell for the same reason."[26]

Unlike Martin King, who hardly uttered a sound when he was whipped by his father, Malcolm, when he was punished, behaved as if his mother were "killing" him. "For if she even acted as though she was about to raise a hand to me," he recalled, "I would open my mouth and let the world know about it." He used the same tactic when his mother refused his request for "a buttered biscuit or something." Unlike his siblings, especially his oldest full-brother, Wilfred, whom his mother praised "for being nice and quiet," Malcolm was quick to make his wishes known: "I would cry out and make a fuss until I got what I wanted." He "learned early that crying out in protest could accomplish things." "If you want something," he contended, "you had better make some noise."[27]

In his autobiography and in several interviews and speeches, Malcolm said that his father was murdered, "thrown under a street car" by the Black Legionnaires. But during a speaking engagement at Michigan State University, in January 1963, he reported that his father's death was accidental. A coroner's inquest also listed his death as accidental.[28] Whether the cause of the death was murder or a mishap, Malcolm's father's absence had a profound effect upon the economic and emotional well-being of the Little family. Louise Little was forced to try to survive with eight children during the depression years of the 1930s. The pain of hunger became a daily experience for the Little family. "Our family was so poor," Malcolm recalled, "that we would eat the hole out of a doughnut." He described the hunger in greater detail: "We would be so hungry we were dizzy. My mother would boil a big pot of dandelion greens, and we would eat that. I remember that some small-minded neighbor put it out, and children would tease us, that we ate 'fried grass.' Sometimes, if we were lucky, we would have oatmeal or cornmeal mush three times a day. Or mush in the morning and cornbread at night."

Against her pride Malcolm's mother was forced to accept public relief and the humiliating implications that she was mentally incompetent to care for her children. "Psychological deterioration" set in as the Little family had to recognize that they were destitute. Malcolm began to steal, because, as he said, "I was so hungry, I didn't know what to do." The welfare agents began to exert their authority, which undermined the family's mutual support and unity. Malcolm's memory of them partly explained his intense antipathy toward whites in his later life: "They acted as if they owned us, as if we were their private property. As much as my mother would have liked to, she couldn't keep them out. She would get particularly incensed when they began insisting upon drawing us older children aside, one at a time, out on the porch or somewhere, and asking us questions, or telling us things—against our mother and against each other."[29]

The welfare workers or "home wreckers," as Malcolm called them, succeeded in breaking up the Little family. Louise Little suffered a mental breakdown and was placed in the state hospital at Kalamazoo. The eight children became "state children." The younger ones, including Malcolm, were placed in several homes. Looking back on that painful event, Malcolm said:

> I truly believe that if ever a state social agency destroyed a family, it destroyed ours. We wanted and tried to stay together. Our home didn't have to be destroyed. But the Welfare, the courts, and their doctor, gave us the one-two-three punch. . . . We were "state children," court wards; [the judge] had the full say-so over us. A white man in charge of a black man's children! Nothing but legal, modern slavery—however kindly intentioned.[30]

Comparing Malcolm X's and Martin King's early childhood experiences provides a clue to their radically different perspectives on America in their later lives. Martin's parents provided their children with "a very congenial home," including "the basic necessities of life," and important role-models of the race for them to emulate.[31] They also protected them from the worst experiences of white racism. Martin, therefore, was able to develop the inner fortitude, self-confidence, and discipline to overcome his disadvantages in a segregated society.

Malcolm's parents could not protect their children from the violence of white hate groups or from the more civilized violence of institutional racism. Malcolm was only six years old when his father was killed and twelve when his mother was committed to a mental institution. With no parental love to affirm his personhood and to instill in him the self-confidence that he was as good as anybody else, he, though gifted and popular, did not have the emotional strength to cope with a white society that refused to recognize his humanity.

It is important to note the great contrast not only in the family environments of Martin and Malcolm but also in their church and educational experiences during childhood. While Martin attended segregated churches and schools and rarely came in contact with whites, thereby enabling him to develop a sense of himself as a Negro in a white world, Malcolm's church and educational experiences were primarily integrated and thus defined by whites. "I . . . lived a thoroughly integrated life,"[32] Malcolm told Kenneth Clark, as he reflected back on his childhood. Following his father's death, his mother joined a Seventh-Day Adventist church which was mostly white. Malcolm attended three schools in Michigan; two of them were chiefly white, and all three were controlled by whites. What he remembered about the white people he encountered in the schools and the detention home where he resided was the names they called him and other blacks: "Nigger," "coon," "darkie," and "Rastus." He heard these epithets so often they ceased to be insulting; he thought of them as his actual names.

Besides the children of a black family called Lyons, Malcolm was the only one of his race at Mason Junior High School. He studied hard and succeeded in becoming one of the top students in his class. He was also elected the president of the seventh-grade class. The Swerlins, a wife-husband team who ran the detention home where Malcolm stayed, were proud of him. It seemed that everyone—fellow students, teachers, and townspeople—liked him, and he was proud that they did. But despite all the attention Malcolm received, those whites made it clear to him that he was not *white* and thus could not do what others did. He could not date white girls. Malcolm was their *favorite* nigger, but no more.

Going to Boston during the summer of 1940 and seeing so "many Negroes . . . thronging downtown Roxbury at night, especially on Saturdays"—the "neon lights, nightclubs, poolhalls, bars, the cars they drove!"—created, Malcolm remembered, "the sense of being a real part of a mass of my own kind, for the first time." It also caused "a restlessness with being around white people." When he returned to Mason, whites noticed that he was "acting so strange. You don't seem like yourself, Malcolm," they told him.[33] He was struggling with the "Who am I?" question, a perpetual one for a people whose place in the world is defined by others. Because he was not white and was isolated from the masses of blacks, Malcolm not only did not have a clear sense of his identity but was not even in a supportive environment where he could search for it and fight openly against others who denied him that right. Thus when his eighth grade English teacher discouraged him from becoming a lawyer and suggested carpentry as a more "realistic goal for a nigger," his ego was too weak to insist on fulfilling his ambition. "It was then that I began to change—inside. I drew away from white people. I came to class, and I answered when called upon. It became a physical strain simply to sit in Mr. Ostrowski's class. Where 'nigger' had slipped off my back before, wherever I heard it now, I stopped and looked at whoever said it. And they looked surprised that I did."[34]

Malcolm's encounter with his English teacher became the "first major turning point" in his life. It represented the end of his attempt to become integrated into white society. He concluded that no matter what he did he would never be fully accepted by whites and given the same opportunities as they. With that conclusion clear in his mind, from that point on in his life he did not even want to be around them. The Swerlins of the detention home (who not only allowed Malcolm to stay with them so he would not have to go to the reform school but also enrolled him at Mason Junior High and helped him get a job) were particularly puzzled and wanted to know why Malcolm was acting as if he "wasn't happy there anymore." They kept asking him, "What's wrong?," to which he replied, "Nothing." He was a black teenager with no parental support or role-models; he was living in a detention home run by whites who treated him as if he were a "mascot" or a "pet canary"; he was going to a white school where people showed no respect for his humanity— that was what was wrong! Malcolm, of course, could not explain the deep hurt he was feeling inside to the people who were responsible for it. They would not have understood anyway.

At this point in his life, Malcolm had not developed a political or a cultural consciousness to explain his antiwhite feelings even to himself. He was not yet a black nationalist. But his restlessness with being around whites and the unpleasant encounter with his English teacher pushed him in that direction. Black nationalists do not like whites, and they *especially* love being around their own kind. This is why they are called separatists in contrast to integrationists, who seek to be accepted by whites. As a student at Mason Junior High, Malcolm was very successful academically and quite popular in his social relations with others. He was a model integrationist. He thus deeply resented it when his English teacher recommended carpentry for him while he "encouraged" the less intelligent whites to pursue "what they . . . wanted."

For middle-class Negroes who have the support of strong, successful parents and who live in a vibrant community of their race, a note of discouragement from a white teacher would likely serve only to strengthen their determination to enter a profession. In viewing the racial struggle they would probably become integrationists or possibly moderate nationalists. Malcolm later looked at this turning point from a different angle: "If Mr. Ostrowski had encouraged me to become a lawyer, I would today probably be among some city's professional black bourgeoisie, sipping cocktails and palming myself off as a community spokesperson for and leader of the suffering black masses, while my primary concern would be to grab a few more crumbs from the groaning board of the two-faced whites with whom they're begging to 'integrate.' "[35]

As it was, Malcolm, only fifteen, dropped out of school and went to live with Ella Mae Little Collins, a half-sister who lived in Boston. There he identified with the black masses and rejected the Negro middle class. Although he appreciated what his half-sister did for him, she could not entice him to associate with the successful "Hill Negroes" of her neighborhood in Roxbury, the "Four Hundred," as they called themselves. They pretended to be who they were not—"breaking their backs trying to imitate white people."

Malcolm was drawn to that part of Roxbury which the "Hill elite" "looked down their noses at," the "town ghetto section." It was "much more exciting," with its "grocery stores, walk-up flats, cheap restaurants, poolrooms, bars, storefront churches, and pawnshops." He "felt more relaxed among Negroes who were being their *natural* selves and not putting on airs." For Malcolm, before and after his conversion to the Nation of Islam, being "natural" meant acting like *black* people—talking, walking, and dancing according to the instincts of their African heritage. It also meant not feeling "any better than any other Negro" and avoiding the "indignity of . . . self-delusion."

Nothing disturbed Malcolm more than to hear Negroes talking, with "phonied up" "black Bostonese" accents, about being in "banking" or "securities," as if "they were discussing a Rockefeller or Mellon," when in fact they "worked as menials and servants." Some "talked so affectedly among their own kind," he said, "that you couldn't even understand them." Malcolm called them "Hill clowns." His utter distaste for the Negro middle class deepened after his conversion to the Nation of Islam, and caused him to unleash a barrage of intemperate statements against King and other civil rights leaders.[36]

As a teenager in Roxbury, however, Malcolm showed his contempt for the Negro middle class and its values by immersing himself whole-heartedly in the violent and self-humiliating world of the black under-class, where he was fully accepted. He identified completely with the world of the hustler from the moment in 1941 when he first arrived in Boston to his conversion in 1948 to Elijah Muhammad's Nation of Islam while in prison. He found himself a "slave" (job) as a shoeshine boy at the Roseland State Ballroom, bought himself several zoot suits, smoked and sold reefers, and got himself a white woman, "too fine to believe," as a status symbol. As a shoeshine boy, he not only shined white cus-tomers' shoes, making his rag "pop like a firecracker" to the rhythm of Benny Goodman's band, he also "whiskbroomed" "white cats" for "a nickle or dime tip" and "for two bits, Uncle Tom[med] a little." Noth-ing, however, revealed Malcolm's contempt for himself more than the faithful "conking" of his hair. Reflecting back on his "self-defacing conk," he said:

> This was my first really big step toward self-degradation: when I endured all that pain, literally burning my flesh to have it look like a white man's hair. I had joined that multitude of Negro men and women in America who are brainwashed into believing that the black people are "inferior" — and white people "superior" — that they will even violate and mutilate their God-created bodies to try to look "pretty" by white standards.[37]

Malcolm was awed when he first visited New York. Harlem mes-merized him. "New York was heaven to me," he recalled. "And Harlem was Seventh heaven!" Small's Paradise, the Savoy Ballroom, the The-resa Hotel, the Braddock Hotel bar, the Apollo Theater, the nightclubs, speakeasies, and other places "wherever Negroes played music" con-sumed every waking hour of his time when he was not working as a "sandwich man on the 'Yankee Clipper' [train] to New York." Harlem was like Roxbury's South End "magnified a thousand times."[38]

It was in Harlem that Malcolm was "schooled" in his hustling trade by the "experts" (such persons as "Sammy the Pimp," "Jumpsteady," "Fewclothes," "Dollarbill," and "West Indian Archie") and succeeded in becoming "one of the most depraved parasitical hustlers" of his time. He learned all about "such hustles as the numbers, pimping, con games of many kinds, peddling dope, and thievery of all sorts, including armed robbery." Malcolm's description of his life in the world of the black underclass is a powerful story of what white society did and still does to those who are its black victims. While in Harlem, he was nearly killed several times by fellow hustlers, and he nearly murdered them. "I would risk just about anything," he recalled.[39]

When Malcolm returned to Boston, old acquaintances (especially his half-sister Ella) were surprised how weird and "uncouth [he] had become." He had a cocaine habit that cost him twenty dollars a day. To support it, he organized a burglary ring which included a friend named "Shorty," their white girl friends, and a "finder" named "Rudy."[40] He later thought himself fortunate to have been caught and sentenced to eight to ten years in prison for burglary, for it was in prison that he encountered the teachings of Elijah Muhammad, teachings that radically transformed his life.

Like Malcolm's natural father, Elijah Muhammad was a Baptist minister. Born on 10 October 1897 on a tenant farm in Sandersville, Georgia, Elijah Poole, as he was known then, left Georgia for Detroit in 1923 after several years of severe encounters with racism in his native state. He left the Christian ministry because he found it to be an ineffective tool for fighting racism. He soon became a disciple of Wallace D. Fard, who was credited with founding the first Temple of Islam on 4 July 1930. Fard bestowed upon Poole the title of "Muhammad." Following Fard's mysterious disappearance in 1934, Elijah Muhammad assumed complete authority over the movement and soon after, because of a contest over his leadership, moved the headquarters from Detroit to Chicago. With a small but faithful following, Muhammad defined the Nation of Islam as antiwhite and anti-Christian. He was convicted in 1942 on the charge of encouraging draft resistance and served three years in the Federal Correctional Institution at Milan, Michigan.

Malcolm was taken to prison just before his twenty-first birthday. At first his behavior in prison was the same as before. He continued to hurl obscenities at whites in authority, especially the "prison psychologist" and the "prison chaplain." His prison inmates named him "Satan" because of his "antireligious attitude." He liked the name, because, as he said, "I considered myself beyond atheism."[41]

After a "vicious reply" to his "religious brother" Philbert, who had written to him about the "natural religion for the black man," the process of Malcolm's radical conversion to the teachings of Elijah Muhammad began when his younger brother Reginald wrote him a letter which said, in part: "Malcolm, don't eat any pork, and don't smoke any more cigarettes. I'll show you how to get out of prison." The information surprised Malcolm and captured his attention like nothing else, because, as he said, "I wanted out so badly." Thinking that his brother, who had lived for a time with him in New York, "had come upon some way I could work a hype on the penal authorities," Malcolm gladly followed his instructions as he anxiously waited for Reginald to provide the solution to the riddle. His sudden change in behavior shocked his fellow inmates and also made him feel proud that he had overcome the white stereotype that blacks "couldn't do without pork." He also later identified his change as "unconsciously, my first pre-Islamic submission."[42]

Even before Malcolm received his brother's letter, he had taken steps to transform his life. He was greatly impressed with the wide-ranging knowledge of Bimbi, a self-educated fellow inmate. "Out of the blue one day," Malcolm recalled, "Bimbi told me flatly, as was his way, that I had some brains, if I'd use them." That was the beginning of Malcolm's own self-education, which transformed his life. Hearing Bimbi's discourse on religion, Malcolm began to develop a different attitude toward it. "Bimbi put the atheistic philosophy in a framework, so to speak. That ended my vicious cursing attacks. My approach sounded so weak alongside his, and he never used a foul word." "He was the first man I had ever seen command total respect . . . with his words."[43]

By introducing Malcolm to a world of books, Bimbi prepared him to receive his brother's message about the "natural religion for the black man," commonly known by believers as the "Nation of Islam," but by the public as the "Black Muslims," a phrase coined by sociologist C. Eric Lincoln, who wrote the authoritative text on the movement. What Malcolm's brother told him about the teachings of Elijah Muhammad, "the Messenger of Allah," reinforced what he read in history books in the libraries of Massachusetts prisons. In the Nation of Islam, Malcolm discovered for the first time the respect for himself as a human being that had heretofore escaped him.

Malcolm's conversion occurred in 1948, the same year that King was ordained and entered Crozer Seminary. While Martin King described his conversion to Christianity as "unconscious," the "gradual intaking of the noble ideals set forth in my family and my environment,"[44] Malcolm's conversion to Islam was striking and instantaneous. He said that when his brother Reginald first told him of Muhammad's teachings about the devil white man and the brainwashed black man, he was "left rocking with some of the first serious thoughts of my life." The truth of Muhammad's teachings was like a "blinding light." "Every instinct of the ghetto jungle streets, every hustling fox and criminal wolf instinct in me, . . . was struck numb." "It was as though all of that life [as a hustler] merely was back there, without any remaining effect, or influence." Later he read in the Bible "over and over, how Paul on the road to Damascus, upon hearing the voice of Christ, was so smitten that he was knocked off his horse, in a daze." While he did not liken himself to Paul, he said: "I do understand his experience." Malcolm's interpretation of his conversion experience was similar to that of a typical preacher in black church history, particularly the Baptist tradition, which both his natural and spiritual fathers had represented. "The truth can be quickly received, or received at all, only by the sinner who knows and admits that he is guilty of having sinned much. . . . The very enormity of my previous life's guilt prepared me to accept the truth."[45]

However, Malcolm's self-degradation tells only half of the story of his sudden, radical transformation. The religion of transformation had to be one derived from the world in which he lived. It had to be a religion of the black ghetto experience. The public images of Christianity were both middle-class and white—including those of God, Jesus, and all the angels—so no preacher of Christianity, be he ever so black, had a chance with Malcolm. In contrast stood the Nation of Islam, which Elijah Muhammad defined as "God's religion" for the "Original People"—black people. Everything about it was black, including God and all of God's followers. It was a religion specifically directed to "the Negro in the mud"—dope addicts and pushers, pimps and prostitutes, prisoners—all of those blacks who saw no way out of the hell of their daily lives. According to Muhammad, Islam would "wake-up," "stand-up," and "clean-up" these "deaf, dumb, and blind" "so-called Negroes" and then set them on a course toward "freedom, justice, and equality."

Two central claims of the Nation of Islam attracted Malcolm: its definition of the white man as the devil and its affirmation of black history and culture. When one considers Malcolm's personal history with whites and the impact of books that he read in the prison library about slavery in the Americas and colonialism in Africa, it is no surprise that the claim "the white man is the devil" rang true to him. Many, if not most, African-Americans would acknowledge the statement as true: not naturally true, as Elijah Muhammad said, but *historically* true. Initially, Malcolm was completely persuaded that it was true in both senses; after his break with Muhammad, he dropped the idea of the white man as the devil by nature.

However, the rejection of whites would not have been enough to sustain Malcolm's deepest commitment. For him, the most persuasive element of the Nation of Islam was its affirmation of black people's cultural history, going back to the continent of Africa, before the European slave trade and the infamous "peculiar institution" in North America. Lack of self-knowledge leads inevitably to self-destruction, as shown in the hipster life style of lower-class blacks and in the pretentious behavior of those in the Negro middle class. The devil white man, according to Muhammad, has brainwashed the so-called Negroes so that they do not know who they are. Malcolm recalled that Reginald's words moved him deeply:

You don't even know who you are. . . . You don't even know, the white devil has hidden it from you, that you are of a race of people

of ancient civilizations, and riches in gold and kings. You don't
even know your true family name, you wouldn't recognize your
true language if you heard it. You have been cut off by the devil
white man from all true knowledge of your own kind. You have
been a victim of the evil of the devil white man ever since he
murdered and raped and stole you from your native land in the
seeds of your forefathers.[46]

These two ideas—the utter rejection of white values and the embrac-
ing of black history and culture—lay at the heart of Elijah Muhammad's
teachings, and they became the center of Malcolm's philosophy. However, Malcolm was converted not only to Elijah Muhammad's ideas but
to the man himself. Absolute submission to Allah, as the Nation of Islam
demanded, also meant complete obedience to the "Honorable Elijah
Muhammad," who was Allah's Messenger. Malcolm gladly gave himself
in complete obedience to following the precepts of the Nation of Islam
as defined solely by Muhammad. "I have never been one for inaction,"
he said. "Everything I've ever felt strongly about, I've done something
about." All of his intelligence and determination were locked into devotion to Elijah Muhammad, his spiritual father, whom he regarded as
divine.

Malcolm's devotion to the Nation of Islam served as a powerful stim-
ulus to his moral self-reform and self-education so he could be an example to others and an effective evangelist in spreading the good news of
what Islam could do for "the caged-up black man." No one had sunk
lower than he had sunk in the white man's society. If Islam could reform
him, it could reform anybody. Malcolm knew, however, that he could
not tell his story effectively and thereby spread "Mr. Muhammad's
teachings" unless he had the adequate knowledge and a speaking style
that was persuasive for the black people of the prisons and ghetto.

Envious of Bimbi's "stock of knowledge," Malcolm taught himself
how to read and write with understanding by copying words out of the
dictionary. Slowly and painfully, he acquired an adequate penmanship
and knowledge of English, and that enabled him to write letters to Elijah
Muhammad, his brothers and sisters, and hustler friends. Becoming a
Black Muslim increased tremendously Malcolm's passion for knowledge
because the acquisition of learning meant that he could "document
[Muhammad's] teachings in books." He devoured books rapidly, like a
hungry lion eating its prey. "Let me tell you something," Malcolm said,
as he reflected upon the "new vistas that reading opened up" to him.
"From then until I left that prison, in every free moment I had, if I was
not reading in the library, I was reading on my bunk. You couldn't have
gotten me out of books with a wedge." "No university would ask any

student to devour literature as I did." Time passed quickly as Malcolm forgot that he was even in prison. "In fact, up to then," he said, "I never had been so truly free in my life." He read everything—books on sociology, history, religion, and philosophy—written by W. E. B. Du Bois, Carter G. Woodson, J. A. Rogers, Herodotus, Schopenhauer, Kant, Nietzsche, and Spinoza. History was his favorite topic because it focused on the "facts." He read late into the night, using "a corridor light that cast a glow in [his] room." He participated in prison debates, presenting the pro and con on all kinds of subjects, as he honed his skills in the art of argument. No matter what the subject was, he always managed to find a way to tell the history of the "monstrous crime" that the "collective white man" had committed against "the world's collective non-white man."[47]

Malcolm was paroled from prison in August of 1952, just as Martin King was about to begin his second year of graduate studies at Boston University. Malcolm journeyed by bus to Detroit to live with the family of his brother Wilfred, who had gotten him a job at a furniture store. In Wilfred's home, he was introduced to the life style of a Black Muslim family. He liked the order and discipline, with the man, as the head of the household, taking the lead, setting an example for his wife and children. At Temple Number One, he met the members, became acquainted with the Black Muslim worship style, and was given more information about the teachings of Elijah Muhammad. He was especially moved by the members' treatment of each other, the honor and the respect they showed toward each other, calling one another "Brother" and "Sister" and "Ma'am and Sir." This was a great contrast to what Malcolm had experienced among blacks in the ghettos of Boston and New York.

Less than a month after Malcolm arrived in Detroit, he met Elijah Muhammad for the first time when Temple Number One visited Temple Number Two in Chicago, the headquarters of the Nation of Islam. No experience, before or after, made as much of an emotional impact on him as seeing and hearing "this little, gentle, sweet, brown faced man," the Messenger of Allah, talk about his great sacrifices—even going to federal prison for three and a half years—and preach the truth about the so-called Negroes in America. Shortly after Malcolm's first visit to Chicago, Muhammad gave Malcolm his "X," symbolizing the "African family name that he could never know." It replaced "Little," a name derived from "the white blue-eyed devil" who owned his "paternal forebearers." From that point, he became known as Malcolm X, the name which still defines his identity to most people.

Malcolm spent all his spare time recruiting or "fishing," as the Muslims called it, for the temple. While he was angered by the slow progress he was making toward persuading "my poor, ignorant, brainwashed black brothers" to respond to the teachings of Muhammad, others were greatly impressed with his passion and success in converting the "Lost Sheep" to the Nation of Islam. In a remarkably short time Malcolm's work came to the attention of Muhammad, who took a liking to him. Muhammad invited him to Chicago to live with him as a member of his family, so he could personally "train" Malcolm in the Islamic faith. Malcolm was such a fast-learning student in the knowledge and communication of the teachings of Muhammad that he soon became his chief representative.

Muhammad also treated him as a son, and Malcolm came to regard him as his father, replacing the one he lost at the age of six. Their close relationship eventually led to Malcolm being perceived as the "number two" man in the Nation of Islam; it also created the conditions that led to his downfall.

In the teaching of the Messenger (and in Garvey's before him) rejection of white values was expressed in hostility toward integrationism. The solution to the problem of race is separation, not integration. Black nationalism thrives among poor blacks who have lost all hope in white society and its claims about freedom and justice for all. They know the difference between words about freedom in religious and political documents and their experience of being locked in the ghetto. Unable to see any good whatsoever in whites, black nationalists turn to their own cultural heritage for support of their identity as human beings in a white world that does not recognize black people as persons.

Malcolm's experience in the ghetto taught him that the black masses could be neither integrationist nor nonviolent. Integration and nonviolence assumed some measure of political order, a moral conscience in the society, and a religious and human sensitivity regarding the dignity and value of all persons. But since the masses in the ghettos saw no evidence of a political order that recognized their humanity or a moral conscience among white people, an appeal to integration and nonviolence sounded like a trick to delude and disarm poor blacks, so whites would not have to worry about a revengeful response to their brutality.

Integration was the way of the college-educated, the professional Negro elites whose value system and preoccupation with success were similar to the whites with whom they were seeking to integrate. In the ghetto, where survival was an arduous task and violence was an everyday experience, nonviolence was not a meaningful option and most even regarded the promotion of it as a sign of weakness and lack of courage. Malcolm's early life made it impossible for him to accept nonviolence as a philosophy of social change. He grew up in a society characterized by violence — which included both the violence of white hate groups and the structural violence which led to hunger and the mental breakdown of his mother. Both forms of violence affected him deeply. Malcolm could barely contain his rage when he thought about his mother in the mental hospital: "And knowing that my mother in there was a statistic that didn't have to be, that existed because of society's failure, hypocrisy, greed, and lack of mercy and compassion. Hence I have no mercy or compassion in me for a society that will crush people and then penalize them for not being able to stand up under the weight."[48] Malcolm's experience led him to believe that he too, like his father and five uncles, would die by violence. Such a person was not a likely candidate for belief in the philosophy of nonviolence.

Malcolm's social and intellectual development also shows why, during most of his Muslim ministry, he could not believe in the possibility of good residing in white people. To be sure, like Martin, Malcolm had some pleasant experiences with whites during his early years, particularly during his stay at the Swerlins' detention home, at Mason Junior High, and at the restaurant where he worked as a dishwasher. Although the whites called him "nigger" and "coon," they were not trying to insult him, as Malcolm himself acknowledged. Mr. Ostrowski, his eighth-grade English teacher, also liked him and "meant well" when he told him to "be realistic" in choosing his vocation. Malcolm also had pleasant experiences with whites in Boston and in New York. The most notable Boston experience in this regard was his intimate relationship with a white woman he called Sophia; apparently this was the only meaningful intimate relationship with a woman that he had before he met his wife, Betty. In New York, his most important relationship was with a Jewish male friend named Hymie. Malcolm said Hymie "had been good" to him. When his brother Reginald told him of Muhammad's teaching that "without any exception" "the white man is the devil," Malcolm was dumbfounded. "What about Hymie?" he asked.[49]

While Martin King's pleasant experiences with whites softened his negative attitudes toward them, Malcolm's early positive experiences with whites served only to intensify his later negative feelings about them. One reason Malcolm could easily dismiss his early positive encounters with whites was that his personal experience of racism during childhood and early adulthood was much more severe than Martin's. This comment may appear strange to persons who have been led to believe that the South was much more racist than the North. In some ways it was, but in others it was not. Regarding Martin and Malcolm, their social location made the great difference in the kind of racism they encountered and the resources they had to fight against it. Martin was six before he even became aware of racial discrimination. And his worst experience was being forced to give up his bus seat to whites and ride ninety miles standing in the aisle.

Though significant, Martin's experiences with racism during childhood could hardly be compared with Malcolm's. It is perhaps ironic that nothing symbolized this difference more than their skin color. Martin was *black,* which meant that his immediate family history had not suffered the violence of rape, as had the families of so many African-Americans. Malcolm was *red* because his maternal grandmother was raped by a white man. His reddish color, therefore, was always a constant reminder to him of the violence that the white man had committed against his family and his people. "You see me," he said, pointing to his facial complexion while lecturing to an audience at the Detroit Temple, "well, in the streets they called me Detroit Red. Yes! Yes, that raping, red-headed devil was my *grandfather*! That close, yes! My *mother's* father!" Rape was a central theme in Malcolm's early lectures because his color was a symbol of it. "If I could drain *his* blood that pollutes *my* body and pollutes *my* complexion, I'd do it! Because I hate every drop of the rapist's blood that's in me!" "*Think* of it," he often shouted to his audience. "Turn around and look at each other, brothers and sisters, and *think* of this! You and me, polluted all these colors — and this devil has the arrogance and the gall to think we, his victims, should *love* him!" Sometimes Malcolm could hardly contain his rage. "I would become so choked up," he said, "that sometimes I would walk in the streets until late into the night. Sometimes I would speak to no one for hours, thinking to myself about what the white man had done to our poor people here in America."[50]

Martin King was well-educated and quite successful in the white man's world. That was one of the reasons he could be so optimistic about whites, could believe that meaningful change was gradually taking place, and could think that eventually justice and freedom would be achieved for all. He was given many awards to promote that belief. In contrast to King, Malcolm was self-educated and looked with disdain upon the white man's world. He spoke for the poor blacks of the North who were jam-packed in the urban ghettos, struggling daily against unemployment, rats, dope, and police brutality. Thus, Malcolm could not share the optimism of the Negro professional class which King symbolized. There was nothing in Malcolm's experience or that of the black poor to support the view that whites were people of good will who would share power and privilege with the oppressed blacks in their society.

Malcolm's early life as a hustler made it difficult for him to trust not only whites, but blacks as well, including associates in the Black Muslim movement and later the ones who separated with him. He kept people at a distance, remaining professional and businesslike, refusing to allow them to get too close to him. According to Malcolm, "the hustling society's first rule" was "that you never trusted anyone outside of your own close-mouthed circle, and that you selected with time and care before you made any intimates even among these." He told Alex Haley, with whom he collaborated on his autobiography, "I don't *completely* trust anyone, not even myself. . . . You I trust about twenty-five percent."[51] A few days before his assassination, he revised the percentage to 70 percent. Many persons who knew Malcolm testify to his reserved style.

As Martin King's dream was influenced by his social origins, Malcolm X's nightmare was affected by his. Life, of course, is too complex and too ambiguous to enable one to be certain what Malcolm or Martin would have become had their early life-circumstances been different. But the great dissimilarity in their social and intellectual development certainly provides a clue to their different views regarding America and the black struggle for freedom in it. Malcolm and Martin came from different backgrounds of class, familial support, political tradition, geography, religious tradition, and education. All these factors made them different persons, approaching the black freedom struggle in diverse ways, with contrasting temperaments and personality traits. Almost everything that separated them in their later lives, including their speaking styles and the content of their message, is traceable to their early lives.

3

"I HAVE A DREAM"
(1955–64)

We are simply seeking to bring into full realization the American dream—a dream yet unfulfilled. A dream of equality of opportunity, of privilege and property widely distributed; a dream of a land where men no longer argue that the color of a man's skin determines the content of his character; the dream of a land where every man will respect the dignity and worth of human personality—this is the dream. When it is realized, the jangling discords of our nation will be transformed into a beautiful symphony of brotherhood, and men everywhere will know that America is truly the land of the free and the home of the brave.

> Martin Luther King, Jr.
> Washington, D.C.
> 19 July 1962

THE CONTEXT OF MARTIN'S VISION

Three factors formed the context for Martin King's idea of the American dream: (1) the images of the "North" and "South" in the consciousness of black and white Americans during the 1950s and 1960s; (2) the emergence of a resistance movement among the southern black masses; and (3) the resurgence of black nationalism in the North, especially as defined by the Black Muslims and Malcolm X.

The images of the North as free and of the South as unfree have long been in the minds of blacks and northern whites. During the antebellum period, the South was "Egypt," the land of oppression, while the North was "Canaan," the land to which slaves longed to flee and where black and white abolitionists struggled against slavery. The contrasting images continued after the Civil War and Reconstruction as

58

slavery was replaced by white terror groups and Jim Crow laws. Blacks were disfranchised, humiliated, and often murdered.

Repressive and violent measures against blacks persisted into the twentieth century and became the chief motivating force behind the rise of the modern civil rights movement. Like the nineteenth-century abolitionist movement, the twentieth-century civil rights movement was initiated by a small group of northern whites and elite blacks who were determined to apply the principles of the Declaration of Independence and the Constitution against the violence that was being perpetrated daily against the masses of black people, mostly in the South. They were particularly concerned about lynchings, disfranchisement, and segregation. In short, they wanted to put an end to southern barbarism and broaden the processes of liberal democracy so blacks could live without fear and also share in the sociopolitical development of America according to their interest and individual abilities.

The 17 May 1954 Supreme Court decision, which declared school segregation unconstitutional, symbolized the North, and the brutal lynching of a fourteen-year-old Chicago youth, Emmet Till (28 August 1955, in Money, Mississippi) symbolized the South. The chief advocates for the North were the white liberals and the NAACP. The most vocal spokesmen for the South were the members of the sophisticated, business-oriented White Citizens Council and of the cruder Ku Klux Klan. Both groups were fighting to make their own view the norm for the country as a whole. How could America, the white liberals and the NAACP asked after the Second World War, be the leader of the "free world" if Negroes remained segregated, and thus unfree, in the South? How could the white race, the Klan and the White Citizens Council retorted, remain free of "race-mixing" and thus safe from the "sin of mongrelization" if the "niggers" were allowed to associate freely with the whites? This was the atmosphere in which Martin King developed his idea of the American dream.

King's dream was also developed in the presence of a new black resistance movement. Many blacks had fought and died in the Second World War, and this truth made the majority of southern blacks increasingly reluctant to resign themselves to their second-class status in the society. Inspired by the struggles against colonialism in the Third World (especially in Africa) and by America's claim to be the leader of the free world, the southern black masses rose above the fear of violence and economic reprisal and let the world know that they too were ready to strike a blow for freedom. First came the Montgomery bus boycott in 1955–56. It was followed by the sit-ins (1960), the freedom rides (1961), the Albany Movement (1961), the Birmingham Campaign (1963), the great March on Washington (1963), and many other demonstrations throughout the South. The myth of a peaceful South and a contented Negro was shattered as blacks by the thousands, young and old, "Ph.D. and No.D.," proudly marched for freedom, showing no fear of brutal jails or even death. Without an aroused black community, willing to risk their lives for freedom, there would have been no fertile soil for the development of King's dream.

King also developed his idea of the American dream in opposition to the rise of black nationalism in the North, a voice in the black freedom movement that was just beginning to make itself heard. Although black nationalists were mainly influenced by the legacy of Marcus Garvey, they were during King's time chiefly followers of Elijah Muhammad, whose most articulate representative was Malcolm X. Nationalists did not share the integrationists' sharp distinction between the South and the North. Malcolm X contended that there was no difference between the whites in Mississippi and the ones in New York, no difference between Senator James O. Eastland and Governor Nelson Rockefeller, except the former was openly racist and the latter camouflaged his racism with smiles and pats on the back. Eastland and his allies were honest about their intention to "keep the niggers in their place." But Rockefeller and his cohorts pretended to be the friends of blacks, lulling them to sleep, so that they could make blacks think that they were moving toward freedom when in fact they were becoming more and more dependent upon white people.

Contending with Malcolm's angry voice, King and other integrationists could hardly believe that some Negroes did not want to put an end to segregation. Their first reaction was to ignore the nationalists and to treat them as rabble-rousers whose public statements did not warrant a response. But Malcolm's verbal skill and public visibility forced King to take notice of him and to develop his perspective on the American dream not only in opposition to white supremacists in the South, but also against persons whom he initially referred to as black supremacists in the North.

The contrasting images of the North and South, the revolt of the southern black masses, and the nationalist voice of Malcolm X—all shaped the social and political environment in which Martin King developed his dream.

KING AND THE AMERICAN DREAM

Despite similarities with the views of other integrationists, King's idea of the American dream was distinctive in its content, its complexity, and the compelling way in which he advocated it. His thinking on the American dream went through several changes and can be divided into two major periods. The first began with the Montgomery bus boycott in December 1955 and ended with the enactment of the Voting Rights Bill in August 1965. The second began in the fall of 1965 as King began to analyze more deeply the connections between racism, poverty, and militarism in the policies of the U.S. government. In both periods his ideas were defined by his faith in the God of justice, love, and hope. The difference between the periods was a marked shift of emphasis among these attributes. In this chapter we shall look only at the first period, examining the second period in chapter 8.

INTERRELATIONSHIP OF JUSTICE AND LOVE

During the first period, King's thinking was defined by an optimistic belief that justice could be achieved through love, which he identified with nonviolence. At the beginning of the Montgomery bus boycott, he placed justice at the center of his thinking, defining it in contrast to the southern system of segregation. Justice meant white people treating Negroes with the dignity and respect accorded other human beings in the society. In King's first major speech (Holt Street Baptist Church, 5 December 1955), speaking as president of the newly formed Montgomery Improvement Association and with only twenty minutes of preparation time, he focused on Negroes' "right to protest for right," based upon the American democratic tradition of freedom and the biblical notion of the justice of God. Contrary to King's later report of his speech in *Stride toward Freedom,* and contrary to scholarly interpretations of the speech, the major theme of his address was *not* love. He was not primarily concerned about Negroes loving white people. The speech assumed that Negroes love whites because of Negroes' Christian identity and because of the absence of retaliatory violence in the Negro community. King did not think he needed to tell Negroes to love whites; rather he believed he had to tell them to have "the moral courage to stand up for their rights" against whites who humiliated and assaulted them only because of their race. Speaking intimately, as one who knew their pain, King told his audience of nearly five thousand Negroes:

And you know my friends there comes a time when people get tired of being trampled over by the iron feet of oppression. There comes a time my friends when people get tired of being flung across the abyss of humiliation where they experience the bleakness of nagging despair. There comes a time when people get tired of being pushed out of the glittering sunlight of life's July, and left standing amidst the piercing chill of an Alpine November. We are here this evening because we are tired now.

The applause was deafening, requiring a long pause before King could resume speaking. He spoke like a God-sent prophet of the Negro community who articulated clearly and forcefully their impatience with the indignity of their treatment on the city buses. Martin King let them know that they did not have to take white abuse and insults anymore. Since Negroes composed 75 percent of the riding public, they could and should demand their rights as citizens of America by "substituting tired feet for tired souls." They should boycott the buses until white people agreed to show Negroes the respect that they themselves demanded.

At that time King was concerned mainly about inspiring Negroes to take a stand for justice, which he understood as the right to ride the city buses of Montgomery free of "the paralysis of crippling fear," a "problem [that] has existed over endless years." "We only assemble here," he said, "because of our desire to see right exist. My friends, I want it to be known that we're going to work with grim and firm determination to gain justice on the buses in this city."

King also wanted to let Negroes know that there was nothing wrong with their protest. The right to protest against mistreatment was both a constitutional right and a biblical principle. Again receiving thunderous applause and cheers, King proclaimed:

> We are not wrong in what we are doing. If we are wrong, then the Supreme Court of this Nation is wrong. If we are wrong the Constitution of the United States is wrong. If we are wrong God Almighty is wrong. If we are wrong Jesus of Nazareth was merely a utopian dreamer and never came down to earth. If we are wrong justice is a lie. . . . And we are determined here in Montgomery to work and fight until justice runs down like water and righteousness like a mighty stream.

Drawing upon the distinction between love and justice he found in the theological writings of Paul Tillich and Reinhold Niebuhr, King explicitly made the principle of love secondary to justice:

> I want to tell you this evening that it is not enough to talk about love. Love is one of the principal parts of the Christian faith. There is another side called justice. . . . Justice is love correcting that which would work against love. The Almighty God . . . is not . . . just standing out saying, "Behold thee, I love you Negro." He's also the God that standeth before the nations and says: "Be still and know that I am God, that if you don't obey me I'm gonna break the backbone of your power. . . ." Standing beside love is always justice. And we are only using the tools of justice. Not only

are we using the tools of persuasion but we've got to use the tools of coercion.[1]

I emphasize the theme of justice as King's starting point because of its importance in identifying the developmental changes in his understanding of the American dream. No interpreter of King has identified justice as the primary focus of his thinking at the start of the Montgomery bus boycott. Most are so eager to stress love as the center of his thought and actions (as King himself did when he reflected on the event) that they (like King) fail to note that this was a later development in his thinking.

Another important reason for noting the justice emphasis is that it shows that Martin King and Malcolm X shared an important idea when they began their public ministries. Though far apart in many ways, Martin and Malcolm both insisted that black people stand up and demand their rights.

Blacks in Montgomery made three specific demands to the bus company and city commission: (1) first-come, first-served seating, with blacks starting from the rear and whites from the front; (2) courteous treatment from the bus drivers at all times; and (3) access to jobs as drivers for bus service in their neighborhoods. King was clear that integration was not their goal. "We are not asking for an end to segregation," he told reporters. "That's a matter for the legislature and the courts. . . . All we are seeking is justice and fair treatment in riding the buses. We don't like the idea of Negroes having to stand when there are vacant seats. We are demanding justice on that point."[2]

Of course, King, like other blacks in Montgomery and elsewhere, believed in integration. He believed that human beings were created for community with each other and not for separation from each other. "We began with a compromise when we didn't ask for complete integration," he acknowledged during the third week of January 1956. "Frankly, I am for immediate integration. Segregation is evil, and I cannot, as a minister, condone evil."[3] But Martin also knew that he could not openly advocate social integration in the Deep South in 1955 and still live to talk about it.

But when the NAACP began to register its concern about the narrow limits of their demands; when Glenn Smiley of the Fellowship of Reconciliation and Bayard Rustin, an associate of the labor leader A. Philip Randolph, began to provide assistance in relating Mahatma Gandhi's philosophy of nonviolence to the Montgomery Movement; and when Martin King and the movement began to receive national and international acclaim and support, King then began to see that the bus boycott and his leadership had powerful symbolic significance beyond the achievement of justice for Negroes in Montgomery. The Montgomery Movement, he said in January 1956, "is a part of a world-wide movement. Look at just about any place in the world and the exploited people are rising against their exploiters."[4]

When King began to view the Montgomery Movement from a global perspective, he began to articulate a vision of humanity that had a much larger scope than the question of Negro-white relations in the South. "This is not a war between the white and the Negro," King proclaimed to a Montgomery rally, "but a conflict between justice and injustice. This is bigger than the Negro race revolting against the white. We are not just trying to improve Negro Montgomery. We are trying to improve the whole of Montgomery."[5] As he traveled throughout the United States and later to other countries, King began to develop a philosophy of history that was informed by a world perspective. The oneness of humanity, informed by creative divine love, began to move to the center of his thinking. When that happened, justice within a segregated system was no longer acceptable, and integration became the primary goal of the movement. On Sunday, 26 February 1956, following the indictment of the boycott leaders, King preached a sermon entitled "Faith in Man."

> Integration is the great issue of our age, the great issue of our nation and the great issue of our community. We are in the midst of a great struggle, the consequences of which will be world-shaking. But our victory will not be a victory for Montgomery's Negroes alone. It will be a victory for justice, a victory for fair play and a victory for democracy. Were we to stop right now, we would have won a victory because the Negro has achieved from this a new dignity. But we are not going to stop. We are going on in the same spirit of love and protest, and the same dignity we have shown in the past.[6]

To be sure, justice was still important, but now it was applied in a larger context and was shaped by a higher goal — love. Love did not displace justice or make its achievement less important. Quite the opposite was the case. Love bestowed a deeper significance upon justice, making its achievement more urgent than ever before.

There was a close interrelationship between love and justice in King's thinking: Love — and its political expression, integration — occupied the center of his thinking, while justice — and its political expression, desegregation — became the precondition or the means of achieving love. But looking at the problem from another angle, King also advocated that love, expressed in nonviolent protest, was the only means of achieving justice, which he equated with desegregation.

After 381 days of walking in heat and cold, rain and glaring sun, enduring sore feet and tired bodies, police harassment, the mass indictment of their leaders, several bombed homes, and daily telephone threats against their lives, King and the Montgomery Negroes achieved their goal of desegregated bus service. The Supreme Court's order ending segregation was served on the white officials on 20 December 1956. By that time, King had become an international figure, highly praised for his leadership in keeping fifty thousand Negroes nonviolent in their struggle for justice. Some called him an "American Gandhi." Others thought of him as "Moses," the one who would deliver his people from the bondage of segregation to the Promised Land of integration in America. Many groups invited him to tell the "Montgomery Story." Several religious and secular magazines printed his version of it, including *U.S. News & World Report*.[7] He also received many awards, including the distinguished Spingarn Medal of the NAACP (28 June 1957). Major northern newspapers, magazines, and other media carried prominent and favorable stories about King and the boycott. Calling the boycott the "miracle in Alabama," the *Nation* said that it "represents a fulfillment of the American dream . . . of freedom and equality and the dignity and worth of every human being."[8] The 18 February 1957 issue of *Time* magazine carried King's picture on its cover and a favorable, detailed account of his life and leadership of the boycott. King became the most discussed African-American of his time and was compared to Frederick Douglass and Booker T. Washington. In the eyes of many whites and the majority of his race, King was now the spokesman for *all* Negroes in America. Indeed people sought his advice not only regarding the "Negro problem" but also about the problem of injustice in many parts of the world.

Even Malcolm X privately applauded King for his courage to stand up to southern whites. But he was not pleased with the praise and financial support that whites bestowed upon him, nor with King's promotion of integration and nonviolence respectively as the goal and method of the black freedom movement. When whites initially queried him about the Montgomery bus boycott, Malcolm did not criticize King but rather the society that made the boycott necessary. "Now just *imagine* that! This good, hard-working, Christian-believing black woman, she's paid her money, she's in her seat. Just because she's *black*, she's asked to get up! I mean, sometimes even for *me* it's hard to believe the white man's arrogance!"[9] However, the contrast in Martin's and Malcolm's developing philosophies would soon cause Malcolm to attack Martin directly, forcing Martin to respond to Malcolm indirectly. The dream and nightmare images provided the context for their public debate.

Unlike Malcolm, Martin was a very young man when leadership was thrust upon him. King's rise to national prominence so soon after the beginning of his ministry required him to develop quickly his ideas about *what* freedom meant for blacks and *how* they should struggle for it. To meet this need, Martin, with some prodding from his advisers (especially Ella Baker, Stanley Levison, and Bayard Rustin), called upon black ministers from all over the South to meet at Ebenezer Baptist Church in Atlanta on 10–11 January 1957. A follow-up meeting was convened a month later in New Orleans on 14 February. These meetings led to the founding of the Southern Christian Leadership Conference (SCLC), with King as the president. Its purpose was to "redeem the soul of America" by destroying the ugly disease of segregation. Nonviolent direct action was chosen as the method, because the ultimate goal was integration, that is, the creation of a "beloved community" where Negroes and whites could live together as brothers and sisters. King's success in Montgomery made him believe that what happened there could be achieved in America as a whole, indeed throughout the world.

The American Dream and the White Public

The phrase "American dream" began to appear in Martin King's addresses in the late 1950s. He talked about a "dream of our American democracy" in the presence of Vice President Richard Nixon, in an address to a meeting of the Committee on Government Contracts, a meeting held at the Sheraton Park Hotel in Washington, D.C., on 11 May 1959. By the beginning of the 1960s the phrase had emerged as a frequently used symbol of his perspective on America and the black struggle in it, as seen in such titles of his addresses as "The Negro and the American Dream" and "The American Dream."[10]

King derived the meaning of the expression "American dream" from two sources: the American liberal democratic tradition, as defined by the Declaration of Independence and the Constitution, and the biblical tradition of the Old and New Testaments, as interpreted by Protestant liberalism and the black church. During the second half of the 1950s and first half of the 1960s, King drew these sources into a coherent and powerful image of the nation's future.

Martin King was deeply moved by the assertions of the Declaration of Independence "that all men are created equal; that they are endowed by their Creator with certain inalienable rights; that among these are life, liberty, and the pursuit of happiness." He often quoted this statement, in order to challenge Americans to implement the idea of freedom that existed from the beginning of their nation.

Two concepts in the statement attracted King. One was its "amazing universalism." "It does not say all white men, but it says all men, which includes black men. It does not say all Gentiles, but it says all men, which includes Jews. It does not say all Protestants, but it says all men, which includes Catholics." The other concept was the "divine origin" of human rights. According to Martin King, the one thing that made the American form of government different from totalitarian regimes was its recognition that "each individual has certain basic rights that are neither conferred by nor derived from the state. . . . They are God-given."[11] Therefore every person has worth and dignity which must be recognized and respected. The dream that King articulated was not nationalistic; it was universal, that is, grounded in eternity and not given by people.

Recalling King's speeches about the American dream, it is important to keep in mind his audience and what he expected them to do to realize the dream. The dream metaphor was directed mainly to the white public — the federal government, southern moderates, northern liberals, and religious communities — because he believed they had the material resources and the moral capacity to create a world based on the principles that they claimed to live by. King assumed that the moral sensitivity of whites would not allow them to violate the ideals of democracy and the moral vision of the Jewish and Christian faiths. He believed that they needed only to be shamed and challenged to put into practice what they publicly proclaimed.

King chose the third anniversary of the Supreme Court's school decision (17 May 1957) as the time to make his first major speech to the nation. The *place,* the Lincoln Memorial, symbolized the audience to whom he wanted to speak — different segments of the white community who could be aroused to implement justice on behalf of all people. The *time* symbolized the message he intended to deliver — the urgent necessity of integrating Negroes into the mainstream of American life. Although he did not use the American dream phrase in his "Message Delivered at the Prayer Pilgrimage," its core meaning was plainly stated. As the last speaker to an audience of approximately 25,000 blacks, King proclaimed the "urgent need for dedicated and courageous leadership" so justice could be fully achieved for Americans of African descent.

To the executive branch of the federal government, King said: Enforce the law of the land! Protect the rights of all citizens! He believed that the judicial branch of the government provided quality leadership with its 1954 decision which outlawed school segregation. But no "positive leadership" had come from the executive or legislative branches of the government. "In the midst of the tragic breakdown of law and order, the executive branch of government is all too silent and apathetic."[12] King could not understand why President Eisenhower would not make a speech in a major southern city and urge whites to obey the law of the land as a *moral* imperative and then move quickly to enforce the Supreme Court's school decision. King was also troubled that Eisenhower did not accept the civil rights leaders' recommendations to appoint a Negro to cabinet rank as "Secretary of Integration" and set in place a "Bureau of Negro Affairs." The president ignored the "Reverend," as Eisenhower called King, even refusing to do anything which suggested that he endorsed integration.[13]

Later, expecting much more executive initiative from President Kennedy, King urged him to establish "equality now," but within a year the president was "fumbling on the New Frontier."[14] He did not understand why Kennedy ignored his recommendation to issue a "Second Emancipation Proclamation," outlawing all forms of racial discrimination with the stroke of his pen. How can American presidents be the symbol of freedom among the political leaders of the world, especially in Africa and Asia, if they will not enforce the laws of equality in their own country?

In his "Prayer Pilgrimage" address, King also expressed disappointment with the "stagnant and hypocritical" leadership of the Congress, a problem he said was not "confined to one particular party." He said that both Democrats and Republicans had betrayed American ideals by "capitulating to the prejudices and undemocratic practices of the southern dixiecrats" and "to the blatant hypocrisy of right-wing, reactionary northerners." "We come humbly to say to the men in the forefront of our government that the civil rights issue is not an ephemeral, evanescent domestic issue that can be kicked about by reactionary guardians of the status quo," King proclaimed. "It is rather an eternal, moral issue which may well determine the destiny of our nation. . . . The clock of destiny is ticking out. We must act now before it is too late."

In relation to its inhabitants of color, said King, America has violated its own principles of democracy and freedom. He let the president and the members of Congress know that the United States could not continue to exist with the contradiction of "proudly profess[ing] the principles of democracy," and then "practic[ing] the very antithesis of those principles." Slavery and segregation have been strange paradoxes in a nation founded on the principle that all people are created equal. According to King, this "schizophrenic personality" is "America's dilemma." King believed that it is the responsibility of government leaders to heal the sickness of America by making and enforcing laws that bestow freedom upon all its citizens.

To southern moderates, King said: Break your silence and speak up for the cause of democracy and justice which you know in your heart to be right. Do not allow the Ku Klux Klan and the White Citizens

Council to define the image of the South. When you speak up for right and human decency, the "closed-minded, reactionary, recalcitrant group" will have to shut up, because you are the majority. "God grant," he said, "that the white moderates of the South will rise up courageously, without fear, and take up the leadership in this tense period of transition."

To northern liberals, King said: Quit "straddling the fence," "looking sympathetically at all sides," and "fail[ing] to become committed to either side." On the issue of racial justice, there were only two sides: right and wrong, truth and error, integration and segregation. All persons must declare where they stand. "We call for a liberalism from the North which will be thoroughly committed to the ideal of racial justice and will not be deterred by the propaganda and subtle words of those who say, 'slow up for a while, you are pushing too fast.' "

Although King did not single out white churches in his "Prayer Pilgrimage" address, he believed that they had a special responsibility for the implementation of the American dream. This was so because racial injustice was not primarily a political problem but rather a *moral* problem. "America must rid herself of segregation not alone because it is politically expedient, but because it is morally right!" As we will see in greater detail in a later chapter, King challenged the white churches, especially their ministers, to assume leadership in healing the moral sickness of the nation.

Against the claim that morality could not be legislated, King responded that behavior nevertheless could be regulated. "You can't legislate integration," he agreed, "but you can certainly legislate desegregation."[15] The government could not make white bigots love Negroes. The churches and schools had to do that. But the government could stop white bigots from lynching Negroes. "And I think that's pretty important also!" King was fond of saying. What America needed were courageous and intelligent leaders dedicated to serving *all* its citizens.

Martin King's articulation of the American dream, then, was primarily for the white public. He wanted to prick their consciences and motivate them to create a society and a world that were free of racial discrimination. Unlike Malcolm, who had given up on white America, Martin believed that it could be redeemed. Martin could be as critical as Malcolm regarding the inhumanity of whites. But he always left the door open for reconciliation, and he actively worked for it. Martin was optimistic that his dream of a beloved community of blacks and whites, working together for the good of all, could be realized even in the most racist states in the nation. As Malcolm trusted no whites, Martin refused to give up on any segment of white America.

PURSUING THE DREAM: THE ROLE OF THE NEGRO PEOPLE

ORGANIZING FOR ACTION

Although blacks were not the primary audience for his addresses on the American dream, King believed that they also had a large role to play in its realization. Unlike whites, blacks did not have to be convinced that America had reneged on its promise of freedom to its citizens of color. They did not have to be convinced of the inhumanity of segregation. All Negroes, whether rich or poor, the ones who graduated from "Morehouse or Nohouse," as King often said, knew from personal experience what it meant to be insulted, kicked in the seat of the pants, and spat upon by white people. What they needed was to be inspired and taught the most effective way, morally and practically, to fight for justice. For many years, as King saw it, the masses of Negroes acquiesced in their situation of oppression because they did not feel that they could do anything about it, except pray to God and root for the NAACP. But with the success of the Montgomery bus boycott (and later the sit-ins, freedom rides, vigils, and countless other demonstrations throughout the United States), the masses of Negroes discovered that they could do a great deal for the cause of freedom.

King was always careful to praise the NAACP for its legal work in gaining equal rights for Negroes, partly because he knew that Roy Wilkins and other NAACP officials were envious of him. But "a court order can only declare rights," King told a Virginia audience of Negroes on 12 March 1961 during the Southern Christian Leadership Conference's People to People tour. "It cannot deliver them. Only when people themselves begin to act are the rights which are on paper given life-blood. Only when a people in mass begin to act are they able to make all these laws real and meaningful."[16]

As King became the symbol of the civil rights movement, he felt an obligation to guide it in a creative direction that would help realize the American dream. "At times I think I'm a pretty unprepared symbol," he said in an interview for *Life* magazine. "But people cannot devote themselves to a great cause without finding someone who becomes the personification of the cause. People cannot become devoted to Christianity until they find Christ, to democracy until they find Lincoln and Jefferson and Roosevelt, to Communism until they find Marx and Lenin. . . . I know that this is a righteous cause and that by being connected to it I am connected with a transcendent value of right."[17] When he addressed whites, therefore, he frequently spoke as if he were speaking for the entire Negro community in the United States and not just for his organization. When he appeared before blacks, he often spoke as a "messianic" figure, that is, as one who had been called by a divine power in history to give his life for the cause of their freedom. King believed deeply that "the Negro is God's instrument to save the soul of America."[18] He urged his people to accept their redemptive role by pursuing five objectives: self-respect, high moral standards, whole-hearted work, leadership, and nonviolence.

THE FIVE OBJECTIVES

Self-respect

King declared that Negroes must "maintain a continuing sense of dignity and self-respect." With a history of 244 years of slavery and a century of segregation, King realized that it was easy for many Negroes to feel that they did not belong or were not significant. "Let no force, let no power, let no individual, let no social system," he told them, "cause you to feel that you are inferior." King was greatly concerned about complacent Negroes who had lost their sense of somebodyness, adjusting to segregation, accepting the place whites assigned to them, and internalizing the words of the blues singer, "Been down so long, down don't bother me." He told them that "if we are going to be prepared for this new order in this new world that is emerging, we must believe . . . that [we] are somebody," "made in God's image."[19] King frequently quoted the poem:

> Fleecy locks and dark complexion
> Cannot forfeit nature's claim.
> Skin may differ but affection
> Dwells in black and white the same.
> Were I so tall as to reach the pole
> Or to grasp the ocean at a span,
> I must be measured by my soul,
> The mind is the standard of the man.

King's emphasis on self-respect touched on Malcolm X's most distinctive contribution to the black freedom movement. King's disciples are correct when they reject Malcolm's devotees' contention that King showed no concern for the self-respect of African-Americans. Integrationists have always made self-respect the center piece of their philosophy. But there is an important difference between Martin and Malcolm that should be noted here and will be explored further in chapters 9 and 11. For Malcolm, self-respect was linked with Africa, i.e., *blackness,* as the nationalists shouted during the age of Black Power. But for Martin, self-respect was connected with being an American citizen, with being treated with the same regard as others and without any reference to color. Segregation was evil precisely because it defined human beings on the basis of color, with whites on the top and Negroes on the bottom. To change the ruling group by putting Negroes on the top and whites at the bottom would not result in self-respect for Negroes. Genuine self-respect means seeing yourself not as a Negro but as a human being.

Therefore, despite segregation, which denies the essential worth of its victims, King told Negroes that "we must have the spiritual audacity to assert our somebodyness. We must no longer allow our physical bondage to enslave our minds. He who feels that he is nobody eventually becomes nobody. But he who feels that he is somebody, even though humiliated by external servitude, achieves a sense of selfhood and dignity that nothing in all the world can take away."[20]

High Moral Standards

King emphasized that Negroes must "make ourselves worthy of the respect of others by improving our personal standards." King told Negroes that "our standards have lagged behind at many points." "Negroes constitute 10 percent of the population of New York City and yet they commit 35 percent of the crimes. Missouri Negroes constitute 26 percent of the population and yet 76 percent of the persons on the list for Aid to Dependent Children. . . . We've got to lift our moral standards at every hand and every point." This point was emphasized much more during his pastorate in Montgomery than after his move to Atlanta in January 1960. On this point, Malcolm thought King was guilty of using the moral standards of criminals — that is, whites — to evaluate the behavior of their victims. Why should the victims of crime, Malcolm would ask him, try to make themselves worthy of the respect of criminals? King realized that not everything that whites said about Negroes was true and that much of it was "maliciously directed." But he thought that self-criticism is a sign of maturity. Therefore "we must pick out the elements of truth and make them the basis of creative reconstruction. We must not let the fact that we are the victims of injustice lull us into abrogating responsibility for our own lives."[21]

Wholehearted Work

King also urged Negroes to "make full and constructive use of the freedom we already possess," refusing to "use our oppression as an excuse for mediocrity and laziness." He frequently pointed to the Jews as an example of a people who did not allow discrimination and suffering to prevent them from achieving excellence. Being Jews did not prevent Spinoza, Handel, and Einstein from achieving excellence in the fields of philosophy, music, and science. Neither should being Negroes prevent people from achieving distinction in their chosen fields of study. King quoted repeatedly the words of Ralph Waldo Emerson: "If a man can write a better book, or preach a better sermon, or make a better mouse trap than his neighbor, even if he builds his house in the woods the world will make a beaten path to his door." King's point was that if Negroes were going to be ready for the new age of integration, then they had to strive to be the best that they could be and not simply strive to become "good Negro teachers, good Negro doctors, good Negro ministers, good Negro skilled laborers. We must set out to do a good job, irrespective of race, and do it so well that nobody can do it better."

The street sweeper image was another one of King's favorite images: "If it falls your lot to be a street sweeper, sweep streets like Michelangelo painted pictures, like Shakespeare wrote poetry, like Beethoven composed music; sweep streets so well that all the host of Heaven and earth will have to pause and say, 'Here lived a great street sweeper, who swept his job well.'" King often cited past and current examples of Negroes who had performed their jobs with excellence so his people would have an existential knowledge of what he was talking about. Booker T. Washington as a race leader, Roland Hayes and Marion Anderson as singers, and Joe Louis, Jackie Robinson, and Jesse Owens as athletes were some of his favorite examples of excellence.

King's analysis of excellence called forth the scorn of Malcolm X and other black nationalists, because King's standard was again derived from the dominant white community. All of his examples of achievement were either white or persons who had succeeded in the white man's world. Why not point to persons who resisted white domination, such as Nat Turner, David Walker, Paul Robeson, or W. E. B. Du Bois? Excellence for Malcolm was linked with cultural affirmation and physical resistance, and not with cultural alienation and physical passivity. "It's important . . . for us to be reestablished and connected to our roots," Malcolm insisted. "[Frederick] Douglass was great. I would rather have been taught about Toussaint L'Ouverture. We need to be taught about people who fought, who bled for freedom and made others bleed."[22]

During the first stage of his civil rights activity, in sharp contrast to Malcolm, the only occasion on which King deviated from his standard list of Negro excellence was in an Atlanta address where he referred to David Walker, Nat Turner, Denmark Vesey, Gabriel Prosser, and "other unsung heroes [who] plotted and planned and fought and died to make the American dream a reality for their people."[23] It is clear that King was well aware of the contradiction of using persons who advocated and used violence as examples of excellence in a movement that identified freedom with integration and nonviolence.

Leadership

In his "Prayer Pilgrimage" address, King also emphasized the "urgent need for strong, courageous, and intelligent leadership from the Negro community." He urged Negroes to shun both the Uncle Tom, who has acquiesced to the system of segregation, and the hot-headed "rabble-rouser," who is led astray by emotionalism. "We must realize that we are grappling with the most weighty social problems of this nation, and in grappling with such complex problems," he said, "we must be sure that our hands are clean in the struggle."[24]

While many whites thought King was an extremist, he saw himself as "stand[ing] in the middle of two opposing forces in the Negro community": The conservative, middle-class persons who had "adjusted to segregation" and the bitter black nationalists who came "perilously close to advocating violence."

King was greatly concerned about complacent, Uncle Tom Negroes in both the middle class and among the masses. He told Negroes that "leaders are needed . . . in every community all over this nation. . . . Not leaders in love with money, but in love with justice. Not leaders in love with publicity, but in love with humanity."[25]

Often conservative Negro leadership opposed King and did not allow the SCLC to stage demonstrations against segregation. It was ironic that Atlanta, King's birthplace and place of residence and pastorate, was never singled out by him as a "testing ground." Initiated by students, he reluctantly participated in a sit-in at Rich's Department Store (19 October 1960). But Atlanta's conservative Negro leadership, of which Daddy King was a prominent member, made it quite clear to King, Jr., that Atlanta was off-limits for SCLC-type demonstrations.

King also met opposition in Birmingham. When the SCLC set in motion "Project C" (the "C" was for *Confrontation*), challenging the city's segregation ordinances, local Negro leaders were less than enthusiastic. Some even labeled King an "outsider." After the struggle was joined and in an effort to unify the Negro community, King called several meetings and appealed to business and professional people and the preachers, emphasizing the need to take a stand for justice. Like whites, the established Negro leadership did not wish to disturb the status quo. Segregation might have been bad, but they were fearful that things could get worse. As with whites, King often had to shame them into supporting the cause of justice. He was especially critical of conservative Negro preachers. He repeatedly told them:

> I'm sick and tired of seeing Negro preachers riding around in big cars and living in big houses and not concerned about the problems of the people who made it possible for them to get these things. It seems that I can hear the Almighty God say, "Stop preaching your loud sermons and whooping your irrelevant mess in my face, for your hands are full of tar. For the people that I sent you to serve are in need, and you are doing nothing but being concerned about yourself." Seems that I can hear God saying that it's time to rise up now and make it clear that the evils of the universe must be removed. And that God isn't going to do all of it by himself. The church that overlooks this is a dangerously irrelevant church.[26]

It was difficult for Negro preachers to listen to King and not respond to his call.

On the other hand, no group in the black community disturbed King more than Elijah Muhammad's Black Muslims, particularly Malcolm X. Though King did not deny the cogency of Malcolm's condemnation of white America, he saw Malcolm as a hot-headed radical with a dangerous emotional appeal. King was troubled both by Malcolm's separatist solution to the problem of white racism and by the method he chose to achieve it. These he regarded as the result of frustration and despair.

As early as 1959, King made public his strong opposition to the Black Muslims. "Dr. King, Keating Blast Muslim Group" reported the *Pittsburgh Courier.* King was careful, however, to support "legitimate" "racial pride." "Too many Negroes," he said, "consider it a curse of fate that they were born colored and are ashamed of their black and brown skin." Thus in his Detroit address, 23 June 1963, he expressed his admiration for a "magnificent new militancy" in the black community that was to a large extent due to the influence of Malcolm X. Martin liked the spirit of determination in it, with Negroes standing up declaring that they were proud to be black and determined to be free. But he saw a danger that it would cause Negroes to distrust "every white person." "There are some white people in this country," Martin said, "who are as determined to see the Negro free as we are to be free." But he was even more concerned about the "doctrine of black supremacy," as he often called it, which he saw in Malcolm's work. "I can understand . . ., we've been pushed around so long," Martin told his audience. "I can understand from a psychological point of view why some caught up in the clutches of the injustices surrounding them almost respond with bitterness and come to the conclusion that the problem can't be solved within. And they talk about getting away from it in terms of racial separation." Still he could not imagine any solution more wrong or dangerous than the Black Muslims' idea of territorial separatism. "But even though I can understand it psychologically," he continued, "I must say . . . that . . . black supremacy is as dangerous as white supremacy. . . . God is not interested merely in the freedom of black men and brown men and yellow men. God is interested in the freedom of the whole human race."[27]

For Martin King, an affirmation of the oneness of humanity had to precede an acknowledgment of any form of particularism. Segregation was an expression of particularism—one race asserting a claim to superiority, and thereby injuring not only the other but itself. He did not want to be associated with any movement in the Negro community that even suggested excluding whites. "I think it would be very dangerous and even tragic," he said regarding white people's participation in the civil rights movement, "if the struggle in the United States for civil rights degenerated to a racial struggle of blacks against whites. . . . It is a tension between justice and injustice."[28] Anyone, therefore, who believed in justice must be welcomed in the civil rights movement.

Nonviolence

King also told Negroes that "we must plunge deeper into the whole philosophy of nonviolence." No advice was offered more often and more passionately, and nothing separated him more from Malcolm X than his commitment to nonviolence.

Yet King did not begin the Montgomery bus boycott with a personal commitment to nonviolence. This commitment came later as he shifted the primary focus of his thinking from justice to love. Before his shift to the primacy of love and following the bombing of his house (30 January 1956), King had armed guards around his house and even applied for a permit to carry a gun in his car. But when he made the shift to love, nonviolence became more than just a practical way for an oppressed people to achieve justice; it also became a way of life, a total commitment.

King urged Negroes to follow his example and to accept nonviolence as a way of life. But even if they could not accept nonviolence as an affirmation of faith, he urged them to accept it as the only practical way of achieving justice in America. Violence will not achieve freedom for Negroes, King argued. It will merely get a whole lot of them killed and also serve as an excuse for the whites not to do anything about oppression.

Malcolm was unmercifully critical of Martin's advocacy of nonviolence, and we will examine his reasons for it in the next chapter. Here it is important to state what Martin meant by nonviolence and why he advocated it. No aspect of his philosophy of social change was more important than nonviolence. It was the beginning and the end of everything that he stood for—both politically and religiously. Though the political and the religious dimensions of nonviolence cannot be separated in Martin's thinking, here we will focus mainly on the relevance of nonviolence for social change in America and in a subsequent chapter examine its religious meaning.

For Martin, nonviolence did not mean passivity or doing nothing, as so many critics have suggested. His philosophy was nonviolent *direct action.* And no one was more actively involved in the struggle for justice than Martin. Indeed Malcolm and the Black Muslims were often criticized for talking loud but doing nothing. Not so with Martin. He put his *body* on the line and risked his life for what he believed in. Whatever critique one might make against him, he cannot be justly criticized for not acting or for not being involved.

Martin's philosophy of nonviolence was strongly influenced by Jesus and Gandhi, with the former providing the religious motive that was persuasive in the Negro religious community and with the latter providing the practical method that was effective in the South. Martin often said that "Christ furnished the spirit and motivation, while Gandhi furnished the method."[29]

Contrary to Malcolm, who contended that nonviolence disarmed the oppressed, Martin claimed that it disarmed the oppressor. "It weakens his morale" and "exposes his defenses. And at the same time it works on his conscience. And he just doesn't know what to do," Martin told an audience of Negroes. "Now I can assure you," he continued, "that if we rose up in violence in the South, our opponents would *really* know what to do, because they know how to operate on this level." They are experts on violence. "They control all the forces of violence." But nonviolence confounds the oppressor. "If he beats you, you develop the power to accept it without retaliating. If he doesn't beat you, fine. If he throws you in jail in the process, you go on in there and transform the jail from a dungeon of shame to a haven of freedom and human dignity. Even if he tries to kill you, you develop the quiet courage of dying if necessary without killing." The oppressor ends up frustrated. "This," King said, "is the power of nonviolence."[30]

Nonviolence, therefore, was not a sign of weakness or of a lack of courage. Quite the contrary. King believed that only the strong and courageous person could be nonviolent. He advised persons not to get involved in the civil rights struggle unless they had the strength and the courage to stand before people full of hate and to break the cycle of violence by refusing to retaliate. "The reason I can't advocate violence is because violence ultimately defeats itself," he told Negroes who had experienced the brutality of Bull Connor's dogs and water hoses. "It ultimately destroys everybody. The reason I can't follow the old eye-for-an-eye philosophy is that it ends up leaving everybody blind. Somebody must have sense and somebody must have religion." He urged Negroes to "meet hate with love," "physical force with soul force."[31]

King connected nonviolence with the new order of freedom which he believed was being inaugurated by God through the liberation struggles of the oppressed. In an essay for *Christian Century* he took up this theme and wrote: "Hence the basic question which confronts the world's oppressed is: How is the struggle against the forces of injustice to be waged?"[32] King saw only two alternatives: Violence or nonviolence. Negroes in America, he argued, must choose nonviolence because it is the only practical and moral course to follow. How could a 10 percent Negro minority with no access to the weapons of warfare ever expect to wage a successful violent revolution against a white majority with the military technology of the United States? For King the idea was so silly that he did not even wish to discuss the matter. Talking tough would only arouse the genocidal instincts in white people. And these instincts had been clearly revealed in what Hitler did to the Jews and in what white Americans did to Indians and slaves.

Although King pointed out the practical fallacy of violence, it was, however, the *moral* power of nonviolence that was most important for him. Nonviolence was connected with his idea of the American dream, a dream of a place where Negroes and whites could live together as brothers and sisters. Violence destroys the enemy, but nonviolence has the power to transform the enemy into a friend. "This refusal to hit back will cause the oppressors to become ashamed of their own methods and we will be able to transform enemies into friends."[33] But even if nonviolence does not immediately transform the oppressor (King eventually saw that it did not), its power is primarily found in what it does "to the hearts and souls of those committed to it. It gives them new self-respect. It calls on resources of strength and courage that they did not know they had." King emphasized that violence never creates the conditions for reconciliation; it only breeds more of the same. The American dream is possible only if Negroes struggle for justice with a method that has reconciling power built into it. Nonviolence "helps you to work for something that is morally right, namely integration and the brotherhood of men, with methods that are morally right." King deeply believed that "in the long run of history, destructive methods cannot bring about constructive ends." Why? Because "ends are pre-existent in the means."[34]

Martin's most serious difficulty with Malcolm was on the question of violence. During his early years, Martin viewed Malcolm and the Black Muslims as the black counterpart of the white supremacists. He accepted much of the white media's portrayal of the Muslims as "merchants of hate." Even after Malcolm broke with the Muslims and discarded their racist views, Martin was still reluctant to associate himself with him. It was not a personal issue because Martin liked Malcolm as a person. The issue was violence. When Alex Haley asked Martin his opinion of Malcolm in December 1964, he acknowledged that Malcolm was "very articulate," but, he continued, "I totally disagree with many of his political and philosophical views." The more Martin listened to Malcolm the more he realized that his nemesis was more than just a rabble rouser—he was a serious actor in the struggle for justice. Yet it was hard for him to acknowledge the truth of what Malcolm said about America without also being accused of advocating, along with Malcolm, the right of Negroes to retaliate violently against their white oppressors. "I don't want to seem to sound self-righteous, or absolutist, or that I think I have the only truth, the only way," Martin told Haley.

> Maybe he *does* have some of the answer. I don't know how he feels now, but I know that I have often wished that he would talk less of violence, because violence is not going to solve our problem. And in his litany of articulating the despair of the Negro without offering any positive, creative alternative, I feel that Malcolm has done himself and our people a great disservice. Fiery, demagogic oratory in the black ghettos, urging Negroes to arm themselves and prepare to engage in violence, as he has done, can reap nothing but grief.[35]

THE AMERICAN DREAM AND THE DREAM FOR THE WORLD

King's dream spilled over the boundaries of the United States. King urged Americans to "develop a world perspective." The American dream could not be realized apart from "the larger dream of a world of brotherhood, and peace, and good will." We cannot be free in America, King believed, unless people are free in the Third World nations of Africa, Asia, and Latin America. "We must all learn to live together as brothers," he said, "or we will all perish together as fools. We must come to see that no individual can live alone; no nation can live alone. We must all live together; we must be concerned about each other."[36]

Martin King became especially critical of the United States after he traveled to Ghana and India and saw many homeless and starving people. He was also greatly disturbed by the poverty he saw while vacationing in Mexico. Remembering that the U.S. government spends more than a million dollars a day to store surplus food, King said he knew where "we can store that food free of charge—in the wrinkled stomachs of the millions of people who go to bed hungry at night." He believed deeply that all "life is interrelated." No person or nation can be free or at peace without everyone being free and at peace.

> We are caught up in an inescapable network of mutuality, tied to a single garment of destiny. What affects one directly, affects all indirectly. As long as there is poverty in this world, no man can be totally rich even if he has a billion dollars. As long as diseases are rampant and millions of people cannot expect to live more than twenty or thirty years, no man can be totally healthy, even if he just got a clean bill of health from the finest clinic in America. Strangely enough, I can never be what I ought to be until you are what you ought to be. You can never be what you ought to be until I am what I ought to be.[37]

King's words may not sound radical or original today because we have accepted his way of putting it, and we have even elevated him to the status of a national hero. But, unlike the American government and many persons who pay homage to him, King believed those words. Just as talk of integration was a radical departure arousing fear and anger in many whites, so also speaking about the oneness of humanity was not innocent Sunday-school talk. It was a direct, courageous challenge to all those in the South who advocated segregation as legally sound and morally right. It was also a moral challenge to white northerners to put into practice the principles of justice and fair play by working together with Negroes toward the creation of a fully integrated society where every person would be treated equally. It was a challenge to the American government to use its economic resources to feed the hungry people of the world. And it was a challenge to the Negro community of the South and North: reject despair on the one hand and violence and separatism on the other; go forth knowing that you as a people have been called by God to redeem the soul of America.

BIRMINGHAM AND THE MARCH ON WASHINGTON

Between 1960 and 1965 King worked on portraying and implementing his American dream. At first he was reluctant to become an active participant. He stayed on the sidelines, giving speeches and writing essays about events that others initiated. For example, the sit-ins were started by college students and the freedom rides by CORE. When the freedom riders pleaded with King to join them on a bus from Montgomery, Alabama, to Jackson, Mississippi, to their great disappointment, he said no. A little later (December 1961), speaking at Shiloh Baptist Church in Albany, Georgia, King allowed Dr. William G. Anderson, an old friend of Ralph Abernathy, to draw him into the Albany Movement. Planning only a one-night appearance, he was carried away by the enthusiasm of the audience, which sang, "I woke up this morning, / With my mind set on freedom, / Hallelu . . . hallelu . . . hallelu. . . ." After giving a standard but rousing speech on the need to struggle and suffer for freedom, King found himself agreeing to Anderson's plea to the audience to return the next morning: "Bring your marchin' shoes, and Dr. King is gon' to march with us."[38]

Many observers claimed Police Chief Laurie Pritchett outsmarted King in Albany. Knowing that King wanted "to overcrowd our jail conditions, thus making us give in," Pritchett said he "made arrangements" to put demonstrators in other jails as far as a hundred miles away. He also instructed his officers to follow the principle of "nonviolence."[39] When King had himself arrested to draw national attention to the movement, Pritchett released him and falsely claimed that "a Negro male made his bond."[40] Assisted by "fractious internal rivalries in the black community," soon afterward the movement lost its momentum and King departed Albany without gaining any of the demands that the movement sought. Pritchett was credited with giving King his first major defeat.

Feeling the need to redeem nonviolence from its failure in Albany, King decided to accept Fred Shuttlesworth's invitation to use Birmingham as the "testing ground." About fifteen of the SCLC's inner circle gathered at a two-day retreat in Dorchester, Georgia (10–11 January 1963), to assess their mistakes in Albany and ways to avoid repeating them in Birmingham. They were determined to show that, against the contentions of their critics, Albany was not a failure but, in the words of Wyatt Tee Walker, the executive director of the SCLC, a "first step" "in the early stage of the nonviolent revolution."[41] Careful preparations paid off. Birmingham proved to be King's first significant success since the Montgomery bus boycott, which had ended six years earlier. With Public Safety Commissioner Eugene "Bull" Connor as his highly visible adversary, King was able to demonstrate to the world that segregation was so evil that it could not be tolerated in a nation that claimed to stand for freedom and justice for all. While the white community did not actually concede very much in the "Birmingham Truce Agreement," the moral victory for King was beyond calculation. After the media coverage of the fire hoses, the dogs, the beastlike behavior of Bull Connor's policemen, and the jailing of more than four thousand people, most of whom were children, millions of whites were ready for change, even for federal intervention. In response to Birmingham and the crisis at the University of Alabama, President Kennedy went on national television (June 11) to declare civil rights a "moral issue" "as old as the Scriptures and as clear as the American Constitution. The heart of the question," he said, "is whether all Americans are to be afforded equal rights and equal opportunities; whether we are going to treat our fellow Americans as we want to be treated." In the address, Kennedy announced his intention to "ask Congress . . . to make a commitment it has not fully made in this century to the proposition that race has no place in American life or law."[42]

While Malcolm ridiculed Kennedy's address as a "mealy-mouthed speech," "only in the stage of words," Martin was elated with the president's address. Although it was not the "Second Emancipation Proclamation" he had urged Kennedy to issue, he still praised it as "the most earnest, human and profound appeal for understanding and justice that any President has uttered since the first days of the Republic."[43] It seemed that King had pricked the conscience of America. On 19 June Kennedy submitted his new Civil Rights Bill to Congress.

Birmingham proved to be a turning point in the civil rights movement and for Martin King. Malcolm X was the only public figure in the African-American community who was sharply critical of the tactics and goals of Martin in Birmingham. Malcolm commented: "An integrated cup of coffee is not sufficient pay for 400 years of slave labor."[44] But blacks turned a deaf ear to Malcolm and extolled Martin as their leader.

Soon afterward Martin and other civil rights leaders began to organize the largest demonstration against segregation and for integration in the history of America. While the idea for a "March on Washington for Jobs and Freedom" originated with A. Philip Randolph of the Brotherhood of Sleeping Car Porters and focused at first mainly on *jobs,* King's success in Birmingham redirected it toward *freedom,* that is, "the passage of the Kennedy Administration's civil rights legislative package — 'without compromise or filibuster.' "[45] "Freedom Now" emerged as the chief slogan of the civil rights movement.

On 22 June 1963, King, Randolph, Wilkins of the NAACP, and Whitney Young of the Urban League met with President Kennedy to talk about his proposed Civil Rights Bill and the forthcoming March on Washington event. Seeking to ease the anxiety of a concerned president, the Negro leaders told him that although they expected 100,000 people to attend, they were confident that they had everything under control. Everyone would remain nonviolent.

To the surprise and great joy of the civil rights leaders, nearly 250,000 people gathered at the Washington Monument and marched to the

Lincoln Memorial to declare their support of civil rights for Negroes. Each marcher wore a "twenty-five cent button, displaying a black hand clasping a white hand," and together the marchers sang "We Shall Overcome," the only song permitted at the march. There was not even a hint of violence during the entire day. An estimated one-third of the participants were white. Nothing could have pleased King more, for it vindicated his claim that the civil rights movement was a nonviolent struggle for justice that transcended race. Despite claims by members of Congress that they would not be influenced by the march, no politician could ignore such a powerful witness of black and white Americans.

Malcolm was present at the march as an "uninvited observer," and to anyone who would listen he demeaned the significance of the march. But few people took Malcolm's diminutions seriously. They were anxiously waiting for the imminent coming of the "great age of integration," and they believed that Martin King was the "messiah" who would usher that dream into reality.

On 28 August 1963, King delivered the "I Have a Dream" speech, the most memorable of his many addresses on the American dream. King was the last person to speak in a long program of speakers on a hot summer day, but the melodious and melancholy sound of his baritone voice recaptured the attention of the crowd. "I am happy to join with you today in what will go down in history as the greatest demonstration for freedom in the history of our nation." Out of the combined intellectual traditions of the militant Negro church and liberal Protestantism, Martin King stated his dream with the sermonic power of a prophetic black preacher.

Speaking in the shadow of the Lincoln Memorial, slowly and from his memory of a carefully prepared text, King talked about "a great beacon light of hope" which Lincoln's Emancipation Proclamation gave to Negro slaves "who had been seared in the flames of withering injustice." "But one hundred years later," he proclaimed, "the Negro still is not free" but is "sadly crippled by the manacles of segregation and the chains of discrimination," living "on a lonely island of poverty in the midst of a vast ocean of material prosperity."

No one could describe the moral and political contradiction of America's democracy and its treatment of citizens of African descent as effectively as Martin King. His language cut deeply into the conscience of white America as he spoke of the "shameful condition" in which Negro people have been condemned to live. America has not lived up to its promise of freedom to Negro people. "Instead of honoring its sacred obligation, America has given the Negro people a bad check; a check which has come back marked 'insufficient funds.' " But Martin King "refused to believe that the bank of justice is bankrupt," and he challenged everyone to make the U.S. government cash the check that would bring "the riches of freedom and the security of justice" to all its citizens. That was why he said that "we have . . . come to this hallowed spot to remind America . . . [that] now is the time to rise from the dark and desolate valley of segregation to the sunlit path of racial justice."

As he came to the end of his prepared text, King was deeply moved by the sight of so many Negroes and whites, Protestants and Catholics, Jews and Gentiles together in the nation's capital, symbolizing the beloved community that he had proclaimed for nearly eight years. Like a black preacher being told to "go on!" by an enthusiastic audience, Martin may have heard Mahalia Jackson shout, "Tell us about your dream, Martin!" Whether he did or not, he could not resist the "pull of the crowd." "I have a dream today!" he said, his voice moving toward an inspiring crescendo, as he began to speak on the theme that had become his trademark. "I have a dream that one day . . . right there in Alabama, little black boys and black girls will be able to join hands with little white boys and white girls as sisters and brothers." "I have a dream today!" he repeated, increasing the volume of his voice, using the language and rhythm defined by his black Baptist tradition. "I have a dream that one day every valley shall be exalted, every hill and mountain shall be made low. The rough places will be plain and the crooked places will be made straight, 'and the glory of the Lord shall be revealed, and all flesh shall see it together.'"

By now the crowd was shouting and moving to the rhythm of his voice. Moving past the prescribed ten-minute limit, King expressed his optimistic faith that Negroes and whites together would "transform the jangling discords of our nation into a beautiful symphony of brotherhood." He concluded with a clarion call of freedom, encouraging the people to complete the task that had brought them to Washington:

> Let freedom ring from the prodigious hilltops of New Hampshire; let freedom ring from the mighty mountains of New York; let freedom ring from the heightening Alleghenies of Pennsylvania; let freedom ring from the snowcapped Rockies of Colorado; let freedom ring from the curvaceous slopes of California. But not only that. Let freedom ring from Stone Mountain of Georgia; let freedom ring from Lookout Mountain of Tennessee; let freedom ring from every hill and molehill of Mississippi. "From every mountainside, let freedom ring."

And when this happens, and when we allow freedom to ring, when we let it ring from every village and every hamlet, from every state and every city, we will be able to speed up that day when all of God's children, black men and white men, Jews and Gentiles, Protestants and Catholics, will be able to join hands and sing in the words of the old Negro spiritual: "Free at last. Free at last. Thank God Almighty, we are free at last."[46]

Caught up in the ecstasy of that moment, Martin King described the march as "the greatest demonstration for freedom in the history of the nation."[47] He and many other Americans of all races left Washington that August convinced that the beloved community of integration would soon be realized.

AFTER WASHINGTON

Two weeks after King's great speech, white racists in Birmingham sent King and other Negroes an unmistakable message that they wanted no part of his dream. They bombed the Sixteenth Baptist Church, killing four girls. The tragedy stunned the nation. Though deeply shaken by the ghastly event, King refused to allow his hope for a reconciled America to be shattered. In his eulogy for three of the girls, he said that "these children . . . were the victims of one of the most vicious, heinous crimes ever perpetrated against humanity. Yet they died nobly." In their death, King saw a message for America: "They say to each of us, black and white alike, that we must substitute courage for caution. They say to us that we must be concerned not merely about *who* murdered them, but about the system, the way of life and the philosophy which *produced* the murderers. Their death says to us that we must work passionately and unrelentingly to make the American dream a reality."

King was convinced that "they did not die in vain . . . [because] unmerited suffering is redemptive." Instead of causing him to doubt his dream, King said that their deaths

> may well serve as the redemptive force that will bring new light to this dark city. . . . The death of these little children may lead the whole Southland from the low road of man's inhumanity to man to the high road of peace and brotherhood. These tragic deaths may lead our nation to substitute an aristocracy of character for an aristocracy of color. The spilt blood of these innocent girls may cause the whole citizenry of Birmingham to transform the negative extremes of a dark past into the positive extremes of a bright future. Indeed, this tragic event may cause the white South to come to terms with its conscience.[48]

Martin King's faith in America seemed unshakable, and it continued to separate him from Malcolm X, who did not believe that America could be changed significantly through an appeal to the conscience of its white citizens. Tensions and conflicts between Martin and the young activists in the SNCC continued to deepen because the latter were moving more and more toward Malcolm, especially in regard to their attitudes about whites. But no matter who disagreed with him, Martin held firm to his faith in the American dream, which meant, as the theme song of the civil rights movement said, "we shall overcome, black and white together." Thus at the funeral of the murdered children, King could still urge Negroes "not to despair," "become bitter," or "harbor the desire to retaliate with violence." "We must not lose faith in our white brothers," he said. "Somehow we must believe that the most misguided among them can learn to respect the dignity and worth of all human personality."[49]

Many blacks agonized over King's continued commitment to nonviolence in the face of such an atrocity. Perhaps nonviolence is not the way, many suggested. Maybe Malcolm X, who ridiculed the March on Washington and nonviolence, was right. Whites did not seem to have a conscience. How could any human being bomb a church? Diane Nash of the SNCC and Jim Bevel of the SCLC proposed moving nonviolence to a new level: namely the mass civil disobedience of thousands of protesters, designed to shut down completely the capital city of Montgomery. They wanted to organize a "nonviolent army" and stage "sitdowns on highways, airfield runways, and railroad tracks."[50] But King did not think that the movement was ready for that and treated the Nash-Bevel suggestion as a joke. King merely threatened to resume demonstrations in Birmingham if meaningful changes did not result from the reconciliation initiatives of the president's emissaries to Birmingham.

White Americans and Europeans, however, applauded King for what he said to Negroes about love and nonviolence. They rewarded him with hundreds of prizes and awards and invited him to speak at many distinguished occasions. *Time* named him "Man of the Year" in 1963, the first African-American to achieve the distinction since the magazine started picking persons in 1927. A year later he received the Nobel Peace Prize, the youngest winner since it was first awarded in 1901. En route to receive the award, King stopped in London and four thousand Britons packed St. Paul's Cathedral to hear him deliver the first evensong ever given by a non-Anglican. In London, Oslo, and Paris, he told Europeans that he had an " 'abiding faith in America' and refused to believe that mankind was 'so tragically bound to the starless midnight of racism and war that the bright daybreak of peace and brotherhood can never become a reality.' " The chairman of the Norwegian Parliament's Nobel Committee, Gunnar Jahn, hailed King as an "undaunted champion of peace," and the "first person in the Western world to have shown us that a struggle can be waged without violence." King's name became a household word throughout the world, and world leaders sought his opinions on many topics.[51]

Upon his return to the United States, King was acclaimed as a national hero by blacks and whites alike. Joined by Vice President-elect Hubert Humphrey and Governor Nelson Rockefeller, Mayor Wagner of New York City awarded him the city's Medallion of Honor. Later a gathering of eight thousand met at the 369th Artillery Armory to salute him. President Johnson also gave him an audience. Though white Atlantans initially objected to honoring King, they joined with blacks and gave a testimonial dinner in King's honor and praised him as "Georgia's first winner of a Nobel Prize." "I take great pride," Mayor Ivan Allen, Jr., said, "in honoring this citizen of Atlanta who is willing to turn the other cheek in his quest for full citizenship for all Americans."[52]

King was deeply moved by the public attention he received, and it gave him much hope that full equality for African-Americans would soon be achieved. "The response to our cause in London, Stockholm, and Paris, as well as in Oslo, was far beyond imagination," he told a New York City audience. "These great world capitals look upon racism in this nation with horror and revulsion, but also with a certain amount of hope that Americans can solve this problem and point the way to the rest of the world." In a television interview, he predicted that "the United States might have a Negro President within 25 years." "I am very optimistic about the future," King said. "Frankly I have seen certain changes in the United States over the past two years that surprised me."[53]

While King was very pleased with the attention he received, he sincerely felt he had not earned it. He believed the recognition should be given to the civil rights movement as a whole. That was why he divided the Nobel Prize money ($54,000) among the civil rights organizations. In his acceptance speech and on other occasions celebrating his achievement, he spoke often of the "unknown ground crew," comparing his many supporters to the nameless workers who prepared an airplane for its flight. Although they did not get recognition like the pilot, excellence in their work was just as essential. King saw himself as one of the pilots of the civil rights movement, and he was deeply grateful to the ground crew of the movement who were sustaining him in his hope that his dream was being realized. "Most of these people will never make the headlines and their names will not appear in *Who's Who*," he said in his Nobel acceptance speech. "Yet [when] the years have rolled past and when the blazing light of truth is focused on this marvelous age in which we live, men and women will know and children will be taught that we have a finer land, a better people, a more noble civilization because these humble children of God were willing to suffer for right-eousness' sake."[54]

During the period demarcated by the Montgomery bus boycott and the events at Birmingham, King was a "reluctant leader," responding to the initiatives of others. But after Birmingham, he concluded that he could not avoid the great responsibility which had been placed upon him. Before Birmingham, according to Andrew Young, King even considered an offer from Sol Hurok's agency of "a guarantee of one hundred thousand dollars just to be a lecturer."[55] But after Birmingham, the Washington March, and the Nobel Peace Prize, King realized that he could drift no longer. He had been chosen as the symbol of the black freedom struggle and he could not escape it. "History has thrust me into this position," King told reporters who had gathered to get his reaction to being awarded the Nobel Peace Prize. "It would be immoral and a sign of ingratitude if I did not face my moral responsibility to do what I can in this struggle."[56]

So, despite the Birmingham church bombing and the Kennedy assassination, King held fast to his belief that America's unfulfilled dream would soon be realized. He was encouraged by the passage of the Civil Rights Bill, the huge margin of victory of Lyndon B. Johnson over Barry Goldwater, and the international recognition that the civil rights movement was receiving in his name. King's successful Selma March, which led to the passage of the Voting Rights Acts on 6 August 1965, was his last great burst of hope.

4

"I SEE A NIGHTMARE" (1952–63)

Unemployment and poverty have forced many of our people into this life of crime; but . . . the real criminal is in City Hall downtown. The real criminal is in the State House in Albany. The real criminal is in the White House in Washington, D.C. The real criminal is the white man who poses as a liberal—the political hypocrite. And it is these legal crooks, posing as our friends, [who are] forcing us into a life of crime and then using us to spread the white man's evil vices among our own people. Our people are scientifically maneuvered by the white man into a life of poverty. You are not poor accidentally. He maneuvers you into poverty. You are not a drug addict accidentally. Why, the white man maneuvers you into drug addiction. You are not a prostitute accidentally. You have been maneuvered into prostitution by the American white man. There is nothing about your condition here in America that is an accident.

Malcolm X
Harlem, New York
10 August 1963

What is looked upon as an American dream for white people has long been an American nightmare for black people.

Malcolm X
New York City
1 May 1962

THE CONTEXT OF MALCOLM'S VISION

No one can understand the full meaning of Malcolm X's nightmare without first gaining an awareness of what blacks' lives were like in the urban ghettos of the North prior to and during Malcolm's life. The great migration of blacks from the rural South to the urban North, which began before the First World War and continued through the 1950s, marked a significant change in the context and texture of their lives. The contrast between what blacks expected to find in the "promised land" of the North and what they actually found there was so great that frustration and despair ensued, destroying much of their self-esteem and dignity. Blacks expected to find the *freedom* which had eluded them for so many years in the South; that is, they expected to have—like other Americans—the right to live wherever they chose and to work and play with whomever they chose. Instead they found themselves crammed into small ghetto sections of the cities, paying to white land-lords and merchants exorbitant prices for rent, food, and clothing, and being policed by white cops who showed no more respect for black life than the "white law" they knew so well in the South.

Blacks also encountered white hostility and hate as the ghetto expanded to make room for the continuous influx of their relatives from the South. Northern whites did not welcome blacks as neighbors or as competitors in the workplace. White resentment often led to mob violence, creating what is known as urban race riots, in which most of the victims were black.

As de jure segregation defined black life in the South, de facto segregation was a way of life in the North. Blacks were confined to the ghetto, with no future to look forward to except an endless repetition of mental and physical pain and suffering. In church, school, and their social lives, blacks and whites lived in separate and unequal worlds, having even less contact with each other than in the South. As was true of the South, it seemed that everything that was good about America belonged disproportionately to whites and everything that was bad, the things which exploited humanity physically and mentally, fell mostly to blacks. Of course, there were a few northern whites who, unlike southern whites, talked about freedom and justice for all and also participated in and contributed to their favorite civil rights organizations, socializing with black professionals; but it is important to note that white liberal talk and socializing with the black bourgeoisie did not improve the quality of life for the black masses in the ghetto. On the contrary, black existence continued as an unabated process of deterioration.

Some people claimed that for blacks the quality of life in the North was even worse than that in the South, because of the devastating effects of the ghetto upon the personalities of its inhabitants. Ghetto existence was defined primarily by unemployment and underemployment, dirty streets and overcrowded, rat-infested tenements, pimps and prostitutes, drug pushers and dope addicts, black-on-black crime, and police brutality. It was difficult to live daily in the squalor and filth of the ghetto and also think of oneself as a human being. Though a few managed to get out, the great majority could only carve out a meager existence. For many life was made bearable because of the hope that they received from their daily talks with Jesus. However, many others found the religion of Jesus weak and unrelated to their needs. Removed from the southern context, it seemed too white, too outdated, and too other-worldly for coping with ghetto life. In place of Jesus, savior of the main-line black churches, they often talked with the readily available saviors who touched the psychic depths of their identity as *black* people and thereby rendered their existence worthwhile. Father Divine, Daddy Grace, and Elder Lightfoot Micheaux were well-known for creating a life of meaning for poverty-stricken blacks in the urban ghetto. Black nationalist philosophies also were highly visible as alternatives to traditional black Christianity. In that regard, Marcus Garvey made an immense impact on the black masses. But during the 1950s and 1960s no force affected black life as did the ministry of Malcolm X, a ministry devoted to Elijah Muhammad's Nation of Islam. As Martin King's dream was developed in the context of black people's fight against segregation in the South, Malcolm X's nightmare was shaped in the context of their fight for dignity and respect in the North.

MALCOLM AND MUHAMMAD

Informed observers of the Black Muslims agree that Malcolm X was most responsible for the impact that the sect made upon black American life. While Elijah Muhammad, the "Messenger of Allah," was the sole and absolute authority in the Nation of Islam, Malcolm X was his most effective missionary, "the St. Paul of the Black Muslim movement." Malcolm's years as "Minister Malcolm," Elijah Muhammad's fiery spokesman, the angry critic of liberal whites and bourgeois blacks, are the subject of this chapter. Later we will examine his year of independence after his break with the Messenger.

When Malcolm X was paroled from Charlestown State Prison in 1952, Martin King was still a graduate student and Elijah Muhammad's Nation of Islam was a small religious sect. It had approximately four hundred followers and ten temples, and was unknown even to most students of black religion. In the summer of 1953, Malcolm was made the assistant minister of Temple Number One in Detroit for his excellent work in recruiting new members. Soon after, he was sent to organize a temple in Boston and then in Philadelphia. As a reward for his outstanding service to the Nation, Malcolm was appointed the head minister of the influential Temple Number Seven in New York City in June

1954, three months before King began his full-time ministry at Dexter Baptist Church.

From the time of Malcolm X's sudden and radical conversion in 1948 to his declaration of independence in March 1964, Malcolm's thinking was defined by his total commitment to Elijah Muhammad. Everything he said and did, politically and theologically, was approved by the Messenger, the only person, according to Black Muslims, who had seen Allah ("in the person of Wallace D. Fard"). Malcolm's complete submission and absolute obedience to the Prophet Muhammad in all things were symbolized by the frequent prefacing of his remarks with the phrase: "The Honorable Elijah Muhammad teaches us that . . ." Malcolm said that he was like the dummy Charlie McCarthy, dependent for speech on Elijah Muhammad as Charlie depended on the famous ventriloquist Edgar Bergen. "If Bergen quits talking, McCarthy is struck dumb. . . . This is the way it is with the Messenger and me. It is my mouth working, but the voice is his."[1]

Malcolm accepted the authoritarian character of the Black Muslim movement. He freely and happily submitted his total self to the person and teachings of Elijah Muhammad, the supreme judge in everything affecting the lives of Black Muslims. They developed a genuine father-son relationship. Malcolm's public and personal behavior was entirely subject to the approval of Elijah Muhammad. Malcolm even submitted when his brother Reginald was sentenced to "isolation" from all other Muslims. "I considered that I was a Muslim before I was Reginald's brother."[2] Malcolm sought Muhammad's blessings for his marriage to Betty in 1958 and also named the third of six daughters after him—Ilyasah, Arabic for Elijah.

Signs of differences between the two men appeared in the early 1960s, and Malcolm at the end saw his commitment to the Messenger as a great mistake. But for most of his years as a Muslim, Malcolm expressed unqualified love and respect for Elijah Muhammad, who "rescued me when I was a convict" and then "trained me in his home, as if I was his son." "I had more faith in Elijah Muhammad than I could ever have in any other man upon this earth." "I worshipped him," because "to us [Black Muslims], the Nation of Islam was Mr. Muhammad."[3] He considered Muhammad a *divine* teacher, one who could not err. He often said that he believed in Muhammad more than Christians believed in Jesus.

Malcolm's commitment to Elijah Muhammad should be seen within the larger context of his devotion to the freedom of black people and the religion of Islam. "The Honorable Elijah Muhammad gave me the ability to respect myself" as a black person, Malcolm said. "Before hearing of him . . ., I had nothing, knew nothing, and was nothing. I was

addicted to and enslaved by the evils and vices of this white civilization —
dope, alcohol, adultery, and even murder." He believed that Elijah
Muhammad's Nation of Islam offered a community and a value system
which bestowed meaning upon his life as a *human being* and upon blacks
as an *African* people. Muhammad had picked him up from "the very
bottom of the American white man's society," where, he said, "I . . . was
buried up to my neck in the mud of this filthy world, with very little
hope, desire or intention of amounting to anything." "I was walking on
my own coffin."⁴ Muhammad cleaned Malcolm up, stood him up on his
feet as a proud black man, and then gave him a platform from which
to speak on behalf of justice for black people. Elijah Muhammad's most
significant influence upon Malcolm was his teaching about blacks and
whites, using his own special version of Islam as the religious justification
of it. Malcolm's commitment to Muhammad was a religio-cultural passage through which he traveled as he developed the political implications of his "pledge" to tell white people about their crimes and black
people about their brainwashed condition.

OPPRESSION AND JUSTICE

INDICTMENT OF AMERICA TO BLACK AUDIENCES

Malcolm was a gifted thinker and leader whose perspective was
defined by his uncompromising solidarity with the victims of history. He
saw America as "the little people in the street" saw it: oppressive and
insensitive to the basic needs of weak and helpless people, especially
the black poor in the ghetto.

From 1953 to 1959, Malcolm was unknown in the white community.
As King talked primarily to whites, Malcolm directed his message almost
exclusively to blacks. As Elijah Muhammad's tireless and most effective
evangelist, he traveled from coast to coast, organizing new temples,
encouraging floundering ones, and representing the Messenger whenever and wherever he requested. Malcolm spoke in homes, temples, and
churches, at street rallies and community meetings, and wrote a weekly
column, entitled "God's Angry Men," for the New York *Amsterdam
News*, *Los Angeles Herald Dispatch*, and other African-American newspapers. His message was the same everywhere: it was deeply religious
and focused on the brainwashed condition of the "so-called Negroes"
who seemed totally unaware of the satanic nature of the white man.
"We so-called Negroes here in America are in pitiful shape, our 'illness'
being more unique than that of any people in recorded history." "We
have become like a puppy sleeping at the slavemaster's feet; or a watch
dog for him, not willing to bite him, but ready to CHEW UP the first

of OUR OWN KIND who comes to awaken us."

Mental slavery was the great problem of the Negro. "He is so deaf and dumb and blind, he can't hear the truth when it is told to him, he can't speak up for himself and he is so blind he can't see that the white man is the devil and his enemy. We are so much in love with him we still think he is our friend." "There is no one who could love someone who has treated them as the white man has treated you and I, but a fool." Malcolm understood his task as that of "waking up a dead people," using the truthful message of Elijah Muhammad. "A junkie can never start to cure himself until he recognizes and accepts his true condition."

Malcolm spoke in a conversational style, addressing blacks personally, as if he were a teacher uncovering the truth for his pupils. "Master Teacher" is what Peter Bailey, a disciple, appropriately called him. Malcolm knew that blacks were not ready to accept his perspective on America. Thus he anticipated their objections and then shrewdly undermined them.

> You hear us talking about the white man and you want to go away and tell him we have been subversive. Here is a man who raped your mother and hung your father on his tree, is he subversive? Here is a man who robbed you of all knowledge of your nation and your religion and is he subversive? Here is a man who lied to you and tricked you about all things, is he subversive? Today Elijah Muhammad is subverting him. He is pulling the covers off of this snake and giving us his true identity. This is the man who the Almighty God Allah is subversive against . . . and you come in here and get mad at us. You better listen or you will be taken off the planet along with the devil.[5]

Although Malcolm was well-known in Black Muslim circles, it was the Hinton Johnson incident in April 1957 which brought him to the attention of the larger black community, especially in Harlem. It was one thing to talk "bad" at Temple Number Seven and quite another to back it up in a confrontation with the "powers that be." One evening Hinton Johnson, a Muslim, was severely beaten and hauled off to jail by several policemen, an act which editor James Hicks of the *Amsterdam News* called "a flagrant case of police brutality." Within minutes, Malcolm X assembled over one hundred members of the Fruit of Islam (a paramilitary group of Black Muslim men) in front of the police precinct in Harlem. Soon, other blacks increased the crowd to eight hundred, "some of them teenagers with zip guns." The police officials became very worried about the possible eruption of a race riot. With the help of Hicks, who was a friend of Malcolm's, the police arranged a meeting with Malcolm to enlist his "influence against violence." "Guarantee that our brother will get medical treatment," Malcolm snapped. "Pledge that the men who beat him will be punished." After the "police gave him their promise" and Hicks assured him that "their word could be trusted," Malcolm did something that stunned the police and established him as a leader in the black community who must be reckoned with. "He strode to the head of the angry, impatient mob, stood silently, and then flicked his hands. Within seconds, the street was empty." Seeing that, a policeman said: "No man should have that much power."[6]

From that incident onward, the black community began talking about Malcolm X and the Black Muslims. People began to flock to hear him at Temple Number Seven and other places where he was speaking. Many joined the Nation of Islam because of Malcolm's magnetic presence. Black civil rights leaders, preachers, and politicians started to take notice of him and accepted his invitations to appear at Harlem street rallies. Among them were Manhattan borough leader Hulan Jack, Congressman Adam Clayton Powell, Jr., Pastor Gardner C. Taylor of Brooklyn's Concord Baptist Church, labor leader A. Philip Randolph, and civil rights theoretician Bayard Rustin.

With a larger audience for his message, Malcolm stepped up his attack on the "white man," his favorite target of ridicule. "Much of what I say might sound bitter, but it's the truth," he told Harlem blacks. "Much of what I say might sound like it's stirring up trouble, but it's the truth. Much of what I say might sound like it's hate, but it's the truth. . . . The best thing to put the white man to fright is the truth. He can't take the truth."

Malcolm was committed to telling the truth as he felt it and with the simplicity, clarity, and passion of an angry biblical prophet. He frequently quoted Jesus' saying, "You shall know the truth and the truth shall make you free." No one believed that saying more than Malcolm. "We don't care who likes this or not, as long as we know it's the truth," he told his audiences. "If you are afraid to tell the truth, why you don't deserve freedom. Just tell the truth."

The truth which Malcolm felt he had to tell to blacks was about the hypocrisy of the northern white liberals. He referred to them as "shrewdly camouflaged racists." They pretended to be blacks' friends and supporters, "eager to point out what the white man in the South has been doing to us while they themselves . . . are doing the same thing." Malcolm called the northern white liberals "foxes," in contrast to the whites in the South whom he referred to as "wolves." "I prefer the candor of the southern segregationist to the hypocrisy of the northern integrationist," Malcolm said, because, the former "always let you know where you stand." "I'd rather walk among rattlesnakes, whose constant rattle warns me where they are, than among those northern snakes who grin and make you forget you're in a snake pit." Southern segregationists were honest about what they believed. "The wolf doesn't act friendly and therefore ... has more difficulty in getting the lamb chops on his plate." But "a fox acts friendly toward the lamb and usually the fox ends up with the lambchops on his plate." "These northern foxes," Malcolm declared, "pose as your benefactor, ... as your employer, ... as your landlord, ... as your neighborhood merchant, ... [and] as your lawyer trying to help you." They are hypocritical and "even more cruel and vicious than the white [wolves] in the South." "They use integration for infiltration." White liberals "[try] to pat you on the back and tell you how much progress you are making when you are catching more hell today than your grandfather caught a hundred years ago." "By joining you, they strangle your militant efforts toward freedom, toward justice, toward equality."[7]

Unlike Martin King, Malcolm did not try to support his assertions with the kind of evidence that whites would accept, because he was not trying to persuade them. He was talking from a *black* point of view, and he merely wanted to identify the enemies to black people so they would know whom they had to fight against in their struggle for dignity. He argued that it was no accident that the great number of blacks lived in rat-filled slums and the majority of whites lived in luxurious apartments in the city and beautiful homes in the suburbs. "It was," Malcolm said, "a part of the science used by the white man to keep us in bondage, in ignorance, in poverty, in slavery, twentieth century slavery." Malcolm did not shrink from naming white people as the ones primarily responsible for black suffering in the ghetto. He wanted blacks to know it and whites to know that they knew it. He therefore used language and spoke in a style that was intended to infuriate whites (especially policemen and the media who attended his Harlem rallies). The more enraged they became about what he said the happier he was, because he wanted them to know how blacks felt. He called whites every scurrilous name he could think of: "blue-eyed devils," "two-legged snakes," "international thugs and rapists," "white apes and beasts." "I love to talk about them," Malcolm said with a big smile to a Harlem rally. "They should be able to take it. Why, when I was a little boy they called me nigger so much I thought that was my name." Malcolm wanted to give whites an "inkling of how we feel"; he wanted to experience the justice of giving them a taste of their own medicine. He, therefore, let loose a verbal barrage against whites, especially the government, that frightened many blacks. "Anytime you live under a flag that does not protect you," he told a Los Angeles audience, "that flag isn't any more than an old dirty rag. Oh, yes, some of you people out there are scared and saying I'm going to jail for talking like this. But the hell that the 'so-called Negroes' have gone through for these many years in North America will make the inside of a jail house look like the best suite in the Waldorf-Astoria Hotel."[8]

Malcolm's claim that "white people are a race of devils" was not mere name-calling, intended to get himself publicity, as many of his critics suggested. On the contrary, his intention was to speak nothing but the truth, the "truth that is not dressed up." His was not just a religious truth, revealed only to Black Muslim believers. It was a historical, objective truth, available to any thoughtful and morally sensitive human being. "When I say the white man is a devil," proclaimed Malcolm in a sermon at a Muslim meeting, "I speak with the authority of history." "That's right," the audience responded, as though they knew through experience the truth about which he spoke. "The record of history shows that the white men, as a people, have never done good," Malcolm continued. "He stole our fathers and mothers from their culture of silk and satins and brought them to this land in the belly of a ship—am I right or wrong?" "You are right, God knows you are right," was the resounding response.

Malcolm regarded the white people's crime against black people as the worst in human history. He called it "the world's most monstrous crime." Using his imagination combined with his study of history, he spoke often of the physical brutality that whites committed against blacks:

I know that you don't realize the enormity, the horrors, of the so-called *Christian* white man's crime.... Not even in the *Bible* is there such a crime! God in His wrath struck down with *fire* the perpetrators of *lesser* crimes! *One hundred million* of us black people! Your grandparents! Mine! *Murdered* by this white man. To get fifteen million of us here to make us slaves, on the way he murdered one hundred million! I wish it was possible for me to show you the sea bottom in those days—the black bodies, the blood, the bones broken by boots and clubs! The pregnant black women who were thrown overboard if they got too sick! Thrown overboard to the sharks that had learned that following these ships was the way to grow fat! Why, the white man's raping of the black race's woman began right on those slave ships! The blue-eyed devil could not even wait until he got them here! Why, brothers and sisters, civilized mankind has never known such an orgy of greed and lust and murder....[9]

Although Malcolm identified whites as the ones most responsible for the suffering of blacks, he did not absolve the victims from responsibility. He often appeared more angry with blacks for accepting exploitation than he was with the whites who he claimed were responsible for it. His reference to the truth as "sharp," "like a two-edged sword," was applied primarily to blacks. "It cuts into you," he told them. "It causes you great pain, but if you can take the truth, it will cure you and save you from what otherwise would be certain death."

Malcolm was especially critical of the civil rights leaders, like King, who, he contended, allowed themselves to be used by their enemies. However, it is important to note that, in the interest of unity, Malcolm, following the advice of Elijah Muhammad, at first sought to avoid public criticism of King and other civil rights leaders. During most of the 1950s, he seldom mentioned anyone by name, even though much of what he said was an implicit, and sometimes explicit, critique of the civil rights movement. Even though their philosophy of black separatism and pride contradicted the prevailing mood of integration, Black Muslims were deeply concerned about black unity. Elijah Muhammad offered King a serious invitation to speak, at a date of the latter's own choosing, in March or April 1958 "before the Moslems of Chicago . . . [and] other citizens in a Free Rally." Malcolm also offered him several invitations to appear at Harlem rallies. Martin's secretary always gave a form letter reply, acknowledging the "receipt of your letter" and informing Malcolm that "Dr. King is out of the office for several days."[10] King himself never made any public effort to meet with Malcolm. He made private initiatives without success after Malcolm's break with Muhammad.

Martin's avoidance of Malcolm, as well as his and other civil rights leaders' critique of the Black Muslim movement as a philosophy of black supremacy, angered Malcolm, and he pleaded with Muhammad to allow him to respond to their criticisms. In the early 1960s, after Muhammad gave him the green light, Malcolm let loose an avalanche of criticisms against civil rights leaders that destroyed any future possibility of a black united front. Malcolm was often as severe and as unrestrained in his castigation of black, middle-class advocates of integration as he was when he talked about white liberals. He referred to them as "these old white-minded," "brainwashed, handkerchief-head, twentieth-century intellectual Negroes." He also called them "puppets and parrots" who had been "endorsed, sanctioned, subsidized, and supported by white liberals." He said that as "Negro stooges," civil rights leaders, like their white liberal masters, are clever. The unsuspecting observer, therefore, is often fooled by them. "Today's Uncle Tom doesn't wear a handkerchief on his head," said Malcolm. "This modern . . . Uncle Thomas now often wears a top hat. He's usually well-dressed and well-educated. He's often the personification of culture and refinement." He "sometimes speaks with a Yale or Harvard accent . . . [and] is known as Professor, Doctor, Judge, and Reverend, even Reverend Doctor." Malcolm called him "a *professional* Negro," and then went on to clarify himself: " . . . by that I mean his profession is being a Negro for the white man."[11]

Since Martin King was the symbol of the civil rights movement and the one whom whites promoted as the leader of blacks, Malcolm X singled him out as a special object of criticism. "The white man is our first and main enemy. Our second enemy are the Uncle Toms, such as Martin Luther King and his turn the other cheek method."[12] He called him a "religious Uncle Tom," a "traitor," a "chump," and the "Reverend Dr. Chickenwing." Of course, Martin never responded in like manner; he merely moved further away from any meeting with Malcolm. As Martin continued his policy of ignoring Malcolm, the latter reacted to every major media event in which Martin was engaged.

While many middle-class blacks reacted to Malcolm in a fashion similar to liberal whites, the black poor reveled in his courage to be "blunt speaking" and "frank talking." "Oooooh, he *burnt* that white man," Alex Haley overheard an excited woman say about Malcolm's lecture in Temple Number Seven, "burnt him *up,* chile . . . chile, he told us we descendin' from black kings an' queens—Lawd, I didn't know it!" Malcolm also enjoyed speaking to them, and these speeches often went on for two hours or more. "I think I could be speaking blindfolded," Malcolm said, "and after five minutes, I could tell you if sitting out there before me was an all-black or all-white audience. Black audiences and white audiences feel distinguishably different. Black audiences feel warmer, there is almost a musical rhythm, for me, even in their silent response."[13]

When Malcolm went into the black community to speak, he was in his natural habitat; it was analogous to throwing "Br'er Rabbit" in the "briar patch." He felt at home among blacks because they accepted him as one of their own, as one who cared enough for them to speak the truth about America even if it cost him his life. He was also severe in his critique of blacks. Love and criticism were linked together. Blacks knew that Malcolm had to have great love for them to say what he said. They also knew that he would never "sell them down the river" for status or money. They urged him on, saying "Yes, that's right brother," "You, tell'em like it is Malcolm," "Make it plain." Like Martin King's preaching in a black church, the eloquence and conversational style of Malcolm's speaking added to the cogency of his analysis and somehow empowered poor blacks to cope with their present, miserable situation, creating the confidence in them that they could make a better future for themselves. No one could speak the truth to "the bottom-of-the-pile Negroes" as effectively as Malcolm. "My hobby," he often said, "is stirring up Negroes."[14] He told it as he felt it and as he lived it, and they liked what they heard, because he was an incarnation of the truth about which he spoke.

INDICTMENT OF AMERICA TO WHITE AUDIENCES

In his indignation Malcolm eagerly awaited a time when he could look directly at whites—with fire in his eyes and accusatory right index finger pointing—and tell them what he thought about their Western civilization. The opportunity came in late 1959 with the airing of a television documentary on black nationalism entitled "The Hate That Hate Produced," researched by Louis Lomax for the "Mike Wallace Show." White Americans saw and heard Malcolm X for the first time and were deeply shocked by what most of them believed was nothing but the preaching of black supremacy. Many had thought that Martin King was a dangerous radical, especially when they compared him with the moderate leadership of Roy Wilkins of the NAACP and Lester Granger of the National Urban League. But Malcolm X and the Black Muslims made King look like a harmless conservative and therefore more than acceptable to the liberal establishment in the North, whom Malcolm had singled out as the special object of his righteous indignation. In order to offset Malcolm's appeal to the black community, Martin was adopted as the darling of the white liberal community and was portrayed by the media as the ideal black leader.

Malcolm's style of speaking was as important as the content of his message; more accurately, his style was an essential part of his message. He was angry, and his anger was reflected in the passion and rhythm of his voice, which in turn informed the logic of his analysis. "You should not be angry with me if I raise my voice," Malcolm said to a Boston University audience. "When you see a man on a stove and he yells, 'ouch!', why, he should be allowed, because he knows what it feels like to suffer." Malcolm spoke from his heart and exposed whites to his deepest and most passionate feelings. He wanted the world to know that he was angry and could not understand how anyone could be a human being and *not* be angry about what white people had done to black people in America. He was proud to be known as the "angriest Negro in America."[15]

"The white man is the devil" whose "time is up." This was Malcolm's often-repeated central claim. It offended and agitated whites more than anything else he said. Knowing this, Malcolm was pleased that he, with words alone, could upset white America. The more whites described him as a racist demagogue, the more he was determined to accuse them of the terrible deeds which they had committed against blacks. With the singlemindedness of a biblical seer, he proclaimed Allah's intention to destroy "the wicked white race in the war of Armageddon." In media interviews, on television and radio panels, and as a frequent lecturer at colleges and universities, Malcolm declared that "the entire white race is a race of devils" and "the common enemy of all dark mankind."

When whites heard or read Malcolm's fiery words, they often accused him of being "antiwhite," "anti-Christian," and a "teacher of hate" no different from the Ku Klux Klan. Malcolm, however, was ready for that criticism, and he got a great deal of satisfaction responding to it, holding his own in debates with articulate white intellectuals and scholars. "It's not a case of being antiwhite or anti-Christian," he said in an interview for *Playboy.*

> We're anti-evil, anti-oppression, anti-lynching. You can't be anti-those things unless you're also anti- the oppressor and the lyncher. You can't be anti-slavery and pro-slavemaster; you can't be anti-crime and pro-criminal. In fact, Mr. Muhammad teaches that if the present generation of *whites* would study their own race in the light of their true history, they would be antiwhite themselves.[16]

Malcolm was a master of debate, and he loved to engage in it. He responded to white questions in different moods and from different angles, bobbing and weaving, moving from position to position as if he were a verbal boxer, sizing up the assumptions of his opponents. He was always in control of the discussion, moving it in the direction of his own intellectual strengths so he could deliver the knock-out blow at the moment of his choosing. His white opponents sometimes recognized what he was doing and tried to avoid the impending disaster, but they seldom succeeded.

Martin and other civil rights leaders, like Roy Wilkins and Whitney Young, were well aware of Malcolm's debating skills and avoided appearing with him in public. Nothing would have pleased Malcolm more than to get Martin in a debate before an audience. Martin, however, went to great lengths to make sure that it would never happen. He threatened to cancel his scheduled appearance on the "David Susskind Show" when he heard that Malcolm would appear as a guest with him. When Frank Clark, speaking for Radio station KDIA of Oakland, California, invited Martin to debate Malcolm, Martin's secretary wrote to Clark to inform him that King had "taken a consistent position of not accepting such invitations because he feels that it will do no good. He has always considered his work in a positive action framework rather than engaging in consistent negative debate." Wyatt Tee Walker, then executive director of the SCLC, did appear with Malcolm.[17]

After several unfavorable appearances with Malcolm, Wilkins forbade any staff member from debating Malcolm. Wilkins and Young also tried to talk James Farmer out of meeting Malcolm in debate before white audiences. Malcolm developed much respect for Farmer, Bayard Rustin, Louis Lomax, and other integrationists who had the courage to debate him in public. However, he chuckled as he reflected on his public debates with Bayard Rustin, and commented "poor Bayard," suggesting that he, with his Oxford-sounding accent, did not have a chance with him.

Malcolm was so effective in debates that James Hicks of the *Amsterdam News* called him the "giant killer." He was referring to Malcolm's debates with Kenneth Clark and John Davis, both professors at City College, Reverend Milton Galamison, a prominent Brooklyn community leader, and Gloster Current of the National Urban League. "Malcolm X figuratively murdered Ken," wrote Hicks, "and Ken virtually confessed at the end of the program."[18] The others fared even worse.

Whites suffered even more than blacks in debates with Malcolm. He regarded his encounters with them as a verbal battle between the oppressed and the oppressor. "It was like being on a battlefield—with intellectual and philosophical bullets," he said, as he reflected on his college and university appearances. "It was an exciting battling with ideas. I got so I could feel my audiences' temperaments. . . . It's a psychic radar. As a doctor, with his finger against a pulse, is able to feel the heart rate, when I am up there speaking, I can *feel* the reaction to what I am saying." When Malcolm knew he was about to make a telling point that his audience might find too controversial to accept, sometimes he would say, in a cool and calm manner, "Let us not be emotional; let us reason together." At other times he would keep pounding one point after another until even his fiercest opponents would acknowledge the truth of his claims with dead silence and a sheepish grin.

Malcolm was particularly angered by white people's assertion that he was teaching hatred. "History is not hatred," he often shot back.

As soon as the white man hears a black man say that he's through loving white people, then the white man accuses the black man of hating him. The Honorable Elijah doesn't teach hate. The white man isn't *important* enough for the Honorable Elijah Muhammad and his followers to spend any time hating him. . . . The white man has brainwashed himself into believing that all the black people in the world want to be cuddled up next to him. When he meets what we're talking about, he can't believe it, it takes all the wind out of him. When we tell him we don't want to be around him, we don't want to be like he is, he's staggered. It makes him reevaluate his

300-year myth about the black man. What I want to know is how the white man, with the blood of black people dripping off his fingers, can have the audacity to be asking black people do they hate him. That takes a lot of nerve.[19]

Although Malcolm spoke often to white groups and gave hundreds of interviews to the news media, he, unlike Martin King, was not attempting to convert them to his point of view. Whites were devils, and he did not expect devils to become angels. Unlike Martin who based his view of America on faith, Malcolm's perspective was defined primarily by history. "Historically," he often said, as he invited whites to offer contrary evidence, "I think, the weight of the evidence is against them if you're looking for angelic deeds." As one would expect, many whites reacted *personally* to being called "white devils."

Most of the time, Malcolm was pleased when whites reacted negatively to his analysis of American history. "The more the white man yelps," he told Alex Haley, "the more I know I have struck a nerve." Sometimes, however, he tried to assure whites that he was speaking collectively and not individually:

Unless we call one white man, by name, a "devil," we are not speaking of any *individual* white man. We are speaking of the *collective* white man's *historical* record. We are speaking of the collective white man's cruelties, and evils, and greeds, that have seen him *act* like a devil toward the non-white man. Any intelligent, honest, objective person cannot fail to realize that this white man's slave trade, and his subsequent devilish actions are directly *responsible* for not only the *presence* of the black man in America, but also for the *condition* in which we find this black man here. You cannot find *one* black man, I do not care who he is, who has not been personally damaged in some way by the devilish acts of the collective white man!

Malcolm's explanation may have helped some whites, but for most, it did not eliminate their resentment of his analysis of the historical record. They did not like his concentration on the evil deeds of the past and tried to get him to focus on the present situation. To that Malcolm replied, "You can't solve a problem by dealing with the current situation. You have to go to the roots as to how that racial mythology developed."[20]

Whites were looking for hope, which they always received when they heard Martin King speak. But Malcolm refused to accommodate the white need for hope and instead told them that neither their historical past nor their present deeds warranted the belief that the social evils about which he spoke would be eliminated by the people who created them. Because Malcolm would not knuckle under to whites' need "to feel 'noble' about throwing crumbs" to black people, he was portrayed by the white media as a "black devil," and whites were much more successful than Malcolm in making the label stick, even though the latter's judgment was closer to the truth.

GOD'S JUSTICE

Malcolm's idea of justice differed from that held by Martin, who defined it in the light of Jesus' command to love the enemy. Malcolm's idea of justice was defined by the concept of "an eye for an eye, a tooth for a tooth, and an arm for an arm, and a head for a head, and a life for a life." God, Allah, would exact stern justice against white people for the evil deeds they had committed against the "Lost-Found Nation of Islam, the so-called Negroes, here in 'this wilderness of North America.' " In contrast to Martin's call for forgiving love, Malcolm envisioned an even-handed justice. White Americans would suffer punishment in exact proportion to their crimes against black people. "Just as Egypt had to pay for its crime that it committed for enslaving the Hebrews, the Honorable Elijah Muhammad teaches us that America has to pay today for the crime that it committed in enslaving the so-called Negroes."

It is important to note that God is the executor of justice in Malcolm's perspective. "The white man is going to be destroyed," he proclaimed, "*not* by us, but by the Almighty God, whose name is Allah. We don't have to do anything but live a righteous life." This emphasis led to passivity in the realm of political action. This passivity contrasts sharply with King's political activism. While King shared Malcolm's belief that God is the ultimate executor of justice, his accent on God's righteousness led him into exhausting efforts to establish justice in the world. Malcolm, on the other hand, believed that the "solution" to the problem of racial injustice "will never be brought about by politicians," but "it will be brought about by God."[21]

Although Malcolm's position on this matter seemed to encourage political passivity, he still remained troubled by the Muslims' political non-engagement, especially as it reduced his credibility among the grassroots people of the ghetto whom he wanted to influence. "I've never been one for inaction. Everything I've ever felt strongly about, I've done something about it." Nevertheless, following Muhammad's doctrine, he limited the exercise of his gifts as a leader and organizer to the Nation of Islam. Until the last year of his life, the outside world knew him mainly through his proclamation of God's justice.

UNITY, SELF-KNOWLEDGE, SELF-LOVE, SELF-DEFENSE, AND SEPARATION

UNITY

Though Malcolm was more famous for his scathing critique of whites, his call for unity among blacks was actually the dominant theme of his ministry. Unity depended on genuine love for each other. If blacks were going to achieve the unity necessary for the attainment of their freedom, then self-hate—according to Malcolm the number one problem in the black community—had to be replaced with a love of themselves. However, genuine love of each other was possible, in Malcolm's view, only to the degree that blacks were able to acquire a true knowledge of their history and culture. Malcolm told blacks that they were "culturally dead," alienated from their past and from each other. That was why they did not love each other and could not achieve the unity that was necessary for their freedom. *Freedom, unity, love,* and *knowledge,* he insisted, were bound together as interdependent elements in black people's struggle to make a creative future for themselves. In Malcolm's perspective, black people should not even think about uniting with or loving any other people until they first learn how to come together with love and with respect for each other.

SELF-KNOWLEDGE

Nothing pained Malcolm more than black people's alienation from each other, which he saw as the most damaging element of the legacy of slavery. While physical servitude was terrible, mental slavery was worse, because when the mind is damaged, one cannot act in the best interest of the whole self. Other peoples have suffered physical slavery, but no people has had its history and culture taken away from it like black people. "We are a lost people," said Malcolm in an address at the Philadelphia temple. "We don't know our name, language, homeland, God, or religion. . . . Any other people, no matter where they live or [are] naturalized, they know where they come from." But *not* the so-called Negroes. They think that they are Americans. They even still use their " 'slave names' given by the slavemaster to our fathers during slavery time": "Jones, Smith, Powell, King, Bunche, Diggs, and Dawson, etc." According to Malcolm, black people are "spiritually dead, in the graves of ignorance," "like DRY BONES IN THE VALLEY."[22]

Another indication of black people's cultural ignorance was their use of the word "Negro" as a self-designation. Malcolm despised it. Hence his frequent use of the phrase "so-called Negro." "You were re-named 'NEGRO,'" he told a Los Angeles audience. "You were re-named Negro by the same man, the same white man, who had kidnapped and robbed you of your own culture." Malcolm preferred the designations "African," "black," and "Afro-American." "You ain't nothing but an African," he frequently told blacks. "You were denied knowledge of the oldest culture man knows."[23] As the representative of Elijah Muhammad, Malcolm's task was to raise black people up from the graves of mental bondage so that they would come together in love based on a true knowledge of themselves.

One can always tell whether a people know who they are by whether they know the identity of their enemies. Although blacks knew that whites kidnapped them from Africa, enslaved, lynched, raped, and seg-regated them in North America, blacks did not want to identify whites as their enemies. Why were blacks so reluctant to name whites as their enemies? Why did they regard whites as their friends when whites, as a people and a nation, had not acted friendly toward black people? With one word, Malcolm gave the answer: Brainwashed! Only a brain-washed people hate themselves and love their enemies. "The white man [has] so thoroughly brainwashed the Negro that he wants to be like everyone but himself."[24] "Brainwashing" was a powerful image that ordinary black people could understand, and Malcolm was very effective in his use of it.

Without knowledge of themselves, black people could not think for themselves. Even blacks with college and university degrees do not know who they are and thus do not use their intellectual skills for the benefit of their community. The black person, Malcolm often told white and black university audiences, "hasn't been educated, he's been trained," like a lion in a circus doing "tricks for his master whenever the whip is cracked." "When a man is educated, he can think for himself." But the black person "believes exactly what he has been taught in school." For example, "it's like a watchdog," Malcolm told a Boston University audience—"you don't give him credit for being intelligent, you give him credit for being well-trained." He bites only "whenever you say sic'em. . . ."

> Well, this is the situation you have with the black man in America. Why, you can tell him sic'em and he bites the Japanese. You tell him sic'em and he'll bite anybody you say. He would go to Korea and be the bravest man on earth and the best soldier you ever had. But he'd come right back here in Mississippi and see a cracker coming in the door to rape his mother and he'd sit there in the corner with his knees knocking. Why? You weren't there to say sic'em, he won't bite anybody unless you say sic'em.[25]

SELF-LOVE AND SELF-DEFENSE

Malcolm felt that the goal of loving your enemy was insane, and he could not understand how any intelligent person could advocate it. It pained him that Martin and other civil rights leaders made loving the enemy the cornerstone of their philosophy. He did not see whites doing that; they only used Martin to promote nonviolence in the black community, but not in the white community. "You never find the so-called white liberal advocating peaceful suffering, nonviolence, to white people, . . . only Negro masses."[26]

"Don't love your enemy," Malcolm told blacks, "love yourself." He talked about self-love and black unity because he saw so much black self-hate in the slums: drugs, prostitution, and blacks killing and robbing each other. As long as blacks wanted to be like whites, they would hate and kill each other while being passive and nonviolent toward whites. That was why Malcolm insisted on the right of self-defense and was sharply critical of Martin King for advocating nonviolence. "Any Negro who teaches Negroes to turn the other cheek in the face of attack is disarming that Negro of his God-given right, of his moral right, of his natural right, of his intelligent right to defend himself," he said when Kenneth Clark asked him about Martin King. "Everything in nature can defend itself and is right in defending itself except the American Negro."[27]

Malcolm felt that nonviolence was "unmanning," a defeatist philosophy. He called it "this little passive resistance or wait-until-you-change-your-mind-and-then-let-me-up philosophy." A people who had been victimized by fear of the oppressor needed an aggressive, assertive approach and not a "mealy-mouth, beg-in, wait-in, plead-in kind of action."

How could blacks gain self-respect if their leaders would not allow them to fight back in self-defense when their enemies attacked them? Was it not true that the Ku Klux Klan and other white hate groups—including the police—attacked the black community because they knew that blacks would not fight back? Was it not true that blacks fought each other because they were afraid to fight white people? Was that not self-hate, the worst enemy of human dignity? "Love each other," Malcolm told Kenneth Clark, "this is all black people need to be taught in this country because the only ones whom we don't love are our own kind." Malcolm was extremely critical of King and the civil rights movement because of his concern for the health of the personality of black people. He did not believe that it is possible to consider oneself "a normal human being" while at the same time loving "a man whose chief purpose in life is to humiliate you."[28] He did not believe that one could be a *person* without defending his or her life. That was why he contended that a leader who taught black people not to defend themselves had to be a "traitor" to the race, a tool of their enemies—white people. He put Martin in that category. "Men like King," said Malcolm, "their job is to go among Negroes and teach Negroes 'Don't fight back,' " which actually meant, "Don't fight the white man." "He doesn't tell them, 'Don't fight each other,' " "because the followers of Martin Luther King will cut each other from head to foot." Malcolm viewed Martin as a handpicked leader who was chosen and promoted by the white liberal northern community:

> *White* people follow King. *White* people pay King. *White* people subsidize King. *White* people support King. But the masses don't support Martin Luther King. King is the best weapon that the white man, who wants to brutalize Negroes, has ever gotten in this country, because he is setting up a situation where, when the white man wants to attack Negroes, they can't defend themselves, because King has put this foolish philosophy out—you're not sup- posed . . . to defend yourself.[29]

SEPARATION

Since "Almighty God ALLAH has declared that HE HIMSELF shall remove . . . this murderous, beast-like, wicked white race . . . from the planet earth," Malcolm wrote in a column for the *Los Angeles Herald Dispatch,* no blacks should want to integrate with them. We should "get unto our own kind" and seek "to get on God's side and to integrate with God and imitate God instead of running around here foolishly trying to integrate with the white man."[30]

For Malcolm separation was not a temporary, tactical position but rather an ideological commitment. God demanded separation; the desire to integrate was a sign of self-hatred. Malcolm urged blacks to show love for themselves by separating from "the blue-eyed white man." His vituperative language against whites did not mean that he hated whites or that he was trying to make blacks hate them. Rather his purpose was to wake blacks up to the need to love each other. What some called "hate teaching," Malcolm called "love teaching." "If I didn't love you," he told an audience of Harlem blacks, "I wouldn't tell you what I'm telling you. I wouldn't stick my neck out. . . . This is love talk. We love you, but we don't love him [the white man]. We want to unite with you, but we don't want to unite with him. We recognize you as our brother, but we don't recognize that old blue-eyed thing as our brother. Let him go out and be a brother to himself."[31]

As love was linked with black people's relationship to each other, justice was linked with whites. Justice meant punishment, white people reaping the harvest that they have sown against black people. According to Malcolm, "a day of great separation is at hand," "the handwriting is on the wall for America." "God is going to judge it and destroy it" "in a lake of fire." Only a fool would seek integration with a sinking ship.

Malcolm totally disagreed with Martin's identification of freedom with integration. Integration meant begging whites to accept blacks into their schools. "No one respects or appreciates a beggar."[32] Insofar as Martin equated freedom with the recognition of the dignity and worth of black people as human beings, Malcolm regarded him as an ally. They parted company when Martin advocated that integration with whites would bring about self-respect for blacks. Malcolm regarded that belief as nonsense. Black people, he contended, would never be regarded as human beings as long as that regard was dependent upon their association with white people. If whites can be human without being integrated with blacks, then blacks can be human without associating with whites.

This contrasted with Martin's view that integration was essential for the full development of blacks. Commenting on the 1954 Supreme Court decision, Martin said: "If it had been possible to give Negro children the same type of buildings as white children, the Negro children [note he did not say white children!] would have still confronted inequality in the sense that they would not have had the opportunity of communicating with all children."[33] Nothing pained Malcolm more than to hear black leaders talk like that. It was as if they believed that blacks could not be human unless they were rubbing up next to whites who alone set the criteria of humanity. Malcolm was so disgusted that he felt justified in advocating the reverse side of integration, that is, advocating that whites could never be human until they accepted blacks' criteria of humanity. But the crux of Malcolm's view was his insistence that blacks are worthy independent of their association with whites. "If white children can go to an all-white school and the absence of Negroes doesn't affect them, why should black children be affected by all-black schools?" Malcolm queried those who doubted the validity of separatism. He contended that there could be no unity among the different races based on equality until there was first a unity of particular races among their own kind. Black people, according to Malcolm, were the *only* people who had absolutely no unity. White people had unity, and that was why they enslaved blacks and why blacks continue to be objects of their victimization. Integration with whites, therefore, could only mean disunity among blacks. It could only mean black people wanting to be like and with white people and not like and with themselves. It was a perpetuation of mental slavery—the worst kind of exploitation imaginable because the victims did not even recognize what was happening to them. "Any Negro trying to integrate is actually admitting his inferiority, because he is admitting that he wants to become a part of a 'superior' society."[34]

Furthermore, contended Malcolm, the only kind of integration that whites will permit is "tokenism," which is nothing but a substitute for the real thing. It is a "false solution." Malcolm also called integration a "hypocritical approach," "a tricky scheme devised by [whites] and propagated by [their] Negro puppets." The masses of black people will remain in the poverty of the ghetto while a "handful of handpicked, high-class Uncle Toms" enjoy the benefits of being "turned loose in a white community. . . . But if all black people went into the white community, over night you would have a race war."[35] Since whites will *never* grant genuine freedom to blacks, even as integrationists defined it, the two races must be completely separated.

The media and the civil rights leaders presented Malcolm as a black segregationist, despite his contrary claims. "Many of you misunderstand us," Malcolm often said to black audiences, "and think that we are advocating continued segregation. No! We are as much against segregation as you are. We reject segregation even more militantly than you do. We want *SEPARATION,* but not segregation." According to Malcolm, "segregation is when your life and liberty is controlled (regulated) by someone else. . . . Segregation is that which is forced upon inferiors by superiors; but *SEPARATION* IS THAT WHICH IS DONE VOLUNTARILY."[36] Despite Malcolm's efforts to clarify the distinction between separation and segregation, most blacks did not acknowledge the difference between them. In the prevailing ethos of integration, the two terms meant the same thing. This was true at least until the rise of Black Power, which did not appear as a significant force until after Malcolm's death. Malcolm, therefore, found himself speaking against the dominant mood not only in white America but in the black community as well.

Aside from his unquestioning devotion to Elijah Muhammad, nothing puzzled blacks more than Malcolm's advocacy of territorial separation of black and white people. His appeal to white America to either help establish separate states or face the judgment of God was so weird to most blacks that they simply did not regard it as a serious political proposal and therefore left it in the realm of religious mythology. Many blacks liked Malcolm not for the political solution he proposed but for his trenchant critique of America and its defenders, especially black civil rights leaders like Martin King. Malcolm kept them honest and pushed them much further to the left than they otherwise would have dared gone.

AMERICA AS A NIGHTMARE

MALCOLM AND THE DREAM

During the time that Martin King was preaching his American dream, Malcolm X offered a challenging critique of him by proclaiming that America, for the vast majority of blacks, was not a dream but a nightmare. More than any other images, "dream" and "nightmare" best summarize the differences between Martin King's and Malcolm X's perspectives on America. They also illustrate that Malcolm was primarily a *reactor* to Martin, for his use of the nightmare image did not appear prominently in his speeches until he responded to Martin's well-known "I Have a Dream" address at the March on Washington event.

Because of Elijah Muhammad's political nonengagement policy, Malcolm was limited to the role of a commentator on events that Martin and other civil rights leaders initiated. It was a difficult situation for him to be in, because he was an action-oriented person. But Malcolm played his role as social critic and gadfly exceedingly well, for he helped Martin to see what his middle-class, integrationist, black church origins had prevented him from seeing, namely the depth of racism in America—not just in Mississippi and Alabama but in New York and Washington, D.C., Malcolm was *the* master critic of America and of civil rights leaders and their liberal white supporters. No one analyzed the shortcomings of American society and its programs of social uplift from the perspective of black people "at the bottom of the social heap" "in the big city ghetto" as validly and as incisively as Malcolm X.

At no time was Malcolm's critical contribution more needed than when Martin King was preaching his dream of an integrated society of blacks and whites, the sons and daughters of former slaves and slave owners living and working together as brothers and sisters. It was a magnificent dream, a splendid hope that captured the imagination of many blacks and whites, making them feel good about the possibilities of America. For the first time in the history of the United States, a significant number of blacks and white northern liberals joined forces to destroy the ugly face of segregation which had been so humiliating to the self-respect and dignity of black people in the South.

As a black person who was born and grew up in the South, during the time that "Jim Crow" ruled the land, I can personally attest to the great difference that the ministry of Martin King made to the quality of life for both blacks and whites in that region. We know each other today in ways we never could have known each other without the great work of the civil rights movement.

But Martin's great contribution to the South notwithstanding, he did not understand, in either his head or his gut, the *depth* of the problem of racism in the northern, urban ghettos of America (at least not during the first stage of his civil rights activity). For if he had known racism in the North as Malcolm knew it, intellectually and existentially, he would not have given that dream speech in Washington, D.C. Others might have given it, even knowing that the Civil Rights Act would have no appreciable effect on the wretched conditions of blacks in the North, but *not* Martin King. He had too much integrity for that.

Malcolm saw, more clearly than anyone else, the great limitations of Martin's dream. What did Malcolm see that Martin's historical and social origins prevented him from seeing? Briefly stated: the depth of the exploitation and restlessness of the black masses in the big city ghettos and the hypocrisy of white liberals. Malcolm's insight into these two realities was nothing short of profound.

THE MARCH ON WASHINGTON

The year 1963 was a major turning point in Malcolm's career. He had become the second most sought after speaker for colleges and universities. (Interestingly, the first was Senator Barry Goldwater.) His enormous public popularity added fuel to his growing crisis with Muhammad and the Black Muslim leadership in Chicago. They were jealous of the attention he received from the black and white publics, overshadowing the Messenger of Allah. Malcolm's lectures and rallies were widely covered in the daily press, and he was invited frequently for radio and television talk shows. He had become a "star," and, despite his contrary claims, the media continued to refer to him as "the number two leader of the Black Muslim movement," the heir apparent to the ailing Muhammad.

The widespread rumor about Muhammad's extramarital relations encouraged Malcolm to become less religious and more political in his public utterances. Speaking at MUST Radio Hall in Washington, D.C., he was sharply critical of Martin's advocacy of nonviolence in Birmingham. "Martin Luther King . . . is a fool," he shouted when informed of a riot in Birmingham despite the agreement that ended the demonstrations. "You need somebody who is going to fight, . . . you don't need any kneeling-in or crawling-in." He was equally critical when Martin used children in the demonstrations. "Real men don't put their children on the firing line." Malcolm also attacked Martin for his financial connections to the "hypocritical whites in the North" who allowed him to go just so far but no further. Noting the resistance of bystanders, not under the orders of Martin's SCLC, Malcolm proclaimed the end of black people's commitment to nonviolence. "The lesson of Birmingham," he said, "is that the Negroes have lost their fear of the white man's reprisals and will react today with violence if provoked." And he declared: "Black people are not going to take no more stuff no more."[37]

Malcolm also berated the Kennedy administration's motivation for sending the troops into Birmingham. "President Kennedy did not send troops to Alabama when dogs were biting black babies," he told a *New York Times* reporter. "He waited three weeks until the situation exploded. He then sent troops after Negroes had demonstrated their ability to defend themselves." Furthermore, "in his talk with Alabama editors," Malcolm continued, "Kennedy did not urge that Negroes be treated right because it is the right thing to do. Instead, he said that if the Negroes aren't well treated the Muslims would become a threat. He urged a change not because it is right but because the world is watching this country. Kennedy is wrong because his motivation is wrong." At a Harlem rally of 2,000, about six weeks later, he also assailed President Kennedy "for talking about freedom in Europe when 20,000,000 black [people] have no freedom here." "Right now," he asserted, "representations of the American government are in Nazi Germany complaining about the Berlin Wall, but haven't done anything about the Alabama Wall."[38]

The March on Washington was a special object of Malcolm's derision. He criticized it even before it took place. At a Harlem unity rally (8 August 1963), purposely staged to distract attention from the forthcoming Washington March, Malcolm talked about how the white man joined the march when he discovered that he could not stop it.

The astounding success of the march did not cause Malcolm to reevaluate his perspective. Rather it fueled his critique of the march. While civil rights leaders were basking in the successful display of black and white unity, Malcolm called the march a "Chump's March" and a "Farce on Washington." He compared it to "the Rose Bowl game, the Kentucky Derby, and the World Series." According to Malcolm, the march was "subsidized by white liberals and stage-managed by President Kennedy." "The President and the Administration in Washington should get an Academy Award for directing the best show of the century." Probably under orders from Muhammad, Malcolm avoided criticizing King and other civil rights leaders directly. "The Negroes spent a lot of money, had a good time, and enjoyed a real circus or carnival-type atmosphere," Malcolm told an *Amsterdam News* reporter. "Now that the show is over," he snorted, "the black masses are still without land, without jobs, and without homes. . . . Their Christian churches are still being bombed, their innocent little girls murdered. So what did the March on Washington accomplish? Nothing!"[39]

"Message to the Grass Roots"

Two months after the March on Washington, a nationalist meeting, the Northern Grass Roots Leadership Conference (held 9–10 November 1963), was hastily called in Detroit by the Reverend Albert B. Cleage, Jr., pastor of the Shrine of the Black Madonna, in collaboration with the Group On Advanced Leadership (GOAL) and the Freedom Now Party, an all-black political party formed in August 1963 to support black candidates for national and local political offices. The occasion was precipitated on 9 November when the chairman of the Detroit Council for Human Rights, Reverend C. L. Franklin (a King loyalist), and other integrationist members attempted to exclude black nationalists from a meeting of the Northern Leadership Conference. The integrationist gathering of approximately three thousand at Cobo Hall was addressed by Congressman Adam Clayton Powell, Jr. Malcolm was the main speaker for the nationalist five-hour rally of approximately two thousand held at King Solomon Baptist Church. Appearing on the program with him were civil rights activist Gloria Richardson of Cambridge, Maryland, Reverend Cleage, William Worthy, journalist and New York leader of the Freedom Now Party, and James and Grace Lee Boggs, Detroit militants. Approximately twenty whites attended the rally and were "segregated" into one section of the church sanctuary.[40]

Malcolm's resounding "Message to the Grass Roots" can be viewed as his answer to Martin's dream speech and a signal of his forthcoming break with Elijah Muhammad. In it he spoke not primarily as a Black Muslim, but as a leader of the masses, outlining what was needed for black freedom. Malcolm used the stock phrase, "The Honorable Elijah Muhammad teaches us that . . .," several times when delivering the speech. But the evidence shows that he already saw the forthcoming break with Muhammad (see chapter 7). "That was when I really wondered how long it would be before he would break with them [the Black Muslims]," Gloria Richardson recalled, as she reflected back on Malcolm's address, "because in my mind he was doing that part like his heart wasn't really in it, you know? Like he was just repeating something. A mechanical kind of thing." Furthermore the political content of the speech was outside the boundaries of Muhammad's teaching. (Later, after the break, Malcolm asked his friend Milton Henry to delete all references to Muhammad from the tape-recording of the speech. This explains the absence of such references from the widely distributed recording. It also shows that Malcolm believed that the speech expressed his post-break thinking.)[41]

"Message to the Grass Roots" was the most "political" talk that Malcolm had given. He began his speech informally, speaking in a conversational style and in a "down to earth" manner that the average black person could understand. "We want to have an off-the-cuff chat between you and me, *us*," he told his audience. "America's problem is us," because "she doesn't want us here." And "once you face this as a fact, you can start plotting a course that will make you appear intelligent, instead of unintelligent."

The course that Malcolm urged blacks to follow was unity, a familiar theme. He pleaded with them to "learn how to forget our differences" and come together on the basis of what they had in common.

> You don't catch hell because you're a Baptist, and you don't catch hell because you're a Methodist. . . . You don't catch hell because you're a Democrat or a Republican, you don't catch hell because you're a Mason or an Elk, and you sure don't catch hell because you're an American; because if you were an American, you wouldn't catch hell. You catch hell because you're . . . black. . . . You catch hell, all of us catch hell, for the same reason.

Referring to the 1955 Bandung conference of Third World nations, Malcolm urged blacks in America to follow the Third World example by identifying their "common enemy" as "the white man." (Malcolm had called for a "Bandung conference" among African-American leaders as far back as 1959.)[42] "At Bandung all the nations came together, the dark nations from Africa and Asia." Although they represented many different religious and political orientations, they could come together because "they excluded the white man." They

> submerge[d] their petty differences and agreed on one thing: That where one African came from Kenya and was being colonized by the Englishman, and another African came from the Congo and was being colonized by the Belgian, and another African came from Guinea and was being colonized by the French, and another came from Angola and was being colonized by the Portuguese, . . . [the colonizers] were all from Europe, . . . blond, blue-eyed and white skins. . . . They realized all over the world where the dark man was being oppressed, he was being oppressed by the white man; . . . so they got together on this basis — that they had a common enemy.

Malcolm also made his well-known distinction between "the black revolution and the Negro revolution." "The black revolution," he said, "is world-wide in scope and nature." He identified it with the Mau Mau in Kenya, with the Algerian "bloody battle" with France, the Cuban revolution, and the liberation struggles throughout the continent of Asia. The Negro revolution, in contrast, was not even a revolution. Malcolm ridiculed blacks for calling the struggle for integration a "revolution." "The only revolution in which the goal is loving your enemy is the Negro revolution. It's the only revolution in which the goal is a desegregated lunch counter, a desegregated theater, a desegregated park, a desegregated public toilet; you can sit down next to white folks — on the toilet." "Imagine that!" Malcolm said in his Harlem unity speech where he made the same point. Integration means "you'll have a chance to go to the toilet with white folks — why, you're out of your mind! Only way I want to go to the toilet with him is if I can flush him down with the rest of that stuff. Flush him right down the drain with the rest of his kind." Going to the toilet with white people was not a revolution. "Revolution is bloody," Malcolm told his Detroit audience; "revolution is hostile, revolution knows no compromise, revolution overturns and destroys everything that gets in its way."

Malcolm linked his distinction between the Negro revolution and the black revolution to another of the distinctions he often used — that between "the house Negro and the field Negro back during the time of slavery." He used both distinctions to express the contrast between himself and the civil rights leaders of the March on Washington. "I am a field Negro," he proudly proclaimed. "The masses are the field Negroes." Malcolm characterized the house Negroes as the Uncle Toms who "lived near the master," "in the attic or the basement," with the privilege of eating his leftover food and wearing his discarded clothes. They identified completely with the master, sharing his joy and sorrow, with no thought of trying to escape to freedom. "If you came to the house Negro and said, 'let's run away, let's escape, let's separate,' the house Negro would look at you and say, 'Man, you crazy. What you mean separate? Where is there a better house than this? Where can I wear better clothes than this? Where can I eat better food than this?' "

But the field Negroes, the majority of the slaves, were different. They did not eat the master's food or live in his house. They worked long, gruelling hours and "caught hell" daily from the whip of the overseer. Their distinguishing mark was their hate for the master and their will to escape "by any means necessary." Malcolm went on: "When the [master's] house caught on fire, [the field Negro] didn't try to put it out; that field Negro prayed for a wind, for a breeze. When the master got sick, the field Negro prayed that he'd die. If someone came to the field Negro and said, 'Let's separate, let's run,' he didn't say, 'Where we going?' He'd say, 'Any place is better than here.' "

Identifying himself with the field Negroes and the black revolution, Malcolm identified King and other civil rights advocates — the leaders of the Negro revolution—as the contemporary manifestations of the house Negroes. He compared King's message of nonviolence to the Novocaine used to deaden a tooth and gum before a tooth is pulled. The drug makes patients feel numb, as if nothing is happening to them, even though blood is running down their jaws. In other words, the message of nonviolence was: "Don't stop suffering—just suffer peacefully."

Malcolm was particularly critical of the March on Washington because it was not a gathering of the field blacks but rather of the house blacks and the liberal whites walking hand-in-hand, singing about being free some day. "Whoever heard of a revolution where they lock arms . . . singing 'We Shall Overcome'? You don't do that in a revolution. You don't do any singing, you're too busy swinging."

The heart of Malcolm's critique, however, focused on the white and black leaders of the march. He called it a "picnic" and a "circus," with "white clowns and black clowns." "It was a sellout . . ., a takeover" by white liberals in government, labor, and the churches. "They controlled it so tight," Malcolm railed, "they told those Negroes what time to hit town, how to come, where to stop, what signs to carry, what songs to sing, what speech they could make, and what speech they couldn't make; and then told them to get out of town by sundown. And every one of those Toms was out of town by sundown."

Malcolm's language was harsh, but it was the truth. The March on Washington was controlled by the black bourgeoisie and indirectly by the white liberals who financed it. Whites exerted their power when they needed to, forcing John Lewis of the SNCC to rewrite his prepared speech because it was regarded as too offensive to the Kennedy administration. "When James Baldwin came in from Paris," said Malcolm, "they wouldn't let him talk, because they couldn't make him go by the script. Burt Lancaster read the speech that Baldwin was supposed to make." Baldwin told Gil Noble in a television interview that he withdrew rather than "create another hassle back stage," similar to the uproar about Lewis's speech.[43] No one was allowed to give a speech that was critical of white liberal supporters of the Civil Rights Bill. King did not object to white liberals' control of the event because he viewed them as allies. Malcolm said that United Auto Workers' president Walter Reuther and "those other three devils," Protestant notable Eugene Carson Blake, Rabbi Joachim Prinz, and Catholic layman Mathew Ahmann, "should get an Academy Award for the best actors because they acted like they really loved Negroes and fooled a whole lot of Negroes." The award for the "best supporting cast" should be given to the six Negro leaders (Martin King, Roy Wilkins, James Farmer, A. Philip Randolph, Whitney Young, and John Lewis) because they allowed themselves to be used by the white liberals in the circus.

At a rally in Philadelphia, Malcolm continued his scathing critique of the march: "What is the so-called Negro revolution? Is that what you call Uncle Tommin' in Washington . . . walkin' up and down between two dead Presidents [Lincoln and Washington], while the live President sits up there behind closed doors rockin' in his chair?" The three hundred blacks who attended the rally roared back, "teach, Malcolm, teach," as he addressed them as "Toms": "And what are you 'Toms' doing all this demonstrating and picketing for? . . . A desegregated cup of coffee? . . . This is no revolution. . . . This is a 'beg-olution.' . . . You 'Toms' are begging the white man for a cup of coffee at a lunch counter."[44]

Malcolm lashed out at the march every chance he got, even after the Kennedy assassination. At a New York rally, he said:

> The late President has a bigger image as a liberal, the other whites who participated have bigger liberal images also, and the Negro civil rights leaders have now been permanently named the Big Six (because of their participation in the Big Fix?) . . . but the black masses are still unemployed, still starving, and still living in slums . . . and, I might add, getting angrier and more explosive every day.[45]

There are no doubt many persons, especially whites and middle-class blacks, who believe that Malcolm's judgment was too harsh, and perhaps it was. But we cannot understand Malcolm unless we also know what pained him: black people jammed up in ghettos, dying from filth; white liberals blaming the victims; and black leaders urging them to be loving and nonviolent with no protection from the government. Malcolm could not stand by and watch black people die daily from "that dreadful needle—heroin, morphine, cocaine, opium"; he could not hear of black babies being gnawed by rats and not name *who* was responsible. Malcolm once showed Alex Haley a newspaper clipping of a black baby who had been bitten by a rat. In a moment of deep anger, he railed: "Now just read that, just think of that a minute! Suppose that was *your* child! Where's that slumlord—on some beach in Miami!"[46]

What most people did not like about Malcolm was actually his strength: speaking the truth about the black condition in America in clear, forceful, and uncomplicated language. He was not tactful because he believed that "diplomacy fools people." "It's better to be frank," he said, "then you know how each other thinks." But whites, as well as many blacks, did not like Malcolm's frankness. It merely made it easy for most of them to dismiss him as a fanatic or an extremist. Malcolm did not mind the labels that people put on him as long as he knew he was telling the truth. When accused of being an extremist, he shot back: "Yes, I'm an extremist. The black race in North America is in extremely bad condition. You show me a black man who is not an extremist and I'll show you one who needs psychiatric attention!"[47]

The dream and nightmare images, therefore, were derived from the lives that Martin and Malcolm lived. They were also derived from their religious imaginations. To that subject we turn in chapters 5 and 6.

5

"WE MUST LOVE OUR WHITE BROTHERS"

I am first and foremost a minister. I love the church, and I feel that civil rights is a part of it. For me, at least, the basis of my struggle for integration — and I mean the full integration of Negroes into every phase of American life — is something that began with a religious motivation. . . . And I know that my religion has come to mean more to me than ever before. I have come to believe more and more in a personal God — not a process, but a person, a creative power with infinite love who answers prayers.

Martin Luther King, Jr.
Redbook
September 1961

Martin King's dream and Malcolm's nightmare were primarily defined by two distinct religious traditions in the African-American community. One was Christian, imported from Europe but redefined in the light of black people's struggle for dignity in American society. The other was Muslim, originally Asian and African but reshaped to express the hostility of American blacks to white oppressors. Despite some nationalist expressions, black Christianity was associated with the integrationist tradition. The Nation of Islam, on the other hand, was outspokenly nationalist — antiwhite and problack. With roots in the "invisible institution" (the secret church of the slaves) and the free black denominations of the North, black Christianity was the dominant religion of the black population. Despite a Muslim presence among the slaves, the Nation of Islam was a twentieth-century phenomenon unknown to most southern rural blacks. But the urban poor responded to it in significant numbers in the 1950s and 1960s. It accented the

African identity of black people that could not be assimilated by white Europeans.

Despite the contrasts between the two religious traditions, they were also closely related by their common past, involving continuous struggle for justice in a white American society that did not recognize blacks as human beings. Both traditions were more *black American* than either African or European, which means that one's search for an understanding of their meaning should begin in the rural South and urban North and not on the continents of Africa or Europe.

No two persons better illustrate the centrality of the black struggle for justice in defining black religion than Martin King and Malcolm X. In this chapter and the next one, I will examine the influence of their religious perspectives upon their contrasting images of America, as well as examining the two men's impact upon their religious traditions.

THE IMPACT OF KING'S FAITH AND THEOLOGY UPON HIS DREAM

Martin King's dream was defined by two movements of American Protestant Christianity. These two movements—the black church and white, Protestant liberalism—were embodied in his life, respectively, in the black Baptist church of his southern childhood and youth and in the northern seminary and graduate school he attended.

King's faith was primarily Christian in the black Baptist tradition, but unlike most ministers of that community, he had a long experience among Protestant liberals which reshaped his theological interpretation of his primary faith.

Although the two traditions will be examined separately, they both reinforced the central assumption of King's dream: that America was a Christian nation which had failed to live out the true meaning of its destiny. That destiny was defined by the nation's moral vision of freedom and justice and its religious identity as the Kingdom of God, the "beloved community" that King referred to so often.

The Black Religious Tradition

King received his faith at Atlanta's Ebenezer Baptist Church, joining at the early age of five. He thus became part of the largest black religious group in North America. When speaking of King as a black Baptist, it is important to note that the word "black" was more important in defining his faith than the word "Baptist," even though King did not refer to his faith in racial terms. King's faith was derived primarily from his people's suffering and struggling in a society where whites talked of freedom and justice, while blacks experienced slavery and segregation. A separate faith emerged among black Christians in the United States because they believed that the God of the Exodus, the prophets, and Jesus did not condone the mistreatment they received from whites. They believed that the God of the Bible was no respecter of persons. All races of men and women were created to live together on this planet as brothers and sisters and as children of God. Therefore, color and other physical features were secondary to our universal humanity grounded in God's creation and redeemed in Jesus' suffering on the cross. This is the faith that King encountered in black Baptist churches, and it was also found in black Methodist churches and among blacks in other denominations. It was a black faith that emphasized God's will to make right what white people made wrong, so that the rule of love would be established among all races of people. This was the hope that encouraged black Christians to bear witness, through public protest, to God's creation of them as human beings, just like white people, and not as slaves or as second-class citizens.

The *faith of the black experience* began to shape King's idea of God during childhood, and it remained central to his perspective throughout his life. This point needs emphasis because many interpreters have failed to acknowledge the *decisive* role of the black religious tradition upon King's thinking. Without denying other important influences— liberal Protestantism, Gandhi, Niebuhr, among others—we still must emphasize that no tradition or thinker influenced King's perspective as much as the faith which blacks created in their fight for dignity and justice.

Faith created in the black struggle for dignity provided the link that connected King not only with black Christians in other denominations but also with the faith of Malcolm X. As different as Martin's and Malcolm's religious communities were, Martin's faith, nonetheless, was much closer to Malcolm's than it was to that of white Christians, and Malcolm's faith was much closer to Martin's than it was to that of Muslims in the Middle East, Africa, or Asia; this was true because both of their faith commitments were derived from the *same* black experience of suffering and struggle in the United States. Their theologies, therefore, should be interpreted as different religious and intellectual responses of African-Americans to their environment as they searched for meaning in a nation that they did not make.

While King was in seminary and graduate school, liberal Protestant theology provided the intellectual framework for the public expression of his faith. But when he became the pastor of Dexter Avenue Baptist Church in Montgomery and later was chosen the leader of the bus boycott, the faith of the black church emerged at the center of his public discourse about God. What King really thought about God is not found in the essays or even the Ph.D. dissertation he wrote in graduate school. He was merely trying to meet the expectations of his professors, which is the reason much of what he wrote reflects standard texts on the subject. King's faith is not found even in some of his published essays and books about the civil rights movement. Again, trying to meet the expectations of a white public, some of the essays and books that bear his name were ghostwritten. One discovers King's faith primarily in his *preached word* (chiefly the unpublished sermons) delivered at Dexter Avenue, Ebenezer, and other black churches and in his *practiced word* during many of his nonviolent, direct-action demonstrations, mainly in the South. It is foolish to deny the cogency of King's theology merely because it is not framed in the customary forms of academic theologians. He did not develop his theology in the classroom, teaching graduate students, or in professional theological societies, reading learned papers to professors of theology. Rather King's theology was *embodied in his life,* that is, in what he did and said about justice and love between blacks and whites and about God's will to realize the American dream, reconciling, as brothers and sisters, the children of former slaves and former slaveholders. King was not an academic theologian; he was a theologian of action, a theologian of liberation (in the best sense) whose thinking about God was developed in his efforts to achieve freedom and dignity for black people.

To understand the meaning and the significance of King's faith and theology, the place to begin is with the year-long bus crisis in Montgomery, which was started not by King but by the black Christians of the city. They asked him to represent them, to be their leader, because they needed someone who could converse with the whites on "their level" and articulate the concerns of the black community. King was deeply moved by their choice of him as their leader and also by the spirituality which empowered them to protest. It was clear to him that the blacks of Montgomery decided to protest because they believed that God did not will the daily abuses which they received on the city buses. Blacks believed firmly in the dignity and worth of their personhood, even though whites, with few exceptions, refused to treat blacks as human beings.

The spirituality that enabled blacks to know that they were human beings was not derived from Europe, even though black Christians often used the language of white Christianity to express their ideas about God. Rather it originated from their African culture and was then forged in the struggle to make sense of their lives in a nation of white so-called Christians. When blacks read the Bible and listened to its stories, even when told by whites, they heard a message of freedom and applied it to their own situation in America. They refused to accept white people's attempt to limit the Bible's message of freedom to a spirituality removed from the everyday relations between black and white people. If God created all races as children of the divine, which even whites did not deny, then we are all brothers and sisters, and nobody has the right to mistreat another.

After his sojourn in the North, King was reintroduced, in a practical manner, to the God of the black experience; this reintroduction occurred through his experience as pastor of Dexter and especially as a leader and participant in the biweekly community meetings of the bus boycott. But, it was not until the crisis of 27 January 1956, several weeks into the boycott, that King appropriated the God of the black experience "for his own personal life," as they say in the black church.

Shortly after midnight, just home from a steering committee meeting of the boycott, King got a telephone call. "Nigger," the voice said, "we are tired of you and your mess now, and if you are not out of this town in three days, we're going to blow your brains out and blow up your house." Though he had received many similar threats (about forty daily), for some reason that one stunned him, preventing him from going to sleep. He began to realize that his wife and newly born baby daughter could be taken from him or he from them at any moment. He went to the kitchen, "thinking that coffee would give me a little relief." In the midst of one of the most agonizing experiences of his life, King searched for a place where he could stand. "Rationality left me," he remembered. "I started thinking about many things. I pulled back on the theology and philosophy that I had just studied in the universities, trying to give philosophical and theological reasons for the existence and reality of evil, but the answer didn't quite come there." Unable to cope with his frustration and despair, King turned to the God of the black experience that he had been taught about as a child:

Something said to me, you can't call on daddy now; he's in Atlanta, a hundred seventy-five miles away. . . . You've got to call on that something, on that person that your daddy used to tell you about, that power that can make a way out of no way. And I discovered then that religion had to become real to me and I had to know God for myself. And I bowed down over that cup of coffee. I never will forget it. Oh yes, I prayed a prayer. And I prayed out loud that night. I said, "Lord, I'm down here trying to do what's right. I think I'm right. I think the cause that we represent is right. But Lord, I must confess that I'm faltering, I'm losing my courage, and I can't let the people see me like this because if they see me weak and losing my courage they will begin to get weak."

It was in the midst of this crisis of faith that King experienced a heavy burden being lifted from his shoulders, and he felt the liberating presence of God as never before. "Almost out of nowhere I heard a voice," he said. "Martin Luther, stand up for righteousness. Stand up for justice. Stand up for truth. And lo, I will be with you, even until the end of the world." After that experience, he said, "I was ready to face anything."[1]

Three nights after his "vision in the kitchen," as he called it, Ralph Abernathy, his closest friend, came up to him during a meeting and said, "Your house has been bombed." To everyone's amazement, King was not visibly shaken. "I accepted the word of the bombing calmly," King said later, because "my experience with God had given me new strength and trust. I knew now that God is able to give us the interior resources to face the storms and problems of life." He quietly left the meeting and when he arrived home, he found his wife and baby safe, but an angry crowd of blacks had gathered with guns and other weapons and were prepared to retaliate. "Now let's not get panicky," King said to them. "We cannot solve this problem with retaliatory violence. We must meet violence with nonviolence.... We must love our white brothers no matter what they do to us.... Remember, if I am stopped, this movement will not stop, because God is with the movement."[2]

King's faith that "God is with the movement" deepened his commitment to justice and sustained him in his struggle, free from fear for his life or for his family. From that point onward, King never doubted God's presence in the struggle for justice, reassuring him that love and nonviolence, despite the odds, would triumph over hate and violence.

When twelve sticks of unexploded dynamite were found on his porch a year later, he recalled, in his Sunday sermon, how his "vision from heaven removed my fears" "early one morning a year ago." Using language that was similar to that which he used the night before his assassination in Memphis, King spoke without fear: "Tell Montgomery that they can keep shooting and I'm going to stand up to them; tell Montgomery they can keep bombing and I'm going to stand up to them. If I had to die tomorrow morning I would die happy because I've been to the mountaintop and I've seen the Promised Land, and it's going to be here in Montgomery. The old Montgomery is passing away and segregation is dying."[3]

JUSTICE, LOVE, HOPE, AND THE CROSS

What were the faith claims implied in King's spirituality? They were similar to the faith affirmations of the black Christian tradition as a whole, from slavery to the present. The accent was upon three themes:

justice, love, and hope. According to the black religious tradition, the biblical God is the one who establishes justice on behalf of the weak and helpless of the land. That was why King heard a voice saying: "Stand up for righteousness. Stand up for justice." That voice was deeply rooted in his life experience during childhood; in his kitchen experience he merely claimed it as his own faith. One cannot be a Christian, according to the black church tradition, without making the establishment of justice for the poor the heart of the gospel. To emphasize the justice theme, black Christianity focuses more on the Old Testament than the New and more on the Exodus and the prophets than the wisdom literature.

King also heard the voice say: "Stand up for truth." For him, truth, first and foremost, meant love—the love of God and human love. God created blacks and whites for each other and not for separation from each other. That religious claim was also deeply rooted in King's early experience. According to black Christianity, we are all sisters and brothers because "God made of one blood all nations of people to dwell on the face of the earth." As God's justice is grounded in God's creative and redeeming love, so human justice is grounded in love. Neighborly love, especially for the enemy, defines the means by which justice is established and also the goal of the struggle for freedom, namely the beloved community.

"And lo," the voice said to King, "I will be with you, even until the end of the world." The promise of divine presence in the midst of the trials and tribulations of life was also a central element in the black faith which King appropriated. Hope is well-known as a central theme in black religion, even though it has often been misinterpreted as religious escapism. For King, however, hope was not a withdrawal from the world but rather a manifestation of the Christian's faith that "the contradictions of life are neither final nor ultimate." "God is able," he often proclaimed in his sermons, "to make a way out of no way, . . . to transform dark yesterdays into bright tomorrows."[4]

King's belief that "God is able" did not make him passive; rather it empowered him to fight for justice through love no matter what his enemies did to hinder him. His faith sustained him even when his allies failed to give him the moral support he needed to cope with the ever-present dangers of his ministry. "When you know God," King proclaimed in a sermon at Ebenezer Baptist Church, "you can stand up amid the agonies and burdens of life and not despair. When you know God, you can stand up amid tension and tribulation and yet smile in the process. . . . When you know God, you have on some shoes that can help you walk through any muddy place."[5] Here King was using the language and faith of black Christians who believed that they had come "this far [through slavery and segregation] by faith, leaning on the Lord." They say that "God did not bring us this far to leave us." We have a future that no one, not even whites, can destroy, because "the builder and the maker is God."

Justice, love, and hope — these three themes shaped the heart of King's faith and theology. Each theme must be interpreted in the light of the other two, and all three must be defined in the light of Jesus' suffering and death on the cross. The centrality of the cross for King's faith was what separated him from liberal theology and placed him solidly in the heart of the black religious tradition. Not even Martin Luther of the sixteenth century or any of his modern-day interpreters explored the power of the cross in the freedom struggle of the poor as passionately and as profoundly as did Martin Luther King, Jr. For him the cross of Jesus was not primarily a religious idea to be explicated in a theological text or proclaimed in a sermon, or even something one summoned in Sunday worship so as "to get right with God." "The cross is an eternal expression of the length to which God is willing to go to restore broken communities," King proclaimed in a sermon at Dexter Baptist Church. "Through our sin, through our evil and through our wickedness, we have broken communities." Segregation was the most blatant expression of brokenness between human beings in America. For King, the cross was God's way of saying no to segregation and yes to integration, no to the alienation between blacks and whites and yes to their reconciliation. "What is the cross," he asked, "but God's way of saying to a wayward child, 'I still love you . . . and . . . if you will see within the suffering Christ on the cross my power, you will be able to be transformed, you will be redeemed'? "[6]

In King's theology, however, the cross was more than what God did to reconcile people through Jesus. The cross was also the suffering that defined the way of life for men and women who are transformed by its power. "Jesus Christ gave his life for the redemption of this world," King told a European assembly of Baptists in Amsterdam, "and as his followers, we are called to give our lives continuing the reconciling work of Christ in *this* world." In America, Christ's reconciling work was identical with the work of the civil rights movement, its struggle being to break down the dividing walls of segregation for the purpose of creating the beloved community between black and white people. The cross was the suffering that Christians freely assumed in their fight for the political freedom of the poor. We "must be willing to bear the burden of the cross," King told his European audience. Not only are individual Christians called to suffer but "whole churches may be crucified."[7]

King did not just talk about suffering and freedom; he lived them. "This cross," he wrote in a letter to his wife, referring to his confinement and four-month sentence in a Georgia prison, "we must bear for the freedom of our people." He also frequently reminded blacks that they must be prepared for a "season of suffering." While King's emphases on the themes of justice, love, and hope shifted throughout his ministry, with one achieving dominance at a given time, the cross, in contrast, remained constant as the center of his faith, always defining his interpretation of other faith claims. "The cross is something that you bear," he told his SCLC staff, "and ultimately that you die on."[8] For King, the cross was the essence of the Christian faith, emphasizing that suffering was an inherent part of the Christian life in the struggle for freedom.

King's theological claim about the cross and the suffering of Jesus was the source of his absolute commitment to nonviolence. Many persons have misunderstood his commitment to nonviolence because they separated it from his faith in God. It was true that he encouraged persons without his faith to endorse nonviolence for the practical reason that blacks did not have the military weapons to wage a violent fight for freedom. But King's personal commitment to nonviolence was derived from his faith in a loving and just God who created us for each other and for eternity. He did not believe that one could participate with God in the creation of the beloved community and at the same time use violent methods. In his view physical violence was an irreconcilable contradiction of the faith that we live in a world that is under the control of a God whose power is disclosed in Jesus' suffering love. Christians, who claim to believe in the God revealed in Jesus' cross, must, like Jesus, be willing to suffer for the cause of freedom. "There can be no resurrection without the crucifixion," he told an assembly of European Baptists, and "no freedom without suffering," a claim he often made to blacks and their supporters in the civil rights movement. Why? Because "the cross we bear precedes the crown we wear. To be a Christian one must take up his cross, with all of its difficulties and agonizing and tension-packed content and carry it until that very cross leaves its marks upon us and redeems us to that more excellent way which comes only through suffering." King deeply believed and frequently proclaimed that "unmerited suffering is redemptive," because God will not allow evil to triumph over good. "At the center of the faith of Christians is the fact of the death and resurrection of Jesus Christ—our reminder that though evil may triumph on Good Friday, it must ultimately give way to the triumph of Easter," King told an assembly of the National Council of Churches. "Evil may so shape events that Caesar will occupy a palace and Christ a cross, but one day that same Christ will rise up and split history into A.D. and B.C., so that even the life of Caesar must be dated by his name."[9]

Nothing was more central to King's religious convictions than the idea that oppressed people must use moral means to achieve just ends. Whether he spoke of the civil rights movement in the United States or even of the Third World liberation struggles, he was certain that non-violence was the "Christian way of life in human relations." He was pleased that Ghana and other African nations had achieved their independence with little or no violence. Gandhi's success in India had an even greater impact upon King. "I left India," he said, "more convinced than ever before that nonviolent resistance is the most potent weapon available to oppressed people in their struggle for freedom."[10]

But much more important than the success of nonviolence in India or Ghana or even the civil rights movement was King's faith in a God of justice, love, and hope—a faith centered on the cross of Jesus Christ. Violence is derived from hate, and hate contradicts God. People who use violence have lost faith in the God of love and thus have lost faith that the beloved community can be created. King's faith and theology enabled him to reject violence absolutely, while at the same time granting him the conviction that freedom for the poor will be achieved. His affirmation of nonviolence was derived from his deep conviction that the cross of Jesus revealed a personal, creative, divine power in the world establishing freedom in and through the nonviolent actions of the poor and their supporters.

King's theological views about suffering and nonviolence separated him not only from white Christians; they also separated him from many blacks in the freedom movement, especially Malcolm X. Most blacks in the movement, including SCLC staffers, accepted nonviolence as an effective strategy for achieving constitutional rights for blacks but not as a way of life, as King did. Malcolm rejected both King's religious and practical views on nonviolence and insisted that the right of self-defense was essential in the definition of a human being. Martin, however, was so convinced that nonviolence was the only moral and political option available to blacks that he hardly bothered to observe Malcolm's and other nationalists' distinction between self-defense and violence. Martin regarded Malcolm's perspective as being grounded in nothing but the despair prevalent among those blacks in the northern ghettos who had lost hope in America. All Americans had better learn how to live together, Martin often informed whites and reminded blacks, because, contrary to what a few Black Muslims said, "we Negroes ain't going nowhere!"

"We ain't going nowhere" was Martin's most telling point against the Black Muslims' program of absolute separation and in support of his own movement for full integration. If blacks could not leave America— contrary to what Malcolm and the Black Muslims were advocating—did it not make sense for blacks, whites, and other citizens to figure out a *just* way to live together in peace? Was not complete separation totally impractical? The strength of King's faith was its *practicality,* his assumption that the great majority of blacks were going to stay in the land of their birth. Even when blacks did not share King's faith that whites and blacks were created by God for each other, they nonetheless shared his assumption that blacks were not leaving America and that, *practically speaking,* whites and blacks together (as well as others) must learn how to internalize the principle of mutual respect for each other's humanity or no one would survive.

As Martin King did not acknowledge Malcolm X's distinction between violence and self-defense, Malcolm did not acknowledge Martin's theological definition of love as *agape* (redemptive goodwill) in constrast to *eros* (romantic love) and *philia* (reciprocal affections). But Martin's definition of love as agape was the heart of his perspective on nonviolence. "Now we say in this nonviolent movement that you've got to love this white man," he told a Birmingham audience. "And God knows, he needs our love. . . . And let me say to you that I'm not talking about emotional bosh when I talk about love." That would have been eros or even philia, both of which involved a mutual liking of or affection for the other. For Martin, agape was derived from God. It was identical with Gandhi's *satyagraha* and the Christian idea of the redemption accomplished in Jesus Christ. It meant that "you love those who don't love you. You love those that you don't like. You love those whose ways are distasteful to you. You love every man because God loves him."

Malcolm was not a student of Protestant theology. His strength was his devastating critique of white America, pointing out the enormity of its sins against black people. His weakness, however, was his failure to advance a program for freedom based on the assumption that the great majority of blacks would not leave the land of their birth. King did not deny the truth of Malcolm's critique of America, and he conceded in his *Playboy* interview that "maybe he [Malcolm] *does* have some of the answer." But King rejected absolutely the Black Muslims' program of separation as the solution to the injustices of the past. Instead of separation (which King viewed as just another form of segregation), he advocated desegregation, which he understood as the first step toward full integration. With desegregation and integration, or the just society and the beloved community, as the goals of the freedom movement, it becomes clear why King advocated the development of a relationship of "love and understanding," even "forgiveness," between blacks and whites, a religious idea that was utterly revolting to Malcolm X. "We Muslims never forget [the brutality of whites against blacks]," he often said. "We love you [black people] but we don't love him [the white man]."[11] These words sounded good to the ears of a crowd of oppressed blacks in Harlem, but they did not provide the remedy to their oppression. What is the *solution* to the political domination, the economic exploitation, and the social degradation of black people? That was King's major preoccupation, and he criticized Malcolm for not dealing with that question in a straightforward, rational, and creative way. King believed that the solution to the problem of racism was not hate but love, not vengeance but forgiveness. It had to be a solution based on the assumption that the black minority and white majority must learn how to live together as brothers and sisters *in America.*

King was aware that many young blacks were strongly influenced by Malcolm's objections to nonviolence, namely that it disarmed black people, leaving them defenseless against the brutality of white people. As a matter of fact King did not deny the right of self-defense for any individual in the privacy of his or her home or any other place. But he contended that self-defense should not be advocated as a program of freedom for the poor; he held that position because he believed that in a public demonstration it was too difficult to distinguish defensive violence from aggressive violence. The posture of self-defense would only invite violence from the oppressor and thereby confuse the moral issue at stake. Freedom, King believed, is not a gift. The Negro must be willing to suffer nonviolently for it. Imitating the oppressor, using retaliatory violence, will not gain freedom for the oppressed, King contended. It merely escalates the violence and makes it more difficult to achieve peace among people. Martin criticized Malcolm and other nationalists for rejecting white values in everything except their views on violence. Regarding the use of violence, Malcolm and whites were in total agreement with each other and against Martin. But Martin was completely unmoved by the odds against him. He did not care that whites advocated nonviolence only for Negroes and not for themselves; neither did he care how many Negroes rejected nonviolence as a sign of weakness or how many labeled him as a "religious Uncle Tom." Martin's absolute commitment to nonviolence was a matter of faith. He just did not believe that a world fit for human habitation could be created with violence.

The major difference, therefore, between Martin and Malcolm was their faith commitments. While each appealed to the practical side of their perspectives, the bottom line for both was faith and not pragmatism. Malcolm's faith was defined by the *particularity* of his blackness and Martin's by the *universality* of his humanity.

White, Liberal, Protestant Theology

Although King appropriated black faith for his personal life and used it in sermons to black church congregations, white, liberal, Protestant theology was very important in providing him with the intellectual resources to express the universality of his faith in published writings and public addresses to white Americans. King thought of himself as a liberal, philosophical theologian who opposed the narrow "fundamentalism" of his Baptist upbringing and its more sophisticated expressions in the neo-orthodox theology of the Swiss theologian Karl Barth. He rejected the inerrancy of Scripture, Jesus' virgin birth and bodily resurrection, and other fundamentalist views of Christianity that were firmly held by his father, "Daddy King," but which contradicted his university-acquired, liberal Protestant faith. King enthusiastically embraced liberal theology's accent on the social gospel and the need to work toward the building of a just society on earth, which many referred to as the Kingdom of God. He also accepted the philosophy of personalism, using its language to communicate his beliefs about the dignity and worth of the human person.

King used liberal, Protestant theology to articulate the religious dimensions of what he believed about America, because he knew that its language about God was more acceptable to white people than the spirituality of black people. Besides, he saw no major conflicts between liberal theology and black faith. In King's view, the former was intellectual and universal and therefore more accessible to people from a variety of cultural backgrounds. The latter was more emotional and particular, and its meaning was not easily available to those who had not experienced slavery and segregation.

King was particularly attracted to liberal theology's belief in the goodness of humanity and its optimism regarding the ability of the people of Western civilization to make a world that was morally good. His American dream was partly derived from his liberal faith, which said that if white people knew what was right they would do it. While white, liberal theologians pointed to the rise of democracy and scientific and technological improvements in European societies as evidence of human progress, King, incorporating that same theme, also emphasized the struggles for justice among the oppressed in the United States and throughout the world as proof that humanity was moving toward the ideal, the beloved community. He believed that the spirit that led the Negro fight against segregation in America was identical with the spirit that led Third World peoples in Africa, Asia, and Latin America to revolt against their European colonizers.

King referred to the struggles for justice among the poor as the "birth of a new age." His optimism about the new world order was portrayed with passion and excitement in his early speeches. "Those of us who live in the Twentieth Century are privileged to live in one of the most momentous periods of human history," he said in an address to the

First Annual Institute on Nonviolence and Social Change in Montgomery. "It is an exciting age filled with hope. It is an age in which a new social order is being born. We stand today between two worlds — the dying old and the emerging new."[12]

King was aware that not everyone shared his euphoria about the coming new age, especially the guardians of the old vanishing order. White segregationists liked things the way they were. King knew that; but he also believed that the diehard racists were in the minority and that the white American public in general was sympathetic with his views about the elimination of segregation. His first task, as he saw it, was to show whites that he understood their fears of the worldwide freedom movement:

> I am aware of the fact that there are those who would contend that we live in the most ghastly period of human history. They would argue that . . . the deep rumblings of the discontent from Asia, the uprisings in Africa, . . . and the racial tensions in America are all indicative of the deep and tragic midnight which encompasses our civilization. They would argue that we are retrogressing instead of progressing.[13]

King thought his second task was to persuade whites that their fears were groundless. The movement of freedom, like the developments in science and technology, was for the good of all. He employed the classic liberal proposition that pain always accompanies change:

> Far from representing retrogression or tragic meaninglessness, the present tension represents the necessary pains that accompany the birth of anything new. Long ago the Greek philosopher Heraclitus argued that justice emerges from the strife of opposites, and Hegel, in modern philosophy, preached a doctrine of growth through struggle. It is both historically and biologically true that there can be no birth and growth without birth and growing pains. Whenever there is the emergence of the new we confront the recalcitrance of the old. So the tensions which we witness in the world today are indicative of the fact that a new world order is being born and an old order is passing away.[14]

Of course, King was aware that oppressors do not grant freedom voluntarily to the oppressed. He was also aware that white segregationists and European colonists had much more military power than their victims. Yet he contended that the coming of the new world order of freedom was inevitable. His certainty about the future was supported not only by the black church's faith in the God of justice, love, and hope, but additionally by a parallel theme in liberal Protestantism: divinely directed progress toward moral perfection. No idea or strategy that King advocated can be understood correctly apart from his deep faith in the Christian God as defined by the black Baptist and liberal Protestant traditions. The new age is coming and cannot be stopped because God wills that the oppressed be liberated. In the language of the liberal tradition King could say:

> Oppressed people cannot remain oppressed forever. The urge for freedom will eventually come. This is what happened to the American Negro. Something within has reminded him of his birthright of freedom; something without has reminded him that he can gain it. Consciously and unconsciously, he has been swept in by what the Germans call the *Zeitgeist,* and with his black brothers of Africa, and his brown and yellow brothers of Asia, South America, and the Caribbean, he is moving with a sense of cosmic urgency toward the promised land of racial justice.[15]

King often used the German word *Zeitgeist* to refer to his belief that "the universe is under the control of a loving purpose, and that in the struggle for righteousness [we have] cosmic companionship." This was what he had in mind when he said that Rosa Parks "had been tracked down by the *Zeitgeist* — the spirit of the time." He made a similar statement in relation to himself when he offered his resignation to Dexter Avenue Baptist Church in Montgomery: "I can't stop now. History has thrust upon me a responsibility from which I cannot turn away." King was referring to a historical movement of freedom that was rooted in ultimate reality and thus was not exclusively dependent on human decisions. In King's perspective, the American dream was an aspect of the new age of freedom that was bursting forth throughout the world, and both, the "dream" and the "new age," were the immanent, creative, revolutionary hand of God at work in the world, reconciling blacks and whites, poor and rich, Europe and its colonized peoples. King felt that he had been chosen by God as an instrument for the coming of freedom. When he received the Nobel Peace Prize in 1964, it reinforced this belief and deepened his commitment to global justice and peace. "I have the audacity to believe," he said in his acceptance speech, "that people everywhere can have three meals a day for their bodies, education for their minds, and dignity, equality and freedom for their spirits."[16]

For King, the Nobel Prize was an "unutterable fulfillment," given in recognition of those fighting for freedom all over the world. His dream of a coming new age of freedom was eloquently expressed in his Nobel Lecture, "Quest for Peace and Justice":

> What we are seeing now is a freedom explosion. . . . The deep rumbling of discontent that we hear today is the thunder of the disinherited masses, rising from dungeons of oppression to the bright hills of freedom. . . . All over the world, like a fever, the freedom movement is spreading in the widest liberation in history. The great masses of people are determined to end the exploitation of their races and land. They are awake and moving toward their goal like a tidal wave. You can hear them rumbling in every village, street, on the docks, in the houses, among the students, in the churches and at political meetings.[17]

King believed that because God was involved in the freedom struggles, they could not be halted. Victory was inevitable. Successes in the civil rights and Third World liberation movements and King's own deep faith in God's loving justice combined to give him an optimistic hope that freedom was not too far away. King's faith that the freedom movement was initiated and sustained by God's liberating Spirit also encouraged him to expect white and black churches to join the struggle for justice throughout the world.

KING'S IMPACT UPON THE AMERICAN CHURCHES

SOUTHERN AND NORTHERN WHITE CHURCHES

No religious leader has made a greater impact upon American society and its churches than Martin King. That distinction can be interpreted as either a strength or a weakness, depending on one's view of the achievements of the civil rights movement, which King persuaded many white churches to support. King's appeal to whites and their religious values was the chief reason why he became an influential leader in the society and was subsequently elevated to the status of a national hero. The religious ethos of America was defined primarily by white Protestant Christianity. No one, especially not a member of a minority group, could acquire the moral influence King possessed without identifying with and appealing to the spirit and teachings of Christianity as preached in white churches and taught in white seminaries.

Malcolm X and other black nationalists stood outside of the sphere of moral power defined by white Christians, and that was the chief reason why Malcolm was not as influential as Martin in appealing to the religious and moral sensibilities of whites. However, when Martin

King shaped his message to appeal to the religious consciousness of white America, and when Malcolm shaped his for the cultural sensitivities of the black masses in the ghetto, both lost and gained in the process. Martin gained the ear of white America, especially its churches, and blacks in the South, while losing most of the northern, urban unchurched black poor and the black nationalists. Malcolm gained what Martin lost, and lost what he gained.

King's understanding of the Christian faith as a universal message of freedom influenced his attitude toward white churches and his expectations about the role they should play in the black struggle against segregation. When he became the leader of the Montgomery bus boycott, he expected white churches and their ministers to support blacks in their fight for justice. He knew that many of the ministers had studied in reputable seminaries, and, therefore, were keenly aware that the gospel of Jesus demanded justice for the poor and the reconciliation of all persons as brothers and sisters. But to King's surprise, only one white minister in Montgomery, Robert Graetz, publicly supported the boycott, and he was the pastor of a black congregation, the Trinity Lutheran Church. Other white ministers either remained silent or openly joined the forces of segregation and accused King of mixing religion and politics. For example, E. Stanley Frazier, an outspoken segregationist, pastor of St. James Methodist Church, and a member of the negotiating committee to find a settlement of the Montgomery boycott, reminded King that "the job of the minister . . . is to lead the souls of men to God, not to bring about confusion by getting tangled up in transitory social problems."[18]

Initially, the refusal of white southern churches to support the civil rights movement did not dishearten King. He had a tendency to blame himself for his lack of patience and understanding regarding the deep resistance to social change in the South. After all, slavery and segregation had been realities in America for more than three centuries. King's liberal optimism encouraged him to believe that, in time and with sympathetic understanding and adequate patience, the moderates of the South, especially ministers, through an appeal to the gospel, could be persuaded to join the civil rights movement.

In many addresses and writings to white churches, King perceived that his task, as a minister of the gospel and as a citizen of America, was to inform them of their responsibilities in the Negro struggle for justice. At the Conference on Christian Faith and Human Relations, which was sponsored by eighty-five southern religious leaders of both races and was held in Nashville, Tennessee, on 23–25 April 1957, King gave what became his standard address to white church bodies. He began by lauding America's great advances in science and technology, enabling us to "cure dreaded diseases," to "carve highways through the stratosphere," and to "build the greatest system of production the world has ever known." But, said King, "there is another side to our national life which is not bright." He was referring to the "racial conflict," "the chief moral dilemma of our nation," as he frequently called it. "In the midst of all of our scientific and technological advances," King told white ministers, "we have not learned the simple art of loving our neighbors and respecting the dignity and worth of all human personality. Through our scientific genius, we have made the world a neighborhood, but through our moral and spiritual geniuses, we have failed to make our Nation a brotherhood." The great gap between our science and our morality, our technology and our theology presents the church with a "tremendous challenge," because, as he said in a similar presentation to the Southern Baptist Theological Seminary, "the church has a moral responsibility of being the moral guardian of society." "The broad *universalism* standing at the center of the Gospel," said King in his Nashville address, "makes brotherhood morally inescapable. Racial segregation is a blatant denial of the unity we have in Christ. Segregation is a tragic evil which is utterly un-Christian."[19]

King realized that his claim about the un-Christian nature of segregation was not as obvious to white ministers (especially in the South) as it was to Negro ministers. Patient in his faith, he often repeated three reasons for his point of view. "First," he said, "segregation inevitably makes for inequality"; second, "it scars the soul of both the segregator and the segregated"; and third, "it ends up depersonalizing the segregated." King carefully explicated each reason, using the Bible and recent studies in the human sciences to support his claim.

As King saw it, the racial problem could be solved through education, with church leaders "taking a forthright stand," urging the nation to make "brotherhood a reality." Racism was due to ignorance. The role of the church was to reconcile people by "keeping the channels of communication open" so whites and Negroes could get to "know each other," and thereby create the beloved community. Although King was critical of the white clergy's practice and tolerance of segregation, telling them how "appalling" it was that "11 o'clock on Sunday morning . . . is the most segregated hour in Christian America," he still appealed to their good will by always acknowledging that "much progress has been made toward the goal of a non-segregated society," and by encouraging them, firmly and lovingly, to build on that progress by opening the door of reconciliation, without delay, to their Negro sisters and brothers.

When a few white moderates in the South began to voice their support for the civil rights movement (one of the most notable being theologian Will D. Campbell), King was elated, thinking that their actions would encourage a significant number of others to follow suit. At the Nashville conference, he openly praised them for their "determined courage . . . to suffer and sacrifice for truth," standing "unflinchingly amid threats and intimidation, inconvenience and unpopularity, and even at times amid sheer physical danger." But King told the vast majority of white ministers who seemed tied to the cultural mores of the South that they were "citizen[s] of two worlds." He told them they not only had to "answer to the mores," but they had also to "give account to God." He went on: "Every minister of the gospel has a mandate to stand up courageously for righteousness, to proclaim the eternal verities of the gospel, and to lead men from the desolate midnight of falsehood to the bright daybreak of truth."[20]

Despite King's repeated appeals, most white clergy remained unmoved in the early 1960s, and King began to express his impatience. He gave a sharp critique of their "abysmal silence" during the crisis precipitated by James Meredith's entry into the University of Mississippi. After federal troops had quelled white rioters, King wrote in *The Nation* (13 October 1962), "Where was the cry of the Lord's prophets?" He could not understand the silence of the white clergy. King recalled his travels through Mississippi where he had seen "tall church spires and sprawling brick monuments dedicated to the glory of God." With segregation as a way of life, he wondered then about the people and the God they worshiped in their churches. He wrote: "When I review the painful memory of the last week at Oxford and cannot recall a single voice 'crying in the wilderness,' the questions are still the same: 'What kind of people worship there? Who is their God?' "[21]

King's concern about the white churches did not abate but increased as he and others stepped up their involvement in the civil rights movement, initiating nonviolent direct action demonstrations throughout the South. During the Birmingham demonstrations, eight white clergy decided to oppose him openly by making a public statement. Included among them were bishops in the Catholic, Episcopal, and Methodist churches, a moderator in the Presbyterian church, a Jewish rabbi, and a prominent Baptist pastor. These clergymen were not the "regular run of mill" ministers one would have found at a Klan rally or even at a White Citizens Council meeting. King acknowledged them as "men of genuine good will" and as persons of prominence in the white community. They referred to him, however, as an "extremist" and an "outsider" and said that the "demonstrations [were] unwise and untimely." The clergymen called for "law and order and common sense," as they praised Bull Connor's police for "the calm manner in which these demonstrations have been handled."[22]

King was deeply disturbed by their statement. He knew that their opinions were not isolated, but represented the feelings of a significant number of whites in the church, not only in Alabama but throughout the South and much of the North. His reply, therefore, was written with the American white church as his primary audience. The title, "Letter from Birmingham City Jail," was purposely chosen to evoke the memory of the Apostle Paul, who was jailed many times "for the sake of the gospel of Jesus." Next to Jesus, no biblical character engenders as much respect among Christians as does Paul. At the Dexter Avenue Baptist Church on 4 November 1956 King had preached a sermon entitled "Paul's Letter to American Christians." It contained most of the points found in his own "Letter," including his central theological claim that "unmerited suffering is redemptive" because "love is the most durable power in the world," a claim derived from his interpretation of Paul's view of Jesus' death.[23]

The time was right for his "Letter," just as the moment was right for his "I Have a Dream" speech a few months later. White America was ready to hear King and he was ready to give them the "Word from on High," as they say in the black church. Despite the opposition of southern religious leaders, King persuaded many white northern ministers that segregation was a denial of the gospel. The months before the "Letter" showed rising levels of support for King's efforts. The northern ministers responded to his call for support during the Albany Movement, and several distinguished theologians and church leaders participated in the sit-ins and freedom rides. They also began to deliver sermons and addresses against racism and to write essays and books uncovering the long history of the practice of segregation in their churches. Many northern, white church leaders and theologians were very critical of their southern brothers and sisters for not seeing the moral issue and the urgent need of the church to clean its own house or lose its credibility as a church of Jesus Christ.

The most important event that set the stage for King's "Letter" was the National Conference on Religion and Race, which represented, "for the first time in the United States, the formal cooperation of our major faith bodies on a common moral and social problem." There were seventy participating organizations and 657 delegates. It was held in Chicago (14–17 January 1963), the home of the headquarters of the Black Muslims, but, significantly, none was invited, a glaring omission that did not escape Malcolm's critical observations. In an address at Michigan State University on 23 January 1963, he claimed that the conference participants "didn't get to the meat of the issue," because the Muslims were not present.

White and black religious leaders were well aware of the Black Muslim presence in Chicago and in the ghettos and prisons throughout the nation. But they were not interested in providing a platform for the Muslim "hate teachings," which they regarded as little different from those of the Ku Klux Klan. The people who met in Chicago were interested in arousing the conscience of the nation in support of integration. The highlights of the conference were King's address, "A Challenge to the Churches and Synagogues" (which was similar to the Nashville address and other addresses to white church leaders), and a common statement of the participants, entitled "An Appeal to the Conscience of the American People." Their statement said what King had been waiting for the white church to say for a long time. They invoked the image of Abraham Lincoln and expressed their regrets that even one hundred years after his Emancipation Proclamation racism, "our most serious domestic evil," was still deeply rooted in America. They also said that "racial discrimination and segregation are an insult to God, the Giver of human dignity and human rights." Even worse, they went on to acknowledge, religious bodies have participated in perpetuating racism. They asked for God's forgiveness and also for that of the victims of racism. They called upon "all the American people to work, to pray and to act courageously in the cause of human equality and dignity while there is still time, to eliminate racism permanently and decisively, to seize the historic opportunity the Lord has given us for healing an ancient rupture in the human family, to do this for the glory of God."[24]

Thus by the time King wrote his "Letter," he had gained the support of the great majority of white, northern church leaders in the view that segregation, as it was practiced in the South, was a moral contradiction that no Christian or American could tolerate.

King's "Letter" was an eloquent and now classic statement of his theological and political views. It contained nothing new, nothing that he had not said in other sermons, addresses, and essays to white America, but when he restated what he had been saying for nearly eight years, it acquired a moral power that shook the conscience of the members of the white churches in America, especially northern liberals. King stated that nothing was more tragic for the church and the American dream than the continued existence of segregation. He saw segregation as a double contradiction: of America's democratic faith and of its religious heritage. Of the two contradictions, according to King, the religious one was the worst. He was severely critical of white ministers who tolerated segregation in their churches and remained silent about its practice in the society. Instead of being uncompromisingly prophetic in their denunciation of segregation and their support of integration, "all too many have been more cautious than courageous and have remained silent behind the anesthetizing security of stained-glassed windows." "I have heard numerous southern religious leaders admonish their worshippers to comply with a desegregation decision because it's the law," King said, "but I have longed to hear white ministers declare: 'Follow that decree because integration is morally right and because the Negro is your brother.' " He accused the church of being content to "stand on the sideline and mouth pious irrelevancies and sanctimonious trivialities" during the present Negro revolution.

In the South a few white ministers joined the civil rights movement, and some of them lost their churches. But by this time, King's hope of persuading the white moderates in the South—a group he thought was in the numerical majority—had been shattered. It deeply disappointed him that the white clergy seemed incapable of understanding that the demands of the gospel transcended the mores of the South. "I have been greatly disappointed with the white Church and its leadership," King wrote in the "Letter." He acknowledged that, though he had hoped for the support of the white clergy of Birmingham, their opposition was consistent with the past behavior of the white church leadership.

> I had the strange feeling when I was suddenly catapulted into leadership of the bus protest in Montgomery several years ago that we would have the support of the white Church. I felt that white ministers, priests, and rabbis of the South would be some of our strongest allies. Instead, some have been outright opponents, refusing to understand the freedom movement and misrepresenting its leaders. . . . But in spite of my shattered dreams of the past, I came to Birmingham with the hope that the white religious leadership of this community would see the justice of our cause. . . . But again I have been disappointed.

Despite his disappointment with the white church, King did not abandon his faith commitment and its link with the universal church. King was a universalist who believed that the gospel of Jesus demanded freedom for all. The white church's failure to follow the mandates of the gospel did not invalidate it. Rather the white church's failure, King believed, obligated him and other Christians to bear witness more than ever to the universal message of the gospel so that the world might know that true Christianity is not only concerned with heaven over yonder but also with the quality of life *here* on earth.

Although most southern ministers disappointed King, a significant number of their northern brothers and sisters lifted his spirit and gave him hope that the beloved community was not too far away. The Chicago conference was the first major, highly visible support of white religious bodies for the civil rights movement. More than one million copies of King's "Letter from Birmingham Jail" were published and distributed, mainly in northern churches. Soon after, the National Council of Churches urged the thirty-one denominations that were its members to initiate "nationwide demonstrations against racial discrimination." The NCC general board said: "Words and declarations are no longer useful in this struggle unless accompanied by sacrifice and commitment."[25] About two months later, white churches offered significant contributions and participation toward the success of the March on Washington. Major Protestant denominations began to set up "Commissions on Race," with the NCC leading the way. Embarrassed by the opposition and silence of their southern colleagues, northern church leaders were determined to let the world know that they supported King in his identification of segregation as a moral evil which must be exterminated from the church of Jesus Christ and from American society. Reflecting back on the events of 1963, King said: "I think that 1963 brought a coalition of conscience we had never seen before. For example, church groups came out in 1963 in a way they never had come out in the past—in terms of active participation by white clergymen and many of the lay leaders in white churches."[26]

But the high-water mark of the white church's participation was the Selma March in 1965. James J. Reeb, an outspoken Boston Unitarian minister, was killed, and others were wounded as many marched with King and other blacks in the struggle for the ballot. In an address to the General Synod of the United Church of Christ on 6 July 1965, about four months following the successful march from Selma to Montgomery, King was still elated about the support the civil rights movement was receiving from white churches. In his closing statement, he was euphoric:

> It is encouraging to be able to close an address to a national Church body on an optimistic note for in the past year we have seen the Church of Jesus Christ rise up as never before and join the thunderous procession of committed souls in behalf of racial justice. One of the most inspirational moments of my life was the memorial service for the Reverend James Reeb, when an Episcopal bishop, a Methodist bishop, a Greek Orthodox archbishop, the president of the Unitarian-Universalist National Conference, a Roman Catholic monsignor, and two Baptist preachers conducted services in an A.M.E. church, with twenty to thirty top ranking officials of labor and civil rights organizations seated in the choir stand saying amen. I was sure that this alliance of conscience could only be a sign of the coming kingdom.[27]

There was an extremely sharp contrast between Martin's and Malcolm's attitudes toward Christianity in general and the white American church in particular. The same was true in regard to their perspectives on the black church. I will save Malcolm's comments on Christianity and the churches for the next chapter and will conclude this one with an interpretation of Martin's perspective on the black church.

BLACK CHURCHES AND THE CIVIL RIGHTS MOVEMENT

While white churches were slow to become involved in the civil rights movement, black churches, to a large degree, embraced it. This was particularly true of their ministers. The name and purpose of King's organization were deliberately chosen to accent the faith of black ministers—the name: Southern *Christian* Leadership Conference; the purpose: "to redeem the soul of America." Black preachers and the members of their churches made up the staff of the organization and were its chief financial supporters in the black community. From the time that King accepted the leadership of the Montgomery bus boycott and later founded and became the president of the SCLC, he viewed his work in the civil rights movement as a part of his ministry in the church and invited persons to join his staff who had similar convictions. The civil rights movement, therefore, was not thought of as something separate from the church; rather it *was* the church living out its obedience to Jesus Christ's calling "to preach good news to the poor," "to proclaim release to the captives," and "to set at liberty those who are oppressed" (Luke 4:18, RSV).

Unlike white churches, which separated religion and politics when the racial question was involved, black churches have always viewed them as belonging together, *especially* in regard to race. When their dignity was being disregarded, blacks used religion and anything else in their possession in order to fight for their right to be treated as human beings. Religion was their best weapon, and no one used it as effectively as Martin King. Black churches were the base of his operations, and their ministers supported him more than any other group.

As a young minister in Arkansas, I remember clearly the impact the civil rights movement made upon me and others in the black churches. No one I knew, in any black denomination, ever separated Christianity from the right to be free in the society. Some, however, were braver than others, preaching and practicing what everyone else believed but might have been too afraid to say or do. Fear is the major reason black churches often have been passive in regard to the struggle for racial justice. What Martin King did more than anyone else, by word and example, was to infuse courage into black ministers, thereby enabling them to do the same for their congregations. Young people were particularly responsive.

This is not to deny the presence of the otherworldly, "heaven over yonder" theme in black churches and the role it has played in encouraging blacks to withdraw from the affairs of this world. "You may have all this world, give me Jesus" was interpreted by some blacks to mean that whites could run the political affairs of the world as long as blacks were free to worship Jesus in their churches. But the otherworldly theme in black churches must be placed in historical context to be understood correctly. During slavery, heaven served as that element in the slaves' religion which enabled them to believe that they were somebody even though there was nothing in this world that recognized their humanity. It was a spirituality that affirmed their personhood in a society which denied it. That was why they could hope for freedom and even struggle for it, even though the odds were against them achieving it. As long as black slaves believed that they were children of God, they also knew that they were not created to be the slaves of white men. Heaven, therefore, far from creating passivity among black slaves, more often than not created the desire to be free, not only in the next world, but also in this one.

Following slavery, the theme of heaven often became an end in itself. The reasons were understandable, though unfortunate. With nearly four million newly freed slaves, formerly small black denominations became large and many new ones were founded. It was not easy to help feed, clothe, house, and educate their illiterate brothers and sisters and still confront a powerful, hostile white community who regarded their former slaves as less than human. Because of their fear of confrontation with white society, some black ministers used heaven as a replacement for being concerned about justice on earth. Others used it to manipulate the congregation for personal financial gain. But despite these distortions, heaven's true meaning, though dormant, was still present in the churches, and Martin King merely recaptured it and then creatively applied it in the civil rights movement. He did not create black spirituality; he simply appropriated it in the struggle for justice more effectively than anyone else before, during, or after his time.

When the Montgomery bus boycott began, I was a student at Shorter College, a small school run by the AME Church and located in North Little Rock, Arkansas. I was in charge of reporting "current events" to the daily assembly in the chapel. During the early months of 1956, I remember hearing and reading about King and the boycott in Montgomery. The more I researched the event and reported the news of it to the college community, the more the spirit of the Montgomery Movement influenced my identity as a black person and my vocation as a minister. King's faith commitment and his courage to stand up to white folks made me proud to be a minister and to be black. His education made me more determined to continue my own beyond the undergraduate level. As I participated in the black church, I believed, as did others I knew, that fighting for justice was as important as preaching the gospel on Sunday morning. Indeed I believed that was the chief way to determine whether preachers really believed what they were saying or whether they were "just talking" or "entertaining" to earn status or a living and nothing else.

I always thought it was strange that white Christians, especially ministers, did not recognize that the truth of the gospel meant that all persons were created equal. I felt that the Christian identity of whites was in jeopardy since none seemed to see what was obvious to blacks. I experienced an even greater shock when I discovered that in Chicago and in Evanston (where I attended Garrett Theological Seminary) and in the surrounding area whites were just as racist as they were in the South. They were, of course, a little more subtle but just as vicious and sometimes even more so. I had not yet discovered Malcolm X, but I had started to feel about the North what I later heard him articulate so eloquently. In the late 1950s, I was still trying to understand how my ministry could make sense in a white world that claimed a Christian identity but whose understanding and practice of it excluded my humanity. Martin King was my primary resource on how to think about the gospel and the black struggle for freedom.

My first shock in graduate school was the small number of black students attending Garrett, a Methodist seminary that was trying to lure King as a professor of systematic theology. Another surprise was the blatant expressions of racism by some of my professors and the failure of all to deal with it as a blatant contradiction of the Christian faith. It was, of course, difficult to stay in graduate school with the civil rights movement in full swing, defining segregation as America's chief moral dilemma. My brother left school, as did many others, including Jesse Jackson. Black ministers not only left divinity schools; they also left prominent positions as pastors of churches to devote full time to the civil rights movement, which they regarded as ministry. Wyatt Tee Walker, an executive director of the SCLC, was a prominent example.

No religious group has been more divided by denominationalism than the black church. But during King's leadership in the SCLC, black ministers' commitment to the cause of black freedom enabled them to transcend the denominational barriers that separated them. King, Ralph Abernathy, and Wyatt Walker were Baptists; but Joseph Lowery and Andrew Young were Methodist and Congregationalist, respectively. The array of ministers representing different black denominations in the civil rights movement was vast. They came together in their support of the movement and of King because the bottom line for most was the liberation of black people from their political domination by whites. The attitudes of most black and white churches toward the civil rights movement, therefore, were literally as different as the colors black and white.

Although many black ministers supported the civil rights movement, a few did not. The most prominent was Joseph H. Jackson, then head of the National Baptist Convention, the largest organization of black churches. It is important to note that Jackson initially supported King by sending financial aid to the Montgomery movement and urging others in his organization to do the same. He also attended the First Annual Institute on Nonviolence and Social Change in Montgomery and gave the major address for the occasion. King also became an officer in the National Baptist Convention. But King's increasingly radical politics as well as his rapidly developing influence in the black and white communities alienated Jackson.

J. H. Jackson was one of a very few black ministers who openly opposed King. While the great majority of black ministers did not openly oppose King, some, due to fear of white reprisals, refused to allow organizations to use their churches when he was invited to speak. "Ga. Church Group Afraid of Dr. King" was the headline of an article in the *Pittsburgh Courier*. The article told of the Reverend A. R. Smith and the officers of St. James AME Church of Columbus refusing to allow the Prince Hall Masons to use the auditorium to present Dr. King. When asked about the refusal, Reverend Smith said that "Dr. King's appearance might stir up racial friction here." However, the Reverend A. W. Fortson of Friendship Baptist Church "flung wide the doors of his church."[28]

When King and his SCLC staff went to Birmingham in the early months of 1963, most black ministers opposed him. However, after a few talks with them, King was able to persuade many to support the movement. Similar problems emerged in other cities, and King's conversations with reluctant black ministers usually convinced them of the wisdom of joining the civil rights movement. It was nearly impossible for black ministers to listen to King and not be persuaded by the power of his presence, example, and proclamation of the gospel. His words cut deep into the Christian conscience of black ministers. He was to black church leaders what Malcolm was to the people of the ghetto—a voice of truth to whom they could not turn a deaf ear. Like Malcolm in relation to the people of the ghetto, King loved the black church and its ministers because he was one of them; but he was also different from them because of the integrity of his commitment and the critical posture he assumed in relation to the church he loved so much. No person's commitment to the gospel or to black freedom exceeded his (and that included Malcolm's). No person in the black church and only a few outside of it (Malcolm was one) were more critical of it than King.

Repeatedly King made two main criticisms of the Negro church: its one-sided, anti-intellectual focus on the heaven theme to the exclusion of problems on earth, and its class snobbery. Negro churches guilty of the first weakness "[burn] with emotionalism." They often reduce "worship to entertainment" by placing "more emphasis on volume than on content" and by confusing "spirituality with muscularity." According to King, "the danger in such a church is that the members may have more religion in their hands and feet than in their hearts and souls."[29]

King was particularly critical of Negro ministers for being both apolitical and anti-intellectual. Urging Negro ministers to get ready for the new age of integration, he told them that "we can't spend all our time learning how to whoop and holler. We got to study some. . . . We've got to have ministers who can stand up and speak the gospel of Jesus Christ." For King, the true gospel was "not a Negro gospel!" It was "not a gospel merely to get people to shout and kick over [benches] but a gospel that will make people think and live right."

When the clergy were reluctant to become involved in the civil rights movement, King reminded them that "a minister cannot preach the glories of heaven while ignoring social conditions in his own community that cause men an earthly hell." Many blacks were accustomed to depending on prayer to change the social conditions of injustice; to them King said what he said to whites: "We are gravely misled if we think the struggle will be won only by prayer. God who gave us minds for thinking and bodies for working would defeat his own purpose if he permitted us to obtain through prayer what may come through work and intelligence." King frequently told all Christians that "any religion that professes to be concerned with the souls of men and is not concerned with the slums that damn them, the economic conditions that cripple them, is a spiritually moribund religion in need of new blood."[30]

King's most effective critique of the Negro church's excessive concern with the next world was delivered in sermons to black congregations. In a sermon entitled "Remember Who You Are," preached at Ebenezer, he said:

There's something wrong with any church that limits the gospel to talkin' about heaven over yonder. There is something wrong with any minister . . . who becomes so otherworldly in his orientation that he forgets about what is happening now. There is something wrong with any church that is [so] absolved in the hereafter that it forgets the here. *Here* where men are trampled over by the iron feet of oppression. *Here* where thousands of God's children are caught in an air-tight cage [of poverty]. *Here* where thousands of men and women are depressed and in agony because of their earthly fight . . ., where the darkness of life surrounds so many of God's children. I say to you that religion must be concerned not merely about mansions in the sky, but about the slums and the ghettos in this world. A proper religion will be concerned not merely about the streets flowing with milk and honey, but about the millions of God's children in Asia, Africa, and South America and in our own nation who go to bed hungry at night. It will be concerned [not only] about a long white robe over yonder but about [people] having some clothes down here. It will be concerned not merely about silver slippers in heaven but about men and women having some shoes to wear on earth.[31]

King also criticized a type of Negro church which "freezes with classism." It brags of being an exclusive, "highbrow church" with a "membership of professional people"—doctors, lawyers, teachers, and businessmen. "In such a church the worship service is cold and meaningless, the music dull and uninspiring, and the sermon little more than a homily on current events." It has no sensitivity for the cultural and religious heritage of Negroes. "If the choir sings a Negro spiritual, the members claim an affront to their class status." According to King, "this type of church tragically fails to recognize that worship at its best is a social experience in which people from all levels of life come together to affirm their oneness and unity under God."[32]

Classism was not as serious a problem in the black church as in the white church. But as more blacks achieved the middle-class status that King's philosophy of integration was fighting for, the more classism became a problem in the black church. King himself was a product of the classism he detested. For him, on the one hand, the gospel was universal and thus was intended for everybody—Negroes and whites, poor and rich. This meant that there should be only one church and not a *Negro* church and a *white* church or a rich one and a poor one. "All [are] one in Christ Jesus" (Gal. 3:28, RSV), as Paul said, a statement which King interpreted as a call for the elimination of preference for race or class. But, on the other hand, whites do not want to worship with blacks and neither do middle-class blacks want to worship with poor blacks. The black bourgeoisie would prefer to be with whites and, failing that, would rather be alone with those blacks who share a similar respect for "dignity" and education. King attacked the Negro-white problem by advocating integration, which he often interpreted as Negroes having the same opportunity as whites, living with them, going to school with them, and becoming like them. He often communicated the idea that unless Negroes are in the same schools with whites and socialize with them, they cannot be free or equal to whites. But by becoming integrated with whites, a few (and *only* a few) blacks acquired middle-class income, status, and values which separated them from the black masses, especially their religion. For integration, by its very definition, alienated blacks from their cultural history and thereby from those religious values that empowered them to fight for freedom. To be "free" meant to *become white,* and to be white in America has always meant the opposite of being black. King's American dream had to be "universal," that is *white,* before it could capture the imagination of the majority of white people in the United States. In fact, the success of black persons in the mainstream of America is primarily dependent upon their willingness to deny their African identity and become *just* an American.

King was caught between two worlds—one was made up of whites and middle-class blacks and the other was composed of poor blacks. His education linked him with the world of the whites and the black middle class. But his faith (appropriated in his Montgomery kitchen and tested on the battlefields of Albany, Birmingham, St. Augustine, and Selma against armed white segregationists) placed him in solidarity with poor blacks. When he reflected upon the truth of the gospel in the context of the civil rights movement, his primary resource was the black church whose suffering, at the hands of white racists in the South, he often compared with the persecution of the early church. "The Negro church today, by and large, is a glorious example in the history of Christendom," he said in his *Playboy* interview. "For never in Christian history, within a Christian country, have Christian churches been on the receiving end of such naked brutality and violence as we are witnessing here in America today. Not since the days of the Christians in the catacombs has God's house, as a symbol, weathered such attack as the Negro churches."[33]

The Christian gospel, as King viewed it, was inseparably connected with the cross and the suffering of Jesus. That was why he urged Negroes to follow nonviolence. There was no way anyone could be the kind of Christian that King's theology called for without being willing to suffer on behalf of the "least of these," a biblical reference he often used to describe the poor. He could not understand how whites expected to live the Christian life without suffering on behalf of their Negro brothers and sisters in their fight against segregation.

The essence of the Epistles of Paul is that Christians should *rejoice* at being deemed worthy to suffer for what they believe. The projection of the social gospel . . . is the true witness of a Christian life. This is the meaning of the true *ekklesia* — the inner, spiritual church. The church once changed society. It was then a thermostat of society. But today . . . the [white] church is merely a thermometer, which measures rather than molds popular opinion.[34]

More than any other American of his time, King embodied the best in the Christian religion. But the best in Christianity was not good enough for Malcolm's religious needs, because Christianity was still too closely identified with the "white man's culture." He had to have a *black* religion, one that could restore his wounded self-image and connect him with his African roots. To that subject we turn in the next chapter.

The arrest of Rosa Parks on December 1, 1955, for failing to yield her seat to a white passenger on a city bus, touched off the Montgomery bus boycott.

March 22, 1956, supporters cheer Martin Luther King after his conviction for leading the Montgomery bus boycott. Beside him is his wife, Coretta Scott King.

Malcolm X with his wife and daughters.

Malcolm X at an outdoor rally in Harlem.

Martin preaching at Ebenezer Baptist Church, Atlanta, Georgia.

Malcolm at a Harlem street rally.

Malcolm with Elijah Muhammad at a Muslim convention in Chicago, 1961.

Malcolm leads protest against police harassment of salesmen of *Muhammad Speaks*, Times Square rush hour, February 13, 1963. Hundreds of Muslims participated.

Martin leading a Civil Rights march through downtown Detroit, June 1963.

Malcolm addressing a Harlem rally.

1963 March on Washington.

August 1963, Martin delivers his "I Have a Dream" speech at the Lincoln Memorial.

Malcolm interviewed for *Playboy* by journalist Alex Haley, with whom he later collaborated on his *Autobiography*.

From the *Playboy* interview with Alex Haley.

Martin in Birmingham jail, 1963.

In Birmingham, Alabama, firehoses
are turned on demonstrators.

Martin, holding his son, views cross
burned in front of his Atlanta home.

Malcolm with his daughters.

Malcolm announces break with Nation of Islam at a news conference in New York City, March 12, 1964.

Robert Parent/Pathfinder

The only meeting of Malcolm and Martin took place on March 26, 1964 at the U.S. Capitol. Both were attending the Senate debate of the Civil Rights Bill.

Library of Congress

Malcolm meets reporters upon return from travels in Africa and pilgrimage to Mecca, May 1964.

Malcolm at Kennedy Airport upon return from meeting of the Organization of African Unity in Cairo, November 24, 1964.

Malcolm at the founding of the Organization of Afro-American Unity at the Audobon Ballroom in Harlem, June 28, 1964.

Moments after being shot in the Audobon Ballroom in Harlem, Malcolm is rushed from the scene. February 21, 1965.

Funeral for Malcolm X, Faith Temple in Harlem, February 27, 1965.

Malcolm X.

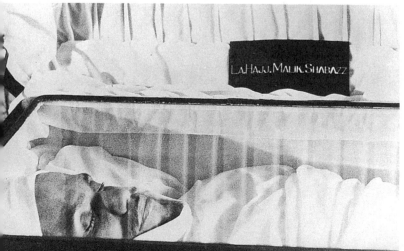

LAHAJJ.MALIKSHABAZZ

Taking his message north, in January 1966 King moved into a slum
tenement in Chicago.

On April 15, 1967 Martin addresses
a large rally protesting the Vietnam
War in front of the United Nations.

March 1968, Martin joined striking sanitation workers in Memphis.

Memphis, April 3, 1968, the day before his assasination on the same motel balcony, Martin is flanked (left to right) by Hosea Williams, Jesse Jackson, and Ralph Abernathy.

Jesse Jackson after the
assassination.

Martin's funeral service in Sister's Chapel at Spelman College, April 9, 1968

Intersection in Harlem,
125th St. and Lenox Ave.

6

"WHITE MAN'S HEAVEN IS A BLACK MAN'S HELL"

Brothers and sisters, the white man has brainwashed us black people to fasten our gaze upon a blondhaired, blue-eyed Jesus! We're worshiping a Jesus that doesn't even look *like us! Oh, yes! Now just bear with me, listen to the teachings of the Messenger of Allah, The Honorable Elijah Muhammad. Now just think of this. The blond-haired, blue-eyed white man has taught you and me to worship a* white *Jesus, and to shout and sing and pray to this God that's* his *God, the white man's God. The white man has taught us to shout and sing and pray until we* die, *to wait until* death, *for some dreamy heaven-in-the-hereafter, when we're* dead, *while this white man has his milk and honey in the streets paved with golden dollars here on* this *earth!*

Malcolm X
Harlem, New York
June 1954

Martin King's faith is not hard to understand or communicate to most people, black or white. We may disagree with particular theological points, or even reject his faith entirely; but that faith is not completely alien to our religious and intellectual sensibilities. That is because King's faith and theology were strongly influenced by European Christianity, the dominant religion of the privileged race in America. We have often heard language like his from religious, educational, and political leaders.

Malcolm X's faith, on the other hand, is more difficult to understand and communicate to the majority of both blacks and whites because it was derived primarily from Elijah Muhammad's Nation of Islam, a minority religion of an underprivileged class of a minority race. Malcolm's faith was marginal not only in America as a whole but in the African-American community itself. This places Malcolm's religious

151

perspective at a great disadvantage, compared with King's, regarding our openness to understand what he believed and why he believed it. The idea that a person from the black underclass, with no university or seminary education, could teach the people of America something about their God and country was and still is today almost unthinkable for the vast majority of whites and blacks. What could a former convict and dope pusher teach us about things holy and divine? To be sure, some Americans find Malcolm's works, particularly the *Autobiography* and his recorded speeches, stirring and relevant. But even the members of that small group, not to mention all the other Americans, do not see Malcolm's religious statements as an important exploration into the meaning and purpose of human existence. When they encounter his religious faith, they find it narrowly sectarian and thus alien to their religious and cultural sensibilities. Nevertheless, Malcolm was a deeply religious person who identified his life's work as a mission from God, mediated through the Messenger. His highest aspiration was to be one of God's ministers.

Malcolm's alienation was so deep that he could derive no positive meaning from Christianity as he knew it. How then does a black Christian preacher and theologian like me understand and communicate the religious message of a Black Muslim minister like Malcolm? The most important thing that we have in common was also the source of his faith: *the experience of being black in a white, racist society.* Our common blackness and resistance to racism always empowered me to listen to him, over and over again, until I found myself deeply engaged by his message. The more I read his writings and listened to his cogent and passionate oratory, the more I understood his message and was persuaded by it. This was especially true in the area of religion. As much as I am persuaded by the truth of the gospel of Jesus, I am equally persuaded that living and preaching Jesus' gospel in America require the exacting test of Malcolm's nationalist critique.

THE IMPACT OF MALCOLM'S FAITH AND THEOLOGY UPON HIS NIGHTMARE

HOME TO ALLAH, HOME TO BLACKNESS

Malcolm's faith, like Martin's, was a product of the African-American religious experience. Unlike Martin's, it was defined by his total rejection of the religion of Christianity as he experienced it in black and white communities and as he reflected upon it.

Malcolm's alienation from Christianity began at an early age. When he went with his father to church as a child, what he saw and heard "confused and amazed" him. "I would sit goggle-eyed at my father jumping and shouting as he preached, with the congregation jumping and shouting behind him, their souls and bodies devoted to singing and praying." While his brother Philbert "loved church," Malcolm could not. "Even at that young age, I just couldn't believe in the Christian concept of Jesus as someone divine."[1]

More important for his rejection of Christianity than his befuddled experience in the black church were his experiences of violence and humiliation from "the good Christian white people" of Omaha, Nebraska, and Lansing, Michigan. He saw clearly the contradiction between what they said about Christian love, and how they treated his parents and other blacks, including himself. Even white people's best behavior toward blacks (for example, the Swerlins' kindness toward him) was more like their care of favorite pet animals than a mutual and loving relationship with human beings. "It just never dawned upon them," Malcolm said, reflecting back upon how the Swerlins treated him, ". . . that I wasn't a pet, but a human being. They didn't give me credit for having the same sensitivity, intellect, and understanding that they would have been ready and willing to recognize in a white boy in my position." The Swerlins and the other "good people" of Lansing treated him as if he were invisible, "talk[ing] about me," he said, "or about 'niggers,' as though I wasn't there, as if I wouldn't understand what the word meant. A hundred times a day, they used the word 'nigger.' " "Thus they never did really see *me.*"[2] Malcolm experienced not only "kindly condescension" but also the violent hate of white Christians who burned down his family's house, and harassed his mother until she lost her mind. Malcolm's rejection of Christianity did not arise so much from intellectual doubt as from his personal experience of being treated as less than human by white Christians.

Though Malcolm could not embrace his father's Christianity, he was pleased to share his father's enthusiasm for Marcus Garvey's "back to Africa" movement. Malcolm spoke of how the two of them attended Garveyite meetings together. "I remember seeing the big, shiny photographs of Marcus Garvey that were passed from hand to hand," he recalled with delight.

> The pictures showed what seemed to me millions of Negroes thronged in parade behind Garvey riding in a fine car, a big black man dressed in a dazzling uniform with gold braid on it, and he was wearing a thrilling hat with tall plumes. I remember hearing that he had followers not only in the United States but all around the world, and I remember how the meetings always closed with my father saying, several times, and the people chanting after him, "Up, you mighty race, you can accomplish what you will!"[3]

The death of Malcolm's father ended his attendance at the meetings of the Garveyites, the only group which made him proud to be black. His mother's mental breakdown left him without parental support and guidance as he searched for meaning for his life. His search took him from Lansing to the ghettos of Boston and New York. In both places, Malcolm's rejection of Christianity was expressed in the immoral and illegal life he lived and in his utter disdain for the life style of the "snooty" blacks and their churches. "No religious person," Malcolm said, ". . . could tell me anything. I had very little respect for most people who represented religion." He "sunk to the very bottom of the American white man's society." Malcolm described himself as a "predatory animal," a "vulture," "nervy and cunning enough to live by my wits, exploiting any prey that presented itself."[4]

Malcolm's life as a hustler and burglar landed him in a Massachusetts federal prison where he continued to hurl obscenities against the Christian God and that God's representatives. Then, all of a sudden, Malcolm's life was radically transformed. Through the teachings of Elijah Muhammad, the Messenger, he found Allah and respect for himself as a human being.

One can ask, Why did Malcolm discover self-respect in Elijah Muhammad's Nation of Islam and not in some other religious sect, perhaps even a Christian one? Although there are many perspectives from which to examine this question, I want to use it as an opportunity to make two comments about Malcolm's faith.

First, Elijah Muhammad's Nation of Islam was specifically designed to address the spiritual, social, economic, and political needs of the black underclass, particularly those in prisons and urban ghettos. When Malcolm heard the problack, pro-Islamic, antiwhite, and anti-Christian teaching of Elijah Muhammad, "it just clicked," he said, "a perfect echo of the black convict's lifelong experience." It was as if he had been blind and the "Messenger of Allah," Elijah Muhammad, opened his eyes so he could see the world as it really was. It was then that he began to realize why he hated himself and wanted to be white, as did most blacks. He also discovered why whites hated blacks. Muhammad told Malcolm the "true knowledge" of himself and of the history of black people and white people and of their religions. According to the Messenger Elijah Muhammad, " 'the true knowledge' . . . was that history had been 'whitened' in the white man's history books, and that the . . . Original Man was black, in the continent called Africa where the human race had emerged on the planet Earth." For a black person, for a person who had been treated like he was no more than an unwanted animal, to hear that he was *somebody,* a descendant of a great race of people, the ancient "tribe of Shabazz," was indeed "mind-blowing." It was a revelation that shook the very foundation of the world as Malcolm had known it. Elijah Muhammad gave Malcolm a metaphysical foundation for his affirmation of blackness and rebellion against white Western civilization, which had declared that he was not a human being. With Muhammad's philosophy to guide him, he was now ready to extol African culture and, as he said, "to devote the rest of my life to telling the white man the truth about himself—or die."[5]

Second, as the Nation of Islam was created for the specific needs of blacks, Euro-American Christianity was designed for the particular needs of whites who perceived themselves and their culture as the standard by which all others were to be judged. Therefore, God, Jesus, the angels, and all the heroic biblical characters were portrayed as white, and the devil and sin, of course, were often pictured as black. Malcolm remembered his parents and other black Christians singing, "Wash me and I'll be whiter than snow." With Christian churches and their theologians and preachers defining everything good in this life and the next as *white* and defining everything bad in this world and the next as *black,* how was it possible for that religion to bestow self-worth upon the *black* personhood of a prisoner like Malcolm? It seems that, in Malcolm's case, it was not possible. Only a *black* religion, a black God, could "resurrect" a person like Malcolm from the "dead," from the "grave of ignorance and shame," and stand him on his feet as a human being, prepared to die in the defense of the humanity of his people. As Malcolm testified:

> I, myself, being one who was lost and dead, buried here in the rubbish of the West in the thickest darkness of sin and ignorance (hoodwinked by the false teachings of the Slavemaster)—am able to stand upright today, PERPENDICULAR, on the square with my God (ALLAH) and my own kind ... able for the first time in 400 years to see and hear. ... I bear witness that MESSENGER ELIJAH MUHAMMAD has been taught (raised) by this Great God ALLAH, and today ... is ... teaching us and raising us from the ignorant dead.[6]

As Martin King's commitment to justice cannot be understood apart from his *faith,* Malcolm X's faith cannot be understood apart from his commitment to *justice.* This is a major difference between them. Martin received his faith at Ebenezer Baptist Church prior to his commitment to justice, a commitment that came to maturity in Montgomery. To be sure, his faith empowered and sustained him in that commitment; but his faith was not created in his fight for justice. In contrast to King, Malcolm's faith was indistinguishable from his commitment to justice on behalf of black people. That was why he said, "A Muslim is someone who is for the black man. I don't care if he goes to the Baptist Church seven days a week. The Honorable Elijah Muhammad says that a black man is born a Muslim by nature." Malcolm's faith was not simply a religious perspective that could be applied or related to the life experiences of blacks; rather, it was a *black* faith in the literal sense of having been created by blacks and for the specific purpose of achieving justice for the "Lost-Found Nation in this wilderness of North America." Martin's faith was universal; that is, it was meant to embrace *everybody,* which meant, in the modern world of Euro-America, that it was ultimately defined by *white people* and those who shared their values. Martin had to reinterpret a white religion, designed to enslave blacks, into a religion of black liberation. Malcolm, however, contended that black people "need a religious expression that is not dictated and controlled by their enemies," but rather, by themselves.[7]

Malcolm's religious commitment can be seen not only in his commitment to justice and his obedience to the Islamic moral code but also in his spirituality. In a moving passage of his *Autobiography* he told how difficult it was for him to "Turn to Allah . . . [and] pray to the East."

> The hardest test I ever faced in my life was praying. You understand. My comprehending, my believing the teachings of Mr. Muhammad had only required my mind's saying to me, "That's right!" or "I never thought of that." But bending my knees to pray—that *act*—well, that took me a week. You know what my life had been. Picking a lock to rob someone's house was the only way my knees had ever been bent before. I had to force myself to bend my knees. And waves of shame and embarrassment would force me back up. For evil to bend its knees, admitting its guilt, to implore the forgiveness from God, is the hardest thing in the world. It's easy for me to see and say that now. But then, when I was the personification of evil, I was going through it. Again, again, I would force myself back down into the praying-to-Allah posture. When finally I was able to make myself stay down—I didn't know what to say to Allah.[8]

Malcolm's religious commitment was defined by the important distinction between himself and Muhammad. Elijah Muhammad was often compared with Moses, who spoke for God, and Malcolm was identified with Aaron, who spoke for Moses. As only Moses spoke for God, because God chose him to tell Pharaoh to "let my people go" or suffer the dreadful consequences, likewise, only Elijah Muhammad, the "modern Moses," could speak for Allah today and tell America to let the "so-called Negroes" separate because America's "time is up." As Aaron's power was derived from what Moses told him to say, so Malcolm's power was derived from what Muhammad taught him: "We who represent [the Messenger] as his ministers know only what he has taught us. We know nothing of our own, have nothing of our own, and would be nothing if we were on our own. We are MESSENGER MUHAMMAD'S servants and helpers. HE'S THE MESSENGER. THE MAN! He alone has THE KEY!"[9] When Alex Haley asked Malcolm about the popular view that he was "the real brains and power of the movement," he shot back: "Sir, it's heresy to imply that I am in any way whatever even equal to Mr. Muhammad. No man on earth today is his equal. Whatever I am that is good, it is through what I have been taught by Mr. Muhammad."[10]

Although Malcolm's faith and theology were derived from the teachings of Elijah Muhammad, the latter, though regarded as a divine man, was not considered as equal to Allah. In actual Black Muslim practice, however, believers treated Muhammad with such reverence that it was sometimes difficult to observe any meaningful distinction between Allah and his Messenger. As has been true of many Christians in relation to Jesus and God, some members did not make the distinction. However, Malcolm made it. While he was prepared to die for Muhammad, to hurl "myself," he said, "between him and an assassin," he did discover that "there was something—one thing—greater than my reverence for Mr. Muhammad." The discovery occurred when Malcolm was in Cambridge to appear as a speaker at the Harvard Law School Forum. He happened to look through a window toward the apartment house that had been the hideout for his burglary gang nearly twenty years earlier. Malcolm said the experience "rocked" him "like a tidal wave." He was reminded of his previous "depraved life" and gave all the thanks for his deliverance to the religion of Islam and Allah.

Awareness came surging up in me—how deeply the religion of Islam had reached down into the mud to lift me up, to save me from being what I inevitably would have been: a dead criminal in a grave, or, if still alive, a flint-hard, bitter, thirty-seven-year-old convict in some penitentiary, or insane asylum. Or, at best, I would have been an old, fading Detroit Red, hustling, stealing enough for food and narcotics, and myself being stalked as prey by cruelly ambitious younger hustlers such as Detroit Red had been. But Allah had blessed me to learn about the religion of Islam, which had enabled me to lift myself up from the muck and the mire of this rotting world.[11]

Malcolm's reverence for the religion of Islam and his freedom to speak for the Black Muslims, a freedom bestowed upon him by Elijah Muhammad, gave him the opportunity to develop his own thinking about God, America, and the "so-called Negroes." As Malcolm became a popular speaker and participated in debates and panel discussions with black and white intellectuals, he was asked questions whose answers required more knowledge and imagination than what Elijah had taught him. He also discovered significant differences between the world as he experienced it and as Muhammad described it in his teachings. For a time the differences were small enough to be ignored, and Malcolm continued to represent Muhammad faithfully in everything he said.

"WHITE AMERICA IS DOOMED!"

This was one of Malcolm's most repeated and most controversial claims. It was not, however, an arbitrary assertion, intended merely to express his hatred of whites. Malcolm sometimes did use the language of vengeance, as in the notorious incident when he publicly rejoiced and encouraged others to rejoice in the deaths of 120 white people in an air crash in France.[12] However, the anger that fueled that action was not the source of his frequent statements about the impending destruction of white people. Rather the source of those statements was standard Black Muslim doctrine. According to that doctrine the doom of white America was based on: (1) the Black Muslim myth of Yacob; (2) the biblical theme of justice and judgment, especially as found in the prophets and the Revelation of John; and (3) historical observation.

As a Black Muslim, Malcolm accepted the myth of Yacob, which claimed that an evil black scientist created the devil white race six thousand years ago because they were destined to rule the world for that period of time. But today, according to Malcolm, following the teachings of the Prophet Muhammad, God has declared "the end of white world supremacy," because of whites' crimes against black people. Malcolm's nightmare about America was partly defined by this myth. He referred to it often in his many sermons at Black Muslims temples.[13]

Malcolm, however, seldom referred to the Yacob myth when he spoke to white audiences. Instead, he based his claim upon the biblical theme of justice and judgment and his analysis of the downfall of nations of the past. But whether Malcolm referred to the myth of Yacob, the Bible, or to history, his central claim regarding white America's doom was based upon his belief that "the all-wise Supreme Being" and "the great God of the universe" was also "the God of justice." White America's crime was slavery and segregation, hypocrisy and deceit. According to Malcolm, justice meant that *God* (not Malcolm or the Muslims or black people) must destroy America for its sins.

Of course, most whites and blacks did not want to hear Malcolm talk about America's coming end. In fact, most people were deeply offended by his apocalyptic preachments and labeled him as nothing but a teacher of hate and fomenter of violence. But Malcolm was not naive; he anticipated their rejection of his message. To support his claim, he called their attention to *their* Christian Bible and *their* history books.

> Before your pride causes you to harden your heart and further close your ears, and before your ignorance provokes laughter, search the Christian Scriptures. Search even the histories of other nations that sat in the same positions of wealth, power, and authority that these white Americans now hold . . . and see what God did to them. If God's unchanging laws of justice caught up with every one of the slave empires of the past, how dare you think White America can escape the harvest of unjust seeds planted by her white forefathers against our black forefathers here in this land of slavery![14]

"History," said Malcolm, "is repeating itself today." Just as Noah warned the people of his time of the coming flood and Lot warned the Sodomites of the coming fire, so God raised up Elijah Muhammad as the one to warn white America of its coming destruction. "We believe," Malcolm said, "that we are living in the time of 'prophecy fulfillment,' the time predicted by the ancient prophets of God," when "white nations" would have to stand before the "seat of justice" and be judged "according to the deeds they committed."[15]

Malcolm compared America's coming doom to the "downfall and destruction of ancient Egypt and Babylon." He often preached about the "great Doomsday, the final hour, when the ancient prophets predicted that God himself would appear in person, in the flesh, and with divine power He would bring about the judgment and the destruction of this present evil world." "No one shall escape the doom," said Malcolm, "except those who accept Allah as God, Islam as his only religion, and the Honorable Elijah Muhammad as his Messenger to the twenty-two million ex-slaves here in America."[16]

While Martin's theology focused on love and forgiveness and the hope that blacks and whites could create the American dream, could create the beloved community, Malcolm's theology stressed strict justice and stern punishment and the hope that God would destroy the entire white race and then establish a world of peace and good will among all blacks. "According to the Bible," Malcolm said, referring to Revelation

13:10, "Judgment Day is that final hour when God will cause 'those who led others into captivity to go into captivity themselves' . . . and 'those who killed others with the sword to be killed by the sword of justice themselves.' . . . This is justice!"[17]

Malcolm rejected Martin's idea that blacks should love whites and insisted instead that they should separate from them and get unto their own kind so that they could avoid the coming destruction of Western civilization. He interpreted justice, love, and hope in the light of the all-important symbol of blackness. In Malcolm's theology, God, Jesus, the prophets, and the "Original Man" were portrayed as black, and the devil and all evil things were pictured as white. Of course, to some persons, Malcolm's reversal of the color value system, exchanging the places of black and white, may appear to be nothing but reverse racism. But it was more than that. He was making a theological statement about God which is commonly found among peoples of the world whose religions portray God as being more than a mere extension of the ideology of the ruling class. In a society where blacks have been enslaved and segregated for nearly four centuries by whites because of their color and where evil has been portrayed as "black" and good as "white" in religious and cultural values, the idea that "God is black" is not only theologically defensible, but is a necessary corrective against the powers of domination. A just and loving God cannot be identified with the values of evil people. Indeed, a case could be made that white people created a God of "cheap grace" (to use Dietrich Bonhoeffer's well-known phrase) so that they would not be punished for the enormous crimes they have committed against the colored peoples of the world. What is clear, however, is that Malcolm's theology demands much more attention than the simplistic claim that he was a racist.

Malcolm's emphasis on justice *for* blacks "by any means necessary" in contrast to Martin's stress on justice for blacks through love *for* whites illuminates another important difference between them. From Martin's theology of love emerged his absolute adherence to nonviolence, and from Malcolm's theology of justice emerged his absolute commitment to self-defense. Malcolm despised Martin's "turn the other cheek" philosophy and insisted on "an eye for an eye" as the only language that white oppressors would understand.

ISLAM OF THE EAST

As Martin King was influenced by Western Christianity, Malcolm X was influenced by the religion of Islam in the Middle East, Africa, and Asia. It could be argued that as black church denominations were organized to meet the specific needs of black Christians who found white denominations inhospitable to their presence, the Nation of Islam was founded to meet the needs of black Islamic believers because Moslems from the East (living in the United States) were uninterested in their brothers and sisters in the African-American community. This analogy is only superficially true because while African-Americans had been closely associated with white Christianity, they had never been associated with the Islam of Middle Eastern immigrants.

The Nation of Islam was home-grown, founded in 1930 in the black community of Detroit. There was no direct historical connection between its origins and the worldwide Islamic community, except the Black Muslims' claim that their founder, Wallace D. Fard, came from the Holy City of Mecca. But even granting that dubious claim, it appears that the causes of the rise of the Black Muslims were located not in the historic Muslim lands, but in the United States. Black nationalism generally and Marcus Garvey and Noble Drew Ali in particular were the historical roots of the Nation of Islam. The Nation was a *black* religion whose meaning can best be understood by investigating the social and psychological impact of urban life upon black people in America. The doctrines and practices of traditional Islam were secondary to the main themes of Elijah Muhammad's Nation: the rejection of Christianity as the white man's religion, and the affirmation of Elijah Muhammad's interpretation of Islam as the "natural religion of the black man," this interpretation having been given to Muhammad by Allah ("in the person of Wallace D. Fard") for the purpose of restoring the self-esteem and self-confidence of the "Lost-Found Nation of so-called Negroes in the West."

Locating the origin of the Nation of Islam in the African-American experience is supported by Muhammad's and Malcolm's frequent quotations from the Bible. The Bible, not the Quran, is the central document in the black religious experience in America. Malcolm would never have gained wide acceptance in the African-American community without his profound knowledge and creative use of the Bible, the sacred book for black Christians.

Although Wallace D. Fard was the founder of the Nation, Elijah Muhammad was most responsible for shaping its doctrines and practices. He elevated Fard to the status of "God" or "Allah" and then bestowed upon himself the title of "Messenger," the one who was taught and sent by Allah to "resurrect from the dead" "these poor, dumb, deaf, and blind so-called Negroes" who are like "Dry Bones in the Valley."[18]

Consistent with his background in the Baptist ministry, Elijah Muhammad organized the Nation of Islam in a manner similar to the black church, with ministers who were accountable to him and who were expected to be articulate leaders in the community. His main concern, however, was to address the needs and problems of poor blacks in the urban ghetto, needs and problems which black churches had been incapable of addressing and solving or had simply ignored. The problems in the black community were obvious: drugs, crime, unemployment, prostitution, gambling, juvenile delinquency, and other forms of vice and evil prevalent in the ghetto. The causes of these problems were also obvious: white racism and the lack of self-esteem among black people. To get rid of the problems in the black community, Elijah Muhammad concluded that one must get rid of the causes. He, therefore, designed the Nation of Islam for the purpose of identifying the white man as the enemy who used Christianity as a tool to teach blacks to hate themselves.

Malcolm X thought of himself not only as a minister in the Nation of Islam but also as a part of the worldwide Islamic community. His identity with Islam in the East, however, was not as important to him as Western Christianity was for Martin King. Malcolm's primary religious identity was defined by the teachings of Elijah Muhammad, whom he regarded as the "Second Moses," Allah's last Messenger to blacks in the United States. When Moslem scholars from the East or in the United States questioned the "religious authenticity" of Elijah Muhammad, saying that his teachings contradicted the Islamic precepts of the Quran, Malcolm tenaciously defended the validity of the Messenger's beliefs. As the Nation's "National Minister," Malcolm became its most respected apologist or theologian. While Malcolm acknowledged that Elijah Muhammad's Nation accented different ideas from Muslims in the East, he argued that the different sociopolitical and psychospiritual condition of the so-called Negro in the West justified Muhammad's special emphases. "We are teaching the true Islamic faith," he said, "but we are making it applicable to the peculiar condition faced by the American black man." Furthermore, Malcolm reminded his critics, Muslims throughout the world were not identical in doctrine or practice, but also differed from each other according to their environment. In the final analysis, a Muslim, said Malcolm, was "one who submits to God's will and obeys God's rules for right conduct by living a righteous life."[19] Malcolm did not seek to universalize the doctrines and practices of Muhammad's Nation. Rather, he defended its independence, not only from white America but also from so-called orthodox Islam. Since Elijah Muhammad was appointed as the Messenger to the so-called Negro in the West by Allah himself, not even the Muslims in the East could invalidate his divine mission.

Although Malcolm defended the validity and independence of the Black Muslim religion, he saw sooner than Muhammad the need to build bridges to the worldwide Islamic community. Malcolm's international perspective in religion and politics began in the 1950s. He realized that recognition of the Nation of Islam by historic Islam would effectively counter the frequent criticism that the Nation was the personal cult of Muhammad and not a part of the Islamic community. Malcolm made an exploratory trip to the Middle East and Africa early in 1959 to determine how Muhammad would be received if he went. He had an audience with President Gamal Abdel Nasser of Egypt and other African leaders.[20] Upon his return, he urged Muhammad to take the pilgrimage to Mecca, which he did, along with two sons. This event silenced many critics who had claimed that Muhammad would not be permitted to visit the holy city.

Malcolm also entertained several prominent persons from the Moslem world in Harlem and attended their public affairs, expressing the Black Muslims' solidarity with the Arab countries in their dispute with Israel. Malcolm and the Black Muslims were particularly critical of Ralph Bunche, then Under Secretary of the United Nations, calling him an "international Uncle Tom" and "the George Washington of Israel" for what they suspected was his favoring of Israel in his negotiation of the Arab-Israeli conflict. Malcolm's support of the Arab world was so passionate that he was frequently labeled as anti-Semitic. In a widely reported lecture at Princeton University, Thurgood Marshall denounced the Black Muslims as "being run by a bunch of thugs organized from prisons and jails, and financed, I'm sure, by Nasser or some Arab group." Marshall, of course, was reacting to their public attack upon the "white man" and their seemingly uncritical support of Third World people of color. While no financial connections existed between the Black Muslims and Arab nations, the former leaped at every opportunity to make close public ties with their Moslem brothers and sisters in the Third World. Malcolm was primarily responsible for this international focus. He read to a Harlem rally Elijah Muhammad's cablegram to President Nasser on the occasion of an African-Asian conference, and a few weeks later he read Nasser's response to Muhammad. Malcolm also attended the Third Pakistan Republic Day in Los Angeles. Especially important was the appearance of Mahmoud Youssef Shawarbi — a member of the Supreme Council on Islamic Affairs — at Temple Number Seven in 1960. Speaking before an audience of 2500 Black Muslims, Shawarbi rebutted the story which said that he had "denounced U.S. Muslims for teaching spurious doctrines." "I have denounced no one," he said. "We are all Muslims and Muslims do not denounce each other." Shawarbi went on to salute the Black Muslims for their contribution to the teaching of Islam in the New York community. "I congratulate you," he said, "on the work you are doing, and I thank God that once a week the teaching of Islam can be heard on the radio in this area." He was referring to "Mr. Muhammad Speaks," heard each Wednesday evening.[21]

Malcolm wanted Black Muslims to know that their religion was not "something that . . . Muhammad himself made up," as it was described by the white and black media, but was a part of a worldwide Islamic community. "Simply by accepting the divine leadership of the Honorable Elijah Muhammad," he told a radio audience in Atlanta, "we have 725 million Muslim brothers and sisters in Africa, in Asia, and in the brotherhood of Islam."[22] He also wanted blacks in America to know that they were not alone in their fight for justice but were part of a worldwide black liberation movement in Asia, Africa, and Latin America. He rejected the idea that blacks in America were a minority. Rather he contended that they were a part of the colored majority of the world. Malcolm's contacts with prominent persons in the Moslem world and his dependence upon the doctrines and practices of historic Islam proved to be important for him after his break with Muhammad, which is a subject that will be discussed in the next chapter.

MALCOLM AND MARTIN: RELIGION AND THEOLOGY

Because of Malcolm's public image as an advocate of hate and violence, people did not—and often still do not—acknowledge his profound religious commitment. Even Malcolm's devotees often ignore the central place of religion in his perspective, interpreting him as if his political philosophy can be understood apart from his faith and theology. Malcolm was a deeply religious person who thought of himself as a minister of God (and was pleased to be called "Minister Malcolm") just like the Reverends Martin King and Adam Clayton Powell, Jr.

The reason that sympathetic interpreters often miss the central role of religion in Malcolm's thinking is that religion is commonly separated from struggles for justice. That was why Martin had such a difficult time getting the white church involved in the civil rights movement, and why liberation theologians in the Third World are so controversial today. Many people think that religion has everything to do with an individual's personal relationship with God and nothing to do with society and one's fight for justice in it. When Malcolm X identified the fight for justice as *the central religious act,* his message was usually misunderstood. His friends often avoided the subject of religion and ignored the strict moral code he faithfully obeyed. Malcolm's enemies accused him of using religion as a façade for fomenting hate and violence.

Even though Martin is generally and appropriately credited with deep religious commitment, a case could be made that Malcolm was more religious than Martin, if we evaluated the matter in terms of their obedience to the moral code of the religion they professed. Martin acknowledged that he preached a morality in church that he sometimes violated in the world, while Malcolm faithfully obeyed the strict moral code of the Black Muslim religion, refraining from smoking, drinking, fornication and adultery, and eating pork and corn bread.

However, compliance with their professed moral codes is not the central criterion for judging the degree or quality of the two men's religious commitment. I contend that the depth of any religious commitment should be judged by one's commitment to justice for humanity, using the liberation activity of human beings as the lens through which one sees God. By this criterion both Martin and Malcolm must be considered as deeply religious persons.

Despite Malcolm's public emphasis on the differences between himself and Martin, he could have pointed out important similarities in their theological perspectives. For example, both appealed to the Bible as a major source for their theological claims. They often referred to the same biblical characters, parables, and events: Moses, Daniel, Jesus, Paul, Lazarus, the lost-found sheep, the wheat and the tares, the prodigal son, and the great liberation event—the Exodus. Both frequently preached from the Book of Revelation. They also placed the themes of justice, love, and hope at the heart of their theologies. They frequently talked on the themes of heaven and hell, suffering and the resurrection. Each had a transforming personal vision of God, Martin in his Montgomery kitchen and Malcolm in his prison cell. These striking similarities between them were due chiefly to their common grounding in the African-American religious experience.

The similarities between Martin's and Malcolm's theologies also bring to mind their differences. Although both of them accented justice, love, and hope, they gave different meanings to the three themes and placed them in different relationships to each other. (1) Martin made love his major emphasis among the three and centered his interpretation of them on the cross of Jesus Christ; Malcolm made justice his major emphasis and interpreted the three themes in the light of his views of blackness, the dominant symbol in his theology. (2) While Martin was concerned about justice for black people, he wanted to achieve it through love of the oppressor (that is, through nonviolence). For Malcolm, however, love of black people was primary, and that was why justice occupied the highest priority in his theology. (3) Martin's hope was defined by what he believed about God's love of humanity as he saw it revealed in the cross and resurrection of Jesus. Malcolm's hope was expressed in what he believed about God's love of black people and his "judgment of white America," "the coming DOOM of this wicked land of bondage, because of its mistreatment of God's CHOSEN PEO-PLE (the so-called Negroes . . .)."[23]

Finally, Martin and Malcolm had different theological views of white people. Martin's theology saw whites as essentially good. He expected white Christians, especially ministers, to join him and other blacks in their fight for justice in America. Malcolm's Black Muslim theology and commonsense historical observation convinced him that whites were devils, incapable of doing good. Thus it was useless to try to gain "freedom, justice, and equality" for blacks by appealing to the religious convictions of whites. In Malcolm's view Christianity was proven both false and wicked by its age-old association with white people.

MALCOLM'S EXPOSITION OF RELIGIONS AND RACE

CHRISTIANITY AS THE WHITE MAN'S RELIGION

Malcolm X began his ministry with a scathing attack upon the white man's Christianity and the role it played in the physical, mental, and spiritual oppression of black people. According to Malcolm, whites had no moral conscience that was applicable to their relations with blacks. The morality which whites derived from Christianity was limited to their own kind and never applied to blacks and other Third World people, because whites did not regard them as human beings. Slavery, colonization, and segregation—which were accompanied by the "destruction of the African civilization"—clearly demonstrated the devil-like behavior of whites in Europe and America toward the dark-skinned peoples of the world.

In language reminiscent of David Walker a century earlier, Malcolm contended that Christianity, instead of making whites treat blacks justly, served only as a tool for enslaving them, always trying to make blacks content with happiness in the next world as whites exploited them in this one. That was why Malcolm referred to Christianity as a "perfect slave religion" and a "slave-making lie," "invented by the wicked white race." He claimed that

> Christianity is the white man's religion. The Holy Bible in the white man's hands and his interpretations of it have been the greatest single ideological weapon for enslaving millions of non-white human beings. Every country the white man has conquered with his guns, he has always paved the way, and salved his conscience, by carrying the Bible and interpreting it to call people "heathens" and "pagans"; then he sends his guns, then his missionaries behind the guns to mop up.[24]

Malcolm's opposition to Christianity was not based upon his examination of its creeds and doctrines or the scholarly writings of its theologians. Rather, it was defined by the *practices* of people who called themselves Christians. "If you want to know what [the Christian white man] is, examine his deeds," Malcolm told a Harlem rally. "Forget his words. He's got a whole lot of pretty sounding words. Watch his deeds. His deeds are like the deeds of a snake, . . . the deeds of a beast. Why, nothing but a race of beasts would take dogs and sic them on black children and black women, nothing but a race of beasts." In this speech, Malcolm was angry about the recent events in Birmingham. But whether speaking of some contemporary act of brutality like the use of Bull Connor's dogs or of the inhuman behavior of a slave trader like John Hawkins, who used a ship named *Jesus* to transport his human black cargo, Malcolm was determined to name the criminals who were primarily responsible for the crimes committed against his people. He was not trying to be "objective" in his analysis of Christianity, that is, seeking to present a case against Christianity that would have been acceptable to white Christian oppressors. "Everybody looks at the world subjectively," Malcolm told a University of Chicago reporter, "and the oppressor is bound to look at a situation differently than does the oppressed."[25] Malcolm looked at the world through his experience at the bottom of American society and through his deep commitment to the freedom of his people, combined with historical research and native intelligence — all of which made him deeply suspicious of Christianity and the Bible as they were interpreted and practiced in the white community.

Malcolm's critique of Christianity as white and the Bible as a "poison book" should not be dismissed as uninformed comments of an outsider. Malcolm was a well-informed student of the Bible and a master critic of Christianity. His knowledge of Christianity and of the Bible was derived from both personal experience and disciplined study. The Christianity of his mother and father (and of other black and white Christians in his early experience), his later studies in prison, the tutelage of Elijah Muhammad, and his perpetual study for his evangelistic work as a Black Muslim minister gave him the knowledge to make his the most formidable *race* critique of Euro-American Christianity in the modern world.

Malcolm did not reject Jesus and the Bible as such. Although he did not share the Christian belief in Jesus' divinity, he did regard him as one of the great prophets, like Moses and Muhammad. He believed that the Bible had been "poisoned," that is, used by white theologians to corrupt the minds of Negroes throughout the centuries. "Anything you take that . . . makes you helpless . . . [is] poison," he said. Since the Bible has been tampered with by white translators and interpreters, it should not be read literally. The Bible must be read as a book of divine prophecy that was being fulfilled in the life and teachings of the Honorable Elijah Muhammad. The "ancient Scriptures," Malcolm said, contain "symbolic stories" that "paint a prophetic picture of today, of America, and of . . . 'Negroes' here in America." He identified Elijah Muhammad as a modern Noah or Lot or David, even as a modern Jesus, but most often as a modern Moses. As the emancipator of the Israelite slaves, Moses *separated* them from the Egyptian slaveholders and led them to a land of their own. Moses' message of separation was being realized in the present day in the person of Elijah Muhammad. The Exodus, said Malcolm, was not a historical event which happened in Egypt but rather a symbolic, prophetic picture of what was happening in America through the teachings and work of Muhammad, separating the "so-called Negroes" from their white oppressors. That was why Malcolm said that "history is repeating itself today," because what happened in the story of Pharaoh and the Egyptians was also imminent in present-day America. As Moses tried to warn Pharaoh, so Elijah Muhammad was trying to warn white America: "Let my people go!" Unless the so-called Negroes were allowed to go free and establish their own land, "God will take this entire continent away from [whites]; and [America] will cease to exist as a nation."[26]

For white Christians and others who were influenced by them, Malcolm's theology appeared to be nothing but racism with a black face. But that kind of quick dismissal of Malcolm failed to grasp the central insight of his race critique of Christianity. It was like dismissing Marx's class critique of religion by labeling him an economic determinist or Nietzsche's radical critique by claiming that his philosophy prepared the way for German Nazism. Flaws in a critic's perspective do not necessarily render the whole critique invalid. The task was to discover what was true and false about the practice and the thinking of people who were known as Christians.

Although white Christians did not like what Malcolm said about them, much of what he said was the truth. One of his chief concerns was to uncover the role of European Christianity in the politico-economic exploitation and culturo-spiritual degradation of black people. Malcolm's analysis of the role of white Christianity was so penetrating, so persuasive, and so wide-ranging in its depths that arguments to refute him seemed worthless. Most white Christians did not even try to answer Malcolm. Dumbfounded by Malcolm's attack on Christianity at Boston University School of Theology, a person in the audience asked him about his "image of Christians and Christianity." "Your Christian countries . . . are the countries of Europe [and] North and South America," Malcolm shot back. "Predominately, that's Christianity." Malcolm refused to engage in a theoretical debate about the *theological* identity of Christianity. "Whether that's it technically, I don't know; whether that's it because they practice what Jesus taught, we're not getting into that." Malcolm did not speak as an academic theologian but rather as a grass-roots activist whose critique was defined by his solidarity with the victims of white Christians.

> The Christian world usually is what we call the Western world. Now what do I think, what is my image? The exploitation, colonization of the dark nations or . . . lands was done by nations that today are known as Christian powers. Christians made slaves here in America out of twenty million black people who today are called second-class citizens. . . . The people in Africa . . . today . . . are trying to get free from countries who represented themselves to the Africans as Christian nations. . . . Wherever you find dark people or non-white people today . . . trying to get freedom, they are trying to get freedom from the people who represent themselves as Christians; and if you go to them and ask them their picture of a Christian, they'll tell you "an exploiter, a slavemaster." In America the definition would be one who promises you equal rights for a hundred years and never gives it to you.[27]

Unfortunately, most white American theologians and ministers ignored Malcolm's race critique of Christianity. They continued to teach, preach, and write theological essays as if Malcolm did not exist or was not worth serious consideration. White churches and seminaries often invited Martin King to speak but rarely Malcolm. Located only a few blocks from Temple Number Seven in Harlem where Malcolm preached regularly, Union Theological Seminary, well known for its liberalism on race and other matters, did not invite him to speak to its community. Union's failure to provide Malcolm an opportunity to present his views was surprising since its students and faculty must have been aware, not only of his well-attended unity rallies in Harlem, but of his enormous influence in the black community throughout the country. It would appear that white seminaries and churches did not invite Malcolm to speak because their theologians and ministers did not regard racism as a serious theological problem and thus did not care what blacks in the ghetto thought about their doctrines and theologies. Liberal white theologians and churchpeople were influenced by King's philosophy of race relations, which they viewed as antithetical to everything that Malcolm advocated. Boston University School of Theology was one of the few seminaries which offered Malcolm the opportunity to present his views. He spoke there twice during 1960 (15 February and 24 May).

That was due largely to Malcolm's acquaintance with C. Eric Lincoln, who was then a graduate student writing his Ph.D. dissertation on the Black Muslims. It is also significant that Boston University School of Theology had distinguished itself among white seminaries for having a large number of African-American graduate students.[28]

In contrast to Union and most seminaries, Columbia and Barnard, City, Hunter, and Queens Colleges invited Malcolm to speak, as did many other universities and colleges in New York and in other cities. He spoke three times at Harvard and made lecture appearances at Yale, the University of Chicago, Berkeley, Brown, Cornell, and Michigan State. In fact, Malcolm was one of the most sought-after campus speakers during the 1960s. Sometimes university and college officials cancelled the invitations by student organizations to Malcolm because he was so controversial. Among them were Howard University, City College, Berkeley, and Queens College. In each case, the persistence of students and faculty, appealing to academic freedom, prevailed and Malcolm appeared at a later date. As we will observe in the next chapter, the responses of college and university whites, especially students, to his race critique of America and Christianity had a transforming effect upon his religious perspective, enlarging it and eliminating the worst elements of the Black Muslim separatist theology. Perhaps if white religious scholars and preachers had taken Malcolm's race critique seriously, he could have prepared them for the rise of black liberation theology in the United States and South Africa and other expressions of liberation theology in the Third World. They also might have influenced him to see Christianity in a different light.

Malcolm opposed Christianity not only because of the evil practices of white Christians but also because of the negative effect it had upon black people: "Find a black man who has raped a woman," he bellowed to 1500 blacks in Camden, New Jersey, "a black man who is a drunk, or a black man in the gutter, and you will find a black man who is a Christian!" He blamed the plight of blacks upon their acceptance of Christianity, "a religion concocted by the white man."[29]

Malcolm was especially critical of the negative, *white* images of Christianity. "Our slavemaster gave us a blond, blue-eyed, pale-skinned 'god' for us to worship and admire," Malcolm told blacks. "The religions of other people make them proud of what they are," but Christianity, he said, was "designed to make us look down on black and up at white." It made blacks feel inferior because we were taught that " 'God' cursed us black." This meant that "we are supposed to feel honored while serving the white race of Christians." Christianity was nothing but "white supremacy," completely "designed to fill [blacks'] hearts with the desire to be white." "A white Jesus. A white virgin. White angels.

White everything. But a black Devil, of course."[30]

Unlike Martin King, who accepted the European images of Christianity, Malcolm knew that no people could respect themselves if they worshiped a God who looked like their enemies. That was why he said that we black people "should not worship a man who doesn't look like us, act like us, walk like us or even smell like us." According to Malcolm, "every nationality of people serve their own god. Chinese have Chinese gods, Japanese have Japanese gods, the whites have a white god but the Negroes have only a white god."[31]

ISLAM AS THE RELIGION OF THE BLACK MAN

As Malcolm rejected Christianity as a "white-controlled . . . religion," he accepted Islam as the "true" or "natural religion of the black man." "It is designed," he said, "to undo in our minds what the white man has done to us. It's designed to undo the type of brainwashing that we had to undergo for four hundred years at the hands of the white man."[32]

Following the teachings of Elijah Muhammad, Malcolm, particularly at Black Muslim temple meetings, equated Christianity with "slavery, suffering, and death." It was symbolized by the U.S. flag and "a painting of a black man hanged from a tree" beneath an image of the cross. Islam, however, was symbolized by the "crescent and star" and was identified with "freedom, justice, and equality." "Which one will survive the war of Armageddon?" was the rhetorical question which Malcolm encouraged blacks to ponder, as he proclaimed Allah's imminent destruction of the white man's Christian civilization. As a Black Muslim minister, Malcolm was certain that the only solution to the oppression of black people in America was to separate from white people and their religion of Christianity and to integrate with the "religion of God," Islam, as defined by the teachings and the work of the Messenger Elijah Muhammad.

When in 1954 Malcolm went to Harlem as the head of Temple Number Seven, it was a small storefront with few members. There were many competing nationalist voices attempting to gain the attention of the black community. But the vast majority of blacks in Harlem, as in every city in the United States, were Christians, searching for meaning in a white-controlled society. "I knew the temple that I could build," he said, "if I could get to those Christians." In order to present persuasively the Nation of Islam as the "cure" of "the black man's spiritual, mental, moral, economic, and political sickness," Malcolm reasoned that his first task was to convince blacks that whites were the cause of their deprivation and that Christianity was the tool that whites used to corrupt the minds of black people, thereby preventing them from doing anything about their "extremely wretched condition." As Christians dispersed from their Sunday worship services, Malcolm and other Muslims "fished" for them, passing out leaflets and inviting them to come by Temple Number Seven at 2:00 P.M. and "hear how the white man kidnapped and robbed and raped our black race." To Malcolm's apparent surprise and great delight he discovered that Christians were "the best fishing audience of all, by far the best-conditioned audience for Mr. Muhammad's teachings."[33]

As black Christians began to visit the temple, Malcolm "tailored the teachings for them," speaking in an "emotionally charged" style which blacks called "good preaching." With great analytical skill, he perfected the method of shocking black Christians into a radical questioning of the origin and function of Christianity in their community. He told them that they worshiped an "unknown," "spooky God" and a "white Jesus," both of whom were invented by the white man for the purpose of teaching them to "look into the sky for heaven" as he robbed them "deaf, dumb, and blind" on this earth.

Black Christians bristled when they heard Malcolm's blanket condemnation of their faith. Malcolm, however, anticipated their objections:

> You don't want to believe what I am telling you, brothers and sisters? Well, I'll tell you what you do. You go out of here, you just take a good look around where you live. Look at not only how *you* live, but look at how anybody that you *know* lives—that way, you'll be sure that you're not just a bad-luck accident. And when you get through looking at where *you* live, then you take you a walk down across Central Park, and start to look at what this white God has brought to the white man. I mean, take yourself a look down there at how the white man is living!
>
> And don't stop there. In fact, you won't be able to stop for long—his doormen are going to tell you "Move on!" But catch a subway and keep on downtown. Anywhere you may want to get off, *look* at the white man's apartments, businesses! Go right on down to the tip of Manhattan Island that this devilish white man stole from the trusting Indians for twenty-four dollars! Look at his City Hall, down there; look at his Wall Street! Look at yourself! Look at *his* God![34]

It was difficult not to be persuaded by Malcolm's penetrating analysis. He was adept at exposing the moral contradictions of Christianity. "You think you are a Christian," he said, "and yet you see your so-called white Christian brother hanging black Christians on trees. You say that the white man loves you and yet he has done every evil act against you whenever he has had the opportunity. The white man has everything while he is living and he tells you to be a good slave and when you die you will have more than he has up in Beulah's Land." "We 'so-called Negroes,' are in pitiful shape," said Malcolm, as he pointed to the images of self-hate in the worship of black Christians. "We have been down on our knees looking up and praying to a picture of a white, blond and blue-eyed Jesus. That proves to you that we have been doing nothing but worshiping the white man and are still doing it. Get up off your knees," he told black Christians. "Come out of the sky!" "Stop . . . praying to spirits in the sky." "Build heaven on earth."[35]

Malcolm contended that religion must not be separated from the whole of life. We should evaluate it by the material benefits it bestows upon those who believe in it. "If religion means a way of life, and life's necessities are food, clothing and shelter, then we should not separate religion from economics," he proclaimed over WLIB, a Harlem radio station. "Christianity," he continued, "offers Negroes its economic program of milk and honey (food), white robes, golden slippers (clothing), and mansions (shelter) up in the sky after they die, . . . whereas Mr. Elijah Muhammad teaches us that in Islam we can get all of life's necessities right here on earth in this life if we will awaken, unite, and put forth the necessary effort."[36]

According to Malcolm, Christianity and Islam are radical opposites. Christianity is white nationalism; Islam is black nationalism. Christianity enslaves blacks; Islam liberates them. Christianity divides blacks; Islam unites them. Christianity "teaches that black is a curse"; Islam teaches that "it is a blessing to be black." Christianity urges blacks to love whites and to be nonviolent toward them. Islam encourages blacks to love themselves, turn the other cheek toward each other, but to defend themselves against the violence of their enemies. Christianity teaches that "hell [is] down in the ground to which we go after we die." Islam teaches that "hell is right here in North America." Christianity is a Western religion whose adherents are primarily found in Europe and North and South America. Islam is an Eastern, nonwhite religion whose "vast world" "stretches from the China seas to the sunny shores of West Africa."[37]

Malcolm frequently described Christianity as a "slave-making lie" and Islam as "the true religion." In a lecture on "The Black Revolution," presented to an audience of Christians and Black Muslims at Abyssinian Baptist Church in Harlem, Malcolm said that "Islam is the religion of the *naked truth, naked truth, undressed truth, truth that is not dressed up . . .*," repeating himself each time for emphasis, as his audience responded enthusiastically, shouting, "That's right! That's right!" He continued:

Truth will open our eyes and enable us to see the white wolf as he really is. Truth will stand us on our own feet. Truth will make us walk for ourselves instead of leaning on others who mean our people no good. Truth not only shows us who our enemy is, truth also gives us the strength and the know-how to separate ourselves from the enemy. Only a blind man will walk into the open embrace of his enemy, and only a blind people, a people who are blind to the truth about their enemies, will seek to embrace or integrate with the enemy.[38]

Malcolm was a spellbinding orator with bitter wit, power, and an impressive, down-to-earth intellect. Blacks loved his angry eloquence. Even devout Christians found themselves crying out, "Yes, that's right!," "Amen!" A Harlem woman told black journalist William Worthy: "Honey child, you *know* those Muslims are telling the truth about the white folks. I'm not joining up, but I'm not against them either."[39]

Malcolm understood his calling as truth-telling—telling the "plain," "sharp," "naked," "uncompromising" truth, especially about "hell" and the "devil." Speaking to blacks, he said:

Hell is when you're dumb. Hell is when you're a slave. Hell is when you don't have freedom and when you don't have justice. And when you don't have equality, that's hell. . . . And the devil is the one who deprives you of justice . . . equality . . . civil rights. The devil is the one who robs you of your right to be a human being. I don't have to tell you who the devil is. You know who the devil is.[40]

During the 1950s, the "Negro preachers" were a special object of Malcolm's critique. He referred to them as " 'imps' and 'tools' of the white race." He also called them "Pharaoh's Ordained Magicians," "religious Uncle Toms," "puppets," "parrots," and "religious fakers." His critique of the "ignorant, greedy Negro preacher" was similar to his attack upon the "brainwashed, integration-mad Negro leader" and was nearly as harsh as his comments about "the devil white man." As with the close ties between the Negro leader and the white man, a similar tie existed between the Negro preacher and the white man. Both benefited from the "miserable plight" of the black poor.

Malcolm's critique of Negro preachers can be classified into three main but related points. First, they preached heaven in the sky, with disastrous economic consequences. It was the preachers who urged building churches instead of factories and supermarkets. As poor blacks spend their money on churches, getting ready for heaven, Negro preachers and the white man are living in luxury *now*. "The Negro preachers are pretending to lead you," he told an audience in Los Angeles. "He is leading you into deeper economic slavery. In fact, he is leading you into the pit of Hell. And, above all, he prepares you to die. The Negro preacher is teaching you to look for a better life after death. This theory keeps you disunited and diverts your attention and hinders your development economically." Negro preachers should be urging blacks to acquire economic stability and independence by building supermarkets and factories. Like the white man, blacks, Malcolm contended, must build their heaven on earth by providing food, clothes, shelter, and jobs for their own, thereby relieving themselves of the necessity of begging the white man for basic material necessities.[41]

Second, Negro preachers preached love of whites, with disastrous political consequences. It was the preacher, he said, "who taught us to love, be patient, understanding, forgiving, 'turn-the-other-cheek' to the cruel white Christian slavemaster, who was holding a Bible in one hand and the Lyncher's Rope in the other." Malcolm contended that the same thing was happening in his day. He made a tour of the South in 1960, preaching in such places as Birmingham, New Orleans, Atlanta, and Tampa. The headlines of the *New Jersey Herald News* read: "Malcolm X, Blasts Uncle Tom's in Ga." (17 December 1960), "Malcolm X Stirs South" (31 December 1960), and " 'Dixie Negro Will Revolt' " (7 January 1961). In Atlanta, Malcolm spoke before the Interdenominational Ministerial Alliance and before students and faculty at Gammon Theological Seminary, Atlanta University, and Morehouse and Spelman Colleges. He told everyone that the " 'hat-in-hand' Uncle Tom approach" promoted by the Negro Christian church was out of step with a "changing world today." Malcolm demonstrated the kind of approach needed during his encounter with Arthur Schlesinger, Jr., a prominent Harvard professor and presidential adviser, who called the Muslims racists in a speech at Atlanta University. "Malcolm X Rips JFK Advisor" was the *Pittsburgh Courier* (4 February 1961) headline. The same event was also reported in the *New Jersey Herald News*: "Muslims Give JFK Man a 'Fit': Ga. Muslims, Sympathizers 'Shake Up' Dr. Schlesinger" (4 February 1961).[42] In the encounter, Malcolm demonstrated that Schlesinger was not sufficiently informed to define the Muslims as racists. But more importantly, he showed blacks how to talk to white people.

In Atlanta Malcolm's critique of the black church was somewhat more restrained than that which he unleashed in other parts of the South; this was partly because of the makeup of his Atlanta audiences — college and university students and faculty. In Birmingham, New Orleans, and Tampa, he made a scathing condemnation of Negro preachers. "It is time to throw aside the religious chains placed on our minds by Negro preachers and unite behind Muslim leader Elijah Muhammad, so we can stand up like men and protect our women and children," Malcolm told his Birmingham audience. He accused preachers of making " 'religious cowards' of the oppressed black masses by preaching a gospel of 'nonviolence and peaceful suffering' in the face of increasing white hostility and attacks."

The South was Martin King's territory and Alabama was the state where he led the successful bus boycott. Malcolm was well aware of Martin's dominating presence. Without using Martin's name, Malcolm attacked his philosophy of nonviolence, which was the main motivation behind the sit-ins that were sweeping the South at the time: "If the Negro clergy didn't discourage us from participating in violent action in Germany, Japan and Korea to defend white America from her enemies, why do these same Negro clergymen become so vocal when our oppressed people want to take the same militant stand against these white brute beasts here in America who are now endangering the lives and welfare of our women and children?"[43]

In New Orleans and Tampa, Malcolm continued his attack, warning about the dangers of the " 'cowardice-producing narcotic' of nonviolence and peace suffering which has been camouflaged under a religious label and injected into [the black masses'] brain[s] by the traitorous Negro clergymen." He stated: "If the Negro preacher is going to disarm the oppressed black masses with a doctrine of cowardice disguised as 'Christian love,' who is going to teach the white man to love his enemies, turn the other cheek, and peaceful suffering . . . or is the Negro clergy being paid to disarm our people with the slave master's one-sided religion?"[44]

Malcolm was disturbed not only about the Negro preachers' "turn-the-other-cheek philosophy" but was even more upset about their failure to advocate "love your own kind." Self-hate was the number one crime of the black community against itself, and the Negro preachers promoted it by ignoring it. Malcolm's personal experience of self-hate in the ghettos of Boston and New York fueled his opposition to it. He labeled Christianity the main poison which Negro preachers used to destroy self-respect among their own people. "Churches should be bombed and preachers killed," he railed in a moment of intense rage. Such outbursts alienated Negro preachers from Malcolm and made dialogue nearly impossible. His concern, however, was to emphasize, as strongly as he knew how, the detrimental effect of Christianity upon the black community. "We have more churches and pray more than any other people on earth and are worse off. . . ." Why? Because Negroes had a religion that made them "double cross" themselves. It is "so way out . . . it makes it almost impossible for [Negroes] to use logic in analyzing [their] problems." Thus they were politically dead, completely incapable of developing the unity necessary for nationhood.[45]

Third, Malcolm charged Negro preachers with falsely accusing Elijah Muhammad of teaching hatred. He felt they should be supporting the Messenger instead of parroting the white man. Speaking on WLIB's "Voice of Radio Free Africa" program (20 July 1958), Malcolm declared: "The greedy Negro preachers are the willing tools of the very white man who is responsible for our downtrodden people's wretched condition, and it hurts the preachers to see Mr. Muhammad exposing the guilty slavemaster whom they have grown to trust, love, and idolize." How could they accuse Muhammad of teaching hate and fail to point out the evil deeds of the white man? "The white man brags about how he stole this country from the Indians," he reminded his audience. But Negro preachers do not call that hate.

> If it is not hate to say how the white man stole this country from the Indians, then why is it hate to teach our people how this same white man kidnapped us from the East, brought us here in chains, stripped us of our ancient culture, robbed us of all knowledge concerning our glorious history and then made us his slaves? The white man lynched, murdered, slaughtered our fathers and brothers; he raped and ravished our helpless women at will . . . and then trained the ignorant, greedy Negro preachers to "parrot" his religious lies to us, a "pacifying religion" that was skillfully designed to brainwash us and keep us in "our place." No, Mr. Muhammad is not teaching hate. He is teaching the naked truth that these Negroes need to know, a truth so plain that only a fool would dispute it . . . and the Negro preachers are the quickest to prove themselves to be the biggest fools.[46]

Malcolm's sharp language was designed to gain the attention of the black community regarding the dangers of the Christian message which black preachers advocated. While Martin King was trying to convince the white churches that they should support the civil rights movement as the Christian way to achieve justice for their black brothers and sisters, Malcolm was preaching to black Christians, urging them to get out from under "the clutches of the Negro preacher's disarming influence" and join the Nation of Islam and unite behind Elijah Muhammad, Allah's last prophet. It did not take long before many blacks were talking about Malcolm X, "the brilliant young follower of the Honorable Elijah Muhammad," and "his stinging attack against the actions of Negro preachers." His intemperate language angered many black preachers, causing some to boycott his rallies and others to walk out during his vituperations against them. Others wrote responses to his scathing attacks on Negro preachers in his widely read "God's Angry Men" column. Some preachers sought police aid to protect their members from the "annoyances" of Muslims "fishing" and "hawking" newspapers. Others, according to Malcolm, "threatened their members with expulsion" if they attended Malcolm's lectures. Martin King avoided appearing on the same platform with Malcolm and did not bother to respond directly to his criticisms of the black church and its preachers. Martin merely reminded his audiences that black supremacy was as evil as white supremacy.

The black media covered Malcolm's vitriolic attacks against Negro preachers. Their headlines included: "Moslem Leader Lashes Out at Venal Preachers"; "Negro Preachers Walk Out on Malcolm X"; "Malcolm X Hits Negro Preachers in Radio Talk"; "Malcolm X Hurls Challenge at Negro Preachers"; "Malcolm X Blasts Negro Ministers"; "Christians Walk Out on Moslems"; and "Malcolm X Hits 'Tom' Preachers."[47]

However, a few black ministers did not avoid Malcolm and some even appeared on the same platform and attempted to answer his critique of them. They included: Gardner C. Taylor of Brooklyn's Concord Baptist Church; William James, then pastor of Metropolitan Community Methodist Church; Wyatt Tee Walker, SCLC executive and now pastor of Canaan Baptist Church of Christ; Adam Clayton Powell, Jr.; and the Presbyterian activist-pastor, Milton Galamison. As preachers responded to Malcolm and acknowledged the significance of his ministry in the black community, he tended to soften his critique and thereby created a better atmosphere for dialogue. Black preachers also invited Malcolm to speak at their churches. Adam Clayton Powell, Jr., invited him to Abyssinian Baptist Church several times, and he spoke on such themes as "Which Way the Negro?" and "The Black Revolution." Melvin DeWitt Bullock, pastor of Union Baptist Church in New Rochelle, New York, also invited him to "expound the philosophy of his religion . . . [in] the first of a 'series on great religions.' " J. P. McGowan of Mount Zion Baptist Church in Phoenix converted to the Nation of Islam and brought his congregation with him. Malcolm's main concern was not to make a *personal* attack against black preachers. "We do not condemn the preachers as an individual but we condemn what they teach," he said. "We urge that the preachers teach the truth, to teach our people the one important guiding rule of conduct—unity of purpose."[48]

It is true that Malcolm's language was frequently too harsh. It undoubtedly helped to foster the disunity in the African-American community which so saddened him. However, much of what Malcolm said about black churches and their preachers was the truth, especially their heaven-in-the-sky theology. Therefore, the alienation between Malcolm and black preachers, as between him and the white community, was due more to his refusal to compromise than to the sharpness of his language. Martin King knew that Malcolm was telling the truth, and he acknowledged it and incorporated much of what he said into his critique of the black church and its preachers. So did others in the black church.

It is important to point out that Malcolm, during his years as a Black Muslim minister, viewed the Nation of Islam as a challenge to both the black church and the civil rights movement. He viewed the latter as a grossly inadequate attempt to speak to the *political* needs of blacks and the former as a failed effort to meet their *religious* needs. One erred by advocating integration and the other by preaching "heaven in the sky." Both concepts, "heaven" and "integration," and the organizations which promoted them were designed by whites to keep blacks as slaves.

In contrast to black churches and the civil rights organizations, whose messages of love and integration made Negroes "walking fools," "sanctified beggars," the Nation of Islam, according to Malcolm, was designed to meet both the political and religious needs of blacks. Mr. Muhammad had been given "a divine formula, a special medicine," the type of teaching that would "cure the hopeless condition of the Negroes and expose and forever remove even the very cause of their troubles." Malcolm contended that the Nation's strict morality, doctrine of separation from the white man, and heaven-on-earth theology were the only cure for black people's spiritual and social deprivation. "Islam dignifies the black man," Malcolm wrote in his "God's Angry Men" column for the *Westchester Observer.* It makes black people "for the first time" feel proud to be black. "Islam is the religion of our people by nature. It is not a religion of European origin, nor was it organized by the white man. It is the religion of the Supreme Being, Almighty God Allah." By being a black religion, "Islam makes us know one another and love one another as never before." This knowledge and love of self and of our own kind bestows unity upon us as a people. This unity enables us to achieve freedom, justice, and equality.[49]

The Nation of Islam was not a political organization in that it did not participate in the political options provided by the white American government. It was political in the sense that it viewed religion as speaking to the whole person — to the economic, social, political, and spiritual well-being of blacks. That was why Malcolm invited people to consider the deeds and teachings of Elijah Muhammad. "The Divine TRUTH taught by Messenger Muhammad," he told his readers, "has cured us of drunkenness, dope addiction, reefer smoking and the other evils we engaged in as 'Negro Christians' which were destroying our morals."[50]

Malcolm's devotion to the Nation of Islam and Elijah Muhammad remained firm as long as they consistently preached and lived their accent on an uncompromising commitment to the truth and on black self-esteem, self-love, and independence. But Malcolm's faith in Muhammad and the Nation began to falter during the early 1960s. However it was not until December 1963 and March 1964 that Malcolm's alienation from Muhammad and the Nation became public and eventually went beyond the point of reconciliation. We turn to this development in the next chapter.

7

"CHICKENS COMING HOME TO ROOST" (1964–65)

We are not fighting for integration, nor are we fighting for separation. We are fighting for recognition as human beings.

> Malcolm X
> New York City
> 8 April 1964

A bloodbath is on its way in America.

> Malcolm X
> *Afro-American*
> 18 July 1964

I'm for truth, no matter who tells it. I'm for justice, no matter who it is for or against. I'm a human being first and foremost, and as such I'm for whoever and whatever benefits humanity as a whole.

> Malcolm X
> *Autobiography*
> 1965

Sometimes, I have dared to dream . . . that one day, history may even say that my voice—which disturbed the white man's smugness, and his arrogance, and his complacency—that my voice helped to save America from a grave, possibly even fatal catastrophe.

> Malcolm X
> *Autobiography*
> 1965

181

More than any black leader during the 1950s and 1960s, Malcolm X persistently and passionately warned America about the imminent eruption of the nightmare which African-Americans experienced daily in the ghettos of its cities. He contended that America could not survive as a *segregated nation*, sharply divided between whites and blacks, with the latter being treated as if they were less than human beings. Malcolm informed whites that African-Americans would not remain passive, nonviolent, and law-abiding as the U.S. government crammed them into filthy, rat-infested ghettos which were unfit for human habitation. "Retaliation in self-defense to the maximum degree of our ability," he contended, was a natural reaction and a normal response of human beings whose dignity was not publicly recognized and respected in the nation of their birth.[1]

Malcolm's conception of the nightmare about which he spoke was strongly influenced by the biblical idea of the judgment of God. As a Black Muslim minister, he did not believe that America could continue its exploitation of the poor and the weak, here and abroad, and not experience the full force of the wrath of God as described in the Scriptures and as discernible throughout human history. He believed deeply in the biblical God of justice, the One who "put down the mighty from their seats and exalted them of low degree" (Luke 1:52 KJV). Malcolm was a black prophet who told America, in the language and style of his biblical predecessors, that *repentance now* was the only way to escape God's coming judgment: "If America will repent and do this [justice], God will overlook some of [its] wicked deeds (as in the days of Nineveh) . . . but if America refuses . . . then, like the biblical houses of Egypt and Babylon (slave empires of the bible), God will erase the American government and the entire [white] race . . . from this planet."[2] Repent or die — these are the nation's only alternatives. "White America," Malcolm warned, "wake up and take heed, before it is too late!"[3]

As a follower of Elijah Muhammad, Malcolm did not believe that America would "wake up" in time to avoid "that Great Doomsday." As shown in the preceding chapter, he proclaimed America's coming destruction with the passion and certainty of an eschatological prophet: *"White America is doomed!"* he said, sometimes with apparent delight and at other times with great anger. Malcolm warned the "so-called Negroes" about the "day of slaughter . . . for this sinful white world." He told African-Americans that it was foolish of them to seek integration into a white world that would soon be destroyed in a "lake of fire."[4]

In lieu of integration, Malcolm urged blacks to separate themselves completely from whites and join with their own kind so that they together, under the leadership of Elijah Muhammad, could either return to their African homeland or build a black nation in the Western hemisphere. "God has . . . prepared a refuge," Malcolm explained, "a haven of salvation, for those who will accept his last Messenger and heed his last warning."[5]

As long as Malcolm functioned as the mouthpiece of Elijah Muhammad, he was not allowed to participate in the political activities of the civil rights movement. But after his break with the Nation of Islam, which he announced to the public on 8 March 1964, a new Malcolm began to emerge—independent and free of the narrow straitjacket of the religious philosophy of Elijah Muhammad. His views about America and the black struggle changed. Moreover, he moved toward Martin King (and King toward him, as I will show in the next chapter) and closer to the mainstream of the civil rights movement.

In this chapter, I will examine Malcolm's reluctant break with Elijah Muhammad and his decisive movement toward Martin King during the last and most important year of his life, concentrating chiefly on his warning about the imminent explosion of "America's racial powder keg."[6]

BREAK WITH ELIJAH MUHAMMAD

Malcolm's fanatic commitment to the liberation of the black poor alienated him not only from most whites and many persons in the black middle class, but also, as it turned out, from his own religious community and from Elijah Muhammad as well. In a soul-wrenching experience he was separated from his spiritual father and teacher, the Messenger of Allah, to whom he had given his complete allegiance.

From the moment of his sudden conversion in 1948, Malcolm had defined his whole life in total devotion to building the Nation of Islam into a force to be reckoned with. He promoted Muhammad as the "second Moses," sent by the "Great God Allah" to separate the so-called Negroes from the coming destruction of white America. Often working eighteen to twenty hours daily, he traveled throughout the country, recruiting new members and organizing temples, interpreting Muhammad's teachings, and contributing in other ways to the advancement of the Black Muslim philosophy of separation. He surpassed all his co-religionists, even Muhammad, in time and energy devoted to the organization.

Elijah Muhammad rewarded Malcolm for his outstanding service to the Nation by providing him with a car and house, support for his family, and freedom to travel wherever he wished and to say whatever he thought the occasion demanded. In late 1963 Muhammad bestowed upon Malcolm the title of "National Minister," a unique distinction among his fellow ministers, and one that had never been given. When

Muhammad announced Malcolm's new status before a Philadelphia rally, he embraced him and said: "This is my most faithful, hardworking minister. He will follow me until he dies."[7]

The relationship between Malcolm and Muhammad was so close and their affections for each other were so deep that the mood of one influenced the other. "Mr. Muhammad and I were so close," Malcolm recalled, "that I knew how he felt by how I felt. If he was nervous, I was nervous. If I was relaxed, then I knew he was relaxed."[8] It appeared that the Malcolm-Muhammad bond was unbreakable. Many observers assumed that Malcolm was the heir apparent to the Black Muslim movement. He was frequently referred to as the "number two man" in the Nation.

What went wrong? What precipitated the break? The *official* reason, issued by Elijah Muhammad and spokesmen for the Nation, for Malcolm's ninety-day silencing and later his permanent separation was that he had seriously disobeyed Elijah Muhammad. The episode cited was connected with Kennedy's assassination on 22 November 1963. Muhammad gave his ministers explicit instructions not to comment on the tragedy. On 1 December 1963, Muhammad gave Malcolm permission to replace him as the featured speaker for a Black Muslim rally in New York City. He also reminded Malcolm of his directive regarding the Kennedy assassination.

Malcolm spoke on the subject "God's Judgment of White America." Unlike his "Grass Roots" speech about two weeks earlier, it was a typical Black Muslim speech, similar to many he had given before, and no different from what Muhammad had taught him. It was strong on religion and weak on political engagement. The main theme was "divine justice," that is, "as you sow, so shall you reap," or more specifically, "how the hypocritical American white man was reaping what he had sowed." Although Malcolm referred to the "late President" several times (repeating his standard comments about Kennedy's control of the March on Washington), he did not comment on the assassination in his address.

However, "during the question-and-answer period" after the address, Malcolm made his now-famous characterization of the Kennedy assassination as an instance of the "chickens coming home to roost." "Somebody asked [him] what [he] thought of the assassination of President Kennedy." "Being an old farm boy myself," he said with the wide, merciless smile that had become his trademark, "chickens coming home to roost never did make me sad; they've always made me glad." Malcolm, of course, was referring to "America's climate of hate," "the seeds that America had sown — in enslavement, in many things that followed since then — all these seeds were coming up today; it was harvest time."[9]

Predictably the media were not interested in Malcolm's ideas on either white oppression or God's justice, but only in his apparent disrespect for the assassinated president. The *New York Times* headlines read: "Malcolm X Scores U.S. and Kennedy: Likens Slaying to 'Chickens Coming Home To Roost.' " It also referred to the "loud applause and laughter" of the audience.

Soon afterward, making his "regular monthly visit to Muhammad," Malcolm discovered to his great dismay that the closeness between them had vanished. "Did you see the papers this morning?" Muhammad asked. When Malcolm answered, "Yes, sir, I did," he could feel the tenseness growing between him and "the man . . . who had treated [him] as if [he] were his own flesh and blood." "That was a very bad statement," Muhammad told him. "The country loved this man. . . . A statement like that can make it hard on Muslims in general." Distancing himself even further from his chief spokesman, Muhammad said, "I'll have to silence you for the next ninety days—so that the Muslims everywhere can be disassociated from the blunder."[10]

Malcolm could hardly believe what he had heard. Muhammad knew that silencing Malcolm was like taking a fish out of water. No disciplinary measure could have been worse. It was a cruel punishment, not commensurate with the nature of Malcolm's error in judgment. It was, however, consistent with Muhammad's arbitrary exercise of authority in the Nation.

After his initial shock, Malcolm regained his composure and then reflected momentarily about the "many times" he had said to his "own assistants that anyone in a position to discipline others must be able to take discipline himself." Following his own advice, he accepted his punishment—willingly and completely. "Sir," he said to Muhammad with a contrite and humble attitude, "I agree with you, and I submit, one hundred percent."[11]

However, upon his return to New York from Chicago, Malcolm discovered that more was involved in his suspension than his ill-timed statement about the Kennedy assassination. A conspiracy had been set in motion by the "Chicago officials," as Malcolm referred to them, to oust him from the Black Muslim movement. According to Malcolm and Elijah's son Wallace, who also split with Elijah Muhammad, the Chicago officials wanted Malcolm out because of their jealousy of his public popularity and their envy of his power within the Nation, which was derived from his closeness to Muhammad.[12] "Those officials were jealous of Malcolm's power and popularity," Wallace said, "and they wanted him out of the way. They planted suspicions in my father's mind, telling him that Malcolm wanted to take over the organization."

The Black Muslim leadership was also troubled by Malcolm's black nationalist philosophy, which often involved the Nation of Islam in national and international politics, thereby creating more confrontations with the "white power structure," especially the police and the FBI. "Malcolm abandoned the *religion* to become a *political sociologist,*" said Black Muslim minister Henry X. He and other ministers criticized Malcolm for injecting "the political concept of 'black nationalism' into the Black Muslim movement," which was "essentially religious in nature when Malcolm became a member."[13]

Malcolm's adversaries in the Nation were correct in their accusation that he was moving the organization away from its exclusively religious focus toward an engagement of issues in the mainstream of the socio-political life of America and the world. Malcolm believed that the Nation's philosophy of separation and self-defense was a better method for achieving black unity and freedom than the integrationist, nonviolent philosophy of the civil rights organizations. That was why he claimed that Elijah Muhammad, and not Martin King, was the "most powerful black man in America." Unlike the "Chicago officials," who viewed the Nation mainly as a competitor with Christian churches, Malcolm envisioned it primarily as a competitor with the civil rights organizations. He viewed the Nation as a religio-political organization, the one that was best suited for achieving "freedom, justice, and equality" for blacks in America.

Elijah Muhammad, along with most of his ministers, did not share Malcolm's political philosophy. Elijah consistently refused to allow Malcolm to involve the Nation in the politics of the civil rights movement. The Nation's nonengagement policy caused many blacks to say: "Those Muslims *talk* tough but they never *do* nothing, unless somebody bothers Muslims." The Muslims' acts of physical retaliation were meted out primarily in the black community (especially toward persons who left the Nation), and only *verbal* retaliation was directed toward whites. For example, when the Los Angeles police invaded a Muslim temple, killing a minister and wounding several other people, Muhammad did not allow Malcolm to implement the Black Muslim philosophy of retaliation. Instead he instructed his followers to leave the vengeance to God. As a result several young members whom Malcolm had recruited left the Nation, greatly disappointed with its passive response to blatant police brutality. Even Malcolm found Muhammad's claim that God would punish the white man for his evil deeds difficult to accept and to explain to others. While vigorously denying any differences between himself and Muhammad, Malcolm nonetheless had to admit that he and other younger Muslims were becoming impatient with the exclusively religious teachings of the Messenger. "But I tell you this," he said in an interview with Louis Lomax during his period of suspension, "the Messenger has seen God. He was with Allah and was given divine patience with the devil. He is willing to wait for Allah to deal with this devil. Well, sir, the rest of us Black Muslims have not seen God, we don't have this gift of divine patience with the devil. The younger Black Muslims want to see some action."[14]

It was not that religion was secondary to Malcolm's political concerns. On the contrary, like Martin King, religion was primary in defining Malcolm's life and thought. His religious commitment, however, was inseparable from his concern for the political liberation of blacks. "I believe in a religion that believes in freedom," he told Harlem blacks. "Any time I have to accept a religion that won't let me fight a battle for my people, I say to hell with that religion."[15]

Malcolm viewed the Nation as the "divine solution" to the black people's sociopolitical oppression in America, countering Christianity's antiblack and prowhite ideology that fed the oppression of blacks. The Nation of Islam dealt with the moral decay in the black community, providing African-Americans with the spiritual power to abstain from drugs, alcohol, gambling, and crime. Beyond that, Malcolm thought the Nation was a great *political* force in America. It was this theo-political principle that led him to reject Christianity and to accept the teachings of Elijah Muhammad and later to split with the Messenger and to embrace orthodox Islam. "If I harbored any personal disappointment whatsoever," he said in his *Autobiography,*

> it was that privately I was convinced that our Nation of Islam could be an even greater force in the American black man's overall strug-gle — if we engaged in more *action.* By that, I mean I thought pri-vately that we should have amended, or relaxed, our general non-engagement policy. I felt that wherever black people committed themselves, in the Little Rocks and the Birminghams and other places, militantly disciplined Muslims should also be there — for all the world to see, and respect, and discuss.[16]

Elijah Muhammad and other Muslim officials, however, did not view the Nation of Islam as a political organization. They pointed to "God's solution" as the *only* answer to the problem of injustice that whites inflict upon blacks in America and throughout the world. Muhammad proph-esied that 1970 was the year of the great day of reckoning, the time when Allah would bring the rule of the white race to an end and blacks, the Original People, would inherit the earth.

As the rapidly growing membership eagerly waited for "the War of Armageddon," the "Showdown" between God and the devil, the Black Muslim leadership (especially Muhammad's family) took for themselves an inordinate share of the material benefits of the economic growth of the Nation. Not wishing to lose their new perquisites through confrontation with the white power structure, they were determined to deal firmly with Malcolm's attempt to insert the Nation into the politics of black liberation.

In addition to jealousy and envy in the Nation and to Malcolm's black nationalist politics, Elijah Muhammad's moral hypocrisy contributed significantly to Malcolm's definitive rupture with the Black Muslims. The moral code of the Nation was strict and the punishment for breaking it was severe. For "fornication or adultery," it was not unusual for Elijah Muhammad "to mete out sentences of one to five years of 'isolation,' if not complete expulsion from the Nation." Malcolm internalized deeply the moral principles of the Nation, teaching them "so strongly," he said, "that many Muslims accused me of being 'anti-woman.' The very keel of my teaching, and my most personal belief was that Elijah Muhammad in every aspect of his existence was a symbol of moral, mental, and spiritual reform among the American black people." Malcolm referred to his "own transformation" as the "best example" of "Mr. Muhammad's power to reform" the lives of black people. From the time he entered prison in 1946 to his marriage to Betty in 1958, Malcolm "never touched a woman." He also rigidly observed other moral principles, refusing to smoke or drink alcohol even in the company of close friends outside the Nation. At no time did he trivialize the morality which Elijah Muhammad taught.[17]

However, "as far back as 1955," Malcolm, to his great distress, "heard hints" about the "immoral behavior of Mr. Muhammad." "Why, the very idea made me shake in fear," Malcolm recalled. It was so "insane-sounding" that he could not even consider believing it. He simply ignored it. "*Adultery!* Why any Muslim guilty of adultery was summarily ousted in disgrace," as were Malcolm's brother Reginald, several of Muhammad's secretaries, and many others.[18]

"But by late 1962," it became impossible for Malcolm to ignore the gossip about Muhammad's moral failure. Muslims began to leave the Chicago mosque, and "the ugly rumor was spreading swiftly—even among non-Muslim Negroes." When Wallace Muhammad, Elijah's son, personally confirmed the truth of the accusation against his father, Malcolm became greatly troubled about the moral integrity of the Black Muslim movement. How could he explain to the Nation's membership and to the non-Muslim public the great moral contradiction between what Muhammad said publicly and what he did privately?[19]

Malcolm felt that the survival of the Nation was at stake. "I desperately wanted to find some way—some kind of bridge—over which I was certain the Nation of Islam could be saved from self-destruction," he recalled. In his search of the Quran and the Bible, with the assistance of Wallace Muhammad, he believed that he had found the answer. "Loyal Muslims could be taught that a man's accomplishments in his life outweigh his personal, human weakness." David's and Moses' adultery, Lot's incest, and Noah's drunkenness were less important than the positive contributions they made to their people. Could not the same be true of the Messenger Muhammad? This solution, however, gave Malcolm only temporary relief from his spiritual torment.[20]

Nothing was more important to Malcolm than living according to the message one preached. He regarded America as morally worse than South Africa because the latter practiced what it preached—apartheid. America, in contrast, preached freedom and democracy but practiced racial discrimination against its people of color. He made a similar distinction between southern, white conservatives and northern, white liberals, referring to them respectively as "wolves" and "foxes." What passes for democracy in America, according to Malcolm, is nothing but "disguised hypocrisy," which he also frequently called "tricknology," "a science of tricks and lies." For twelve years, Malcolm, before black and white audiences, on television and radio, vented his rage against the calculated deception of white America. *Now* to discover beyond any doubt that Elijah Muhammad, the "Dear Holy Apostle," was a trickster and that he himself was a dupe shook the foundation of Malcolm's faith. "I can't describe the torments I went through," he wrote in his *Autobiography.*[21]

Malcolm's spiritual crisis was so deep that he also "broke the rule," "looked up," and "talked with three of the former secretaries to Mr. Muhammad" "in 'the isolated state.' " They not only confirmed what he already knew; they also told him what he did not know, namely that Muhammad was deceitful in his relationship with him.

> From their own mouths, I heard their stories of who had fathered their children. And from their own mouths I heard that Elijah Muhammad had told them I was the best, the greatest minister he ever had, but that someday I would leave him, turn against him—so I was "dangerous." I learned from these former secretaries . . . that while he was praising me to my face, he was tearing me apart behind my back.[22]

Early in 1963, feeling that he had to discuss the matter face to face, Malcolm wrote Muhammad a letter "about the poison being spread about him." In April Muhammad invited Malcolm to Phoenix to talk about the matter. "Plainly, frankly, pulling no punches," Malcolm confronted Muhammad with what was being said about him. "And without waiting for any response from him," Malcolm told Muhammad that "with his son Wallace's help" he "had found in the Quran and the Bible that which might be taught to Muslims—if it became necessary—as the fulfillment of prophecy."[23]

Muhammad responded with an expression of appreciation for Malcolm's insight. "Son, I'm not surprised," he said. "You always have had such a good understanding of prophecy, and spiritual things. You recognize that's what all of this is—prophecy." Muhammad then proceeded to give his own theological explanation of his moral laxity. "I'm David," he told Malcolm. "When you read about how David took another man's wife, I'm that David. You read about Noah, who got drunk—that's me. You read about Lot, who went and laid up with his own daughters. I have to fulfill all of those things."[24]

After Malcolm discovered the truth about Muhammad's immorality and found biblical references to explain it as the fulfillment of biblical prophecy, he still found the Messenger's moral failings difficult to accept. He spoke less about the *religion* of the Nation and more about the politics of black liberation. Of course, Malcolm's shift from religion to politics in his preaching did not go unnoticed. It seemed that Elijah Muhammad, under the influence of the Chicago officials, could no longer trust Malcolm. Muhammad, therefore, merely waited for Malcolm "to make a move that would enable him to suspend [his well-known spokesman] and get the support of the public in doing so." The opportunity came with his incautious remark about the Kennedy assassination.[25]

It seems in any case that the break between Malcolm and Muhammad could not have been avoided. Malcolm was too political and honest, and Muhammad was too religious and hypocritical for them to sustain their relationship. Muhammad knew it. But Malcolm was too naive to see it soon enough to avoid its disastrous consequences.

During Malcolm's suspension a chain of events occurred that could be interpreted only as a determined effort by the Nation's leadership to put him out of the Black Muslim movement. He was prevented not only from speaking publicly among non-Muslims but also at Muslim temples, including Number Seven, which he headed.

Malcolm also discovered, to his great surprise and dismay, that his enemies not only wanted to put him out of the Nation but out of existence as well. While the Nation's leadership denied making any attempts against Malcolm's life, there is much evidence to support their complicity and very little to contradict it. According to Malcolm, one plot against his life was revealed to him by the person who was supposed to carry it out. "This first direct death-order was how, finally, I began to arrive at my psychological divorce with the Nation of Islam." "The death talk," Malcolm said, "was not my fear."

Every second of my twelve years with Mr. Muhammad, I had been ready to lay down my life for him. The thing to me worse than death was the *betrayal*. I could conceive death. I couldn't conceive betrayal—not of the loyalty which I had given to the Nation of Islam, and to Mr. Muhammad. During the previous twelve years, if Mr. Muhammad had committed any civil crime punishable by death, I would have said and tried to prove that I did it—to save him—and I would have gone to the electric chair, as Mr. Muhammad's servant.[26]

The experience of betrayal by his religious community was psychologically devastating. "I was in a state of emotional shock," he said. He compared it to "someone who for twelve years had had an inseparable, beautiful marriage—and then suddenly one morning at breakfast the marriage partner had thrust across the table some divorce papers." It affected him physically. "My head felt like it was bleeding inside. I felt like my brain was damaged." He even consulted his physician, who recommended rest.[27]

Fortunately, his newly found friend, Cassius Clay (now Muhammad Ali), who later sided with Muhammad against Malcolm, offered him and his family a vacation in Florida, where he was training for the heavyweight fight against the then-champion Charles "Sonny" Liston. This vacation gave Malcolm time to assess his place in the Nation of Islam and also to start his psychological move toward independence. He did not want to break with Muhammad. "I still struggled to persuade myself that Mr. Muhammad had been fulfilling prophecy." What broke his faith with Muhammad was his moral hypocrisy.

Try as I might, I couldn't hide, I couldn't evade, that Mr. Muhammad, instead of facing what he had done before his followers, as a human weakness or as fulfillment of prophecy—which I sincerely believe that Muslims would have understood, or at least they would have accepted—Mr. Muhammad had, instead, been willing to hide, to cover up what he had done. That was my major blow. That was how I first began to realize that I had believed in Mr. Muhammad more than he believed in himself.[28]

Malcolm's break with Muhammad set him off on his own as a leader with no organization and very few public followers. Even though he had many sympathizers, most were afraid to be associated with him because of his public image as a teacher of hate and fomenter of violence against whites. Since Malcolm had neither initiated nor anticipated his break with the Nation, he had not developed a religious philosophy which clearly distinguished his views from Muhammad's. Even his political philosophy, though partly different from Muhammad's, was closely linked to and dependent upon the Nation of Islam. Malcolm tried desperately to remain a minister within the Black Muslim movement, and failing that, he wanted to separate from it without bitterness or rancor.

But that was not to be. At the end of Malcolm's ninety-day suspension, he wrote a letter to Muhammad asking for clarification of his status in the Nation. Muhammad's reply indicated that his suspension would remain in effect "for an indefinite period." Malcolm concluded that the "national officials" in Chicago had successfully poisoned the Messenger with misinformation against him. He, therefore, decided to make a public break by creating his own movement, which he called the Muslim Mosque Incorporated. He initially conceived the organization as a complement to and not in competition with the Nation of Islam. In a telegram to Muhammad, he told him that "you are still my leader and teacher, even though those around you won't let me be one of your active followers or helpers." Malcolm wanted Muhammad to know that he was pressured out of the Nation and did not leave of his own free will. "I have reached the conclusion," he said on the occasion of his public declaration of independence, "that I can best spread Mr. Muhammad's message by staying out of the Nation of Islam and continuing to work on my own among America's 22 million non-Muslim Negroes." Malcolm's separation from the person who rescued him from the depths and placed him in the religious community which defined his ministry was a painful and difficult decision. He left Muhammad's Nation only because he had no other alternative.[29]

Upon his departure from the Nation, Malcolm did not project himself as a divine man like Elijah Muhammad or as an educated leader like Martin King. "My sincerity is my credentials," he said at the 12 March 1964 press conference at New York's Park Sheraton Hotel.[30]

MOVEMENT TOWARD MARTIN

As he slipped out of Muhammad's "straitjacket" religious philosophy, Malcolm was seen increasingly as an independent political leader of the black masses in the urban ghetto. His thinking moved further toward the politics of black nationalism as the necessary alternative to the integrationist, nonviolent philosophy of Martin King. What is remarkable, however, is that in this final stormy year of his life Malcolm revealed not only differences with Martin but also many similarities. Neither their differences nor their similarities remained static but were constantly in a process of change and development, strongly influenced by their awareness of each other, as they searched for the meaning of black freedom in America and the best method for achieving it.

Before the break, Malcolm's public reactions to the leadership and philosophy of Martin King passed through two stages: "mostly silence" during the 1950s and "open attack" during the early 1960s. In both stages he was complying with Elijah Muhammad's instructions. After Malcolm got the green light to criticize King's movement, his remarks were harsh, particularly in 1963. King was a "chump" for using children in the Birmingham demonstrations, a "traitor" for advocating nonviolence, and a "clown" for participating in the March on Washington, which was controlled by whites.

Having been educated in the streets of Roxbury and Harlem, Malcolm was not accustomed to restraining his language in his attempt to state the truth about black-white relations in America. His language was particularly harsh against King and other civil rights leaders, whom he perceived as adjusting the black liberation struggle to ethical guidelines laid down by whites. His lack of verbal restraint was both an asset and a liability. It was an asset in that it enabled him to speak the truth from the perspective of blacks in the urban ghetto in sharp, uncomplicated language. But it was a liability in that it alienated him from Martin and other civil rights leaders as well as from the vast majority of blacks, especially Christians in the South. In addition Malcolm's straightforward language made it easy for the white media to project him as a demagogue.

As Malcolm moved out of the Nation of Islam and began to plot his own course, he consciously moved toward the politics of Martin King and the civil rights movement. "Now that I have more independence-of-action I intend to use a more flexible approach toward working with others to get a solution to this problem," he said. Malcolm decided to enter the civil rights movement as a supporter of blacks everywhere who were fighting against segregation. While he continued to reject integration and to advocate separation, Malcolm concluded that the return to Africa or the creation of a separate state in the Western hemisphere was "still a long range program." In the meantime, the short range goal must be achievement of "better food, clothing, housing, education, and jobs *right now*."[31]

In order to participate in the civil rights movement, of which Martin King was the most visible symbol, Malcolm realized that he had to change his Black Muslim image. He issued a call for unity among all black leaders and organizations. "I am not out to fight other Negro leaders or organizations," he said. "We must find a common approach, a common solution, to a common problem. As of this minute, I've forgotten everything bad that the other leaders have said about me, and I pray they can also forget the many bad things I've said about them."[32]

"THE BALLOT OR THE BULLET"

Malcolm's classic statement of his emerging political vision is his well-known speech entitled "The Ballot or the Bullet." He gave it many times to mostly black audiences, in such places as New York, Cleveland, and Detroit.[33] It was one of his best talks, rivaling his great "Message to the Grass Roots," especially in terms of the enthusiastic response of his audiences.

Malcolm began "The Ballot or the Bullet" speech by clarifying his religious status: "I'm still a Muslim," he said. "I still credit Mr. Muhammad for what I know and what I am." But in the interest of black unity Malcolm stopped proselytizing or even discussing religion because of its propensity for creating divisions. While he was still deeply committed to Islam as the only true religion of blacks, his negative experiences in Muhammad's Black Muslim movement had showed him the limitations of religious fanaticism. As a consequence, Malcolm turned toward Martin King as a model for the political direction in which he was now moving. "Just as . . . Dr. Martin Luther King is a Christian minister . . . who heads another organization fighting for the civil rights of black people in this country," Malcolm said, "I myself am a . . . Muslim minister" following a black nationalist line of action. "I don't believe in fighting today on any one front but on all fronts," he continued. "In fact, I am a black nationalist freedom fighter."[34]

Using language similar to his "Grass Roots" speech, Malcolm emphasized a concept of unity that was based on the common plight of black people and not on his Islamic religion. "It's time for us to submerge our differences and realize that . . . we have the same problem, . . . a problem that will make you catch hell whether you're a Baptist, or a Methodist, or a Muslim, or a nationalist." As Malcolm saw it, "whether you're educated or illiterate, whether you live on the boulevard or in the alley," the consequences of being black in America were pretty much the same. "We're all in the same boat," he said. "They don't hang you because you're a Baptist, they hang you because you're black. They don't attack me because I'm a Muslim, they attack me because I'm black. They attack all of us for the same reason. All of us catch hell. . . . We're in the same bag. . . . We suffer political oppression, economic exploitation, and social degradation . . . from the same enemy" — "the white man."[35]

"The Ballot or the Bullet" speech was Malcolm's initial attempt to develop a political vision that was continuous with his black nationalist, Muslim past, while also showing the new directions in his thinking that would enable him to enter and expand the civil rights movement. The "bullet" in the phrase represented the *continuity* in Malcolm's perspective. It accented his militancy. It referred to his firm belief that no people can be recognized and respected as human beings if they are not prepared to defend their humanity against those who violate their God-given rights.

On the occasion of his declaration of independence, Malcolm created much controversy when he said: "In areas where our people are the constant victims of brutality, and the government seems unwilling or unable to protect them, we should form *rifle clubs* that can be used to defend our lives and our property in times of emergency." He contended that it is "criminal" to teach nonviolence to blacks when they are routinely the victims of white violence. With these comments, Malcolm wanted the whole world to know that his break with Elijah Muhammad and move toward Martin King and the civil rights movement did not mean that he was going to urge blacks to be nonviolent with people who were violent toward them. He wanted to enter the civil rights movement in order to *expand* it, that is, to give it a "new" and "broader interpretation," thereby making it more militant by including the principle of self-defense or, as he often called it, the "by any means necessary" philosophy.[36]

Malcolm was especially careful to stay within the bounds of the law. He wanted only to affirm the ethical principle of self-survival for African-Americans, a right which whites took for granted, both legally and morally. Malcolm never once advocated aggressive violence against whites. "We should be peaceful, law-abiding," he said during his declaration of independence and on many other occasions. "But the time has come for the American Negro to fight back in self-defense whenever and wherever he is being unjustly attacked." Malcolm knew that whites, especially the government, would not like what he was saying. That was why he concluded his statement with the comment: "If the government thinks I am wrong for saying this, then let the government start doing its job."[37]

Like Malcolm's comment about the "chickens coming home to roost," his reference to "rifle clubs" created quite a stir among civil rights groups, law enforcement officials, and in the media throughout the country. Many interpreted the remark as meaning that Malcolm was advocating violence. "Brother Malcolm: His Theme Now Is Violence" was the headline in *U.S. News & World Report*. The report in the *Chicago Defender* read: "Negroes Need Guns, Declares Malcolm X." The editorial in the New York *Amsterdam News* was entitled "Reckless Orbit." "We don't hesitate to say that the solution to the problems of minorities does not lie in hysterical sword rattling and wild statements about the need and use of shotguns in race relations," the editorial said. "The founding fathers long ago made clear the right of the minority to speak out, demonstrate and protest against injustice. And we stand squarely behind and support such protests when the cause is just and the aim is plain. But," it continued, "in the light of the progress that has been made and is being made through nonviolence, it's downright silly to start preaching violence now." "To Arms with Malcolm X" was the heading for the *New York Times* editorial. The editorial said: "His is a call to break the law; to take the law into one group's own hands that would hold firearms; to erect a private militia. His is a call to arms against duly constituted police forces." Calling him an "embittered racist" and "irresponsible demagogue," the *Times* went on to assure its readers that "Malcolm X will not deceive Negroes in New York or elsewhere."

The FBI alerted its agencies and the local police in many cities to be on the lookout for blacks buying firearms and forming rifle clubs. The New York *Amsterdam News* reported on the organization of a "Negro Rifle Club" in Cleveland by a city employee, Louis Robinson. The FBI in Chicago reported that an unknown Negro placed an order for eleven to fifteen .22 caliber magnum automatic rifles with fixed telescopes, stating that he was organizing a rifle club. According to Ray Davis, a columnist for the *Michigan Chronicle,* Malcolm "denied the leadership of the Medgar Evers Memorial Rifle Club, being formed in cities, but declared the constitutional right of such clubs to exist if they are the only means by which Negroes can secure protection."[38]

The predictable negative reactions to Malcolm's statement about blacks protecting themselves with "rifles and shotguns" confirmed, for him, once again that whites did not regard blacks as human beings. "Not a single white person in America would sit idly by and let someone do to him what we black[s] have been letting others do to us," Malcolm said during his third appearance at the Harvard Law School Forum. "The white person would not remain passive, peaceful, and nonviolent." In an interview with the *Washington Star* Malcolm said that like any white person who would defend his or her humanity at all costs, he "reserve[d] the right to do whatever, wherever, whenever, and however is necessary to get results." He made a similar point in response to a question at the Militant Labor Forum, which had a predominantly white audience: "I'm the man you think you are. . . . If we're both human beings we'll both do the same thing. And if you want to know what I'll do, figure out what you'll do. I'll do the same thing—only more of it."[39]

White people's refusal to acknowledge the right of blacks to defend themselves against persons who violated their humanity was perhaps the main reason that Malcolm could never accept Martin King's idea of nonviolence and its capacity to prick the moral conscience of whites. He urged blacks to stop trying to appeal to the good will of whites because it was useless. "Don't change the white man's mind," Malcolm told blacks. "You can't change his mind, and that whole thing about appealing to the moral conscience of America—America's conscience is bankrupt. She lost all conscience a long time ago. Uncle Sam has no conscience. They don't know what morals are." The only language that whites understand is the language that they themselves use—violence. "They don't try to eliminate evil because it's evil, or because it's illegal, or because it's immoral; they eliminate it only when it threatens their existence."[40]

While Malcolm did not think that it was possible to change white people's minds, he was hopeful that he could revolutionize the political consciousness of black people. As was true with his "Grass Roots" speech, Malcolm's "Ballot or Bullet" talk was designed to inspire blacks to take charge of their own political destiny by reshaping their lives, rejecting their assigned role as passive sufferers, and accepting their God-given role as active freedom fighters. "It was not necessary to change the white man's mind," Malcolm assured blacks. "We've got to change our own minds about each other. We have to see each other with new eyes," that is, "as brothers and sisters. We have to come together with warmth so we can develop unity and harmony that's necessary to get this problem solved ourselves."[41]

To persuade blacks to adopt the self-help philosophy of black nationalism, Malcolm believed that he had to show them that they would never get their freedom as long as they put their trust in the government and white liberals. "The government has failed us—you can't deny that," he frequently said. He knew that many blacks would not accept his sweeping condemnation of the government, especially since the Kennedy and Johnson administrations supported the Civil Rights Bill. Still, he told them how misguided they were to think of the government as their ally rather than their main opponent: "Anytime you're living in the twentieth century and you're walking around here singing 'We Shall Overcome,' the government has failed you. . . . White liberals who have been posing as our friends have failed us. Once we see that all these other sources to which we have turned have failed, we stop turning to them and turn to ourselves."[42]

As Martin King and other integrationists accented their American identity, Malcolm refused to identify with the country of his birth. "We're not Americans, we're Africans who happen to be in America," Malcolm told a Harlem audience. "We were kidnapped and brought here against our will from Africa. We didn't land on Plymouth Rock— that rock landed on us."[43] Without fail, Malcolm aroused the resentful feelings of integrationists when he spoke like that. No persons tried to be *Americans* more than integrationists. They have been called "super

Americans" and "exaggerated Americans." When they heard Malcolm denying his American identity, they were greatly embarrassed because he contradicted what they had been telling whites that blacks wanted. How could the black advocates of integration explain Malcolm's philosophy of separation to their white friends in government and the civil rights movement?

Malcolm, however, could not resist exposing what he regarded as the sheer stupidity of black, middle-class leaders talking about America as if it is *"our* country." "I am one," he said, "who doesn't believe in deluding myself." Malcolm compared being a citizen with being a diner. "I am not going to sit at your table and watch you eat with nothing on my plate, and call myself a diner," he said. "Sitting at the table doesn't make you a diner, unless you eat some of what's on that plate." Likewise, "being born in America doesn't make you an American. Why, if birth made you an American, you wouldn't need any legislation, you wouldn't need any amendments to the Constitution, you wouldn't be faced with civil-rights filibustering in Washington, D.C., right now."[44]

Malcolm reminded blacks that European immigrants do not need legislation to make them Americans. "Those Hunkies that just got off the boat, they're already Americans," he said. "Everything that came out of Europe, every blue-eyed thing is already an American. And as long as you and I have been here, we aren't Americans yet."[45]

NEW DIRECTIONS

While the "bullet" symbolized the continuity in Malcolm's thinking, the "ballot" signaled an important change. It represented his movement away from the narrow skin-nationalism of the Black Muslims to an affirmation of blackness which enabled him to cooperate with Martin King and others in the mainstream of the civil rights movement. "We will work with anybody, anywhere, at any time, who is genuinely interested in tackling the problem headon," he said. "We'll work with you on the voter-registration drive, . . . rent strikes, . . . and school boycotts."[46]

When Malcolm was Elijah Muhammad's minister, his religious beliefs defined the heart of his public discourse about America, while his political ideas were kept private. He had been separated from the American political process and from the civil rights movement which sought to integrate African-Americans into it. His advocacy of complete separation was based on an act of faith and not on an option in the American political process. After his break the situation was reversed. He relegated religion to the "private" sphere and placed politics in the center of his public discourse.

This radical change provided an opportunity for a more fruitful dialogue between him and Martin. Malcolm not only cast aside his "true believer" attitude, which had encouraged Martin to avoid him; he also tempered his critique of Martin and other civil rights leaders. Furthermore he put forward an idea of black nationalism that was exclusively devoted to the political, social, and economic development of the black community. Malcolm compared his advocacy of black nationalism with Billy Graham's preaching of Christianity, which he called "white nationalism." Graham "circumvents the jealousy and envy that he would ordinarily incur among the heads of the church" by limiting his activity to "preaching Christ" and urging the converts "to go to any church wherever you find him." "Well," said Malcolm, "we are going to do the same thing, only our gospel is black nationalism." His point was that once one was converted to black nationalism, he or she was free to join any organization or church where it was preached. "Don't join a church where white nationalism is preached," Malcolm told an audience of blacks in Detroit. "You can go to a Negro church and be exposed to white nationalism. When you go in a Negro church and you see a white Jesus and a white Mary and white angels, that Negro church is preaching white nationalism."[47]

As a Black Muslim, Malcolm normally would have sharpened his critique of the black church, for he saw little liberating potential in it and took many opportunities to say so. The "new Malcolm," however, curtailed his critique of the black church in the interest of black unity, defined by the politics of black nationalism. Using conciliatory language that surprised even some of his critics, he said: "When you go to a church and you see the pastor of that church with a philosophy and a program that's designed to bring black people together and elevate black people, join that church!" Malcolm also applied that same principle to civil rights organizations: "If you see where the NAACP is preaching and practicing that which is designed to make black nationalism materialize, join the NAACP." He also mentioned CORE in the same connection. "Join any kind of organization—civic, religious, fraternal, political or otherwise—that's based on lifting . . . the black man up and making him master of his own community."[48]

It is true that as a Black Muslim Malcolm had issued calls for unity, holding many "Unity Rallies" in Harlem and inviting Martin and other black leaders to present their solutions to the black condition in America. He also spoke on unity at Black Muslim and non-Muslim community meetings throughout the country. The unity theme was the core of all types of black nationalist philosophies. However, it was one thing to issue calls for unity and quite another to create the wholesome conditions necessary for its achievement. For example, as a Black Muslim,

Malcolm's idea of unity was based on the African-American community's acceptance of the Nation of Islam as the true religion of black people and Elijah Muhammad as their leader who was sent by Allah to save them from the imminent destruction of white America. It was not surprising that little unity could be achieved on that basis. Elijah Muhammad had neither the vision nor the integrity to be an appropriate symbol for unity in the African-American community. This insight grew in Malcolm during the 1960s as he began to see the limitations of Muhammad's sectarianism.

Martin King and the civil rights movement were much more successful in establishing solidarity among blacks than were Malcolm and the Black Muslims. Malcolm knew that and was sometimes jealous of Martin's influence in the black community. Despite his own rhetoric Malcolm knew that Martin's influence was not always supported by the federal government and the white media. Martin's prestige in the black community was primarily the result of his ability to transcend many petty differences among civil rights leaders and effectively speak to the everyday needs of black people. Therefore, when Malcolm became an independent leader, his inspiration was derived more from Martin than Muhammad, as he sought to build an organization that could include a broad range of blacks with different political and religious orientations. He tried hard to develop a unity message that would enable him to be involved in civil rights activities which previously had been closed to him. In this aim he was only partly successful.

As one might have expected, there were mixed responses to Malcolm's split from the Black Muslims and his subsequent attempt to enter the civil rights movement. In a *New York Times* article appropriately entitled "Negroes Ponder Malcolm's Move: Differ over Significance of His Political Effort," Fred Powledge reported several reactions among civil rights leaders to Malcolm's attempt to join them. James Farmer of CORE focused on Malcolm's "rifle club" statement and suggested that he was "proposing a race war that Negroes could not win." However, most observers, including Farmer, agreed with Bayard Rustin: "There are many elements in the Negro community . . . who out of frustration with the current situation, have been deeply attracted to Malcolm's analysis . . . of the evils that are being practiced on the Negro people." But only a very few accepted Malcolm's idea of "non-nonviolence." Richard A. Hildebrand, then pastor of Bethel AME Church and president of the New York branch of the NAACP, expressed the sentiments of many: "I welcome anybody who is going to help the civil rights struggle, but I cannot condone violence. Malcolm X is a brilliant person. I have the feeling that we can work together as long as we can contain that philosophy of violence."[49]

Malcolm's initial participation in civil rights activities occurred in the New York area. He supported the school boycott that was led by Milton A. Galamison, a militant civil rights activist who was pastor of Siloam Presbyterian Church in Brooklyn. Malcolm's support was unsolicited. In view of his "violent" image, largely created by the media, Galamison accepted it with much caution. "The boycott is being operated under a philosophy of nonviolence," Galamison said. "I have not talked to Malcolm X. If he adheres to nonviolence, he will be welcome at the boycott. We don't want to reject any legitimate support, but I want it to be legitimate." Malcolm did not march in the picket line. As a "believer in '*non-nonviolence,*' " he explained, "if I got in line, other believers of non-nonviolence would join it, and when we met up with white non-nonviolence believers, there would be violence."[50]

Malcolm also addressed a "rent strike rally" sponsored by the Community Council on Housing under the leadership of Jesse Gray, a militant activist. Gray spoke at several of Malcolm's meetings as well. Both appeared frequently in the pages of the *New York Times* and the New York *Amsterdam News* as harsh critics of Police Commissioner Michael J. Murphy.[51]

Galamison and Gray were among several locally based "militant civil rights leaders" who found the national, established leadership too "conservative," that is, too "anxious 'to please white people.' "[52] They were largely located in the North and still committed to nonviolence. But they were urging more militant confrontations with the white power structure, such as the New York school boycott, initiated by Galamison without the support of the NAACP and CORE. Besides Galamison and Gray, other militants included Stanley E. Branch, head of the Committee for Freedom Now in Chester, Pennsylvania; Lawrence Landry, an organizer of school boycotts in Chicago; and Gloria Richardson, chairperson of the Cambridge [Md.] Nonviolent Action Committee.

The militants invited Malcolm to speak at a meeting in Chester, Pennsylvania. About sixty persons were present. He made his standard comments about the right of blacks to defend themselves when the government failed to protect them in the exercise of their human rights. Although the group was "militant," they gave a cautious response to Malcolm's talk about the "firearms and 'rifle club' organizing bit." The headline of the *Afro-American* read: "Malcolm's Gun Idea Gets Cool Response: Even Militant 'Militants' Fail To Warm Up to Plan." According to Stanley Branch, the group supported Malcolm's desire and aim for racial unity as a "good thing." But "Malcolm's firearms ideology was the 'furthest thing from our minds.' "[53]

However, some persons in the group, such as Gloria Richardson, welcomed both Malcolm's call for self-defense and his cooperation with civil rights groups. "Malcolm is being very practical," she said.

The resisting white community takes advantage of our commitment to nonviolence and uses this against us. Throughout the nation colored citizens are at the boiling point. Self-defense may actually be a deterrent to further violence. Hitherto, the government has moved into conflict situations only when matters approach the level of insurrection. Self-defense may force Washington to intervene sooner.[54]

The "militant civil rights activists" formed a new organization called ACT! (not an acronym) to show its contrast with the "passive" approach of the national Negro leadership. "The sole qualification for membership in ACT! is that one must act or utilize direct action to resolve civil rights disputes," said Lawrence Landry, who was elected president of the group. Using language similar to that of Malcolm X, Landry told the group that "1963 had established the principle that Negroes want to be free, and in 1964, we established the principle that Negroes will do whatever is necessary to be free." ACT! turned to Malcolm for inspiration and named him, along with Adam Clayton Powell, Jr., and Dick Gregory, as a consultant to the group.[55]

Another important development was the invitations Malcolm received to speak at the meetings of several clergy groups, including the Brooklyn Methodist Ministers Association (a mixed group of blacks and whites) and a gathering of about twenty black ministers who called their group the Interdenominational Ministers Meeting of Greater New York and Vicinity. To the Methodists Malcolm spoke on the "gospel of black nationalism," repeating his Billy Graham analogy, and reiterating his affirmation of self-defense. When a white minister asked him "whether he thought there were any good white people," Malcolm replied, "I do not say that there are no sincere white people, but rather that I haven't met any."[56]

At the Interdenominational Ministers gathering, the session was polite, with Malcolm and the ministers "twitting each other." He warned them of the coming nightmare in their own communities. "1964 is explosive," he said, "and I'm afraid that most of the leaders have gotten so out of touch with the people that they don't know the powder keg they're sitting on." Asked if his critical attitude toward Christianity had changed within the last year, Malcolm replied: "I don't care what I said last year. That was last year. This is 1964."[57]

It is important to note that some ministers supported Malcolm and appeared on the platform with him. Albert B. Cleage, Jr., a clergyman of the United Church of Christ and pastor of the Shrine of the Black Madonna in Detroit, was a close friend of Malcolm and appeared with him many times. Malcolm introduced Nelson C. Dukes, pastor of the

Fountain Spring Baptist Church in New York, as a "strong Black Nationalist." The *Amsterdam News* reported that C. Asapansa-Johnson (originally an AME minister from Sierra Leone who organized and became pastor of the Bethel Community Church in Staten Island) agreed "85 percent with Malcolm X." As president of the Interdenominational Ministers Meeting of Greater New York and Vicinity, he contended that "Negroes should fight in defense of their lives, homes and rights because 'until we're willing to die, we'll never receive freedom.' " Like Malcolm, he claimed that no people can gain freedom as long as they are paralyzed by fear. "The majority of Negroes are afraid to die," he proclaimed to an assembly of black ministers. "They're taking it too easy. They must be told they must die—shed blood—for freedom."[58]

Other ministers strongly objected to Malcolm's advocacy of "rifle clubs" and rejected his offer to join the civil rights movement. Among them was Robert M. Kinlock. Kinlock—a highly controversial Harlem community activist who later was appointed and then relieved of his duties as the chairman of the Commission for the Elimination of Racism, which was sponsored by the Council of Churches for the City of New York—"called Malcolm's position ridiculous." According to Kinlock, the so-called new Malcolm is not new. "He's still preaching the same philosophy under a new name." A similar position was taken by Irvin C. Lockman, pastor of Mount Calvary Methodist Church, and W. Eugene Houston, pastor of Rendall Memorial Presbyterian Church, both churches located in Harlem. Houston succeeded Asapansa-Johnson as the president of the ministerial group. Both Houston and Lockman opposed Asapansa-Johnson at the Interdenominational Ministers gathering. "It would be suicidal for minority Negroes to fight majority whites through armed conflict to attain first-class citizenship." Lockman advocated that blacks should follow the "moral leadership of Dr. Martin Luther King, Jr." He even claimed with confidence that "the victory (of the rights struggle) has been won—all we need do now is to mop up."[59]

Of the mainline civil rights organizations, the young activists of SNCC were influenced the most by Malcolm's philosophy of black nationalism. Many of them grew increasingly impatient with Martin King's "conservative," nonviolent, and charismatic leadership role. James Forman, the executive director of SNCC, said that Malcolm's new position "opens up possibilities for people who certainly thought the Muslims had something to say but who reject the whole concept of a separate state and the religion. That cat does have a lot of followers outside the [Muslim] temple." John Lewis, SNCC's national chairman, called Malcolm a "great person," but unlike the majority of other SNCC leaders, he was ideologically closer to King. "SNCC will not support a movement to take up arms," he said, "because we believe in nonviolence as a philosophy of life."[60]

Elsewhere in the civil rights movement Adam Clayton Powell, Jr., who referred to himself as a friend of Malcolm X and invited him to speak several times at Abyssinian Baptist Church, where he served as pastor, said that Malcolm's "suggestion . . . that colored people arm themselves with guns and rifles has run afoul of the civil rights movement." He "labeled the scheme 'totally and completely wrong,' " because "the whole power of the black revolution is based upon nonviolence." Roy Wilkins and Whitney Young shared a similar view.[61]

No one was more concerned about Malcolm's call to arms than Martin King. In his speech to the spring luncheon of the United Federation of Teachers, held at New York's Americana Hotel, Martin acknowledged that "race relations had reached a crisis but that he was certain that 'the white majority was willing to meet the Negro half-way.' " When he was asked about Malcolm's "formation of the Black Nationalist Party and his call for Negroes to arm themselves," Martin said "I think it is very unfortunate that Malcolm X continues to predict violence" because "it would be very tragic . . . for the Negro to use violence in any form. Many of our opponents would be delighted." Furthermore, he continued, "if we would take up arms, it would give them an excuse to kill up a lot of us."[62]

Despite Malcolm's "violent" language, Martin sensed that he should not be taken too literally and thus might be opened to tactical nonviolence since he was no longer accountable to the narrow sectarian philosophy of Elijah Muhammad. That was why Martin told the media that he would probably talk with Malcolm about his "call to arms" and seek to convince him of the futility of violence.[63] Cautious in his initiative, Martin, three months later, took a few more steps toward Malcolm, which we will discuss shortly.

In contrast to Martin's cautious approach, Malcolm was bold in his efforts to meet with Martin. He visited Martin's SCLC office in Atlanta several times, but the latter was never there.[64] Malcolm attended civil rights events that featured Martin as a speaker and frequently talked with SCLC staffers. Malcolm also initiated their only encounter in Washington, D.C., during the Senate debate of the Civil Rights Bill. While Malcolm was trying to meet with Martin in order to form a black united front against racism, Martin was shrewdly avoiding him because of his "violent" image.

Since neither King and the civil rights movement nor Muhammad and the Nation responded positively to Malcolm's overtures of unity and peace, he decided to make the Hajj, the required pilgrimage to Mecca, followed by visits to several independent countries in Africa, in order to search for spiritual and political directions. From 19 April to 21 May, he traveled, read, and conversed with many orthodox Muslims and revolutionary Africans about Islam and the worldwide black liberation struggle.

Malcolm's trip to Egypt, Lebanon, Saudi Arabia, Nigeria, Ghana, Morocco, and Algeria made an enormous impact upon his understanding of Islam and his perspective on the politics of black nationalism. In Mecca he discovered that Elijah Muhammad's Islamic teachings — especially the idea that white people were devils by nature — contradicted orthodox Islam. Malcolm saw white Muslims in Mecca treating persons of other races, including himself, as brothers and sisters, showing no prejudice whatsoever. The experience of racial harmony, among many shades of humanity, from all over the world, shocked him. He was told by many Muslims that Islam, the religion of God, is also the religion of "brotherhood." It requires its adherents to treat all persons as human beings, without regard to race or color. Islam, Malcolm was informed, cannot tolerate any form of racial discrimination.

Malcolm spoke of his experience in Mecca as a "spiritual rebirth" which revolutionized his attitude toward white people. "What I have seen and experienced," he wrote in his *Autobiography*, "has forced me to *rearrange* much of my thought patterns previously held, and to *toss aside* some of my previous conclusions." Malcolm rejected completely the racial ideology which he had advocated as a Black Muslim. He wrote many letters to friends back in the United States, describing the "unexpected drastic changes" in his perspective. "Never before have I witnessed such . . . overwhelming spirit of true brotherhood as is practiced by people . . . here in this ancient holy land." He wrote: "They were of all colors, from blue-eyed blonds to black-skinned Africans. But we were all participating in the same ritual, displaying a spirit of unity and brotherhood that my experiences in America had led me to believe could never exist between the white and the non-white."[65]

Since Malcolm X went to the Middle East in 1959 as Elijah Muhammad's emissary, he must have seen blacks and whites associating with each other in a manner similar to what he saw in 1964. Also, several representatives of Islam had informed him of its principle of "brotherhood" and how it contradicted Muhammad's teachings about whites. Why then did Malcolm act as if he was hearing and seeing these things for the first time? As a Black Muslim, Malcolm was not permitted to think for himself but only for Muhammad. "I had blind faith in him," Malcolm said as he reflected back. "My faith in Elijah Muhammad was more blind and more uncompromising than any faith that any man has ever had for another man. And so I didn't try and see him as he actually was."[66] Thus while Malcolm saw and heard new things about Islam in

1959, he could only view them in the light of his absolute commitment to the Messenger of Allah. After his break, however, Malcolm became a free thinker, in search of new directions. With an openness to hear and see new things, he heard and saw them in Mecca, and they changed his life.

From Mecca, Malcolm journeyed to Nigeria and Ghana. As orthodox Islam challenged his theology of race, his African experience caused him to rethink his politics of black nationalism. Malcolm met many revolutionaries who "to all appearances" were white. His strong talk on black nationalism, stressing black control of the economy, politics, etc., made communication difficult with white revolutionaries in Africa. Malcolm spoke often of his encounter with the Algerian ambassador to Ghana, Taher Kaid, who was, according to his description, an "extremely militant" "revolutionary." "When I told him that my political, social, and economic philosophy was black nationalism," Malcolm recalled, "he asked me very frankly, well, where did that leave him?" An African with "all appearances" of "a white man" showed Malcolm how his black nationalist philosophy was "alienating people who were true revolutionaries." "So," Malcolm said, "I had to do a lot of thinking and reappraising of my definition of black nationalism."[67]

Of course, Malcolm knew that many people (friends and foes alike) would be greatly surprised by the radical change in his views regarding whites. Anticipating their surprised reaction, Malcolm wrote: "You may be shocked by these words coming from me. . . . [But] I have always been a man who tries to face facts, and to accept the reality of life as new experience and new knowledge unfolds it." He discussed his new perspective in several letters to friends and acquaintances and in his published essays, interviews, and *Autobiography*. He also spoke of it many times in speeches before black and white audiences when he returned to the United States. "My whole life had been a chronology of—*changes*," he wrote in his *Autobiography*. "I have always kept an open mind, which is necessary to the flexibility that must go hand in hand with every intelligent search for truth."[68]

Malcolm's trip to Mecca and Africa not only transformed his thinking about race; it also deepened his international outlook, reinforcing his conviction that the black freedom movement in America could not be separated from African liberation struggles on the continent. Malcolm had previously recognized the cultural links between African-Americans and Africans. He had urged the former to "submerge their little petty differences" and create a unity based on a "common enemy," using the Bandung conference as a model. However, after his conversations with African peoples, including several heads of state, Malcolm became convinced as never before that the African-American struggle for freedom in the United States and African liberation struggles on the continent were *one and the same struggle,* with the success of each dependent on the success of all. He believed that no black could be free anywhere in the world until blacks everywhere achieved freedom.

While Malcolm's understanding of "black" referred primarily to persons of African descent, it nonetheless had always included all peoples of color throughout the world. His travels abroad reinforced this international perspective and even enlarged it so that he began to speak increasingly of the "human being" without regard to race or nationality. When he returned to the United States, he spoke less of black nationalism and civil rights and more and more of the human rights of all peoples. "I am not a racist," Malcolm said repeatedly. "I am against every form of racism and segregation, every form of discrimination. *I believe in human beings,* and that all human beings should be respected as such, regardless of their color."[69]

The contrast between Malcolm's perspective before and after his trip abroad attracted the attention of Martin King. In an uncharacteristic move, Martin, with the assistance of his legal counsel Clarence B. Jones, who was also a friend of Malcolm, tried to arrange a meeting between them "as soon as possible on the idea of getting the human rights declaration" of the United Nations to expose America's inhuman treatment of its black inhabitants. Malcolm informed his caller (a woman speaking for Jones) that he was eager to meet with "Rev. King," because he was in the process of launching his recently conceived Organization of Afro-American Unity (patterned after the Organization of African Unity), whose "basic aim . . . is to lift the whole freedom struggle from civil rights to the level of human rights, and also to work with any other organization and any other leader toward that end." Malcolm gave the caller his complete schedule, and they tentatively set the meeting time between himself and Martin for the afternoon of the next day. The meeting did not take place.[70]

About a month later Clarence Jones, in the aftermath of the Harlem and Rochester riots and in light of Martin's and Malcolm's initiatives toward and openness to each other, "forecast eventual cooperation between [them]." The occasion of Jones's prediction was a meeting of "a group of Negro writers and artists and intellectuals." They met in order "to assess the meaning of the Harlem and Rochester riots and their probable effect on the future of civil rights organizations." In a statement to the news media, Jones said: "I think it is an irony and a paradox in terms of the national Negro community that two Negroes of such opposing views as Dr. King and Malcolm X should have such great mass appeal. . . . The Negroes respect Dr. King and Malcolm, because they sense in these men absolute integrity and know they will never sell them out." He predicted that "Malcolm is going to play a formidable role, because the racial struggle has now shifted to the urban North."

Jones was "warmly supported" by the well-known playwright and actor Ossie Davis. "The Negroes," he said, "have depended on the goodwill of the whites to help advance their cause of civil rights. Dr. King's doctrine of nonviolence implied that the white people must do the main job. Cooperation between Dr. King and Malcolm is a possibility."

Novelist John Oliver Killens also predicted cooperation between Martin and Malcolm. "If Dr. King is convinced that he has sacrificed 10 years of brilliant leadership," he said, "he will be forced to revise his concepts. There is only one direction in which he can move, and that is in the direction of Malcolm. . . . Politics make strange bedfellows."[71]

Despite the optimistic forecasts by Jones, Davis, Killens, and others, it was not likely that Martin's white benefactors would have allowed public cooperation between him and Malcolm to take place. Several of his advisers expressed their displeasure to Jones for implying that King and Malcolm would work together. For white liberals Malcolm was still too unpredictable and thus not subject to their control. When Martin and Malcolm merely shook hands in Washington, several white liberals questioned Martin about it, fearing that the white public might view it as a symbolic act of unity.

Malcolm departed for another trip abroad on July 9 in order to pursue his United Nations project. He was not present to ignite, observe, or stop the "Harlem explosion" he had predicted; nor was he present to pursue ways in which he might cooperate with Martin King and the civil rights movement. He flew to Cairo in order to attend the second meeting of the Organization of African Unity. His chief concern was to "appeal to the African Heads of State" on behalf of "the interests of 22 million African-Americans whose *human rights* are being violated daily by the racism of American imperialism." Despite the opposition of the U.S. State Department, especially the CIA and the U.S. Information Agency, Malcolm was given the status of an observer and allowed to submit an eight-page "memorandum" to the delegates.[72]

Malcolm planned to stay abroad only about two weeks, but he got so caught up in his mission of bridging the gap between African-Americans and Africans on the continent that he did not return to the United States until 24 November. Shortly after his return, he gave a major speech at his "Homecoming Rally of the OAAU" (29 November 1964) and then departed again (3 December 1964) for Britain, mainly to participate in an Oxford Union debate and other events. Coincidentally, Martin was also present in London during that time, en route to receive the Nobel Peace Prize. Speaking to four thousand Britons at St. Paul's Cathedral, Martin, with an obvious reference to Malcolm, repeated his standard comment that "the doctrine of black supremacy is as great a danger as the doctrine of white supremacy." The implication regarding Malcolm was false, as King should have known. But the words were pleasing to the white world that had bestowed upon Martin one of its highest honors—Nobel Laureate. Malcolm was of course aware of Martin's presence in London. Desirous of building a black united front, he was restrained in his comments about Martin. The *Manchester Guardian Weekly* characterized Malcolm's comments as "barbedly generous to Mr. King." Speaking to three hundred Islamic students, he said: "I'll say nothing against him. At one time the whites in the United States called him a racialist, an extremist, and a Communist. Then the Black Muslims came along and the whites thanked the Lord for Martin Luther King."[73] In a radio talk, however, he labeled Martin's nonviolence "bankrupt" and referred to South African Nelson Mandela's turnabout as evidence.

Malcolm also was present on 17 December 1964 when Harlem honored King upon his return from receiving the Nobel Prize. Despite his new aims and outlook, Malcolm could not resist commenting negatively. "Imagine that?" he said. "Getting a peace prize . . . and the war's not over!" "If I have to follow a general who is fighting for my freedom and the enemy begins to pin peace medals on him before I've gotten my freedom, I'm afraid I'll have to find another general, because it's impossible for a general to be at peace when his people don't get no peace."[74]

During a lecture engagement at Tuskegee Institute on 3 February 1965, SNCC activists invited Malcolm, against the wishes of SCLC staffers, to speak at a voting rights rally the next day in Selma. There was much tension in the air. Martin was in jail, and SCLC people pondered whether Malcolm would inflame the situation with his militant talk. James Bevel and Andrew Young took Malcolm aside and asked him to focus solely on the single issue of voting. As they walked toward Brown Chapel AME Church where he was to speak, Malcolm said, "Remember this: nobody puts words in my mouth."[75]

During his speech, Malcolm expressed wholehearted support for the civil rights struggle to achieve the right to vote. "I believe that we have an absolute right to use whatever means are necessary to gain the vote," he said. "I don't advocate violence," he told his audience, "but if a man steps on my toes, I'll step on his." "If [Sheriff James] Clark brutalizes Negroes, he should be brutalized." Malcolm also gave his well-known analysis of the house Negro/field Negro during slavery.[76]

As was true in every lecture he gave after his travels abroad, Malcolm was critical of the U.S. involvement in the affairs of Third World nations, especially the Congo; he berated the American government for "slaughtering innocent black men . . . under the guise of a rescue operation" in the Congo. Both blacks and whites raised questions about the relevance of his international perspective for the right of blacks to go to the polls in Dallas County. But for Malcolm the two issues were the same.

Malcolm viewed himself as a warrior against worldwide white supremacy. He wanted whites in Selma to know that they had an alternative. They could either listen to Martin King or they would have to deal with him and other "non-nonviolent" blacks. "Whites better be glad Martin Luther King is rallying the people because other forces are waiting to take over if he fails." By threatening whites with his presence, Malcolm believed that he was helping Martin. Greatly disappointed that his flight schedule to Europe did not permit him to visit Martin in jail, Malcolm told Coretta King: "I want Dr. King to know that I didn't come to Selma to make his job difficult. I really did come thinking I could make it easier. If the white people realize what the alternative is, perhaps they will be more willing to hear Dr. King."[77]

From Selma Malcolm made another trip to Britain "to address the first congress of the Council of African Organizations in London." Then he went to Paris for a scheduled speech for the Congress of African Students, but he was denied entrance into France. "General de Gaulle had too much gall in keeping me out of France," he quipped. Malcolm returned to Britain for a speech at the London School of Economics where he spoke about the "shrewd propaganda" of the press—propaganda that makes the criminal look like the victim and the victim look like the criminal. Again his chief examples were U.S. involvement in the Congo and black-white relations in America. Malcolm also went to Birmingham for a private meeting with Islamic students at Birmingham University. During his stay, the British Broadcasting Corporation was assailed for "conducting" Malcolm "around Smethwick," the town on the outskirts of Birmingham that has become a symbol of Britain's racial problems. "If the colored people here continue to be oppressed," Malcolm said, "it will start off a bloody battle."

Malcolm arrived back in New York on Saturday, 13 February. A few hours later, "Sunday morning about 3:00 A.M. somebody threw some bombs inside [his] house." Fortunately no one was hurt. (Malcolm was convinced that it was the work of the Black Muslims.) After he got his family a place to stay, he left again for Detroit and gave a speech which has been called "The Last Message." "Clad in a loose-fitting gray suit without a tie," exhausted and heavily dosed with medicine (due to his exposure to the cold when he hurriedly vacated his bombed house), Malcolm, speaking to "a small gathering at Ford Auditorium," rambled as he talked about the "African revolution" and proclaimed that "1965 will be the longest and hottest and bloodiest year of them all. It has to be, not because . . . I want it to be . . ., but because the conditions that created these explosions in 1963 . . . [and] in 1964 are still here." The next day he lashed out at Elijah Muhammad and the Muslims in a talk at the Audubon Ballroom in New York City, one of the few times he spoke out publicly against his mentor.

During the last week of his life, he went to Rochester, New York, for lectures at Colgate-Rochester Divinity School and Corn Hill Methodist Church. He reminded both audiences that "our problem was no longer a Negro problem or an American problem but a human problem." He also rejected nonviolence: "We don't believe that we can win in a battle where the ground rules are laid down by those who exploit us. We don't believe that we can carry on our struggle trying to win the affection of those who for so long have oppressed and exploited us. . . . Our fight is just." He stated that the criminals were those people who exploit black people. Therefore, "we believe that we're within our rights to fight those criminals by any means necessary."

Back in New York City, Malcolm gave his standard lecture on "The Black Revolution and Its Effect upon the Negroes in the Western Hemisphere" at Barnard-Columbia (Thursday, 18 February 1965) and sat for an important interview the next day with Gordon Parks of *Life* magazine. Knowing that death was closing in on him, Malcolm refused to back down from his commitment to justice for all human beings. "It looks like this brotherhood I wanted so badly has got me in a jam," he told Parks.[78]

As one seeks to understand Malcolm, it is important to keep in mind that his perspective was undergoing a radical process of change and development during the last year of his life. He gradually discarded his Black Muslim beliefs about race and religion and moved toward a universal perspective on humanity that was centered on his commitment to the black liberation struggle in America. He was struck down by assassins' bullets before he arrived at the point of view toward which he was moving. "I am out in outer limbo," he said in June 1964. While acknowledging the limitations of his previous black nationalist views, Malcolm, as late as 18 January 1965, expressed his inability to state precisely his perspective: "I still would be hard pressed to give a specific definition of the overall philosophy which I think is necessary for the liberation of black people in this country."[79]

Eleven months was too short a time to arrive at that definition, particularly as he was trying to save his life from the lethal intentions of the Black Muslims. What was amazing in the circumstances was his ability to do so much so quickly. A similar observation must be made about Martin King. Although Malcolm was severely critical of Martin's nonviolent approach to social change, he realized that both were fighting for the same goal and were equally subject to violent death. "It is anybody's guess which of the 'extremes' in approach to . . . black men's problem might *personally* meet fatal catastrophe first—'nonviolent' Dr. King, or so-called 'violent' me,"[80] Malcolm wrote in his *Autobiography* shortly before his assassination. It was after Malcolm's death that Martin began to make his radical turn away from his vision of the American dream and to gaze at the horror of Malcolm's nightmare.

8

"SHATTERED DREAMS" (1965–68)

In 1963 ... in Washington, D.C., ... I tried to talk to the nation about a dream that I had had, and I must confess ... that not long after talking about that dream I started seeing it turn into a nightmare ... just a few weeks after I had talked about it. It was when four beautiful ... Negro girls were murdered in a church in Birmingham, Alabama. I watched that dream turn into a nightmare as I moved through the ghettos of the nation and saw black brothers and sisters perishing on a lonely island of poverty in the midst of a vast ocean of material prosperity, and saw the nation doing nothing to grapple with the Negroes' problem of poverty. I saw that dream turn into a nightmare as I watched my black brothers and sisters in the midst of anger and understandable outrage, in the midst of their hurt, in the midst of their disappointment, turn to misguided riots to try to solve that problem. I saw the dream turn into a nightmare as I watched the war in Vietnam escalating. ... Yes, I am personally the victim of deferred dreams, of blasted hopes.

> Martin Luther King, Jr.
> Atlanta, Georgia
> 24 December 1967

The judgment of God is on America now!

> Martin Luther King, Jr.
> Atlanta, Georgia
> 6 August 1967

There may be periods where segregation may be a temporary way-station to an integrated society. I'm not sure that it was the best thing in the Methodist Church to get rid of the Central Jurisdiction because

> *power must always be shared power, and if you put me out, you can*
> *integrate me out of power. I don't want to be integrated out of power.*
>   Martin Luther King, Jr.
>   Miami, Florida
>   19 February 1968

More than any other person, past or present, black or white, Martin Luther King, Jr., proclaimed and lived the American dream: the idea that all people, regardless of race, creed, or nationality, are created equal and are therefore entitled to evenhanded justice under the law and social respect under the customs that govern daily behavior.

During the early weeks of the Montgomery bus boycott, as we saw earlier, King assumed that equality under the law and the dignity of the black person could be achieved within the context of a segregated social system. Then, only a few weeks after the beginning of the boycott, he became convinced that justice within a segregated social system was both a legal and an ethical contradiction. Segregation could not be reconciled with either the political ideals of American democracy or the religious principles of the Jewish-Christian Scriptures. "Segregation is evil." Desegregation of the buses, public schools, and all other institutions of public life was the only way to achieve justice for both black and white Americans.[1]

When King's thinking shifted from "justice within segregation" to "justice as desegregation," the Christian-Gandhian idea of love replaced justice as the dominant theme in his theo-political perspective. As justice was equated with desegregation, love was identified with integration and nonviolence. (Earlier he advocated nonviolence more from practical considerations than from a deeply held theological conviction.) When love replaced justice as the predominant theme of his philosophy, desegregation became the first and necessary step toward the ultimate goal of integration, which he equated with the American dream.

The idea of the American dream dominated King's perspective during most of his career as a civil rights activist. When he spoke in theological terms, he referred to it as the "beloved community" of whites and Negroes working together, praying together, struggling for freedom together, and going to jail together, knowing that no one is free until all are free. From 1956 to 1966 King, though sympathetic to many of Malcolm's views, moved in the opposite direction from separatism. He embraced integration absolutely—not only as the true and sole option for democracy but also as God's will for America. He expressed, again and again, his continuous and deepening belief that Negroes and whites together must create a just (desegregated) and loving (integrated) America.

The sight of 250,000 blacks and whites at the Lincoln Memorial in Washington, D.C. (28 August 1963), marching hand in hand, singing and speaking about freedom, reinforced King's conviction. Aside from Malcolm and the Black Muslims, on the one hand, and George Wallace and the die-hard white segregationists, on the other, few publicly denied King's claim that a "new day is coming"—a day when whites and Negroes would transform America into an oasis of brotherhood.

Although there were major challenges to King's optimism—four girls killed in a Birmingham church, Kennedy's assassination, and the killing of civil rights workers—he did not lose hope that a "truly integrated" society could be realized soon in the land of Jim Crow. As there were setbacks, there were also signs of hope: the passage of the Civil Rights Bill in June 1964, the landslide election of Lyndon Johnson as president, and the entrance of the white church, northern liberals, and labor into the civil rights movement.

Nothing, however, strengthened King's optimism about America more than the rise of "a magnificent new militancy within the Negro community all across this nation." With a "new sense of dignity and a new sense of self-respect," acquired from blacks' participation in the civil rights movement, "the Negro all over America is saying he is determined to be free."[2] "Nobody," King repeatedly told his people, "can ride your back unless it's bent." With his energetic and courageous leadership, blacks without fear or shame stood up to white racists and demanded their freedom. King identified the civil rights movement with God's liberating work in history, and he linked it with liberation struggles throughout the world. King concluded that because God created all people as free beings, nothing could stop the march of the oppressed toward the promised land of freedom.

The numerous awards that Martin received from religious organizations, labor unions, universities, and other groups reinforced his belief that the great majority of whites supported the civil rights movement's attempt "to redeem the soul of America."

THE STRUGGLE FOR THE BALLOT: END OF THE FIRST PHASE

Although he was at the summit of his prestige, King in the mid-1960s refused to stay on the "mountain top" of success and so returned to the "valley" of the South to serve the "least of the least of these"—those poor blacks who for years had been denied the right to vote.

Martin believed that the denial of suffrage was the last major barrier to black freedom. "The Civil Rights Act of 1964," he said, "gave Negroes some part of their rightful dignity. But without the vote, it was dignity without strength." Martin contended that with the "sacred right" of the ballot, Negroes would have the political power necessary to gain their freedom, and democracy in America would no longer be "anemic" or "turned up side down."[3]

Martin's emphasis on the importance of the ballot was not new. As pastor of Dexter Avenue Baptist Church, he urged all members to join the NAACP and to become registered voters. Voter registration was also the major focus of the SCLC in its early years. In King's first national address, delivered at the Prayer Pilgrimage in Washington, D.C. (17 May 1957), he appealed to the president and the Congress to "give us the ballot," and "we will fill our legislative halls with men of goodwill." "Give us the ballot and we will place judges on the benches of the South who will 'do justly and love mercy,' and we will place at the head of the southern states governors who have felt not only the tang of the human but the glow of the divine."

Despite the early concern for suffrage, success in this area had been minimal. Following the Nobel ceremonies in Oslo and a triumphant homecoming reception in Harlem, King raised the voting rights issue in an audience with President Johnson. He later recalled the president saying, "Martin, you're right about that. I'm going to do it eventually, but I can't get a voting rights bill through in this session of Congress." The president reminded him of other bills in "my Great Society Program," and "I need the votes of the southern bloc to get these other things through. . . . So it's just not wise or the politically expedient thing to do."[4]

Martin, of course, was not persuaded by President Johnson's line of reasoning. That was the logic of one who had never been denied the right to vote or forced to observe laws which he or she had had no voice in the enactment of. Disappointed with the president's lack of understanding regarding the plight of the black poor, Martin left the White House knowing that he and his supporters had to create a crisis in America by "focusing the attention of the nation and the world on the flagrant denial of the right to vote" and thereby force the president and the Congress to do what the former said could not be done.[5]

About two weeks later, on 2 January 1965, in Selma, Alabama, Martin, along with the SCLC and SNCC, began the fight for the vote. (The SNCC had been in Selma two years before King's arrival.) The fight began on a note of hope. The battle in Selma was not a fight *against* Sheriff Jim Clark or Governor George Wallace, even though they would be skillfully manipulated to disclose "all types of cunning methods [that] are still being used to prevent Negroes from becoming registered voters."[6] As Martin saw it, the Selma campaign was a fight *for America* — its ideals and principles of freedom and democracy.

Martin was sure that he and other black and white freedom fighters would win the battle for justice because love is stronger than hate, truth is more powerful than a lie, right inevitably wins over wrong. "White Americans," Martin said, "cherish their democratic traditions over the ugly customs and privileges of generations."[7]

After many beatings (especially on "Bloody Sunday," the infamous 7 March attack of the police and state troopers at the Edmund Pettus Bridge) and several murders (Jimmy Lee Jackson and James Reeb), eight thousand blacks and whites "started a mighty walk" from Selma to Montgomery, under the watchful eye of a federalized Alabama National Guard, in the "sweltering sun" and rain, "through desolate valleys and across trying hills." When Martin stood before the crowd of 25,000 at the Alabama State Capitol in Montgomery, many were as weary as he was from the long journey. The sight of the large crowd and the knowledge that millions more were watching the televised event inspired Martin to deliver a memorable address, filled with much optimism and rivaling his famous "I Have a Dream" speech at the March on Washington. He began by reminding his audience that "we ain't going to let nobody turn us around." Quoting Sister Pollard, the seventy-year-old woman who turned down an offer for a ride during the Montgomery bus boycott, he said: "My feets is tired but my soul is rested." Martin wanted to let the whole world know that the freedom movement could not be stopped by the forces of evil.

> We are on the move now. . . . No wave of racism can stop us. We are on the move now. And the burning of our churches will not deter us. We are on the move now. The bombing of our homes will not dissuade us. We are on the move now. The beating and killing of clergymen and young people will not divert us. We are on the move now. . . . Like an idea whose time has come, not even the marching mighty armies can halt us. We are moving to the land of freedom.

King believed that the right to vote would open the door to the realization of freedom for all Americans in every segment of the society. "Let us march on ballot boxes," he told the crowd, "until race bigots disappear from the political arena" and "the salient misdeeds of blood thirsty mobs are transformed into the calculated good deeds of orderly citizens." He continued: "Let us march on ballot boxes until brotherhood becomes more than a meaningless word in an opening prayer, but the order of the day on every legislative agenda."

In Martin's mind the Selma March was the beginning of the final lap of a freedom march that had started in Montgomery ten years earlier.

Whites and Negroes struggling for freedom together was a foretaste of the beloved community which he saw coming. "There never was a moment in American history," he said, "more honorable and more inspiring than the pilgrimage of clergymen and laymen of every race and faith, pouring into Selma to face danger at the side of its embattled Negroes." Selma was a deeply moving experience for King, a transfiguration event that dissolved barriers which separated Negroes and whites. It was the first time that whites, in significant numbers (particularly the religious community), ceased being merely sympathetic spectators or financial contributors to the civil rights movement and became active participants, alongside Negroes, under King's leadership. Seeing the active support of whites from all over America and the world and observing the militant determination of Negroes themselves, King, in contrast to Malcolm's earlier gloomy picture, was jubilant about the "prospects of freedom in 1965."

> Let us therefore continue our triumphant march to the realization of the American dream. Let us march on segregated housing until every ghetto of social and economic oppression is dissolved and Negroes and whites live side by side in decent, safe, and sanitary houses. Let us march on segregated schools until every vestige of segregated and inferior education becomes a thing of the past. ... Let us march on poverty ... until no starved man walks the streets of our cities and towns, in search of jobs that do not exist. Let us march on poverty until the wrinkled stomachs in Mississippi are filled ..., the idle industries of Appalachia are ... revitalized, and broken lives in sweltering ghettos are mended and remolded.

King, of course, realized that "there are still some difficult days ahead. We are still in for the season of suffering." But he was confident that the decisive battle against segregation had been won and that the remaining conflicts would represent no more than mopping-up operations. "I stand before you this afternoon," he said, "with the conviction that segregation is on its deathbed ... and the only thing uncertain about it is how costly the segregationists ... will make the funeral."

Somewhat analogous to his "I Have a Dream" speech in Washington, King, in a moment of inspiration, departed from his prepared address and concluded his talk with the sanguine refrain, "How long, not long." "I know you are asking today," he said, "how long will it take? Somebody's asking how long will prejudice blind the visions of men? ... When will justice lying prostrate on the streets of Selma ... and communities all over the South be lifted from this dust of shame to reign supreme among the children of men?"

Speaking with the enthusiasm, rhythm, and language of a black Baptist preacher and with the optimism of a liberal, Protestant theologian, King answered his questions with the eschatological phrases which he frequently used to describe his religious faith. Each time he asked, "How long?," he repeatedly and passionately answered, "Not long!," as if the truth of this claim depended on the spiritual power of his oratory.

> I have come to say to you this afternoon, however difficult the moment, however frustrating the hour, it will not be long, because truth crushed to the earth will rise again. How long? Not long! Because no lie can live forever. How long? Not long! Because you shall reap what you sow. How long? Not long! Truth forever on the scaffold, wrong forever on the throne. Yet that scaffold sways the future and behind the dim unknown standeth God within the shadow, keeping watch over his own. How long? Not long! Because the arc of the moral universe is long but it bends toward justice. How long? Not long! Because mine eyes have seen the glory of the coming of the Lord. He's trampling out the vintage where the grapes of wrath are stored. He hath loosed the fateful lightning of his terrible swift sword. His truth is marching on. He has sounded forth the trumpet that shall never call retreat. He is sifting out the hearts of men before his judgment seat. O be swift my soul to answer him, be jubilant my feet, our God is marching on. Glory Hallelujah, glory hallelujah. Glory hallelujah, glory hallelujah, his truth is marching on.[8]

When Martin concluded the Selma March, he had already been assured by President Johnson and key congressional leaders that a strong Voting Rights Bill would be enacted quickly. With the passage of the Civil Rights Act in 1964, granting blacks social equality in the public life of America, and with assurances about the passage of the Voting Rights Act a few months after Selma, the latter act granting blacks political power, Martin felt certain that the civil rights movement had accomplished its primary goal, and the American dream would soon be realized. He compared the Selma March to "Gandhi's march to the sea." As James Bevel, one of King's key staffers and the brains behind the Selma campaign, told the SCLC convention: the civil rights movement ceased to exist as soon as President Johnson signed the Voting Rights Bill (6 August 1965).[9]

It was Martin King's optimism about America that separated him from Malcolm X and thus made it quite difficult for the two of them to work together in the black freedom movement. Malcolm had no confidence in the federal government and very little in whites as a people. Even after his trip to Mecca and his subsequent denunciation of the "racist" philosophy of Elijah Muhammad, Malcolm remained deeply suspicious of white Americans' moral capacity to treat blacks as human beings. "The criminal action of the United States government in conjunction with Belgium in the Congo," its complicity in the assassination of Patrice Lumumba, the country's prime minister, and its support of Moise Tshombe, "the worst African that was ever born," reinforced Malcolm's belief that white America had no moral conscience in regard to its treatment of black people.

In contrast to Malcolm's views, Martin *believed* in whites because he believed in the goodness of humanity. He believed in humanity because he believed in God, the One who created male and female in the image and likeness of the divine. Therefore, all people, white and Negro alike, have the moral capacity to do the good and to fight against evil. With this faith, Martin contended that the conscience of whites could be awakened to treat Negroes as human beings, as brothers and sisters. While he developed some doubts about how soon the die-hard segregationists might be redeemed, Martin was confident that in time they too would join "the great decent majority" of whites (including the federal government, churches, labor, and white liberals) in their support of equal rights for the Negro people. He sustained his optimism through the Selma March.

The "How Long? Not Long!" address may be regarded as the climax of the first phase of the intellectual development of Martin King's theopolitical perspective. Although he continued to make hopeful statements after Selma, sometimes using identical words and phrases, there was an important change in the quality and expression of Martin's hope. Before Selma his hope was hardly distinguishable from an unsuspecting belief in the goodness of humanity. His perspective on politics and religion was influenced by the black middle-class, integrationist tradition in which he was reared and the liberal theology which he studied in graduate school. With love at the center of his theology, Martin believed that nonviolence had the moral power to "awaken the conscience of the nation" and thereby enable whites and Negroes to create a just and beloved community in America. After Selma, however, the second and most important phase of Martin's thinking began to emerge. This development, until recently neglected by King's interpreters, was characterized by the shattering of his dream and his movement slowly toward the philosophy of Malcolm X.

THE SECOND PHASE: A DREAM SHATTERED

WATTS!

On 11 August 1965, five days after President Johnson signed the Voting Rights Bill, Malcolm X's predicted nightmare exploded in the Watts ghetto in Los Angeles, leaving 34 people dead, 4,000 arrested, and whole blocks of buildings burned to the ground. An army of 14,000 National Guardsmen and 1,600 policemen invaded Watts to restore order. It was like a war zone, with many blacks roaming the streets shouting "Burn, baby, burn" and "Long live Malcolm X." Some blacks, in the spirit and rhetoric of black nationalism, referred to the violence as an insurrection and not as a riot.

Martin King and the entire southern-based civil rights movement were caught completely off guard. Even though he and the SCLC staffers had witnessed earlier disturbances in Birmingham (following the 1963 desegregation "accord") and in Harlem and Rochester in July 1964, they were not prepared for the magnitude of the fury and devastation in Watts. Not since the Detroit riot of 1943, which also killed thirty-four people, had America experienced such outbreaks of violence in the black ghetto. En route to a vacation in San Juan, Martin could not get Watts out of his mind. Staffers advised him to stay away and avoid being associated with the violence. Nevertheless, following a speech to a Disciples of Christ convention in San Juan, he cut short his vacation to accept the invitation of the Los Angeles black clergy to assist them in restoring peace.

Martin was greatly disturbed by what he saw in Watts. After talking with many young blacks who had participated in the riot, he discovered that the problem of racism and injustice in America was much deeper than he had thought. He was surprised to find out also that most of the urban young did not accept nonviolence as the primary method for gaining their freedom. As Paul Williams, a Watts resident, put it: "King, and all his talk about nonviolence, didn't mean much. Watts had respect for King, but the talk about nonviolence made us laugh." The Watts riot and others which followed in the urban centers revealed the great gap between Martin's optimism about nonviolence and the despair found in the random acts of violence in the ghettos of American cities.[10]

During the first ten years of the civil rights movement, Martin King and others had assumed that the blacks of the North would benefit indirectly but significantly from the victories gained in the South. The Watts riot and the dramatic rise in the popularity of the black nationalist philosophy of Malcolm X showed that Martin overestimated the self-esteem that northern blacks would receive from the "straightened up backs" of their southern brothers and sisters. While surveying the devastation of Watts, he was surprised that many blacks there had never heard of him. When he gave a talk to a crowd of three hundred blacks at Westminster Community Center and counseled nonviolence, a man shouted, "Get out of here Dr. King! We don't want you!" Martin was particularly troubled when he heard a group of young blacks boasting, "We won." "How can you say you won," Martin retorted, "when thirty-four Negroes are dead, your community is destroyed, and whites are using the riots as an excuse for inaction?" "We won because we made them pay attention to us," they shouted at him. When Martin reflected on that response and the hostile reactions to his message of nonviolence, he began to realize that the Civil Rights and the Voting Rights Acts did not significantly reduce the problems of racism and poverty, especially in the North. "Watts wasn't suffering from segregation, or the lack of civil rights," Paul Williams asserted. "You didn't have two drinking fountains. . . . When Johnson signed the civil rights bill in sixty-four, nobody even thought about it in Watts. . . . It had nothing to do with us." Northern blacks already could eat in "white" restaurants, could vote, and, in theory, could attend "integrated" schools. But, as Malcolm had pointed out, they had no money for a meal in the white man's restaurant, no representatives of their interests in government, and no control over the de facto segregated schools in their community. Trapped in the ghetto filth, victimized by poverty and police brutality, poor blacks spent most of their time and energy trying merely to survive in a society which had totally neglected them.[11]

The Watts riot initiated a major turning point in Martin King's thinking about America. He began to see that "there are literally two Americas," one beautiful, rich, and primarily white, and the other ugly, poor, and disproportionately black. Martin's encounter with the "other America," as he frequently referred to it, helped him to understand something of the world that created Malcolm X. Bayard Rustin, an adviser to King who met him in Watts, recalled the occasion: "I'll never forget the discussion we had with King that night. He was absolutely undone, and he looked at me and said, 'You know, Bayard, I worked to get these people the right to eat hamburgers, and now I've got to do something . . . to help them to get the money to buy [them].'"[12]

Although Rustin had been telling King, since the March on Washington, that the economic problems of class were greater than the problems of race, only after his brief experience in Watts was King persuaded of the great limitation of his earlier, almost exclusive focus on the elimination of the "legal, overt segregation" of blacks in the

South. "That struck Martin very, very deeply," Rustin said. "I think it was the first time he really understood."[13]

What was it that Martin King understood? First, he realized that formal equality (i.e, the achievement of constitutional rights) did not change the *material* conditions of black people, especially those packed in the ghettos in the North. In fact their poverty continued to get worse, partly because of the progressive displacement of unskilled labor, further eroding their sense of somebodyness. After Watts, Martin concluded that without *economic* justice, the right to a job or income, talk about "life, liberty, and the pursuit of happiness" was nothing but a figment of one's political imagination.

Again against advice King decided that the civil rights movement had to go North and raise the conscience of the nation so that federal, state, and city governments would be pressured to provide the economic resources to eliminate the slums in the central cities. He was determined to prove that nonviolence could work in the North, dealing with the problems of slums as effectively as it had dealt with segregation in the South.

Chicago was chosen as the target city. Moving into a slum apartment on the South Side (in January 1966), Martin did not take long to realize that poverty was no accident but was the consequence of a calculated decision of the wielders of economic power. Using Malcolm's language, Martin began to speak of the ghetto as a "system of internal colonialism." "The purpose of the slum," he said in a speech at the Chicago Freedom Festival, "is to confine those who have no power and perpetuate their powerlessness.... The slum is little more than a domestic colony which leaves its inhabitants dominated politically, exploited economically, segregated and humiliated at every turn." The chief problem is economic, he concluded, and the solution is to restructure the whole society. The anticapitalist sentiments of his graduate school years had long been dormant, but the Watts riot and the Chicago experience activated a cautious but serious examination of socialism as an alternative to the American political economy. "The fire bombs of Watts ... blasted the civil rights movement into a new phase," he told the SCLC convention in Jackson, Mississippi, "and ... Chicago was now the testing ground."[14]

King was careful not to identify himself publicly as a Marxist, partly because of Marxism's materialistic view of history that left no place for God, and partly because of its ethical relativism, which he interpreted as the end justifying the means. But Martin's most important reason for avoiding any public association with Marxism was the deep anticommunist sentiment in America. White segregationists and J. Edgar Hoover, the director of the FBI, constantly harassed him by charging that he had links with the Communist Party or by alleging that he had persons as advisers and on the SCLC staff, such as Stanley Levison and Jack O'Dell, who were party agents.[15]

But despite his caution, it is clear that a radical change was taking place in King's thinking about America, a transformation that was moving him along a revolutionary path that surprised many of his friends and supporters. "Things are not right in this country," he said, over and over again. "Why are there 40 million poor people in a nation overflowing with such unbelievable affluence?" When Martin saw the massive poverty in the ghettos of Los Angeles, Chicago, and other central cities, people living with "wall to wall rats and roaches," with no hope of a meaningful change in their wretched condition, he could not understand why whites assumed that the passage of the recent civil rights legislation meant that Negroes had achieved full equality. He stated: "I am appalled that some people feel the civil rights struggle is over because we have a 1964 civil rights bill with ten titles and a voting rights bill. Over and over again people ask, What else do you want? They feel that everything is all right. Well, let them look around at our big cities."[16]

Many interpreters have declared the Chicago Freedom Movement a failure because it did not produce an enforceable open housing law. However from a viewpoint influenced by Malcolm, one could say that Chicago was one of Martin's great successes, in that it created the most important development in his perspective on America. He began to speak more and more of America as a morally "sick society" and of his dream of 1963 being turned into a nightmare. The only solution, he concluded, was to restructure the whole of America so that all of its people would have food and shelter for their bodies and dignity and self-respect for their spirits.

The new and revolutionary development in Martin's thinking was the chief focus of several SCLC staff retreats and the tenth anniversary convention. Testing his ideas with his staff, many of whom were strong supporters of capitalism, Martin gradually led them to consider the new developments in his thinking:

> We've got to begin to ask questions about the whole society. We are called upon to help the discouraged beggars in life's market place. But one day we must come to see that an edifice which produces beggars needs restructuring. It means that questions must be raised. "Who owns the oil?" . . . "Who owns the iron ore?" . . . "Why is it that people have to pay water bills in a world that is two-thirds water?"[17]

Martin's turn toward economic issues also deepened his global vision and his insights into the links between the sociopolitical freedom of blacks in the United States and the liberation of their brothers and sisters in Africa, Asia, and Latin America. Like Malcolm, Martin believed that Negroes could not be free in America until the poor of the world were set free. Martin recognized that the American identity of the civil rights movement put it in danger of being the enemy of Third World peoples:

> However deeply American Negroes are caught in the struggle to be at last at home in our homeland of the United States, we cannot ignore the larger world house in which we are also dwellers. Equality with whites will not solve the problems of either whites or Negroes if it means equality in a world society stricken by poverty and in a universe doomed to extinction by war.[18]

The urban, black underclass and the poor in the Third World increasingly became the major preoccupation of his practice and reflections.

MOVEMENT TOWARD SEPARATISM

Martin's turn toward the North not only placed the economic question in the forefront of his thinking; it also stimulated a deeper appreciation of Malcolm's philosophy of black separatism.

This is not to suggest that Martin became a closet black nationalist. He did not, because he viewed its advocates as promoters of hate and violence. From the time he accepted love and nonviolence as his philosophy of life, during the Montgomery bus boycott, Martin remained steadfast in his commitment. In fact, it grew stronger rather than weaker. During the time when the summer riots were a regular occurrence, Black Power was on the lips of many young blacks, as they read Franz Fanon's *Wretched of the Earth* and Malcolm's *Autobiography*. Nonviolence began to lose prestige as the most appropriate weapon for social change, especially among the younger generation of civil rights activists and blacks in the northern ghettos. Young blacks began to "yell for the 'white man's blood.' " "Move over whitey or we'll move you over," was a common refrain. Martin King, however, refused to accommodate the mood. "Some people are telling us to be like our oppressor, who has a history of using Molotov cocktails, who has a history of dropping the atom bomb, who has a history of lynching Negroes," he shouted, venting his anger during a civil rights rally in Yazoo City, Mississippi. "Now people are telling me to stoop down to that level," he continued. "I'm sick and tired of violence. I'm tired of the war in Vietnam. I'm tired of Molotov cocktails." King repeatedly said that "if every Negro in the United States turns to violence, I'm going to stand up and be the only voice to say that it is wrong." In one of his last published essays he wrote, "I am committed to nonviolence absolutely." Insofar as black nationalism was defined as "paramilitary movements, back to Africa movements, and 'separate Negro state' movements," which is how it was defined by the white media, King was totally against it.[19]

To say, then, that King was moving toward black separatism is to say that he displayed a new affirmation of black self-esteem and self-determination in politics, economics, and social and religious institutions. After his failure to get an enforceable open housing law in Chicago and other cities, he reluctantly and regretfully began to move toward Malcolm's separatist position. In a revealing speech in Louisville, he said:

> Now I don't believe in black separatism. I'm against it. . . . But I do say this. It seems that our white brothers and sisters don't want to live next door to us. . . . So . . . they're pinning us in central cities. . . . We're hemmed in. We can't get out. They won't pass the fair housing bill here. And that's true in every city in this country. Now, since they're just going to keep us in here, . . . what we're going to have to do is just control the central city. We got to be the mayors of these big cities. And the minute we get elected mayor, we've got to begin taxing everybody who works in the city who lives in the suburbs. I know this sounds mean, but I just want to be realistic.[20]

When he focused on the problems of the inner city, he saw the despair and self-hate that Malcolm had talked about. He saw the drugs and alcohol, prostitution and police brutality, and the often fruitless effort of poor blacks who were trying to survive in an environment unfit for human habitation. "I have never seen such hopelessness," said Hosea Williams, one of King's aides summoned from Atlanta to Chicago to "mobilize 'political power in the Negro community.' " "The Negroes in Chicago have a greater feeling of powerlessness than any I ever saw." "Chicago has been a nightmare."[21] What could integration or the American dream possibly mean for people who saw no hope of getting out of the ghetto?

Martin's move toward black separatism was slow because integration had served as the cornerstone of his perspective for most of his life. Raised in a middle-class family, nurtured in a "highbrow" black church of Atlanta, and educated at the "Harvard" of black colleges and the best schools of liberal theology in the North, Martin found that moving toward Malcolm's position was a difficult step to take. Black separatism contradicted his deep faith in the American dream and his spiritual vision of it as the beloved community. He also knew that white liberal supporters of the civil rights movement would have a great deal of difficulty accepting any perspective that advocated black control of political, economic, and social institutions.

But King also knew that the power of his own organization, the SCLC, was derived primarily from the black church, a separatist institution from the time of its origin in the late eighteenth century. Although he preached integration, Martin did not seek to implement it in the black church or in the SCLC. The leadership in the SCLC was "Southern Negro-oriented," to use Andy Young's description of it. "You are welcome to share in our program, but you can't take it over — that's the way SCLC has always been," Young said. "We didn't have any whites on our board *until* the separatist issue came about. Then to show we weren't being prejudiced, we went out to look for some."[22] But not many. Only two!

Aware of the hegemony of the integration model in both white and black communities, King was reluctant to reveal his separatist leanings. To identify himself and the civil rights movement with black nationalism would have created at least as much difficulty as the communist label. Therefore he embraced certain features of the nationalist tradition while carefully avoiding the nationalist label.

King's movement toward Malcolm's separatist position was a response to two developments: the rise of the Black Power movement and the failure of most whites to support authentic integration.

BLACK POWER

The most important event which contributed to Martin's move toward Malcolm's separatism was the rise of Black Power during the Memphis-to-Jackson Freedom March, organized by the leaders of the SCLC, CORE, and SNCC, following the shooting of James Meredith in June of 1966. Martin was troubled when Stokely Carmichael, SNCC's new chairman, first shouted "black power!" "from the tailgate of a truck" in Greenwood, Mississippi (16 June). Concerned about connotations of hate and violence, Martin told his staff, "When you put *black* and *power* together, it sounds like you are trying to say black domination." He had absolutely no sympathy for black supremacy, and repeatedly said that it was just as evil as white supremacy. He was also troubled because Black Power advocates rejected white support in the black freedom struggle, and even rejected the cherished slogans and ideals of the civil rights movement — such as "we shall overcome," "black and white together," fighting nonviolently for "freedom now," and the realization of the "American dream" — that helped engender that support. "I don't think anything could be more tragic for the civil rights movement," King said, "than the idea that the black man can solve his problems all by himself."[23]

Although King saw some value in Black Power, he often felt that its negative features outweighed its positive contribution. He tried to get Stokely Carmichael, Floyd B. McKissick, CORE's new national director, and other advocates of Black Power to drop the phrase in the interest of unity in the black freedom movement, particularly since Roy Wilkins, Bayard Rustin, A. Philip Randolph, and Whitney Young were vehemently opposed to the phrase. Wilkins, the most virulent critic, attacked Black Power as "the father of hatred and the mother of violence," "a reverse Mississippi, a reverse Hitler, a reverse Ku Klux Klan" that "can mean in the end only black death."[24]

Since the young Black Power advocates said that they needed a slogan with the word "black" in it, King suggested "black consciousness" and "black equality" in lieu of Black Power. They rejected King's suggestions and refused to drop the phrase. In fact, they intensified their use of it, deliberately leaving its meaning vague so it could be manipulated to mean whatever they decided in a given situation. "The intent, initially," explained Cleveland Sellers, SNCC's program director and author of *The River of No Return,* "was not to get boxed into a particular definition. . . . There was a deliberate attempt to make it ambiguous" so that "it meant everything to everybody."[25]

King was greatly troubled by SNCC and CORE's refusal to clarify the meaning of Black Power. "I have heard some Snick members make statements advocating retaliatory violence, and some say they are committed to nonviolence," he told a *New York Times* reporter. "So I am confused about it all." Despite King's denial, his uncertainty about where the Black Power advocates stood on violence prompted him to cancel an address at the annual convention of CORE. He did not wish to appear publicly with any black leader "who might advocate racial violence." That had been the chief reason he refused to appear on the same platform with Malcolm X. Black Power advocates sounded too much like Malcolm for his taste. When he discussed his concern with his staff, he found them divided on the issue.[26]

Meanwhile, the media made Black Power a dominant theme in the news, describing it as "the most disruptive force yet in the rights movement." They emphasized black leaders' confusion regarding the meaning of Black Power. "Nobody knows what the phrase 'black power' really means," a *New York Times* editorial asserted. The media, however, seemed certain that its advocates were antiwhite and promoters of violence as a means of social change. Stokely Carmichael and Floyd McKissick spent much time trying to correct what they called misinterpretations of Black Power. "Black Power is not hatred," McKissick proclaimed at an SCLC rally in Chicago. He said that it "did not mean black supremacy, did not mean exclusion of whites from the Negro revolution, and did not mean advocacy of violence and riots." Rather Black Power meant "political power, economic power, and a new self-image for Negroes."[27]

Despite McKissick's explanations, King remained concerned about the continued use of the slogan Black Power because "it tended to inflame Negroes and alienate whites from the movement." "We need striped power—black and white together," King said. "There is no salvation of the Negro through isolation." King, therefore, searched for a "third road," a "synthesis"—a "middle ground" that would be "militant enough to satisfy the militant, . . . yet [with] enough discipline . . . to satisfy white supporters and moderate Negroes." He walked a tightrope as he tried to keep the civil rights movement unified. Martin invited McKissick to an SCLC rally and proclaimed that "our power is our unity." He "play[ed] both sides of the street," as one of his aides put it, pointing out the good points and weaknesses of the views of both the older civil rights leaders and the young radicals.[28]

After realizing that SNCC and CORE leaders were not going to stop using the phrase Black Power, King tried to invest it with positive meaning. He lauded its emphasis on black self-esteem. "The Negro is in dire need of a sense of dignity and a sense of pride, and I think black power is an attempt to develop pride. And there's no doubt about the need for power—he can't get into the mainstream of society without it." King began gradually to substitute the term "black" for "Negro," often proclaiming in sermons and speeches to African-Americans that he was proud to be black. "Black Power," he said, "means instilling within the Negro a sense of belonging and appreciation of heritage, a racial pride. . . . We must never be ashamed of being black." "Black is beautiful and it's so beautiful to be black" was written on several placards that were prominently displayed at the SCLC's tenth annual convention, held at Ebenezer Baptist Church in August 1967. Many speakers talked about a "sense of negritude" and "Afro-American unity." Bernard Lee, King's constant companion, got himself a natural African hair style. At the convention and in many speeches before and after it, King said that of the 120 synonyms for black in the thesaurus, 60 are offensive but "all 124 synonyms for white were favorable." "They even tell us," he said "that a white lie is better than a black lie."[29]

The most persuasive evidence of Martin's gradual move toward separatism is found in his speeches to blacks in early 1968 during his tour of the South in preparation for the Poor People's Campaign. He accented much more frequently the positive aspects of black culture and its intellectuals.

Before Black Power, white personalities had dominated King's idea of excellence and the black models were the ones whom whites had portrayed as Negroes worthy of emulation (i.e., Booker T. Washington, George Washington Carver, Roland Hayes, Jesse Owens, Joe Louis, Marion Anderson, and Jackie Robinson). King taught a "seminar in social philosophy" at Morehouse College during the first semester of the 1961–62 academic year and did not use one required text written by an African-American scholar. The writings of Plato, Aristotle, Augustine, Aquinas, Machiavelli, Hobbes, Locke, Rousseau, Kant, and Hegel were his choices. During the *Playboy* interview, Alex Haley asked him: "If you were marooned on the proverbial desert island, and could have with you only one book—apart from the Bible—what would it be?" "Well," he said, "I think I would have to pick Plato's *Republic*."

After Black Power, King made fewer references to whites as persons to imitate; he began to name black persons as models of excellence, and those names were less acceptable to whites than the names that had appeared on his earlier list. Speaking about the Poor People's Campaign in Clarksdale, Mississippi (19 March 1968), Martin said:

Every day we are going to have freedom schools . . . [and] black cultural events going, because they've [white people] made us feel that we haven't done anything for the history and the culture of the world. . . . We're going to let our young people know that Shakespeare, Euripides, and Aristophanes are not the only poets that have lived in history. We're going to let our children know about Countee Cullen and Langston Hughes. We're going to let our children know that the only philosophers that lived were not Plato and Aristotle, but W. E. B. Du Bois and Alain Locke came through the universe.[30]

Before Black Power, King referred to Jesus as a white man. When a concerned black person asked King, "Why did God make Jesus white, when the majority of people in the world are non-white?", he replied:

The color of Jesus' skin is of little or no consequence. The whiteness or blackness of one's skin is a biological quality which has nothing to do with the intrinsic value of personality. The significance of Jesus lay, not in color, but in his unique God-consciousness and his willingness to surrender his will to God's will. He was the Son of God, not because of his external biological make-up, but because of his spiritual commitment. He would have been no more significant if his skin had been black. He is no less significant because his skin is white.

After Black Power, Martin's image of Jesus underwent a transformation. "Jesus," he said to a group of black ministers in Miami, "was not a white man." Of course, Martin did not say that "Jesus was black," as Malcolm often said. He gave no religious significance to Jesus' pigmentation; Jesus' meaning transcended color. Now saying Jesus was not white was Martin's way of denying the widespread assumption that everything good and valuable came from Western society. "Christianity is not just a Western religion," Martin said. He urged black ministers to turn toward their own culture and history for the insight and power to revolutionize the world. "We have the power," he told them, "to change America, and give a kind of new vitality to the religion of Jesus Christ." Although he remained a universalist in his views about religion and politics, his thinking was deeply affected by his praxis, causing him to affirm a concept of blackness that was in many respects similar to Malcolm's and clearly absent from his earlier speeches.[31]

Although King was careful not to alienate other leaders of the civil rights movement, especially Wilkins, Young, and Randolph, he was equally concerned not to drive away the advocates of Black Power. For example, he said nothing when Carmichael humiliated Wilkins in a meeting during the Meredith March in Mississippi. According to Carmichael:

> Wilkins came in the meeting and he already had a statement. He was going to make the march to support some legislation, some nonsense that Johnson had. And when he came up with that, everyone else was mad, because they didn't like him much anyway. So I started acting crazy, cursing real bad. I said, "You sellin' out the people, and don't think we don't know it. We gonna getcha." . . . Wilkins couldn't believe it. He went to Dr. King and Dr. King might have been shocked, too, but he didn't say a word.[32]

Martin also refused to attach his name to the statement "Crisis and Commitment," an implicit condemnation of Black Power written by Rustin and signed by Wilkins, Young, Randolph, and three other prominent blacks. He did not want to "excommunicate" SNCC and CORE from the civil rights movement. "Some consider certain civil rights groups conclusively and irrevocably committed to error and wish them barred from the movement," Martin told the *New York Times*. "I cannot agree with this approach because it involves an acceptance of the interpretation of enemies of civil rights and bases policy on their distortion." Martin was referring to whites who interpreted Black Power as black violence, and then used it as a justification of a new wave of white "backlash" and recent civil rights reversals in Congress. White liberals called upon "responsible Negro leaders" to condemn Black Power. Martin responded with an advertisement in the *New York Times.* The caption read: "IT IS NOT ENOUGH TO CONDEMN BLACK POWER." While acknowledging that "the slogan was an unwise choice" because of its "violent connotations," he urged whites to examine its meaning at a deeper level. "Negroes have to acquire a *share* of power so that they can act in their own interests and as an independent social force." With the emergence of the white backlash, however, he soon realized that sharing power with blacks was not an item on the white agenda.[33]

DISENCHANTMENT WITH WHITES

Behind Martin King's affirmation of blackness and his move toward Malcolm X's separatism was a reassessment of the moral quality of whites. He was disappointed that the majority of white moderates in the North and South failed to support the goal of genuine equality for blacks and other poor people. As early as his *Playboy* interview (January 1965), he acknowledged his disappointment.

I have been dismayed at the degree to which abysmal ignorance seems to prevail among state, city and even Federal officials on the whole question of racial justice and injustice. . . . But this white failure to comprehend the depth and dimension of the Negro problem is far from being peculiar to Government officials. . . . It seems to be a malady even among those whites who like to regard themselves as "enlightened." . . . I wonder at [persons] who dare to feel that they have some paternalistic right to set the timetable for another [person's] liberation. Over the past several years, I must say, I have been gravely disappointed with such white "moderates." I am inclined to think that they are more of a stumbling block to the Negro's progress than the White Citizen's Counciler or the Ku Klux Klanner.

When summer riots became a regular occurrence during the second half of the 1960s, Martin became impatient with whites who withdrew their support of the civil rights movement and began to say that "law and order" ought to be the highest priority of government. "I say to you," proclaimed Martin, "the riots are caused by nice, gentle, timid white moderates who are more concerned about order than justice."[34]

What Martin discovered was the limit of white interest in the plight of blacks. The majority of them were willing to support the Civil Rights and Voting Rights Acts, because they were outraged by the brutal behavior of southern bigots, like Bull Connor of Birmingham and Jim

Clark of Selma. "And so," Martin said, "they took a stand for decency, but it was never really a stand for genuine equality for the black man." Genuine equality, he explained, "will cost the nation something," because it involves economic justice. King estimated the cost at 100 billion dollars. "It's much easier to integrate lunch counters than it is to eradicate slums. It's much easier to guarantee the right to vote than it is to guarantee an annual minimum income and create jobs." Many whites who marched with Martin in Selma and other places in the South deserted him when he moved North to fight against the economic plight of blacks and other poor people. The resistance was so great that Martin began to see America through the eyes of the poor in the ghetto. If Martin were going to understand their plight, he had to move closer to Malcolm's perspective and begin to see white liberals as phony advocates of freedom for the black poor. "In Chicago," Martin said, adopting Malcolm's language, "Mayor [Richard J.] Daley's response was to play tricks with us — to say he's going to end slums but not doing any concrete thing."

The more King worked in the North, the more he recognized that it would not be easy to use civil disobedience to place poverty as a moral issue before the nation. It was one thing to break segregation laws in the South and quite another to disobey other state and federal laws. Furthermore, most whites felt that blacks had made much progress and should be satisfied. It was in this context that Martin's views about whites began to change radically, moving closer to Malcolm's. Since only a few whites supported economic equality and the majority were passionately against it, Martin said regretfully, as he spoke to Louisville blacks, "I am sorry to have to say to you that the vast majority of white Americans are racist, either consciously or unconsciously." To his staff, he said, as they prepared for the Second March on Washington: "We live in a confused . . ., sick, neurotic nation." This is quite a contrast from his earlier appeals to "the conscience of the great decent white majority."

During his fight to end legal segregation in the South, Martin could count on the support of the federal government, media, labor, and the churches. His Poor People's Campaign, however, did not mobilize widespread support. Lyndon Johnson was especially angry about the whole idea and prompted several prominent blacks and whites to criticize Martin's views about the Poor People's Campaign and the war in Vietnam. But Martin refused to back down and continued to remind Americans how immoral it was to have 40 to 50 million poor people in the richest nation in the world. He believed that unless America repented by redistributing its wealth so that the poor could have the basic material necessities of life, it would self-destruct.

There is confusion in the land. Now this is why we've made a decision to come to the seat of government, in April, . . . and will seek to say to the nation that if you don't straighten up, and that if you do not begin to use your vast resources of wealth to lift God's children from the dungeons of despair and poverty, then you are writing your own obituary. We are coming to Washington to say to America, "Straighten up, and fly right."[35]

Martin's disappointment with white moderates reached its peak during his preparations for the Poor People's Campaign. According to him, racism was a disease, a cancer in the body politic; while many whites seemed unconcerned about it, Martin deepened his analysis of the "sickness of America." On that sickness he said: "The thing wrong with America is white racism. White folks are not right. Now they've been making a lot of studies about the Negro, about the ghetto, about slums. It's time for America to have an intensified study on what's wrong with white folks. . . . Anybody that will go around bombing houses and churches, it's something wrong with him."[36]

As he realized that whites had no intention of integrating the masses of poor blacks into the mainstream of the society, King began to advocate "temporary segregation." For him segregation and separatism meant the same thing. He ignored Malcolm's distinction that segregation is forced upon blacks by whites while separation is initiated by blacks in order to affirm and to defend their humanity against whites. But even though Martin did not acknowledge the distinction or affirm separation as a goal, his talk about "temporary segregation" was a completely new departure for him. In response to a question at the 1968 annual convention of the Rabbinical Assembly (25 March 1968), he said that "there are times when we must see segregation as a temporary way-station to a truly integrated society." While he rejected separation as an ultimate goal because of humanity's "inescapable network of mutuality," he nevertheless was concerned about being "integrated *out* of power." He was emphatic: "We want to be integrated *into* power." Examples which Martin gave of blacks being integrated out of power included the public schools in the South and the Methodist Church, with its removal of the all-black Central Jurisdiction. Because he realized that whites viewed integration more in "esthetic or romantic terms," Martin said that "it is absolutely necessary to see integration in political terms."

In every city, we have a dual society . . ., two economies, . . . two housing markets, . . . two school systems. This duality has brought about a great deal of injustice. . . . To deal with this unjust dualism, we must constantly work toward the goal of a truly integrated society while at the same time we enrich the ghetto. We must seek to enrich the ghetto immediately in the sense of improving the housing conditions, improving the schools . . ., improving the economic conditions. . . . We must work on two levels.[37]

For Martin King, working on "two levels" meant traveling two roads to freedom: separation and integration. The first road was a temporary but necessary path that blacks had to travel to get to the second road, the main highway of integration. Integration was the ultimate goal, which King called the American dream and the beloved community. He spent most of his years as a civil rights activist traveling on the integration road until he realized that the vast majority of whites, South and North, had no intention of permitting the masses of black people to travel on it. When whites talked about integration they meant tokenism, just as Malcolm had said many years earlier. Martin also saw that, to make matters even worse, white America was playing the same tricks in the international community, talking peace and practicing war— bombing colored men, women, and children in Vietnam. The racism which prevented the realization of the American dream also was destroying the global human community.

THE VIETNAM CRUCIBLE: JUSTICE, LOVE, AND HOPE

King's qualified sympathy with the Black Power movement and his disappointment with whites were reinforced by his growing distress over the war in Vietnam, which became an important theme in his public utterances during the last year of his life. He was gripped by the suffering of the Vietnamese, especially the children; he was angered that Americans would deprive their own poor to pay for an unjust war; and he was saddened that his antiwar position alienated many of his allies, black and white, in the freedom movement. His discouragement over these developments led to an important change in his theology.

Martin's reflections on racism, black empowerment, and the war led to a shift in emphasis and meaning regarding the themes of love, justice, and hope. Except for his justice-centered "Holt Street" address (5 December 1955), love was the focus of the first period of King's spiritual and intellectual development. During that time love was the informing concept, and justice and hope were interpreted in its light. Now as a result of his bleak reassessment of the freedom struggle and his agony over the war, hope became the shining center of Martin's thinking, revealing new interpretations of love and justice. Regarding the idea of hope, the main difference between his early and later years was this: In the early period, King's hope was partly based on the progress of the civil rights movement and the support it received from both the black oppressed (by their active commitment to nonviolence) and the white majority (by their commitment to formal equality). In contrast, Martin's hope in the last years was not based upon the backing he received from whites or even blacks. Rather, his hope was grounded almost exclusively upon his faith in the God of the biblical and black traditions, which told him to stand up for right even if it would cost him his life.

Martin often recalled the time when he was "very discouraged and a little afraid and wondering whether we were going to win the struggle" of the Montgomery bus boycott. Sister Pollard, a devout, elderly woman and an avid supporter of Martin's leadership, noticed that he did not speak with the spiritual "strength and power" which she had become accustomed to hearing from him. "Son, what's wrong with ya?" she asked following a meeting. "You didn't talk strong tonight." Although Martin responded, "Nothing is wrong Sister Pollard, I'm all right," she knew that he was not all right. "You can't fool me," she said. "Somethin' wrong with ya. Is the white folks doin' somethin' to ya that you don't like?" "Everything is gonna be all right," Martin said, as he tried to cover up his depression. Finally, Sister Pollard said, "Come close to me and let me tell ya somethin' one more time, and I want ya to hear it this time. Now I done told ya we's with ya. Now even if we ain't with ya, the Lord is with ya. The Lord's gonna take care of ya."[38]

The encounter with Sister Pollard undoubtedly reminded him of his 27 January 1956 "kitchen experience." However, as long as he received the support of the vast majority of whites, especially the federal government, love seemed sufficient to produce the social change needed to eliminate segregation. But as he began to fight earnestly against poverty, racism, and war, Martin found himself alone and isolated. Sister Pollard's words, "The Lord's gonna take care of ya," became more and more important. "Today," he proclaimed in a sermon, "I can face any man with my feet solidly placed on the ground, my hand in the air, because I know that when you're right, God will fight the battle. Darker yet may be the night, harder yet may be the fight. Just stand up with that which is right."[39]

Instead of trusting human allies to produce a victory over the forces of organized evil, Martin's hope was now a transcendent one, focusing on the biblical God of the oppressed whom he called "a great benign power in the universe . . . [who] is able to make a way out of no way."

Martin's turn toward hope comes out in his critique of the Vietnam War, a critique which he knew would alienate his former allies. America's escalation of the war in Vietnam and its de-escalation of the war on poverty motivated Martin to become one of the severest critics of the domestic and foreign policies of his government during the second half of the 1960s. He began to speak like a prophet, standing before the day of judgment, proclaiming God's wrath and indignation upon a rich and powerful nation that was blind to injustice at home and indifferent to world peace. Instead of speaking of the American dream, as he had done so eloquently before, he began to speak like Malcolm, over and over again, of an American nightmare, especially in Vietnam.

King was slow in making up his mind to take a public stand against the war in Vietnam. With the passage of the Civil Rights Act (1964) and the Voting Rights Act (1965), there was unprecedented support from the federal government and the American people for the black struggle for full citizenship rights in the United States. Respect and acclaim for King were at their peak, and he did nc' elish having to take an unpopular stand. But with the war escalating daily, it became difficult for him to keep silent. As a guest on the CBS television show "Face the Nation," on 29 August 1965, he called for a "negotiated settlement of this very dangerous and tragic conflict." However, with considerable pressure from the Johnson administration, white liberals, and established black leaders, King quietly reduced his criticism of the war. About a year later (January 1967), when he went to Jamaica to write a book (*Where Do We Go from Here: Chaos or Community?*), he "picked up an article entitled 'The Children of Vietnam.' . . . After reading that article," he told his staff, "I said to myself never again will I be silent on an issue that is destroying the soul of our nation, and destroying thousands of little children in Vietnam."[40]

Although King was slow in making up his mind, when he did no one could deter him from the prophetic role to which he felt himself called. "I want you to know that my mind is made up," he proclaimed to his staff at a retreat. "I backed up a little when I came out in 1965. My name then wouldn't have been written in any book called *Profiles in Courage*. But now I have decided. I will not be intimidated. I will not be harassed. I will not be silent and I will be heard."[41]

King's great "Beyond Vietnam" speech, given at Riverside Church in New York exactly one year before his assassination, was heard around the world. In terms of moral courage it was his greatest hour, as he proclaimed America to be the "greatest purveyor of violence in the world today." His public condemnation of America for its criminal involvement in Vietnam, however, did not begin with the Riverside address or end with it. After he made up his mind, for the remaining year of his life, Vietnam remained a chief focus of his attention as he linked it with racism and poverty.[42]

The depth of his distress about the war shows most clearly in the unpublished sermons, delivered at Ebenezer and other black churches.

They include "A Knock at Midnight" (25 June 1967), "Standing by the Best in an Evil Time" (6 August 1967), "Thou Fool" (27 August 1967), "Mastering Our Fears" (10 September 1967), "But, If Not . . ." (5 November 1967), "The Meaning of Hope" (10 December 1967), "Drum Major Instinct" (4 February 1968), and "Unfulfilled Dreams" (3 March 1968).[43] Reading and listening to them reveal the decisive influence of the black and biblical traditions upon them. These sermons were delivered against the advice of many of his friends and followers in the SCLC, the NAACP, and elsewhere, who told him to keep silent about the war because he was alienating President Johnson and the financial supporters of the SCLC. With prophetic passion, typical of the best in the black church tradition, Martin told them: "I'm sorry, you don't know me. I'm not a consensus leader. I don't determine what is right and wrong by looking at the budget of the Southern Christian Leadership Conference, or by taking a Gallup Poll of the majority opinion. Ultimately a genuine leader is not a searcher for consensus but a molder of consensus."

Unlike Malcolm X, Martin King did not enjoy criticizing his government. He loved America deeply, particularly its liberal, democratic, and religious traditions of equality and justice. But he could not overlook the great contradictions of racism, poverty, and militarism. For Martin, there was no greater inconsistency between creed and deed than America's military adventures in Vietnam. He frequently referred to Vietnam as a small nation of people of color which quoted the U.S. Declaration of Independence in its own document of freedom when the people declared their independence from the French in 1945. "Yet," Martin said, "our government refused to recognize them. President Truman said they were not ready for independence. So we fell victim as a nation at that time to the same deadly arrogance that has poisoned the international situation for all these years."[44]

The arrogance that Martin was referring to was racism. "I don't believe," he wrote in "A Testament of Hope," "we can have world peace until America has an 'integrated' foreign policy. Our disastrous experiments in Vietnam and the Dominican Republic have been . . . a result of racist decision making. Men of the white West . . . have grown up in a racist culture, and their thinking is colored by that fact. . . . They don't respect anyone who is not white." Martin also felt that the vehement criticisms that he received from the white community regarding his opposition to the Vietnam War were motivated by racism. He spoke out against his white allies in government and the media who supported his stand on nonviolence during the sit-ins and freedom rides and in Birmingham and Selma and then rejected his position on Vietnam:

They applauded us in the sit-in movement when we nonviolently decided to sit in at lunch counters. They applauded us on the freedom rides when we accepted blows without retaliation. They praised us in . . . Birmingham and Selma, Alabama. Oh, the press was so noble in its applause and . . . praise when I would say "Be nonviolent toward Bull Connor," . . . "Be nonviolent toward Jim Clark." There is something strangely inconsistent about a nation and a press that would praise you when you say, "Be nonviolent toward Jim Clark," but will curse and damn you when you say, "Be nonviolent toward little brown Vietnamese children!"[45]

Many blacks in the civil rights movement, including some of the SCLC staff, joined the chorus of criticisms against King's views on Vietnam, but this opposition did not soften his stand on a war he believed was criminal. For example, when Whitney Young of the Urban League cornered him in public and reprimanded him about his views on Vietnam, he responded sharply: "Whitney, what you're saying may get you a foundation grant but it won't get you into the kingdom of truth."[46]

Like Malcolm during the last year of his life, Martin often found himself alone and isolated. As Malcolm turned to Allah, Martin turned to the God of "Shadrach, Meshach, and Abednego." Just as the "three Hebrew children" refused to worship the King's golden image, accepting instead the flames of the fiery furnace, Martin also took his stand against Lyndon Johnson's war policies and refused to bow down to the political pressures of the White House and the FBI. Martin knew that the fire of criticism against him could be turned into gunfire. But as the pressures increased, he turned to the God of the biblical faith, because he believed that, as was true of the three Hebrews, God could deliver him "if it be so" (Dan. 3:17).

Using the responses of Shadrach, Meshach, and Abednego as a sermon title, "But If Not . . .," Martin made it clear that he was prepared to give his life for the truth of God. The more he was pressured to keep silent, the more forcefully he spoke out against the war. "It is just as evil," he proclaimed in a sermon at Ebenezer, "to kill Vietnamese as it is to kill Americans, because they are all God's children."[47]

Martin refused to accept the idea that being an American citizen obligated him to support his country in an unjust war. He refused to equate "dissent with disloyalty," as many of his critics did. On the contrary he concluded that he was the true patriot because in his opposition to the war, he was in reality defending America's tradition of freedom and democracy that was being violated in Vietnam. Furthermore, as a Nobel Laureate, Martin believed that he was obligated to transcend nationalism, and thereby to take a stand for world peace. But much more important than his obligation as a citizen of America or of the world was his vocation as a minister of God, the Creator of the universe. When people queried him about the wisdom of mixing peace and civil rights, he responded: "Before I was a civil rights leader, I answered a call, and when God speaks, who can but prophesy? I answered a call which left the Spirit of the Lord upon me and anointed me to preach the gospel. . . . I decided then that I was going to tell the truth as God revealed it to me. No matter how many people disagreed with me, I decided that I was going to tell the truth."[48]

For Martin, telling the truth meant proclaiming God's judgment upon America for its failure to use its technological resources for the good of humanity. "Here we spend thirty-five billion dollars a year to fight this terrible war in Vietnam and just the other day the Congress refused to vote forty-four million to get rid of rats in the slums and the ghettos of our country." "The judgment of God is on America now," he said, using language similar to that of Malcolm X. He compared America to the rich man, Dives, who passed by the poor man, Lazarus, and never saw him. And like Dives who went to hell because he refused to use his wealth to bridge that gulf that separated him from Lazarus, "America," Martin proclaimed, "is going to hell too, if she fails to bridge the gulf" that separates blacks from whites, the United States and Europe from Asia, Africa, and Latin America.[49]

Because Martin believed that America's war in Vietnam violated its own democratic values and the moral principles of the universe, he could not keep silent. There comes a time "when silence is betrayal." A nation that spends $500,000 to kill one enemy soldier in Vietnam and only $50 to get one of its own citizens out of poverty is a nation that will be destroyed by its own moral contradictions. "If something doesn't happen soon, I'm convinced that the curtain of doom is coming down on the U.S." The more the American government and its citizens tried to ignore him the more forcefully he proclaimed his message:

America, I don't plan to let you rest until that day comes into being when all God's children will be respected, and every man will respect the dignity and worth of human personality. America, I don't plan to allow you to rest until from every city hall in this country, justice will roll down like waters and righteousness like a mighty stream. America, I don't plan to let you rest until from every state house . . ., men will sit in the seat who will do justly, who will love mercy, and who will walk humbly before their God. America, I don't plan to let you rest until you live it out that "all men are created equal and endowed by their creator with certain inalienable rights." America, I don't plan to let you rest until you believe what you have read in your Bible, that out of one blood God made all men to dwell upon the face of the earth.[50]

Although Martin was often depressed about his government's refusal to stop the war in Vietnam and to eliminate poverty at home and in the Third World, he did not lose hope. "I haven't lost hope," he said about two weeks before his death. "The days ahead are difficult, but I have not lost hope. This is the only thing that keeps me going. . . . I do not yield to the politics of despair. I will continue to work and hope that through that working, we will be able to transform dark yesterdays into bright tomorrows." As Martin watched the widening gulf between America's "promise and fulfillment" of justice for the poor and its fanatical pursuit of an "unjust, evil, criminal war," he separated his dream from the easy optimism of liberal politicians and theologians and grounded it in a black and biblical hope that was carved out of the cross of Jesus and the suffering of his people. "I still have a dream," he proclaimed in "A Christmas Sermon on Peace" at Ebenezer, "because . . . you can't give up on life. If you lose hope, . . . you lose that courage to be, that quality that helps you to go on in spite of all."[51]

It was Martin's hope which sustained him in the midst of controversy, enabling him to make a solidarity with the victims of the world, even though he failed to achieve the justice for which he gave his life. Martin's hope was derived from his religious faith, and it enabled him to see the certainty of victory in the context of an apparent defeat. "When you stand for justice, you never fail. The forces that have the power to make concession to the forces of justice and truth . . . but refuse to do it . . . are the forces that fail. . . . If there is no response from the federal government, from the Congress, that's their failure, not those who are struggling for justice."[52]

King's tenacity in decrying the Vietnam War, racism, and poverty is hard to understand without calling to mind the role of the "preacher as prophet" in the black church community. Interpreters of King have ignored or undervalued his traditional sense of vocation, perhaps because they are unacquainted with the black religious tradition which defined it. When black preachers are true to their "call to the ministry," they must speak the truth of God regardless of who is affected by its judgment or the costs to personal safety. As Martin said in a sermon at Ebenezer:

God anointed! No member of Ebenezer Baptist Church called me to the ministry. You called me to Ebenezer, and you may turn me out of here. But you can't turn me out of the ministry, because I got . . . my appointment from God Almighty, and anything I want to say I'm going to say it from this pulpit. It may hurt somebody. I don't know about that. Somebody may not agree with it, but . . . the Word of God is upon me like fire shut up in my bones and when God gets upon me, I've got to say it. I've got to tell it all over everywhere. And God has called me to deliver those in captivity. Some people are suffering, . . . hungry, . . . [and] still living in segregation and discrimination this morning. I'm going to preach about it. I'm going to fight for them. I'll die for them if necessary, because . . . the God that called me to preach told me that every now and then . . . I'll have to agonize and suffer for the freedom of his children. I may even have to die for it. But if that's necessary I'd rather follow the guidelines of God than to follow the guidelines of men.[53]

King believed that he had been called by God to be a prophet to America. As his advisers continued to urge him to change his position on Vietnam, he tried to explain to them why he could not recant, even if it meant that he would lose his prestige and the SCLC would become bankrupt. What mattered was speaking the truth of God as he saw it. He told Stanley Levison:

At times you do things to satisfy your conscience, and they may be altogether unrealistic and wrong tactically, but you feel better. I just know, that on the war in Vietnam, that I will get a lot of criticism, and I know it can hurt SCLC. But I feel better, and I think this is the most important thing. Because if I lose the fight SCLC will die anyway. . . . And I feel that we are so wrong in the [Vietnam] situation that I can no longer be conscious about this matter. I feel so deep in my heart that we are so wrong in this country, and *the time has come for real prophecy. And I am willing to go that road.*[54]

Living under the daily threat of death, agonizing over the black nationalists' talk about using violence, and frustrated by the U.S. government's continued escalation of the Vietnam war, Martin, in a sermon at Ebenezer, stated why he could not keep silent:

I've decided what I'm going to do. I ain't going to kill nobody in Mississippi . . . [and] in Vietnam. I ain't going to study war no more. And you know what? I don't care who doesn't like what I say about it. I don't care who criticizes me in an editorial. I don't care what white person or Negro criticizes me. I'm going to stick with the best. On some positions, cowardice asks the question, "is it safe?" Expediency asks the question, "is it politic?" Vanity asks the question, "is it popular?" But conscience asks the question, "is it right?" And there comes a time when a true follower of Jesus Christ must take a stand that's neither safe nor politic nor popular but he must take that stand because it is right. Every now and then we sing about it, "if you are right, God will fight your battle." I'm going to stick by the best during these evil times.[55]

Revolutionary prophets, like Malcolm and Martin, often do not live to become old men. They are usually killed by the forces they are seeking to change. Malcolm X was killed by the blacks he loved and was seeking to liberate from self-hate. Martin King was killed by the whites he loved and was seeking to set free of racism. How should we evaluate the success or failure of Malcolm X and Martin King in their missions? This is not an easy question to answer for either person because of the many vantage points from which one could shape an answer. Some persons would say that Martin was very successful and Malcolm was not. Others would argue the opposite. Some would say that both were successful, and others would say that neither was.

While I will not try to answer whether Martin and Malcolm were successful or not from an "objective" or "scientific" point of view, I do want to examine more closely their impact upon each other and upon America, especially the African-American community. Chapter 9 focuses on how they complemented and corrected each other. Chapter 10 identifies two serious flaws in their thinking which were and still today are often present in the African-American and other communities. Chapter 11 and the conclusion examine their contributions as leaders, highlighting their legacies and our need to appropriate their vision of a just society for America and the world.

9

TWO ROADS TO FREEDOM

Today was a dark day in Birmingham. The policemen were mean to us. They got their violent, angry dogs and turned them loose on non-violent people, unarmed people. But not only that, they got their water system working. And here and there we saw the water hose, with water pouring on young boys and girls, old men and women, with great and staggering force. Birmingham was a mean city today. But in spite of the meanness of Birmingham, we must confront her with our kindness and our goodness and our determination to be nonviolent. As difficult as it is, we must meet hate with love. As hard as it is, we must meet physical force with soul force. . . . Just let them get their dogs and let them get their hose, and . . . we will leave them standing before their God and the world covered with the blood and reeking with the stench of their Negro brothers.

> Martin Luther King, Jr.
> Sixteenth Street Baptist Church
> Birmingham, Alabama
> 3 May 1963

You have to understand this about Martin Luther King. If he loses his effort to keep Negroes nonviolent, the result could be disastrous not only in Birmingham but all over the country. Remember, it was King who went around the pool halls and door to door collecting knives, telling people to go home and stay off the streets and to be nonviolent. Compare that with Nashville, where they have pictures of a Negro chasing a white down the street carrying a knife. If King loses, worse leaders are going to take his place. Look at the black Muslims.

> Robert F. Kennedy
> White House Meeting with Alabama Editors
> Washington, D.C.
> 14 May 1963

I'll tell you one of the dangers of Martin Luther King. King himself is probably a good man, means well and all that. But the danger is that white people use King. They use King to satisfy their own fears. They blow him up. They give him power beyond his actual influence. Because they want to believe within themselves that Negroes are non-violent and patient, and long suffering and forgiving. White people want to believe that so bad, 'cause they're so guilty. But the danger is, when they blow up King and fool themselves into thinking that Negroes are really nonviolent, and patient and long suffering; they've got a powder keg in their house. And instead of them trying to do something to defuse the powder keg, they're putting a blanket over it, trying to make believe that this is no powder keg; that this is a couch that we can lay on and enjoy.

> Malcolm X
> Claude Lewis Interview
> Harlem, New York
> December 1964

How should we understand the meaning of Martin and Malcolm for each other? What did they think of each other? What influence did they have upon each other? How shall we see their relationship a quarter-century later? These questions are not easy to answer because Martin and Malcolm had no opportunity for dialogue about the black freedom movement. Their public comments about each other seemed to be based upon media images rather than precise information.

As the "good guy," the darling of the white liberal establishment, Martin stayed away from any public association with "bad guy" Malcolm. He seldom mentioned Malcolm and the Black Muslims publicly because he and his civil rights associates were trying to convince whites that blacks wanted to be integrated into the dominant society. When whites reminded Martin of the presence of the black nationalists, he minimized their significance and explained their existence as a desperate reaction to segregation. He thought that without progress toward full integration, a nationalist "black supremacist" movement became more and more of an alternative for oppressed blacks. Though derived from white supremacy, black supremacy was not to be excused; Martin thought the child was as evil as its parent. He made no attempt to present the positive and creative contribution which Malcolm made to the black freedom movement. When Alex Haley, *Playboy* interviewer, asked him about "the most responsible Negro leaders," he omitted Malcolm and named only the five heads of the major civil rights organizations. If one used only Martin's public statements, the unavoidable conclusion would be that he did not consider Malcolm a significant, creative black leader.

While Martin tried to ignore Malcolm, Malcolm would not let Martin alone, often peppering his speeches and interviews with sharp criticisms of the civil rights leader. Malcolm resented the attention that the media lavished upon Martin and the civil rights movement. Malcolm and the Black Muslims were seldom mentioned in the media until the 1959 television production of "The Hate That Hate Produced," which portrayed them as a black nationalist hate group. From then on Malcolm's visibility in the media was shaped by his antiwhite, anti-Christian, and anti-integration image, placing him in direct opposition to the political and moral values of Martin King and the civil rights movement. As long as Malcolm was saying something negative about Martin or some other civil rights leader, his views were disseminated widely. He gave the media what they wanted, and thus became known as the black version of the Nazi George Lincoln Rockwell.

Martin and the other civil rights leaders knew that Malcolm was in no sense analogous to Rockwell or any other white racist. Likewise Malcolm knew that Martin was not all the names he called him. Both played the roles assigned to them by the white public in hope that they were thereby advancing the black struggle for justice.

Martin's and Malcolm's movement toward each other is a clue that neither one can be fully understood or appreciated without serious attention to the other. They *complemented* and *corrected* each other; each spoke a truth about America that cannot be fully comprehended without the insights of the other. Indeed, if Americans of all races intend to create a just and peaceful future, then they must listen to both Martin and Malcolm.

COMPLEMENTING EACH OTHER

Two Black Worlds

The most important similarity between Martin and Malcolm was the *goal* for which they fought. From the beginning of their ministries, they both sought the unqualified liberation of African-Americans from the bonds of segregation and discrimination to self-determination as a people, from a feeling of inferiority and nobodyness to an affirmation of themselves as human beings. To be sure, Martin's and Malcolm's great differences in historical and social origins led them to choose different paths to the goal, yet the method of each complemented that of the other.

During his year of independence, Malcolm was explicit in identifying his work with that of Martin: "Dr. King wants the same thing I want — freedom!" For both Malcolm and Martin, freedom meant black people affirming their humanity and demanding that whites recognize them as human beings. "We declare our right on this earth . . . to be a human being," Malcolm proclaimed at the OAAU Founding Rally, "to be respected as a human being, to be given the rights of a human being in this society, on this earth, in this day, which we intend to bring into existence by any means necessary."[1]

According to Malcolm, the concepts of "integration" and "separation" were merely different methods which blacks employed in their struggle for freedom. Whites often used these terms to divide blacks, labeling the ones they disapproved of, like Malcolm, as separatists or segregationists and the ones they approved of, like Martin, as integrationists and moderates. Malcolm, however, was adamant in his rejection of these labels. "No," he said in "The Ballot or the Bullet" speech, "I'm not for separation and you're not for integration. What you and I are for is freedom. Only you think that integration will get you freedom; I think separation will get me free. We've both got the same objective. We've just got different ways of getting at it." Malcolm was relentless in making this point, as he sought to bridge the gap that separated him from Martin and other civil rights activists. "It is not a case of our people . . . wanting either separation or integration," he said on a television panel moderated by Irv Kupcinet. "The use of these words actually clouds the real picture. The 22 million Afro-Americans don't seek either separation or integration. They seek recognition and respect as human beings."[2]

"Respect as human beings" was the central theme of both Malcolm and Martin in the black freedom struggle. Initially Malcolm believed that "respect" was found primarily in religio-cultural identity—affirming blackness (Africa) and rejecting whiteness (America). By contrast Martin, though he believed black people's cultural identification with Africa was important, contended that blacks could achieve "respect" only by acquiring social and political power in America, *as Americans.*

The differences between Martin's and Malcolm's approaches were due partly to geography. Each developed a strategy for freedom that was appropriate for the region in which he worked. They complemented each other in that they spoke to different groups of people in their community. King addressed his message primarily to southern black Christians; Malcolm to northern blacks who were either indifferent to or alienated from Christianity.

The nonviolent, direct-action approach, strongly oriented to Christianity, was ideal for challenging legal segregation in the South. It enabled politically powerless blacks to resist virulent racism and thereby let the world know that they would no longer tolerate the daily violation of their humanity by the dominant white society. Their religious faith bestowed upon them the feeling that they were "children of God," and thus just as precious in God's sight as anybody else, including whites. The belief that they were created by God for freedom instilled a rebellious spirit in black Christians, empowering them to fight nonviolently and risk death for their right to be treated as human beings. "We are relying solely on spiritual and moral forces," said E. N. French, pastor of Hilliard Chapel AMEZ Church and a leader in the Montgomery bus boycott, "and we believe that somehow God will give us victory. Whatever the price may be we are perfectly willing to pay it."[3]

Using the Christian idea of the sacredness of human personality as his central religious claim, Martin galvanized southern blacks to take a stand for justice. Fifty thousand African-Americans followed him in Montgomery and even more after that successful "stride toward freedom." They did not follow Martin because he held a Ph.D. degree or because he was a follower of Gandhi, Thoreau, or liberal Protestant theologians. Those persons, though contributing to the coherence of King's thought, were not spiritually and culturally persuasive enough to arouse poor southern blacks to risk their lives for freedom. Martin could motivate blacks to follow him because of the faith he lived and preached, communicating God's life-giving power to the "least of these." Through prophetic preaching of the gospel of Jesus, combined with fearless civil rights activity, Martin inspired ordinary blacks—maids, cooks, and janitors—to believe in themselves as human beings, to stand up to white bigots and demand that the law recognize their humanity. By substituting "tired feet" for "tired souls," they gave birth to a "New Negro" in Montgomery, and their spirit of resistance spread throughout the black community in America.

Demanding the right to ride at the front of the bus, to eat at a lunch counter, and to drink water at a "white only" fountain may not sound radical for people unacquainted with Jim Crow culture in the South. Like Martin, I was born and reared there and still consider it my "home." I know what it meant for blacks to insist on being recognized as human beings among whites who thought of them as nothing more than menial servants. Whites routinely demanded that blacks address them deferentially—"yes sir" and "no ma'am"—but never returned the respect. If blacks and whites approached each other on a sidewalk or street, blacks were sometimes required to cross over to the other side of the street. While no blacks liked the way things were, few challenged it because that meant risking one's life. I heard my mother tell stories about "bad niggers," and she worked hard keeping my father in check, for he was not one to take a step backwards for anyone, except the women of any race.

The last thing white southerners could stomach was "uppity niggers" who violated the "southern way of life" by insisting that blacks should be treated as equals to whites. Only "crazy niggers," "communists," and "outside agitators" could be so bold as to suggest such an outrageous idea. That was why civil rights leaders' most reasonable demands— especially those made by biracial committees of blacks and whites— were almost always bitterly resisted by whites. Masters do not sit down at the "table of brotherhood" and discuss their differences with their slaves. When a prominent Alabama judge was asked whether he saw any "connection between Autherine Lucy's efforts to enter the University of Alabama and the Montgomery nonviolent [bus] protest," his reply was typical of the dominant sentiment of whites in the South: "Autherine Lucy is just one unfortunate girl who doesn't know what she is doing, but in Montgomery it looks like all the niggers have gone crazy."[4]

Because whites controlled the economic and political power in the South, including the state and local police forces, *nonviolent* protest was the only practical alternative for a 10 percent black minority population. For blacks to advocate the use of violence or even self-defense in public demonstrations against racial injustice would have led to a blood bath, with blacks doing most of the bleeding. Many blacks (and a few whites too) suffered and died in the southern civil rights movement, but far fewer in twelve years of intense struggle than the many in the urban riots whose duration was only a matter of days. During the 1950s and throughout most of the 1960s, the only creative method available to blacks in the South to protest segregation was the one that Martin adopted—nonviolent direct action. Martin infused Gandhi's and Thoreau's ideas about nonviolence with the spirituality of the black church and thereby aroused blacks to assert their humanity.

Bayard Rustin, an adviser and astute observer of Martin, referred to him as a "spiritual intellectual."

> What Dr. King delivered to blacks there [in Montgomery], far more important than whether they got to ride on the bus, was the absence of fear, the ability to be men in the same way the Jews in the Warsaw ghetto knew that they couldn't win, but, knowing they were going to die, they said, "Let us go down expressing our manhood, which is to fight back." So Dr. King had this tremendous facility for giving people the feeling that they could be bigger and stronger and more courageous and more loving than they thought they could be.[5]

Fearlessness, which Martin embodied and communicated to black Christians, was derived from the faith of the black church, the belief that the God of Moses and of Jesus was greater and more powerful than the forces of captivity. When poor blacks heard Martin tell the stories of how the biblical God delivered Israel out of the land of Egypt, Daniel from the lion's den, and the "three Hebrew children" from the fiery furnace, that was all the evidence they needed to believe that same God would also deliver them from the Ku Klux Klan and other white hate groups. Faith in the God of the Bible, as revealed in the black religious experience, cast out black Christians' fear of whites and enabled them to take that long, courageous walk toward freedom, singing enthusiastically, "Walk together children, don't you get weary, there's a great camp meetin' in the Promised Land."

The significance of Martin's religious faith in his civil rights activity has often been overlooked and misunderstood. In times of crisis Martin again and again returned to the faith he learned as a child at Ebenezer Baptist Church in Atlanta and appropriated for his life in his kitchen in Montgomery. Martin's advisers and co-workers in the SCLC also testify to his faith that God was involved in the black freedom struggle. According to Bayard Rustin, who was not a Christian, Martin really believed that "if you do the right thing, you must leave the rest to God."[6]

While Martin's secular advisers did not always appreciate his reliance on God, the SCLC clergy and poor African-American Christians understood the logic of his faith, for they too had a similar religious conviction, believing that God had sustained them through many "trials and tribulations" in the unfriendly world of the South. As white brutality and injustice increased, so did the strength of their belief that God had not left them alone in their suffering. Living under the daily threat of death, King often told blacks that there was no greater honor than to suffer or even to die for the cause of justice.

The Bible and the spirituality of the black slave — these were the chief sources of Martin's faith. His black audiences loved to hear him talk about it nearly as much as he loved to preach. One of his most poignant expressions of that faith was repeated many times as the peroration in his sermons.

Centuries ago Jeremiah raised a question, "Is there no balm in Gilead? Is there no physician?" He raised it because he saw the good people suffering so often and the evil people prospering. Centuries later our slave foreparents came along and they too saw the injustices of life and had nothing to look forward to morning after morning, but the rawhide whip of the overseer, long rows of cotton and the sizzling heat, but they did an amazing thing. They looked back across the centuries, and they took Jeremiah's question mark and straightened it into an exclamation point. And they could sing, "There is a balm in Gilead to make the wounded whole. There is a balm in Gilead to heal the sin-sick soul."[7]

What Martin did for poor black Christians in the South, Malcolm accomplished for ghetto blacks in the North. He empowered them to take a stand in the defense of their humanity, affirming their blackness: black self, black action, black culture, and black past. Although this point was never absent in Martin's thought and work, his faith and southern, middle-class origin did not equip him to understand the depth of the deprivation of blacks in the urban ghettos of the North. Grass-roots blacks of the North were the children of Malcolm and Martin knew it. One of Martin's associates, Alfred Duckett, appropriately said that Malcolm "climbed out of the pit of the prison and dope dealing and street hawking of hot goods to become a Daniel for his people, a hot and angry and eloquently persuasive prophet who helped his brothers and sisters be aware that they could, indeed, fight back against the oppressive pressures of racism and persecution." Duckett gives a brief but moving eyewitness account of Malcolm's rallies in Harlem and the impact Malcolm made upon blacks who heard him. Like Martin who stood fearless before Bull Connor and Jim Clark of Birmingham and Selma, Malcolm stood unafraid before the white cops of Harlem "with his searing, almost sneering taunts and bold statements about the law and order troops in their midst, . . . [and] levelled against them the heavy artillery of scorn and ridicule." Other eyewitnesses and videotapes and audiotapes of Malcolm's rallies confirm Duckett's testimony. Duckett called Malcolm "our sage and our saint" who "delighted black audiences with his daring."

> He was not ridiculing these law and order "guardians" for the sake of race baiting. He was letting all of us know that we have no need to fear brutality and injustice when we are guilty of nothing but assembling and standing up for our God-given rights. He was heaping scorn on those blue uniforms to send the clear message to his people that so long as we call police who should act as the paid servants of all peaceful people "the man" — we shall acknowledge that we are less as men and women and indeed deserve to be treated as bad boys and girls.

Harlem blacks loved Malcolm for his courage to speak the truth — bluntly and without compromise. They loved "the power and the magic of his speech, his sense of drama, the exquisite humor which he could invoke to let [the people] see that [they] must stop being frightened of goons who could only justify their existence with billy clubs and guns."[8]

Malcolm inspired Harlem blacks to walk the streets with dignity and to be prepared to die for it: "Treat me like a man, or kill me," he demanded, and blacks knew he meant it. "No one ever called Malcolm a nigger," they said with much pride. As the public defender of black humanity and "witness for the prosecution against white America," Malcolm, in debates with white and black intellectuals, before a variety of audiences, earned the title that Ossie Davis bestowed upon him in his eulogy: "Our Own Shining Black Prince."[9]

Malcolm's power was derived from the African heritage of blacks and not the faith of Christianity. "Our forced importation into this country was not the beginning of our heritage, but a rude interruption." The worst crime white people have committed, Malcolm said, was to teach us to hate ourselves, destroying our past and making us think that our foreparents did nothing but pick cotton. For many years, Africa was dominated by Europeans who "projected [it] in a negative light: jungle savages, cannibals, nothing civilized," so blacks began to hate it. "We didn't want anybody telling us anything about Africa, much less calling us Africans. In hating Africa . . ., we ended up hating ourselves, without even realizing it. Because you can't hate the roots of the tree, and not hate the tree. You can't hate your origin and not end up hating yourself."[10]

Malcolm believed that the self-confidence to live as free human beings could be achieved only through a people's knowledge of its past. "Just as a tree without roots is dead," he said, "a people without history or cultural roots also becomes a dead people." Malcolm ridiculed blacks who said, "I ain't left nothing in Africa." "Why, you left your mind in Africa," he retorted.[11]

As Martin contributed to the development of the New Negro in the South, Malcolm helped to resurrect the dead Negro in the North, creating a proud, angry black — one ready to die in defense of black humanity. Northern blacks already possessed the political rights that their southern brothers and sisters were fighting to achieve. But they were not any better off. Malcolm even suggested that their plight was worse, because the tricky white liberals, who claimed to be the "friends of the Negro," supporting the civil rights movement, were in fact the ones most responsible for the ghettos in the North.

As Martin exposed the brutality of the white southern bigots to the world, Malcolm revealed the hypocrisy of the northern white liberals, identifying them as the worst enemies of black freedom. "Yes, I will pull off that liberal's halo that he spends such efforts cultivating!" he said in his *Autobiography*. "The North's liberals have been for so long pointing accusing fingers at the South and getting away with it that they have fits when they are exposed as the world's worst hypocrites. I believe my own life *mirrors* this hypocrisy. I know nothing about the South. I am a creation of the Northern white man and of his hypocritical attitude toward the Negro."[12]

Long before the eruption of the riots in the urban centers of America, Malcolm warned of their coming, pointing his accusing finger at the white liberal as the one to blame. "Actually, America's most dangerous and threatening black man is the one who has been kept sealed up by the Northerner in the black ghettos—the Northern white power structure's system to keep talking democracy while keeping the black man out of sight somewhere, around the corner."[13]

Malcolm spoke for a group of northern blacks who had lost hope in Christianity and America, the ones "deepest in the mud," as he liked to say. With streetwise, truth-telling oratory, emphasizing the revolutionary and African side of African-American history, he inspired urban blacks to take a good, long look at themselves in the mirror of his analysis and then be transformed by the true knowledge of who they are—the lost children of a proud and mighty African people.

Southern black Christians and northern grass-roots blacks, southern white bigots and northern white liberals—these were respectively the primary audiences and enemies of Martin and Malcolm. Both the black audiences that they wanted to empower and the white enemies that they wanted to expose influenced what they said and how they said it. No one could unmask the great danger of white liberals' participation in the civil rights movement like Malcolm. While civil rights leaders uncritically accepted their contribution and overrated it, Malcolm said that "the ultra New York liberal," who "grins with his teeth," "had more integration problems than Mississippi."[14] On the other hand Martin, though deceived by many white liberals (as he later realized), understood far better than Malcolm the Bull Connors and Jim Clarks of the South. Using the media, Martin, a "master strategist," as Wyatt Tee Walker appropriately called him, made them reveal their brutality as the world looked on in utter disbelief. A Malcolm "macho" approach, emphasizing self-defense, would have led to disaster for the black freedom movement. Martin was right: white racists knew how to deal with violence, and they would have welcomed it as an excuse to kill law-abiding blacks indiscriminately.

CLOSING THE GAP

Martin and Malcolm knew their own limitations and knew also that the limitations of one were the strengths of the other. There is no reason to pit them against each other, debating which of their methods was the most appropriate for the achievement of black dignity—integration or separation, nonviolence or self-defense. Up to a point, both methods were effective in the regions in which they were employed.

Gradually both Malcolm and Martin moved away from the extremes of their original positions and began to embrace aspects of each other's viewpoints, without denying the validity of their own central claims. Malcolm was expelled from the Nation of Islam because he wanted to link its religio-cultural philosophy with the politics of the civil rights movement. His audience among progressive whites (especially young college students) and his panel discussions and debates with integrationists (particularly James Farmer, Kenneth Clark, Louis Lomax, James Baldwin, and Bayard Rustin) convinced him that the approach of the Nation of Islam was too limited. It "took part in nothing that black people in this country were doing to correct conditions that existed in our community," Malcolm said, "other than it had a moral force—that it stopped our people from getting drunk and taking drugs and things of that sort. Which is not enough: after you sober up, you're still poor."[15] He came to see that the religio-cultural approach of the Nation of Islam was complementary and not antithetical to the politics of the civil rights movement.

Malcolm supported several efforts of mainline civil rights organizations, especially voter registration, urging blacks to join the political process and elect black public officials who would represent their interests. "The campaign that they have in Mississippi for voter registration is a good campaign," he said at the second OAAU rally. "It puts them in a position to strike right at the base of all their misery. If our people down there are risking their lives so that they can register . . . what do you and I look like in New York City, with the registration booth only a few blocks away, and we haven't been in it?" Malcolm acknowledged his own past failure in this regard: "You're talking to a man who's guilty of all of this. I've never tried to take part in anything political. Couldn't see it." But after his break with the Nation of Islam he told Harlem blacks that "it's a sin for you and me not to be registered so we can vote in New York City and in New York State, or throughout the North."[16] He spoke at a Harlem rally in support of the Mississippi Freedom Democratic Party and Fannie Lou Hamer and also invited the group to appear at his OAAU meeting that same evening.[17] He also made himself available to appear in support of blacks fighting for political rights throughout the South. He spoke to three thousand students at Tuskegee Institute and the next day at Brown Chapel in Selma, Alabama, in support of Martin (who was in jail) and other blacks fighting for the right to vote.

During Malcolm's last year, one of his most important audiences was Third World nations, particularly the rapidly emerging independent countries in Africa. He spent more than six months abroad in his efforts to convince African heads of state "to bring the United States government before the United Nations and charge her with violating the human rights of 22 million African-Americans." "Our problem is your problem," he wrote in a memorandum which he presented at the second meeting of the Organization of African Unity, held in Cairo, Egypt. "It is not a Negro problem, nor an American problem. This is a world problem; a problem of humanity. It is not a problem of civil rights but a problem of human rights."[18] Surprisingly, Malcolm made an enormous impact in Africa. He was received enthusiastically by students at several universities and was given an audience by several heads of state, including Kwame Nkrumah of Ghana, Julius Nyerere of Tanzania, Jomo Kenyatta of Kenya, and Gamal Abdel Nasser of Egypt.

Malcolm was also influential among several black intellectuals and artists. John O. Killens, Ossie Davis, Ruby Dee, Louis Lomax, C. Eric Lincoln, Lorraine Hansberry, Kenneth Clark, Dick Gregory, and James Baldwin were impressed by the range of his intellect and the depth of his commitment to the black freedom movement. (Martin was influential among many of the same people.) Malcolm's exposure to a variety of perspectives and movements, nationally and internationally, had a profound impact upon his thinking about America and the black struggle for freedom in it. He not only changed how others thought about black freedom; they changed how he thought about it as well. They pushed him toward Martin, the mainstream of black freedom talk and action of the time.

When Malcolm reflected on a debate with Martin, his initial reaction was to smile and say that "the extremist will always ruin the liberals in debate—because the liberals have something too nebulous to sell or something too impossible to sell—like the Brooklyn Bridge. . . . That's why Martin Luther King would lose a debate with me. Why King? Because integration is a ridiculous dream. I am not interested in dreams, but in the nightmare. . . . But then," Malcolm quickly shifting his emphasis, "King and I have nothing to debate about. We are both indicting. I would say to him: You indict and give them hope. I'll indict and give them no hope." As Malcolm became more involved in the mainstream of the black freedom struggle, he realized that King was much more radical than he had initially thought. "Since I've gotten involved," he said as he criticized the exclusivism of the black nationalists, "I am surprised at how militant some of these 'integrationists' are sounding, man; sometimes they put me to shame."[19]

Martin's movement toward Malcolm was just as radical and surprising as the latter's was toward Martin. But because Martin was fearful of tarnishing his nonviolent, integrationist image, especially with the white public (churches, government, labor, northern liberals, and southern moderates), he did not make an explicit public identification with Malcolm. "He always felt that they could not be on the same platform," remarked Andy Young in an interview with Bill Moyers. Young, however, left no doubt that Martin's appreciation of Malcolm increased immensely. He regarded Malcolm as a "tremendously intelligent and dedicated human being,"[20] and an ally in the same struggle for justice, perhaps somewhat similar to his views of Stokely Carmichael and other SNCC radicals.

Among close associates and friends King did not hesitate to concede the truth of Malcolm's analysis of the black condition. He reportedly said to a friend: "I just saw Malcolm on television. I can't deny it. When he starts talking about all that's been done to us, I get a twinge of hate, of identification with him."[21]

With the media, however, Martin was circumspect regarding positive statements about Malcolm, even when it was obvious that he was moving much closer to him. "It was tragic that Malcolm was killed," he said to David Halberstam, who suggested that "he sounded like a nonviolent Malcolm." Of course, Martin denied that his views were similar to Malcolm's, saying that "he could never go along with black separatism. For better or for worse we are all on this particular land together at the same time, and we have to work it out together." That was the response that Martin's white, liberal supporters wanted to hear, and he knew it. However, Martin happily pointed out that Malcolm "was really coming around, moving away from racism. He had such a sweet spirit." He made a similar observation in a Los Angeles news conference immediately following Malcolm's assassination: "I think it is even more unfortunate that this great tragedy occurred at a time when Malcolm was re-evaluating his own philosophical presuppositions and moving toward a greater understanding of the nonviolent movement and toward more tolerance of white people generally."[22]

Equally significant was what Martin did *not* say. He too was re-evaluating his presuppositions and was moving toward a greater understanding of Malcolm, especially regarding black pride, separatism, and white America's lack of commitment to genuine black equality. He began to urge blacks to be proud of their "blackness," a word he almost never used publicly before he turned his attention to the North. The subsequent rise of Black Power deepened his convictions regarding the need of blacks to affirm their somebodyness by identifying with their African heritage. He also started to speak of black oppression in northern slums as "domestic colonialism." To the surprise of many, and perhaps even himself, he concluded that racism was so deeply ingrained in America, especially in the North, that "temporary segregation" was probably the only means of overcoming powerlessness in the black community. These concepts were almost unthinkable before he saw and talked with frustrated black youth after the Watts riots and in the slums of Chicago.

They reflect the indirect and substantive influence of Malcolm upon him, especially through SNCC and Black Power advocates.

Despite Martin's denial of talking like a "nonviolent Malcolm," David Halberstam, and others who heard him, recognized that he was much "closer to Malcolm than [he would admit and] any one would have predicted five years ago — and much farther from more traditional allies like Whitney Young and Roy Wilkins." Halberstam could see that King's split with Young and Wilkins was deeper than their differences on the Vietnam War. "In the split," Halberstam rightly pointed out, "it is King who is changing, not Young and Wilkins." The change in Martin was radical, striking at the root of the civil rights movement's well-known assumption about America and white people. "For years," Martin said, "I labored with the idea of reforming the existing institutions of the society, a little change here, a little change there. Now I feel quite differently. I think you've got to have a reconstruction of the entire society, a revolution of values."[23] Initially Martin thought that most whites were committed to the cause of racial justice, and only a few southern and northern bigots blocked its achievement. But when he took the civil rights movement to the North, he discovered firsthand the white liberals that Malcolm had spoken of so often. Martin's description of the differences between the North and the South was remarkably similar to Malcolm's. Speaking in Clarksdale, Mississippi, in preparation for the Poor People's Campaign, Martin said:

> One thing about the brother down here, he doesn't like us, and lets us know it. . . . It's out in the open. . . . At least you know how to deal with it. I've been up North, you don't know how to deal with it, you know you can't quite get your target. He'll sit there and smile in your face. You go down to see [them in] the office, and they'll serve you cookies and tea, and shake your hand and pose for a picture with you. And at the same time, keeping Negroes in ghettos and slums.[24]

White liberals' condemnation of the urban riots without even acknowledging their causes, their rejection of open housing and school integration, and their seeming indifference to the immorality of the Vietnam War influenced Martin to adopt a view of whites similar to Malcolm's, namely that only a small part of white America was committed to genuine equality. "Most Americans," he said, "were unconscious racists."[25]

When Martin went to the North, he discovered not only the white liberals that Malcolm had talked about; he also found alienated blacks who had little faith in white people. He discovered that he could not gain the trust of blacks without scaring whites. "You can't communicate with the ghetto dweller and at the same time not frighten many whites to death." Caught between the black and white worlds, Martin acknowledged: "I don't know what the answer to that is." Believing that "the lot of the American Negro would not change unless the Negro revolution builds and maintains alliances with the majority white community," he said that "my role perhaps is to interpret to the white world. . . . I've said to gang fellows that I can't use language that will alienate the white majority."[26]

Martin was more interested in influencing European leaders than those on the African continent, largely because he perceived that they were more influential in changing the course of world politics. His philosophy of nonviolence was ignored in many Third World countries as their colored inhabitants took up arms against European colonizers. Martin, however, pleased European listeners when he reminded their Third World victims that "as we struggle for justice and freedom, we must not use second-class methods to gain it." He was, of course, pleading for nonviolence and moderation in the worldwide freedom movement as opposed to the defensive violence and militancy which he associated with Malcolm, who, as we mentioned earlier, also happened to be present in London at the same time. Britons loved what they heard and lavished praise upon Martin. "His speaking with such passion and moderation was a pleasure and a relief," said the *Manchester Guardian Weekly*. "His reputation had gone ahead of him so far that many must have feared he would disappoint. He did not. He said what we had hoped to hear him say. He said it as well as we can hope to hear it said."[27] An even more impressive reception was given for Martin in Oslo, Norway, upon his reception of the Nobel Peace Prize. Later, European audiences were less enthusiastic and frequently hostile when Martin aggressively applied his principle of nonviolence to the relations between nations, especially America's involvement in Vietnam.

Contrary to popular opinion, Martin had great respect for both Malcolm's integrity as a person and the cogency of his analysis of the black situation of oppression. In a telegram to "Mrs. Malcolm X," expressing his sadness over "the shocking and tragic assassination of your husband," Martin (while noting that he and Malcolm "did not always see eye to eye on methods to solve the race problem") acknowledged his "deep affection for Malcolm." He praised Malcolm's ability to put his finger on the root of the problem. "He was an eloquent spokesman for his point of view, and no one can honestly doubt that Malcolm had great concern for the problems that we face as a race."[28]

Alex Haley, a friend and interviewer of both Martin and Malcolm, commented that "both men were intensely interested in each other but their images were such that they were supposed to be adversaries, you know the media made up this, what would happen if they met type of thing." According to Haley,

> Dr. King would always let maybe an hour pass before he'd casually ask, "By the way, what's Brother Malcolm saying about me these days?" I'd give some discreetly vague response, and then back in New York, I'd hear Malcolm, "All right, tell me what he said about me!" to which I'd also give a vague reply. I'm convinced that privately the two men felt mutual admiration and respect.[29]

Martin and Malcolm shared the view that racism was America's main social problem. Both spoke frequently of America as "an extremely sick nation" and attempted to surface the sickness. "When Martin Luther King speaks of social disruption," Malcolm told Carlos Russell, "he is saying the same thing when I say BLOODSHED. He uses big words, and I am direct and to the point."[30]

While whites frequently said that Martin and Malcolm were like "oil and water" with "little if any common ground," blacks often said that they were, as John Killens put it, "kind of a team."[31] When M. S. Handler of the *New York Times* asked about the possibility of "cooperation between Malcolm X and Martin Luther King," Clarence Jones, a friend of both, acknowledged their complementary roles by saying that "it was not beyond the realm of possibility that in the building of a coalition within the Negro freedom movement, Dr. King and Malcolm X might find a common basis of action."[32]

Because of Martin's and Malcolm's profound mutual respect and the tremendous impact that each had upon the other's thinking, James Baldwin claimed that "by the time each met his death, there was practically no difference between them."[33] Others even claim that, as Martin's and Malcolm's daughters, Yolanda and Attallah, are working together today, they would have combined the SCLC and the OAAU into one freedom organization or entered into a coalition somewhat like the SCLC's relationship with other civil rights organizations. I do not share that view because there is another aspect of their relationship that would have precluded it. Martin and Malcolm served not only as a complement to each other, but each also served as a necessary corrective against the other's false reading of what was needed in the black freedom struggle.

CORRECTING EACH OTHER

Since Martin was the most dominant symbol of the black freedom struggle, Malcolm served more as a corrective for him than vice versa.

From the time of Martin's rise to national and international prominence during the Montgomery bus boycott, he was regarded by whites and blacks alike as the symbol of the "New Negro" who was determined to be free from the bondage of racism and segregation in America. Integration and the beloved community emerged as the goals of the black freedom struggle, and nonviolence and love became the means for achieving them. The "Negro revolution," as it was initially called, was defined as a nonviolent revolution, a revolution in which the goal was not to humiliate or defeat white people but rather to convert them, to win them over as friends, as sisters and brothers. Black people's willingness to suffer in order to appeal to the conscience of the white majority and thereby redeem the soul of America defined the heart of Martin's initial message. Paraphrasing the words of Gandhi, he urged blacks to assure whites that

> we will match your capacity to inflict suffering with our capacity to endure suffering. We will meet your physical force with soul force. We will not hate you, but we cannot in all good conscience obey your unjust laws. Do to us what you will and we will still love you. Bomb our homes and threaten our children; send your hooded perpetrators of violence into our communities and drag us out on some wayside road, beating us and leaving us half dead, and we will still love you. But we will soon wear you down by our capacity to suffer. And in winning our freedom we will so appeal to your heart and conscience that we will win you in the process.[34]

Martin's message of nonviolence and love was so pleasing to whites that, for a brief time during the 1950s, many regarded him as more moderate and thus more acceptable than Roy Wilkins of the NAACP and other civil rights advocates. He soon became the most talked about and influential black person in America. The high point of his influence was the time between the Birmingham demonstrations (1963) and the Selma March (1965), during which time he wrote his influential "Letter from Birmingham Jail," delivered his famed "I Have a Dream" speech, was named "Man of the Year" for 1963 by *Time,* and was awarded the Nobel Peace Prize.

Blacks as well praised Martin for his leadership role in their fight for equality in American society. The great majority accepted his advocacy of nonviolence and love (not ideologically but tactically) as the most effective method for the black minority to achieve full integration into the dominant white society in America. Almost no one offered a serious, public challenge to Martin's approach to civil rights. Even Elijah Muhammad and Malcolm were guarded in their criticisms of him during the 1950s and early 1960s. They sought in vain to persuade him to speak at one of their assemblies. This political climate must be kept in mind if one is to understand why Malcolm emerged as an appropriate and necessary corrective to certain dangers posed by Martin's preeminence in the black freedom struggle.

In the early 1960s, Malcolm convinced Elijah Muhammad to let him demonstrate to the world the silliness of the nonviolent approach to freedom. He was merciless in his attack on Martin for urging blacks to "turn the other cheek," calling him a "traitor to his race," an "agent of the white man," and a "religious Uncle Tom." While Malcolm served as a minister in the Nation of Islam, only a few blacks listened to his proposal for a separate territory. Many, however, took notice of his critique of nonviolence and Christian love and of his criticism of how these concepts were taught in the black community by leaders whose organizations were financed by the whites who were themselves extremely *violent* when their interests were threatened. There "wasn't nothing nonviolent about old Pat [Patrick Henry] or old George Washington!" Malcolm frequently proclaimed in his speeches. "Liberty or death" has always been the motto of whites in a contest with their enemies. If whites do not defend their humanity nonviolently, why then should blacks be expected to use that method. "The white man is a damn fool if he thinks we are going to let him hit us over the head, drag us in the street and sic dogs on us and expect us not to put up a fight. If we cannot win, we will die trying." Malcolm called liberal whites who financed the so-called "Negro nonviolent revolution" "hypocrites" and black leaders who accepted their support "puppets."[35]

As Malcolm saw it, the problem with Martin's nonviolent philosophy was that it encouraged whites to commit criminal acts against blacks without fear of retaliation. That was why he initially called it a "criminal philosophy" and why he called the blacks who followed it "subhuman." Malcolm could not understand why Martin, as a leader, advocated nonviolence and was also equally puzzled why blacks followed it. For Malcolm, nonviolence was a coward's philosophy, and no black could ever achieve dignity following it. What blacks needed was not "passivity" but rather the courage to fight for freedom, by any means necessary, so that whites would know that the shedding of blood would be "reciprocal."[36]

In one of his most provocative moments, Malcolm—after listening to Fannie Lou Hamer of the Mississippi Freedom Democratic Party tell how she and other black women were brutally beaten in Mississippi for trying to register to vote—told a Harlem rally of approximately three hundred people that "we need a 'Mau Mau' to win freedom and equality for Negroes in the United States." The Mau Mau was a revolutionary group of Africans in Kenya who led an armed revolt against the British colonial regime. Malcolm called them "the greatest freedom fighters in Africa" in contrast to the *New York Times*'s and *Daily News*'s references to them as "antiwhite terrorists" who "used murder and torture in [their] attempt to drive out whites from Kenya." "I'm against anybody who tells black people to be nonviolent," Malcolm said, "while nobody is telling white people to be nonviolent." Blacks need "to learn the right language to communicate with people." Just as one cannot use French to communicate with someone who speaks only German, likewise, nonviolence is the wrong language to communicate with "brutes." "If the language is a shotgun, get a shotgun. But don't waste time talking the wrong language."

Malcolm's "Mau Mau" comments had the same negative impact on the white media that his "rifle" statement had at the time of his break with the Black Muslims several months earlier. When Arnold H. Lubasch of the *New York Times* reported on Malcolm's speech, the headline of his article read: "Malcolm Favors a Mau Mau in U.S.: At Harlem Rally, He Urges Negroes To 'Even Score.'" Martin and other civil rights leaders were greatly shocked and disturbed by Malcolm's "violent" comments as reported by the white media. They often issued counterstatements, assuring their white supporters that Malcolm did not represent "responsible" black leadership. They sometimes held private strategy sessions about the dangers of his "Ballot or Bullet" and "Mau Mau" speeches and others similar to them.[37]

However, Kenneth Clark, a scholar in the movement, while not endorsing Malcolm's public statements about reciprocal bleeding, saw the great danger of Martin's advocacy of blacks loving their enemies. He contended that loving the enemy created a psychological burden too great for oppressed blacks:

> On the surface, King's [nonviolent] philosophy appears to reflect health and stability, while the black nationalists betray pathology and instability. A deeper analysis, however, might reveal that there is also an unrealistic, if not pathological, basis in King's doctrine. It is questionable whether the *masses* of an oppressed group can in fact "love" their oppressor. The natural reactions to injustice, oppression, and humiliation are bitterness and resentment. . . . It would seem, then, that any demand that the victims of oppression be required to love those who oppress them places an additional and probably intolerable psychological burden upon these victims.[38]

Clark also seemed to have agreed with Malcolm's analysis of why white liberals supported Martin's idea of nonviolence. "It is most disturbing," he said, "to reflect on the possibility that this aspect of Martin Luther King's philosophy has received such widespread and uncritical acceptance among moderate and liberal whites because it is not inconsistent with the stereotype of the Negro as a meek, long-suffering creature who prays for deliverance but who rarely acts decisively against injustices."[39]

Several other black intellectuals also recognized the limitation of Martin's position on nonviolence. They included James Baldwin, John O. Killins, Ossie Davis, and John H. Clarke. "This country is only concerned about non-violence," Baldwin said in an interview with Kenneth Clark, "if it seems as if I'm going to get violent."[40]

Malcolm's critique of Martin had its greatest impact among the black masses in the North who, as Baldwin said, " 'don't go to church no more' and don't listen to Martin." Martin, of course, as Baldwin acknowledged, "still has great moral authority in the South. He has none in the North." The northern masses belonged to Malcolm. When he talked, Baldwin said, he articulated their suffering "which has been in this country so long denied. That's Malcolm's great authority over any of his audiences. He corroborates their reality; he tells them that they really exist."[41]

In place of integration, nonviolence, and love of enemy, Malcolm — via public rallies, radio, television, and newspapers — advocated separation, self-defense, and self-love. He was determined to develop an independent, uncompromising approach to black freedom. He did not believe that whites, who were responsible for black suffering, would also provide the material support for black liberation. Whites financed black organizations, according to Malcolm, so they could control them, and the black leaders who allowed it were either traitors or stupid. Malcolm spent much of his time exposing the hypocrisy of whites and the stupidity of blacks, and he minced no words when he talked about it. Everyone, including many Black Muslims and especially liberal whites and middle-class blacks, was shocked by Malcolm's outspoken language. "Martin Luther King is a fool," he said in reaction to Martin's advocacy of nonviolence in Birmingham, as law-abiding blacks were attacked by Bull Connor's policemen, using fire hoses and dogs. "You need somebody who is going to fight . . ., you don't need any kneeling in or crawling in."[42]

In a taped television interview with Kenneth Clark, Malcolm condemned Martin for " 'disarming' Negroes in their struggle for rights." He told Clark that "King is the best weapon that the white man, who wants to brutalize Negroes, has ever gotten in this country, because he is setting up a situation where, when the white man wants to attack Negroes, they can't defend themselves, because King has put this foolish philosophy out—you're not supposed to fight or you're not supposed to defend yourself." According to Malcolm, self-defense was both a rational act and a moral responsibility.[43]

Malcolm's challenge of Martin's philosophy of nonviolence caused many whites, particularly northern liberals, to reevaluate their view of Martin as moving too fast on the civil rights agenda. Malcolm made Martin and other civil rights leaders acceptable to white America by presenting himself as the "bogeyman" alternative. He also made Martin more acceptable to a larger segment of the black community by pushing him to the left, thereby causing him to become much more militant than he would otherwise have been.

Uncompromising militancy was Malcolm's great contribution to the black freedom struggle. Malcolm played the role of the "bad nigger," refusing to "laugh when nothing was funny" or "scratch when he was not itching." Under the caption "Assertive Spirit Stirs Negroes, Puts Vigor in Civil Rights Drive," M. S. Handler wrote in the *New York Times* in 1963 that "racial pride increases throughout the U.S." and "black nationalism is viewed as [a] powerful force for change." Malcolm and the Black Muslims were given much of the credit for the "new assertive mood," along with the stepped-up militancy of the established civil rights leaders.[44]

In another 1963 *New York Times* article, "Negroes Press Harder for Basic Rights," Anthony Lewis defined the dilemma facing white America: "One urgent question raised by the Birmingham episode is what form the inevitably growing Negro protest is going to take. Will it be the peaceful route of the Rev. Dr. Martin Luther King, Jr.? Or will it be the road of black nationalism preached by the Black Muslims?" According to Lewis, the Kennedy administration, through Burke Marshall, the Assistant Attorney General for Civil Rights, made it clear to the "people of Birmingham, and of the South . . . that if they do not accept Dr. King's way they will get the Muslims' way."[45]

"Kennedy Fears Negro Extremists Will Get Power If Moderates Fail" was the headline of Tom Wicker's account of the president and attorney general's meeting with Alabama editors in Washington. According to Wicker, "Several of the visiting editors reported . . . that the President had expressed concern about Negro extremism. He emphasized . . . that violence might easily follow the failure of moderate efforts, such as the nonviolent movement led by the Rev. Dr. Martin Luther King, Jr."[46]

Martin and other civil rights leaders took advantage of the Black Muslim threat in many of their speeches and writings in order to strengthen their own case for equality. Malcolm's "Black Muslim movement," Representative Adam Clayton Powell, Jr., warned, "will rapidly increase unless the white community rapidly makes way for full equality."[47] Martin spoke often of standing between two opposing forces in the black community: conservatives who were afraid to press for change and extremists, like the Black Muslims, who promoted hate and violence. Martin was very concerned about the separatist and self-defense philosophy of Malcolm and the Nation of Islam. As Malcolm's visibility increased, Martin began to press harder for integration, becoming more militant in order to prevent "black supremacy," as he called it then, from gaining ground in the black community.

Martin's warnings about the dangers of Malcolm's nationalist philosophy had considerable influence not only in the white community but in the black community as well, particularly among northern blacks who seemed inclined toward accepting Malcolm's preachments without critical examination. What Martin was to the civil rights movement, Malcolm was to the black nationalist movement. Malcolm's influence, however, extended far beyond black nationalist organizations. Even blacks in the civil rights movement, especially young SNCC activists, were mesmerized by his oratory. Julius Lester, himself an SNCC member, called them "the angry children of Malcolm X."[48]

Malcolm considered himself a spokesperson of the "field negroes," those blacks who were "trapped in a vicious cycle of ignorance, poverty, . . . sickness, and death." He had no equal in arousing resentment toward the "old blue-eyed, blond-haired, bad-smelling white man," whom he labeled as the "common enemy" of black people. "It's time for you and me to unite," he told blacks, "to get together and get this big white ape off our back." The more Malcolm spoke about the "big white ape named Uncle Sam," using extremely derogatory language, the more poor blacks identified with him, responding enthusiastically with shouts of "Right on!" and "Teach, Brother Malcolm, teach!" as he whipped them into a seemingly uncontrollable frenzy.[49] Blacks admired Malcolm for having the courage to speak the "naked truth" about the "white devil," and most appeared to be ready to take up the gun or knife so as to end the white scourge upon the black community.

Martin King did not regard Malcolm's abusive and vindictive language against whites in general as helpful in the black freedom struggle. Martin asserted that labeling *all* whites as "devils" and "snakes" as if there were no meaningful distinctions between them was not only bad politics but was blatantly false. Whites who participated in the civil rights movement, risking their lives in Mississippi and Alabama during the sit-ins, freedom rides, and voting rights campaigns should not be placed in the same boat with Bull Connor of Birmingham and Jim Clark of Selma or George Wallace and the Ku Klux Klan. There were meaningful distinctions between whites, and eventually Malcolm himself acknowledged them.

As Malcolm considered Martin's views on nonviolence foolish, so Martin viewed Malcolm's self-defense philosophy as foolish. If Malcolm thought nonviolence disarmed blacks, Martin considered Malcolm's "program of 'reciprocal bleeding' " as nothing short of suicidal. It is easy to talk about self-defense in a speech and thereby arouse an oppressed group to rebel violently against their oppressors. But Martin rightly insisted that defensive violence cannot be used by a 10 percent, weaponless minority as a program of social change. Speaking about Malcolm to Alex Haley, in a *Playboy* interview, Martin said:

> Even the extremist leaders who preach revolution are invariably unwilling to lead what they know would certainly end in bloody, chaotic and total defeat; for in the event of a violent revolution, we would be sorely outnumbered. And when it was all over, the Negro would face the same unchanged conditions, the same squalor and deprivation—the only difference being that his bitterness would be even more intense, his disenchantment even more abject. Thus, in purely practical as well as moral terms, the American Negro has no alternative to nonviolence.[50]

Martin's logic was hard to refute, and Malcolm knew it. While Malcolm talked a lot about reciprocal bleeding, he did not implement it into a program. He sent a threatening telegram to George Lincoln Rockwell and frequently talked about the need to "organize self-defense units" in order to give the Ku Klux Klan "a taste of its own medicine."[51] But Malcolm did not even carry a gun and was never known to have done physical harm to anyone. Even when Ronald Stokes, an unarmed Muslim minister, was "shot down in cold blood" by the Los Angeles police, Malcolm did nothing except proclaim the wrath of Allah upon white America. His actions were not that of a person who believed in "an eye for an eye."

Apparently Malcolm thought the threat of violence was sufficient to scare whites into recognizing blacks as human beings. He was wrong about that. It seems that as Martin did not understand as well as Malcolm the psychic disposition of blacks, Malcolm suffered a similar limitation regarding whites.

After his ouster from the Nation of Islam, Malcolm tried with limited success to shed his "black supremacist" image. He went to Mecca, denounced Elijah Muhammad as a "religious faker," and repeatedly rejected racism in any form. While Martin and many blacks were impressed with his change, the media took little notice of it and continued to project him as a teacher of hate and a promoter of violence. Although Malcolm remained a firm believer in self-defense, separation, and self-love, he abandoned the dual anthropology of the Nation of Islam which defined whites as evil and blacks as good by nature. He founded the OAAU in an effort to internationalize the black freedom struggle and to participate more effectively in it, alongside Martin's SCLC and other civil rights organizations. He asked Kenneth Clark to arrange a meeting between him and Martin but was assassinated the Sunday before their scheduled meeting on Tuesday.[52]

The media were not interested in the "New Malcolm," only the old one. They reported only those statements that could be interpreted as "irresponsible," that is, inciting violence, which they usually contrasted with the "responsible" statements of nonviolent leaders of the civil rights movement, especially Martin King. Malcolm's inability to shed his "violent" image among whites prevented him from becoming more deeply involved in the civil rights movement. He spoke of this difficulty in his *Autobiography*: "One of the major troubles that I was having in building the organization that I wanted—an all-black organization whose ultimate objective was to help create a society in which there could exist honest black-white brotherhood—was that my earlier public image, my so-called 'Black Muslim' image, kept blocking me. I was trying gradually to reshape my image. I was trying to turn a corner."[53]

The "turn" that Malcolm was trying to make was in the direction of Martin King. He wanted to be a participant in the mainstream of the black freedom movement so he could expand it beyond the idea of civil rights to human rights. He knew that that would be impossible without the support of Martin King.

Realizing that he could not get rid of his "violent" image, Malcolm decided to project himself publicly as an alternative to Martin so that the "white power structure," which he often called the enemy of black freedom, would be encouraged to negotiate with Martin. This was the meaning of his speech in Selma and his conversation with Coretta King. "You know," Martin said to David Halberstam, as he reflected back on Malcolm, "right before he was killed he came down to Selma and said some pretty passionate things against me, and that surprised me because after all it was my territory down there. But afterwards he took my wife aside, and said he thought he could help me more by attacking me than praising me. He thought it would make it easier for me in the long run."[54]

Wallace D. Muhammad, Elijah's son who like Malcolm was expelled from the Nation of Islam, reported that Malcolm told him that "Martin Luther King has the right answer for the Negro people and that he felt that people like himself were needed for the purpose of letting the white man know the Negro can and will fight if necessary." James Farmer gave a similar report in *Freedom — When?*: "Malcolm felt quite consciously that his extremism helped militant organizations like CORE by making their non-violence respectable in comparison to his own talk of violence. And he did serve this function." Several SCLC people also acknowledged the important role that Malcolm played in the black freedom struggle. "Given a Martin Luther King, Jr., there had to be a Malcolm X," said Wyatt Tee Walker. "In earlier days, Dr. King was considered by most in the national community (circa 1960) a dangerous wild-eyed perverter of religion with demagogic power and obvious Communist sympathies." With Malcolm's emergence, Martin "became more palatable to the American scene."[55]

Malcolm was not always comfortable playing the role of the "bad nigger," since he really did want to join forces with the civil rights movement. He was especially troubled when civil rights leaders showed public resentment toward him. "I don't see why they hate me," he told Ossie Davis. "I raise hell in the backyard and they run out front and The Man puts money in their hands."[56]

Although Malcolm was able to shed much of his black supremacist image in the African-American community, it was not likely that he and Martin could have made a genuine coalition; that outcome was unlikely because of their mutual unwillingness to denounce their respective commitments to self-defense and nonviolence in the black freedom struggle. Martin was absolutely committed to nonviolence and Malcolm was equally committed to self-defense, and both commitments were derived from their faiths. Neither was willing to compromise. Martin, of course, allowed people who did not share his faith to participate in the SCLC's activities as long as they accepted nonviolence as a tactic and pledged an absolute commitment to it in a public demonstration. Malcolm would never have accepted that condition because he would have regarded it as a denial of his humanity. When attacked by an enemy, self-defense was both a human and a religious responsibility. "I am a Muslim," he said at an OAAU rally, "because it's a religion that teaches you an eye for an eye and a tooth for a tooth. It teaches you to respect everybody, and treat everybody right. But it also teaches you if someone steps on your toe, chop off their foot. And I carry my religious axe with me all the time."[57]

Contrary to popular white opinion, most blacks shared Malcolm's view regarding self-defense and not Martin's view on nonviolence. Black history is replete with black Christians who rebelled in self-defense against white brutality. Nat Turner, a Baptist preacher who led a slave revolt that killed sixty whites, was perhaps the most famous in this regard. David Walker's *An Appeal to the Colored Citizens of the World* and Henry Highland Garnet's *Address to the Slaves* were also well-known. There were also many ordinary black Christians, past and present, who quietly but firmly let whites know that they would not remain passive in a situation of a violent attack against their personhood. The "Deacons for Defense" served a similar purpose, protecting many civil rights workers, including Martin King, during the 1960s. Most whites knew whom to "mess with" and whom to leave alone.

The rise of Black Power and black theology was largely due to the influence of Malcolm X. Black Power affirmed the right of blacks to self-defense, and black theology developed a theological justification for it. While both concepts were strongly influenced by Malcolm, they were not his creations. Their origins are deeply embedded in the African-American experience, and Malcolm simply drew upon that experience as he provided a much needed corrective to Martin's absolute commitment to nonviolence.

Like the idea of self-defense, the idea of "survival" is deeply embedded in black history. Nonviolence and love have been employed by African-Americans as a survival tactic but not as an ideology. How does one affirm one's humanity when the assertion of the right of self-defense would mean certain death, not only for oneself but for one's entire family or even the community? This is the question that African-Americans from slavery to the present have been faced with daily. The Malcolms in African-American history have not been very helpful. In this context, Martin King and black Christianity have been most useful. With love and nonviolence, blacks developed a way of living with dignity in a world that did not recognize them as human beings. In a situation of sociopolitical powerlessness, "passivity" was perhaps the only means of black survival. In this sense, Martin's idea of nonviolence served as a corrective to Malcolm's self-defense philosophy.

Martin King provided an important correction against African-American leaders who often got carried away with Malcolm's rhetoric about self-defense. This correction was particularly needed during the rise of Black Power in 1966. "Now we are hearing a lot about violence," Martin told his SCLC staff at Frogmore, South Carolina. "People are talking about 'burn baby burn,' and burning cities down. And the fact is that in spite of all this talk about violence, I haven't seen anybody organize the violent campaign. . . . The riots that have developed always develop spontaneously. . . . The people who stand on street corners and preach about violence always go home at night. . . . And I just think people ought to be honest." For King, honesty demanded that African-American leaders stop using the rhetoric of violence when they themselves were unwilling to "experiment with violence."

On the Meredith March . . . [Charles Evers] was preaching and he really got them up that night, preaching about violence and we ought to take up arms, and what we are going to do to these white folks. After the meeting, I say now Charles, I don't want you to be dishonest. Now, if you sincerely believe in violence, there is a good place for you to start. And that is the shooting of [Byron de la] Beckwith [who shot Evers's brother and was never convicted]. Now if you are not willing to shoot and kill him, then don't come before me preaching any violence, because it's absolutely dishonest.[58]

For Martin, violence was completely impractical for African-Americans. This point was so obvious to Martin that he said that the riots in the cities were nothing but the "language of the unheard," "temper tantrums" of people who had lost hope in America.

Martin's insight into the weakness of violence was much more profound than Malcolm's. On the issue of violence, Malcolm's value system was hardly different from that of the whites he criticized. An eye for an eye philosophy, Martin rightly pointed out, will leave everybody blind. Furthermore, violence "never really deals with the basic evil of the situation." Why? Because

violence may murder the murderer, but it doesn't murder murder. Violence may murder the liar, but it doesn't murder lie; it doesn't establish truth. Violence may even murder the dishonest man, but it doesn't murder dishonesty. Violence may go to the point of murdering the hater, but it doesn't murder hate. It may increase hate. It is always a descending spiral leading nowhere. This is the ultimate weakness of violence: It multiplies evil and violence in the universe. It doesn't solve any problems.[59]

On this point, Martin seems to have history on his side, not only for African-Americans but for everybody. For unless humankind finds a way to put an end to violence, then violence will most certainly put an end to humankind.

Martin and Malcolm represented the two sides in W. E. B. Du Bois's concept of double identity—they represented, respectively, the American and African, the two warring ideas struggling to make sense out of the involuntary presence of Africans in North America. During the early part of their participation in the black freedom movement, their answers to Du Bois's question, "What am I?" were clear, emphatic, and opposite: "American" was Martin's answer and "African" was Malcolm's. The battle between them, to a large extent, was fought in the white media, which portrayed them as adversaries. But they were not. On the contrary, they were like two soldiers fighting their enemies from different angles of vision, each pointing out the other's blind spots and correcting the other's errors. They needed each other, for they represented — and continue to represent — the "yin and yang" deep in the soul of black America.

10

NOTHING BUT MEN

The Negro man in this country ... has never been able to be a man.
Martin Luther King, Jr.
On "Face the Nation"
29 August 1965

You don't have to be a man to fight for freedom. All you have to do is to be an intelligent human being.
Malcolm X
New York City
20 December 1964

There must be a better distribution of wealth, and maybe America must move toward a Democratic Socialism.
Martin Luther King, Jr.
Frogmore, S.C.
14 November 1966

You show me a capitalist and I'll show you a bloodsucker.
Malcolm X
New York City
20 December 1964

We must not romanticize Martin and Malcolm. Like all humans, they had their strengths and weaknesses. To focus on their weaknesses does not detract from their strengths. On the contrary, it enables us to view the men in a larger context and thereby relate to them as human beings who were fundamentally no different from ourselves. Seeing them as human beings, we are encouraged to take up the cause of freedom where they left off, building on their strengths and avoiding, as much as possible, their weaknesses.

272

The "messiah complex" is a danger that pervades the leadership expectations of the African-American community; for African-Americans this complex involves looking forward to the coming of a "modern Moses" or a Christlike figure who will deliver them from the bondage of white racism. When we make Black Messiahs out of Martin and Malcolm, as if they alone knew how to achieve black freedom, we will not be encouraged to complete their unfinished task but rather to wait for another savior to come and liberate us.

Messianic expectation also encourages "self-appointed men and women of God" to manipulate the African-American liberation struggle for their own interests. In order to distinguish true prophets from false ones, it is important to identify a leader's shortcomings. Only false prophets shun criticism, because they do not want their real motives revealed. True prophets welcome the critical opinions of others, because their primary concern is not their public acclaim but rather the cause of freedom for which they speak and act.

Martin and Malcolm were true prophets with impeccable credentials; their status as true prophets was verified by what they did and said for the liberation of African-Americans. Their disciples and admirers have no cause to worry about critical evaluation of the two men. Martin and Malcolm can withstand any test of their leadership, because they were their own most severe critics. They grew in stature, spiritually and intellectually, because they learned from their mistakes, from each other, and from the experiences of friends and enemies.

The messiah complex also contradicts Martin's and Malcolm's own deeply held belief that they were not different from the talented persons who worked beside them. Martin believed that several persons on his staff could have been chosen as the symbol of the civil rights movement. Malcolm's refusal to define himself as a "divine man" separated him from Elijah Muhammad and the other self-described messiahs prevalent in the African-American community. Both Martin and Malcolm believed that the cause for which they were struggling was more important than personal acclaim, and that its achievement required the full commitment of all freedom-loving people. We today can remain faithful to the spirit of their leadership only if we are willing to explore their limitations, in order to understand them better and to deepen our commitment to realize the freedom for which they died.

SEXISM

The most glaring and detrimental limitation of Martin's and Malcolm's leadership was not seeing sexism as a major problem connected with and as evil as racism. Like most white and black men of the 1960s, their attitude toward women was shaped by their acceptance of patri-archal values as the norm for the family and society. Following the pattern of white religious bodies, the black church and the Nation of Islam provided religious justification for the subordination of women. While Martin and Malcolm challenged white values regarding race, their acceptance of black male privilege prevented them from seeing the con-nection between racism and sexism. While both differed sharply with most white men when it came to matters involving race, they shared much of the typical *American* male's view of women. Martin's and Mal-colm's views regarding women's place were not significantly different from those of men of other races. Both believed that the woman's place was in the home, the private sphere, and the man's place was in society, the public arena, fighting for justice on behalf of women and children.

Martin's and Malcolm's views on women were partly understandable, since they lived at the threshold of the rise of feminism in the 1960s and not during its flowering in the 1970s and 1980s. Sensitive and caring as they were, their views would likely have changed if they had lived to encounter the black women who today are developing what Alice Walker calls a "womanist" perspective. But we must be careful as we concede this point, for it can be used to camouflage the deadly conse-quences of sexism. While we black men may understand the reasons for Martin's and Malcolm's or our own sexism, *we must not excuse it* or justify it, as if sexism was not and is not today a serious matter in the African-American community. As we blacks will not permit whites to offer plausible excuses for racism, so we cannot excuse our sexism. Sex-ism like racism is freedom's opposite, and we must uncover its evil manifestations so we can destroy it.

Martin and Malcolm were sexist men, and their sexism hindered greatly their achievement of the freedom for which they fought. They expected their wives, Coretta and Betty, to stay at home and raise their children while they worked for the liberation of black people. King's biographer and friend, L. D. Reddick, said that King believed that "bio-logically and aesthetically women are more suitable than men for keep-ing house." In her important book, *My Life with Martin Luther King, Jr.*, Coretta S. King said that "Martin had, all through his life, an ambivalent attitude toward the role of women," believing on the one hand that "women are just as intelligent and capable as men," but on the other seeing *his* wife as "a homemaker and a mother for his children." When they discussed their impending marriage, "He was very definite that he would expect whoever he married to be at home waiting for him." "I want a wife to respect me as the head of the family," he told her imme-diately following their marriage. "I *am* the head of the family."[1]

A similar but much more rigid perspective on the role of women was held by Malcolm during his Black Muslim years. His view was defined by the "very strict laws and teachings" of the Nation of Islam and by his experience as a hustler and a steerer in Harlem. Interpreting Black Muslim teachings, Malcolm said that "the true nature of a man is to be strong, and a woman's true nature is to be weak, and while a man must at all times respect his woman, at the same time he needs to understand that he must control her if he expects to get her respect."[2] "Respect" and "protect," "love" and "control": these were the words he repeated to hammer home the Nation of Islam teachings about the relations between husbands and wives and brothers and sisters.

Furthermore, Malcolm combined this patriarchal religious doctrine with a misogynic view derived from the ghetto; that combination resulted in his extremely negative attitude toward women. Explaining why he remained single for many years, abstaining from sexual involvement with women, he said, "I'd had too much experience that women were only tricky, deceitful, untrustworthy flesh. I had seen too many men ruined, or at least tied down, or in some other way messed up by women." Malcolm's temple addresses during the 1950s particularly reveal his ultrasexist views, and many sisters in the Nation of Islam complained to Muhammad about his grossly offensive sayings against them. Non-Muslim sisters sometimes walked out rather than listen to his tirade against them, blaming women for the miserable condition of black men.[3]

In 1956 at the Philadelphia Temple, Malcolm gave a series of addresses on black women, accusing them of being the "greatest tool of the devil." "How do you think this black man got in this state?" he asked his audience. "By our women tricking him and tempting him, and the devil taught her how to do this." "The trickiest in existence is the black woman and the white man." "If you go to court with your wife, she will always win over you because the devil can use her to break down more of our black brothers. . . . It is this evil black woman in North America who does not want to do right and holds the man back from saving himself." At this point in his address, he noticed a visiting sister walking out on him. "Look at the sister who just got up and walked out," he said. "Hair five different shades. She's living in a perilous time to imitate that devil woman and when she hears a warning, instead of listening, trying to find out how she can change her ways, she walks out angry."[4]

Like preachers in Christian churches, Malcolm claimed to have derived his view of the woman, in part, from the Bible. "Since the time of Adam and Eve in the garden," he said, "woman has led man into evil and the one she was created to serve became her slave. She rules him entirely with her sex appeal, her clothes are designed by man to accentuate those portions of her body related to sex, and when he fully dresses she undresses."[5]

If we were tempted to make saints out of Malcolm and Martin, their perspectives on women should be more than enough to eliminate that thought forever. Ralph Abernathy's controversial account of King's last night in *And the Walls Came Tumbling Down*[6] was not necessary to show that King was a mortal man and one area of his serious moral failings was in his dealings with women. Like most men of their time, Martin and Malcolm were not only sexist but seemed unduly insensitive to an emerging feminist consciousness in the society.

There were many reasons why Martin and Malcolm turned a deaf ear to the burgeoning women's movement, the most important of which were its perceived identification with "bored white middle-class suburban housewives," its rejection by many black women, the myth of the black matriarchy, and the widespread belief that race, not gender, was the primary factor determining the life chances of black people.

The dominant mood in the black community emphasized the need for black male assertiveness. This theme was strongest in black nationalist groups such as the Nation of Islam, Maulana Karenga's US Organization, and the Congress of African Peoples, led by Imamu Amiri Baraka (LeRoi Jones). But it was emphasized in all groups, expressing itself in the popular myth that black males were victimized more than black women. (Some black men even made the outrageous claim that black women have always been free.) Therefore the woman should "walk two steps behind the man." Some men urged this as a literal practice, but most meant it as a metaphor: letting the man be the head of the family and the front-line fighter in the black freedom struggle.

A number of black men today are quite embarrassed by what they said and thought about women back then. (Unfortunately most have simply learned how to disguise their sexism the way whites cover up their racism.) They regret that they allowed their focus on racism to blind them not only to sexism in the society as a whole but also in the African-American community, hindering their struggle for freedom. I think it is very important to remember our past sins so that we will not be as tempted to repeat them today.

Like most blacks, Martin and Malcolm shared the view that racism was the primary cause of black oppression and that black men should be the leaders of the movements working to eliminate it. Black men, most agreed, needed to assert their masculinity, a view made popular by "The Moynihan Report" (1965) on the black family.[7] Although black men were offended by what they read in that report—they viewed it as a put-down of the black family by a government-sponsored study written by a white man—they did not question Moynihan's assumption that the black man was victimized more than the black woman and that the time had come for him to step forward and for her to step backward. Some black men even claimed to have been victimized ("castration" was the term frequently used) by black women — grandmothers, mothers, sisters, and wives.

During the 1960s black women with few exceptions either openly supported the black male view or at least tolerated it in silence. The reasons for this have been analyzed in several essays and books by black women. Black women did not want to divide the community or minimize the primacy of racism. Neither did they wish to be associated with a movement led by middle-class white women, many of whom were not active supporters of black freedom.

Putting the black man on his feet with a job and status became the primary concern of black leaders. How can the black man be a *real* man, that is, "wear the pants" and control his wife and children, if he does not have a job to support his family? *Authority,* according to this logic, is derived from support and prestige. "When you deprive a man of a job," Martin told a European audience, "you deprive him of his manhood, . . . the authority of fatherhood." In a "Face the Nation" interview, Martin said:

> The Negro man in this country . . . has never been able to be a man. He has been robbed of his manhood because of the legacy of slavery and segregation and discrimination, and we have had in the Negro community a matriarchal family . . . in the midst of a patriarchal society . . . and I don't think any answer to that problem will emerge until we give the Negro man his manhood by giving him the kind of economic security capable of supporting a family.[8]

The focus on "manhood" was one of the main reasons for the low visibility of black women in civil rights and black nationalist organizations, including Martin's and Malcolm's. In an Albany "jailhouse diary," for example, Martin recorded that "Ralph Abernathy and I were arrested again in Albany at 3:15 P.M. . . . We were accompanied by Dr. W. G. Anderson, Slater King, the Rev. Ben Gay and seven ladies." Identities, with names and titles, were given to the men, but the women were rendered invisible even though their number was larger. "One can find scant indication that Dr. King recognized the indispensable work of black women within the Civil Rights Movement," June Jordan has correctly written. "There is no record of his gratitude for Ella Baker's intellectual leadership. There is no record of his seeking to shake the hand of Mrs. Fannie Lou Hamer." King also failed to acknowledge properly the major role that Jo Ann Robinson, Mary Fair Burks, and other women of the Women's Political Council played in the success of the Montgomery bus boycott.[9]

Although Ella Baker was one of the persons who first conceived of the idea of an organization like the SCLC (others included Bayard Rustin and Stanley Levison) and although she served as its "acting director," most of the male preachers were uneasy with her presence because she did not exhibit the "right attitude" (read "submissiveness"?) which they expected from women, an expectation no doubt shaped by the role of women in their churches. Ella Baker's tenure with the SCLC was relatively brief (though longer than she had expected), largely because of her conflicts with King and others regarding their attitude toward women and their leadership style built around the charisma of one person—Martin Luther King, Jr. Baker preferred the group-centered leadership developed by the SNCC, whose founding she initiated.

Fannie Lou Hamer played a major role in the civil rights movement in Mississippi. Her example and courage in the face of extreme white brutality empowered many black women and men to follow in her steps. Self-taught, Hamer, like Malcolm X, was a spell-binding orator who spoke from the authority of her experience. She moved audiences to tears as she told of her efforts to register and vote. She was evicted from a Mississippi plantation, shot at by hooded night riders, and cruelly beaten during her incarceration. There is no mention of Fannie Lou Hamer in any of King's speeches and writings.

Dorothy Cotton, who joined the SCLC's staff in 1960 and became director of the Citizenship Education Program (CEP), was one of two women who served on the executive staff. The other was Septima Clark, who joined the staff in 1961 and served as the director of the workshops of the CEP. In an interview with Howell Raines, Cotton talked about the "male chauvinism that existed in the Movement." When he asked her about Martin's attitude toward women's rights, she laughed and said: "I think that he, too, comes right out of the same society, and he would have had a lot to learn and a lot of growing to do as the Women's Movement took on the momentum that it has taken on."[10]

It is nevertheless important to note that Malcolm's and Martin's views changed significantly in the course of their work, influenced by their wives, women leaders in the movement, and experiences overseas. But their changes were minor when compared with those of two earlier, prominent black advocates of women rights, Frederick Douglass and W. E. B. Du Bois.

Martin's sexism was less obvious than Malcolm's because Martin did not speak often on the theme of women, and when he did, he put his views in the acceptable public discourse of his time. Whatever views

Malcolm held on any subject, he presented them in the most extreme form possible so that no one would be in doubt about where he stood on the subject. When he discovered his error about something, he was as extreme in his rejection of it as he had been in his affirmation. Following his split with the Nation of Islam and his subsequent trips to the Middle East and Africa, Malcolm made an about-face regarding his view on women's rights, as he began to consider the issue not only in the context of religion and morality but, more importantly, from the standpoint of mobilizing the forces needed to revolutionize society:

> One thing that I became aware of in my traveling recently through Africa and the Middle East, in every country you go to, usually the degree of progress can never be separated from the woman. If you're in a country that's progressive, the woman is progressive. If you're in a country that reflects the consciousness toward the importance of education, it's because the woman is aware of the importance of education. But in every backward country you'll find the women are backward, and in every country where education is not stressed it's because the women don't have education. So one of the things I became thoroughly convinced of in my recent travels is the importance of giving freedom to the woman, giving her education, and giving her the incentive to get out there and put that same spirit and understanding in their children. And I frankly am proud of the contributions that our women have made in the struggle for freedom and I'm one person who's for giving them all the leeway possible because they've made a greater contribution than many of us men.[11]

Malcolm also urged women to assume "the chief responsibility for passing on black cultural traditions to the children" and to imbue black men with political militancy. "Educate a man and you educate an individual," Malcolm said, quoting an African proverb. "Educate a woman and you educate an entire family." He called Fannie Lou Hamer "one of this country's foremost freedom fighters." Meeting and hearing her helped Malcolm to realize that intelligence and commitment to freedom are not limited to the male gender.[12]

Against the strong objections of several of the old Muslim men who left the Nation of Islam to follow him, Malcolm began to insist that women must be given clearly defined and prominent leadership roles in the OAAU. For example, Maya Angelou was planning to return from Ghana to work with Malcolm as a leader in the OAAU.[13]

Both Martin and Malcolm were open to change when confronted with experiences which contradicted older or established beliefs. When

Howell Raines asked Dorothy Cotton whether Martin would have resisted the women's movement, she answered:

> No, I don't think he would have resisted. I really don't, because he died saying we've gotta take all oppressed people, and my hope and dream—and maybe it's fantasy—but it is that he would have seen that women are an oppressed class. I don't know how he could have preached what he preached and could not have seen that, too, but it might have been a painful lesson he had to learn. But I think he would have learned it. He would have had to.[14]

CLASSISM

Another major limitation of Martin's and Malcolm's leadership was their failure to identify classism as a problem as harmful to the cause of freedom as racism and sexism; further, they failed to connect classism with the latter two problems. Both men began to analyze the problem of economic injustice during their last years, but the concepts of integration and separation, as they inherited and developed them, did not encourage them to view the American political economy as a primary cause of the oppression of blacks. In fact, it was generally assumed, by both integrationists and separatists, that the American sociopolitical system was basically good and that the *only* thing wrong with it was the exclusion of blacks and other people of color from its benefits. Separatists concluded that whites would never accept blacks into their system on equal terms. Integrationists contended that whites *had* to bring blacks and other minorities into the system because whites' own deepest beliefs demanded it.

Separation and integration became the rallying cries for the two ways which African-Americans sought to attain their freedom. Seldom did either group ask *radical* questions about the moral and economic adequacy of the American system of capitalism, into which some blacks were seeking to integrate and from which others were trying to separate.

Class struggle has not been a major theme in the history of the African-American freedom movement. Since midcentury the main reason for this has been the influence of knee-jerk, witch-hunting anticommunism in American political life. The Cold War and the McCarthy phenomenon discouraged African-Americans from exploring the Marxian theme of worldwide class struggle between poor workers and rich owners of the means of production.

White southerners put the communist tag on anyone who challenged white supremacy. The NAACP was given that label and was declared illegal in Alabama, even though its allegiance to America and almost fanatical rejection of communism could hardly be questioned by any thinking person.

Martin and other civil rights activists also were labeled communist agitators. White southerners knew that if they could convince the American public that the civil rights movement was influenced by communists, the freedom struggle would be discredited and the support of the federal government and private sympathizers would be cut off.

White southerners were not the only ones concerned about a possible communist influence in the civil rights movement. The FBI became concerned when the agency discovered that Stanley Levison, an inactive Communist party member, was Martin's close friend and adviser. The issue also surfaced when Jack O'Dell, who also had previous ties with the Communist party, joined the SCLC's New York staff after being recommended by Levison. Similar concerns were raised from time to time in regard to Bayard Rustin's history of radicalism.

As an integrationist, seeking to persuade whites to include blacks in the mainstream of American society, Martin was nearly as concerned about avoiding the communist label as the white southerners were about getting it to stick to him. He went to great lengths to separate himself and the civil rights movement from any persons or ideas regarded as un-American, particularly those from a radical, leftist tradition. Yielding to pressure from the Kennedy administration, King temporarily severed contact with Levison and terminated O'Dell's employment. Martin sometimes became impatient as he defended himself and the civil rights movement against attempts to pin the communist label on them. "I'm getting sick and tired of people saying this movement has been infiltrated by communists," he said in 1964. "There are as many communists in the freedom movement as there are Eskimos in Florida."[15]

Martin defined the black freedom struggle as an *American* movement, or, as he said at the March on Washington, "a dream deeply rooted in the American dream." The civil rights movement did not receive its motivation from the ideals of Marx, Lenin, or any other communist thinker. African-Americans did not need communism or socialism to tell them that segregation was morally wrong. All they had to do was to read the Bible, the Declaration of Independence, and the Constitution.

In a sermon entitled "How Should a Christian View Communism?" Martin proclaimed that "Communism and Christianity [are] fundamentally incompatible" because the former posits an "atheistic materialism" and the latter a "theistic idealism." Communism is "based on ethical relativism," believing that "the end justifies the means," and "Christianity sets forth a system of absolute moral values and affirms that God has placed within the very structure of this universe certain moral principles that are fixed and immutable."[16]

Initially, Malcolm was even more hostile toward communists than Martin. For Malcolm, communists were *white* radicals who were no more interested in black liberation than their liberal and conservative brothers and sisters. He condemned them not only for advocating just another white philosophy, but also, like Martin, for being atheistic. He regarded himself as a Muslim minister, a devout believer in the One God, Allah.

The interracialism of the communists disgusted Malcolm. He viewed it as just another white ploy, no different from the insincerity of the white liberals. Since communists were marginal in America, with no real political and economic power, and since only a few blacks were attracted to them, Malcolm did not even bother to talk much about them in his speeches.

As long as Martin and Malcolm remained within the first phase of their intellectual and political development, they excluded class analysis or minimized its significance and concentrated their energies on eliminating racism. Initially, both believed that racism was *the* primary evil in America and the world, other manifestations of injustice being secondary to it. This belief blinded them, to some extent, not only to sexism but also to classism in the black community and the society as a whole.

The turning point for Malcolm was his break with the Nation of Islam and subsequent trips to the Middle East and Africa. For Martin it was his trip to Sweden to receive the Nobel Peace Prize and the subsequent violent eruption of the black poor in the northern ghettos, demonstrating that there was something radically wrong with the American system that involved more than racism alone. Both Martin and Malcolm began gradually to recognize that capitalism itself is based upon the exploitation of many poor people by a few rich people.

When Malcolm broke with the Nation of Islam in March 1964, a British reporter asked him whether he would accept communist support. He avoided a direct yes-or-no answer and resorted to one of his familiar parable-type responses. "Let me tell you a little story," he said. "It's like being in a wolf's den. The wolf sees someone on the outside who is interested in freeing me from the den. The wolf doesn't like that person on the outside. But I don't care who opens that door and lets me out." "Then your answer is yes?" asked the reporter. "No," Malcolm replied, grinning. "I'm talking about a wolf."[17]

The Socialist Workers party in New York, a Trotskyite group, invited Malcolm to speak three times at the Militant Labor Forum. Their newspaper, *The Militant*, also reported regularly on his activities in the United States and abroad. During his first appearance at the Militant Labor Forum (on 8 April 1964), Malcolm acknowledged, "I don't know much about Karl Marx."[18] However, his subsequent dialogues with black and white socialists and communists in Africa, Europe, and the United States encouraged him to analyze racism in an international context of human exploitation. He began to see not only the limitations of his own dogmatic black nationalism but also the exploitative nature of American capitalism.

During his second appearance at the Militant Labor Forum (29 May 1964), only a few days after returning from his first trip abroad, Malcolm, while denying any knowledge of socialism, used another parable to present an incipient critique of the American political economy. "It's impossible for a chicken to produce a duck egg—even though they belong to the same family of fowl," he said, and then went on to explain:

A chicken just doesn't have it within its system to produce a duck egg. It can't do it. It can only produce according to what that particular system was constructed to produce. The system in this country cannot produce freedom for an Afro-American. It is impossible for this system, this economic system, this political system, this social system, this system, period. It's impossible for this system, as it stands, to produce freedom right now for the black man in this country.

Using humor to drive home his point, he concluded by saying: "And if ever a chicken did produce a duck egg, I'm sure you would say it was certainly a revolutionary chicken!"[19]

Malcolm's international experience not only softened his affirmation of black nationalism and his blanket rejection of whites; it also made him more receptive to radical ideas from leftist blacks and whites. The more he talked with them, particularly in Africa, the more he realized his need to develop a broader view of injustice than that provided by an analysis based on race alone. His criticisms of capitalism became more frequent and vehement. When Jack Barnes and Barry Sheppard of the Young Socialist Alliance asked Malcolm about "the worldwide struggle . . . between capitalism and socialism," his preference for socialism was clear. "It is impossible for capitalism to survive, primarily because the system of capitalism needs some blood to suck." Malcolm used the analogy of the eagle and vulture to explain why he believed that capitalism's collapse was imminent and inevitable:

Capitalism used to be like an eagle, but now it's more like a vulture. It used to be strong enough to go and suck anybody's blood whether they were strong or not. But now it has become more cowardly, like the vulture, and it can only suck the blood of the helpless. As the nations of the world free themselves, then capitalism has less victims, less to suck, and it becomes weaker and weaker. It's only a matter of time in my opinion before it will collapse completely.[20]

Malcolm's lack of exposure to socialism (its history, development, and various manifestations) prevented him from giving an informed interpretation and critique of it. He tended to speak on the subject only when asked, and that was when he was abroad or in the company of white and a few black leftists at the Militant Labor Forum. Although Malcolm spoke approvingly of socialism and disapprovingly of capitalism, his thinking remained primarily antiracist, and class analysis was always secondary. With only eleven months to think, read, and travel independently, Malcolm did not have enough time to consider socialism comprehensively. He spoke "off the cuff" and in a language which reflected intellectual growth and an undying commitment to the liberation of black people. When a Ghanaian asked him "What do you think about socialism?" Malcolm's reply disclosed his primary commitment. "Is it good for black people?" he asked. "It seems to be," the questioner answered. "Then, I'm for it," Malcolm told him.[21]

Malcolm's receptiveness to socialism was influenced by African socialists like Kwame Nkrumah, then president of Ghana, and Julius K. Nyerere, then president of Tanzania. "All of the countries that are emerging today from under the shackles of colonialism are turning toward socialism," he said in response to the question "What political and economic system does Malcolm X want?" "I don't think it's an accident. Most of the countries that were colonial powers were capitalist countries, and the last bulwark of capitalism today is America." Malcolm focused on the interdependence of capitalism and racism. "It's impossible for a white person to believe in capitalism and not believe in racism. You can't have capitalism without racism. And if you find one . . . that makes you sure they don't have this racism in their outlook, usually they're socialists."[22]

Although Malcolm considered socialism as an alternative to capitalism, he still believed that black people of the world had to find the answers to their own problems and not depend upon the intellectual resources of their former white colonizers. In a Paris interview three months before his death he said: "Many of the African intellectuals that have analyzed the approach of socialism are beginning to see where the African has to use a form of socialism that fits into the African context. Whereas the form that is used in the European country might be good for that particular European country it doesn't fit as well into the African context."[23]

Although Malcolm was open to learn from anyone who was concerned about the liberation of humanity from oppression, he was primarily a *black* revolutionary and not a Marxist revolutionary. Malcolm's hesitation in joining forces with Marxist groups in the United States was due not only to his lack of theoretical knowledge about socialism but also (again in contrast to Martin) to his general distrust of most whites (even after his trip to Mecca) and his belief that blacks and sincere whites could best support each other by working separately in their own communities. When whites join black groups, Malcolm believed, they always end up in positions of leadership, thereby once more instilling in blacks the feeling of inferiority and the idea that they cannot do anything without whites. When blacks join white groups, they usually sever themselves from their community, negating their cultural roots.

Nothing was more important for Malcolm than convincing blacks that through political commitment, intellectual discipline, and racial unity they can solve their own problems. Marxist ideas, as the panacea for the black situation of oppression, did not sit well with him, even though he saw some truth in them. Malcolm believed that African-Americans had to develop their own solution to their problem. "There can be no worker solidarity until there's first some black solidarity," Malcolm told A. B. Spellman. His concern for racial unity caused him to exclude whites from membership in his organizations. "Whites can't join us," Malcolm said, no matter how radical and sincere they were. Contrary to the popular myth about him, Malcolm acknowledged that some sincere whites were "just as fed up . . . as anyone else," "especially at the student level." But this acknowledgment did not prevent him from keeping white Marxists at arm's length in the interest of black unity.[24]

While Malcolm's concern for black unity must be applauded, his tendency to focus primarily on racism was an asset and a liability. It was an asset in the sense that no one can think and act creatively unless his or her perspective takes its point of departure from the *particularity* of his or her own cultural history. It was a liability in the sense that it partly blinded him to class exploitation, and the need for the poor of all races to consolidate their efforts toward the achievement of universal freedom.

Unlike Malcolm, who did not have the opportunity to read Marx, Martin read him "during the Christmas holidays of 1949." He spoke of his "anti-capitalist feelings" in a paper he wrote at Crozer Seminary, and his wife, Coretta, observed the same sentiment in the 1950s. Although he admired Marx's "great passion for social justice," it was not until he went to Sweden that he began to consider a European version of socialism as an alternative to American capitalism. "I am always amazed when I go there," Martin said of Sweden. "They don't have any poverty. No unemployment, nobody needing health services can't get them. They don't have any slums. The question is why? It is because Scandinavia has grappled with the problem of more equitable distribution of wealth."[25]

Martin reflected upon socialism even more seriously when he realized that the black poor (as well as the white poor, a reality that surprised him) were getting poorer and the white rich richer, despite the passage of the much-celebrated Civil Rights Act and President Johnson's War on Poverty. He became explicit about the need for *economic* equality, an "Economic Bill of Rights for the Disadvantaged," which would guarantee a job or an annual income for all Americans. "We are grappling with basic class issues between the privileged and underprivileged," he said in his 1966 Gandhi Memorial Lecture at Howard University. But because he was still deeply aware of the harm that a "communist smear" could do to the civil rights movement, he was very cautious about the dangers of speaking positively of "democratic socialism." "Now this means that we're treading . . . in very difficult waters, because it really means that we are saying that something is wrong with the economic system of our nation," he said in a speech to his staff. "It means that something is wrong with capitalism." During staff retreats, he often requested that the tape recorders be switched off, so he could express his views frankly and honestly about the need for a complete, revolutionary change in the American political economy, replacing capitalism with some form of socialism. What we have had in America is "socialism for the rich and free enterprise for the poor," Martin said often.[26]

Martin's interest in transforming the American political economy is much better known than Malcolm's. Also, unlike Malcolm's, his interest did not arise from his experience in the Third World or from his dialogues with white and black leftists. Martin's interest in socialism was motivated by his readings about it in graduate school, his impressions of Sweden, and by the failure of the civil rights acts and President Johnson's War on Poverty to affect significantly the life chances of the black poor in the urban ghettos of America. The Watts riots and the many others that followed it revolutionized Martin's thinking on America. He began to see that the problem of injustice in America was deeper and wider than racism.

Although Martin and Malcolm began to consider classism as an evil along with and integral to racism, it was still difficult for them to incorporate this analysis into their thinking and activity. Martin's Poor People's March to Washington was intended to achieve solidarity among the poor of all races. Perhaps it would indeed have been a powerful symbol of the solidarity of the poor, if he had not been assassinated while supporting garbage workers in Memphis. Malcolm had not advanced that far in his thinking; but he was trying to turn the corner, to create a new image, defined by his commitment to humanity. If we today are to complete what Martin and Malcolm failed to achieve, then we must identify and correct their weaknesses.

11

Making Their Mark: Legacies

Freedom is not free.

> Martin Luther King, Jr.
> Montgomery, Alabama
> 3 December 1959

The price of freedom is death.

> Malcolm X
> New York City
> June 1964

If a man hasn't discovered something that he will die for, he isn't fit to live.

> Martin Luther King, Jr.
> Detroit, Michigan
> 23 June 1963

Respect me, or put me to death.

> Malcolm X
> New York City
> 5 July 1964

In February 1965 Malcolm's voice was silenced when assassins shot him as he started to speak to a crowd of blacks at the Audubon Ballroom in Harlem. In April three years later Martin, standing on a balcony of the Lorraine Motel in Memphis, Tennessee, was shot by a lone assassin. Both were thirty-nine years old. Both, though mentally and physically exhausted, were still fighting and searching for the freedom that America promised but never delivered.

Since his assassination, Martin has been immortalized as a great *American* leader by blacks and whites alike. During the third Monday of each January, America celebrates his birthday with many tributes and speeches, recounting his contribution to the nation. Similar events are held during the first week of April to mark his assassination. A quarter of a million people returned to Washington to celebrate the twentieth anniversary of the "The March and the Dream," "a day," according to the *Washington Post,* "that altered the Nation."[1] On the twenty-fifth anniversary of "The Great March on Washington," to use the inflated language that most events associated with Martin have acquired, another celebration was held. Still another commemoration was held on the twenty-fifth anniversary of the Selma March. The possibility that there were serious shortcomings in Martin's perspective on black freedom seems to escape most black and white Americans. Saints have no major weaknesses, only minor lapses in judgment to remind us of their humanity.

In contrast to Martin's public acclaim, Malcolm is still forgotten by most Americans. Only a few blacks — and fewer whites — celebrate his birthday on May 19 or remember his assassination. When Malcolm is remembered, his significance is primarily defined as a *black* leader, as if he made little or no contribution to the nation as a whole.

The small group of Malcolm's devotees resent the inordinate attention given to Martin and the obscurity of their hero. In their indignation they often make similar excessive claims about Malcolm, as if his thinking too was self-sufficient and in no need of a complement or correction from anybody, especially from integrationists like Martin. As during Martin's and Malcolm's lifetimes, it is their enthusiasts, the cult worshipers, who exaggerate their differences and individual accomplishments and thereby succeed not only in misrepresenting their significance for the 1950s and 1960s, but more importantly, their meaning for us today. The admirers of Martin and Malcolm must be willing to consider their limitations, just as their critics must be willing to acknowledge their contributions, in order to gain a reasonable and usable picture of them.

Uncritical admirers and unkind critics of Martin and Malcolm have one thing in common: They have not seriously studied either person. Much of what they say about them is misinformation, usually derived from the popular myths about them. For if they had carefully reflected on Martin's and Malcolm's lives and thought, they could easily see that the greatness of each, as an *African-American* leader, is best perceived through an acknowledgment of their humanity. Therefore, to understand their meanings for the black community and for America generally, we must not romanticize or denigrate them but rather see them as they saw themselves and each other: as real human beings, with assets and liabilities that characterize all great leaders.

In this final chapter, we will evaluate the strengths of their leadership, pointing out some important things their legacies teach the African-American community about its struggle for freedom, which are important lessons for other communities as well. The strengths of their leadership are to be assessed in the light of their stated goal: The achievement of freedom for African-Americans in the United States. Our primary concern will be to point out what we today can learn from them in our efforts to complete their unfinished work.

CULTURE

The first area to consider is black culture and consciousness. Though both men participated in this realm, Malcolm was the towering figure. He was a cultural revolutionary who almost singlehandedly transformed the way black people thought about themselves. He was the progenitor of the black consciousness movement that emerged during the 1960s, affecting the whole of black life, including art (black aesthetics), education (black studies), politics (Black Power), and religion (black theology).

Malcolm's most far-reaching impact was among the masses of African-Americans in the ghettos of the cities. He told them, as Baldwin observed, that "they should be proud of being black and God knows they should be. This is a very important thing to hear in a country that assures you that you should be ashamed of it."[2] When Malcolm appeared on the scene in the 1950s, Stepin Fetchit, Aunt Jemima, Amos and Andy, and other demeaning characters dominated the radio, movie, and television images of the black self. Tarzan's Africa, with savages and cannibals, was the only one most African-Americans knew about. Malcolm showed that negative images of Africa were skillfully concocted by whites to make African-Americans hate their African origin. "You know yourself that we have been a people who hated our African characteristics," Malcolm told a Detroit audience.

> We hated our heads, we hated the shape of our nose, we wanted one of those dog-like noses, you know; we hated the color of our skin, hated the blood of Africa that was in our veins. And in hating our features and our skin and our blood, why we had to end up hating ourselves. Our color became to us a chain—we felt that it was holding us back; our color became to us like a prison which we felt was keeping us confined, not letting us go this way or that way. We felt that all of these restrictions were based solely upon our color, and the psychological reaction to that would have to be that as long as we felt imprisoned or chained or trapped by black

skin, black features, and black blood, that skin and those features and that blood holding us back automatically had to become hateful to us. It made us feel inferior; it made us feel inadequate; made us helpless. And when we fell victims of this feeling of inadequacy or inferiority or helplessness, we turned to somebody to show us the way.[3]

Hearing Malcolm analyze the dreadful psychological consequences of black self-hate had a transforming effect upon the consciousness of African-Americans. They began to *think* black and *act* black, because Malcolm, through the power of his oratory, helped them to realize and to accept their *blackness* as the essential element in the definition of their humanity. "All of us are black first," he told African-Americans, "and everything else second."[4]

Malcolm was an artist of the spoken word, "a charismatic speaker who could play an audience as great musicians play instruments,"[5] to use Maya Angelou's apt description of him. Applying this talent, he decolonized the black mind, and thereby transformed "Negroes" into proud black African people. Muhammad Ali proclaimed "I am the greatest," Aretha Franklin started to demand "Respect," James Brown began to sing "I'm Black and I'm Proud," and African-Americans began to say proudly to themselves and to the world that "Black is beautiful, baby." The whole of black America began to walk and talk to the rhythm and beat of a cultural renaissance stretching back to the African homeland. Dashikis and Afros became outward signs of an inward transformation of the black self. New sacred places of worship were erected with African Gods as the objects of adoration, and Black Christs replaced white images of the divine in Christian churches and homes.

Africa emerged as the continent of preference in defining the identity of African-Americans. "It's nation time" and "We are an African people" could be heard in political meetings, casual conversations, and the classrooms of newly founded educational institutions, many of which derived their names from Malcolm. So pervasive was Malcolm's influence that even mainstream civil rights leaders, preachers, and politicians acknowledged his insight and integrity. Though he was assassinated before black consciousness reached its peak, the power of his presence stretched beyond the grave. As Roy Wilkins said of him, "Master spellbinder that he was, Malcolm X in death cast a spell more far-flung and more disturbing than any he cast in life."[6] Blacks today who are proud to claim their African heritage should thank Malcolm. More than anyone else he created the space for them to affirm their blackness. More than anyone else he taught blacks that there can be no freedom for the members of the African-American community in the United States without self-esteem, a high regard for themselves as a *black* people. As a Harlem woman said of Malcolm: "He taught me that I was more than a Little Black Sambo or kinky hair or nigger."[7] That was no small achievement.

The matter of racial pride was never absent in Martin's work. But he did not focus on *black* culture and Africa in his program of social change until he saw the depth of black self-hate, particularly as revealed in the riots of the northern ghettos and the subsequent rise of Black Power.

While cultural affirmation is not the only step which African-Americans must take to gain freedom, it is the *first* and *most important* one. Knowledge of and respect for one's history and culture create unity among people. This is the point that Martin and Malcolm taught in their speeches and demonstrated with their lives. Both leaders emphasized that there can be no freedom for blacks prior to their solidarity with each other. When Martin saw the depth of self-hate and despair among blacks in the urban ghettos, he began to speak strongly in support of black self-esteem. "We must feel that we count," he told an assembly of blacks at Glenville High School in Cleveland, Ohio, "that we belong, that we are persons, that we are children of the living God. . . . We must never be ashamed of our heritage, . . . [or] of the color of our skin. Black is as beautiful as any color. . . . I am black and beautiful."[8]

No people can love others before they first love themselves. No people can love themselves if they want to be somebody else. The great danger of the integration philosophy is its tendency to fill blacks with the desire to be white rather than who they are. White images of the divine define the "spiritual" atmosphere of many African-American churches, communicating the idea that blacks cannot be "saved" except by a white Jesus. Pictures of a white Jesus are prominently displayed on stained glass windows and in the teaching literature of most black churches. It is disheartening to observe that in 1990, twenty-five years after Malcolm's death and twenty-one years since the appearance of black theology, African-American ministers could be so insensitive to the religio-cultural needs of their people. No wonder our youth prefer drugs to religion and laugh at the churches as their ministers continue the routine of building monuments "in the name of God" to satisfy their spiritually warped egos.

African-Americans do not need more church buildings; we need to build lives by creating *pride* in being black. We need to think well of ourselves — of our African history and culture. This is the prerequisite for developing the self-confidence needed to create an alternative to the ghetto and the prison. If one in four black males is incarcerated, it is because America has no respect for black life, and many blacks themselves see no alternative to the self-destructive course they have chosen. Respect for self empowers people to create their own future. Malcolm's life and teachings on black self-esteem are the medicine the African-American community needs to prevent its own self-destruction.

POLITICS

Politics was a second area of strength for Martin and Malcolm. Both leaders participated in politics, but in this arena it was Martin who dominated the scene. Martin was a political revolutionary, not in the Marxist sense of transforming the political economy, but in the racial sense of radically changing the sociopolitical relations between blacks and whites in the South. He was the dominant symbol of the civil rights movement, which changed American politics, creating the conditions for genuine African-American political power in the South. The Civil Rights and Voting Rights Acts were his major achievements. The easiest way to symbolize the transformation of American political life is to point to the large number of black elected public officials and to the Jesse Jackson phenomenon in 1984 and 1988 and the David Dinkins and L. Douglas Wilder accomplishments in 1989. The enormous impact that blacks have made in American political life would be unthinkable without the achievements of Martin King and the civil rights movement.

Although many persons helped achieve this result, it was Martin King who gave the philosophical and political rationale of racial equality. He too was an artist of the spoken word, who inspired poor blacks to risk their lives for freedom and shamed many whites into supporting them. King's moral power transcended racial and national boundaries. Daddy King was correct when he said: "He did not belong to us, he belonged to all the world."[9] He belonged particularly to the world of the poor and the disinherited. His last campaign, the Poor People's March on Washington, which he did not live to complete, symbolized his political dream for America—a dream of a land where blacks, whites, Indians, Asians, Latinos, and others would live together as brothers and sisters, equal under the law and with an Economic Bill of Rights that would guarantee a job or income for all.

Martin taught us that the achievement of African-American unity must lead us to reach out to people of other cultures, including white people. Self-respect and self-love do not mean denigrating or hating other people. On the contrary, when we proudly take that first step toward self-affirmation, the second step must be toward our brothers and sisters of other cultures and histories. Martin extended what he had said about the integration of whites, blacks, and other minorities in America to the relations between nations, especially regarding the

United States and Vietnam. That was why he could not separate the issue of freedom for blacks in the United States from peace in Vietnam.

Martin King became recognized as the moral leader of America (and some would even say of the world) during his time. Commenting on his famed "Beyond Vietnam" speech at Riverside Church in New York, John C. Bennett, then president of Union Theological Seminary, said that "there is no one who can speak to the conscience of the American people as powerfully as Martin Luther King." His foremost contribution as a moral leader and thinker was his penetrating insight into the meaning of justice. As regards race relations in the United States and the world, no one understood justice with more depth or communicated it with greater clarity than Martin King. Because of him, the world is not only more aware of the problem of racial injustice but equally aware of its interrelations with poverty and war. "Injustice anywhere," he constantly reminded us, "is a threat to justice everywhere."

Malcolm came to a similar view. After his split with the Nation of Islam, he spent more than half of the last year of his life in the Middle East, Africa, and Europe, searching for religious and political directions in an attempt to develop a program of black liberation. From his international experiences, he acquired a new vision of freedom that included the human rights of all. Malcolm told a Columbia University audience that "it is incorrect to classify the revolt of the Negro as simply a racial conflict of black against white or as a purely American problem. Rather, we are today seeing a global rebellion of the oppressed against the oppressor, the exploited against the exploiter."[10]

As important as black nationalism is for the African-American struggle, it cannot be the ultimate goal. The beloved community must remain the primary objective for which we are striving. On this point Martin was right: "For better or worse we are all on this particular land together at the same time, and we have to work it out together."[11] Malcolm's reluctance to acknowledge this point was understandable. He did not wish to undermine the need for black self-esteem in the face of a dominant ideology of integration that was hardly distinguishable from assimilation. However, Malcolm's exposure to young whites (mainly college students, who seemed to have more of a moral capacity and will for "brotherhood" than their parents) and his talks with Nasser, Ben Bella, and Nkrumah (all of whom, he said, "awakened me to the dangers of racism") encouraged him to drop the term "black nationalism" and to search for a way beyond it.[12] "I am not a racist," Malcolm repeatedly said, and he meant it.

If European history and culture teach us anything, it is the danger of perceiving the world from the viewpoint of only one culture, as if other peoples' histories do not count. Whether Europeans are discussing world peace, writing history and theology, or organizing for the next revolution, they often act as if other peoples' viewpoints do not have to be taken seriously. If African-Americans or any other people define their freedom struggle in terms of the superiority of their culture over others, they will develop a similarly arrogant and condescending attitude toward others. Martin King was right: We are bound to each other—not just blacks with blacks or whites with whites or Koreans with Koreans, but all races of people in the United States and throughout the world are one human family, made to live together in freedom. We must learn how to live together as brothers and sisters, respecting each other's cultural history, or we will perish together as fools.

Like the world, America is a rainbow. It is a nation of many races, nationalities, and creeds. America is European and African and *much more*. It is the "much more"—Indians, Asians, Latinos, and others—which makes this country a rainbow. Jesse Jackson is right. This rainbow is not a liability. It is our strength. We are the world in miniature, a seed of hope that the people of this planet can live together in peace based on justice. No one provides a better symbol of this hope than Martin Luther King, Jr.

CRITIQUE OF AMERICAN CHRISTIANITY

Martin and Malcolm were master critics of American Christianity. Both focused on racism, with one making a powerful internal critique and the other a devastating external one.

Martin was an internal critic, and as such his race critique was more acceptable to both whites and blacks and thus was more influential in their churches. He challenged white Christians to be true to what they read in their Bibles and affirm in their creeds, namely that God created all people as one human family, brothers and sisters to one another. He challenged black Christians to be obedient to the God they preach and sing about, by refusing to obey laws that discriminate against them.

Before Martin King, white churches ignored the problem of racism, and black churches passively accepted its consequences. Within a short period of time, Martin was able to prick the conscience of both white and black Christians and thereby enlist them into a mass movement against racism in the churches and the society. He made racism the chief moral dilemma, one which neither whites nor blacks could ignore and also retain their Christian identity.

No religious thinker has made a greater impact upon American culture and its churches than Martin King. He has communicated the Christian message of freedom more effectively, prophetically, and creatively than anyone in the United States before or after him. He was a liberation theologian before African-Americans and Latin Americans began to use the term to describe their reflections about God from the perspective of the poor. If American white and black churches had listened more attentively to Martin King, then they would have been better prepared to hear Malcolm X.

Because of Malcolm's unrestrained critique of Christianity and uncritical devotion to Elijah Muhammad's Nation of Islam, white Christians ignored him and black Christians paid too little attention to his critique of their faith. By their turning a deaf ear to Malcolm, the public meaning of Christianity remained almost exclusively identified with the cultural values of white Americans and Europeans. More than anyone else in American or European history (including Marx, Nietzsche, and Freud), Malcolm was the great "master of suspicion" regarding white people's moral and religious values. All Americans, particularly white and black Christians, should incorporate Malcolm's race critique into their understanding of their society and its churches. In clear and forceful language, Malcolm's life and thought tell us about the great difference between Christianity as preached and taught, on the one hand, and about the practice of white and black Christians in their communities, on the other.

I do not think that anyone can be a *real* Christian in America today, or perhaps anywhere else, without incorporating Malcolm's race critique into his or her practice of and thinking about the religion of Jesus. Malcolm's race critique of Christianity is as important for genuine Christian living in the world as Marx's class critique. While progressive white Christians have begun to take Marx's thinking on religion seriously (especially since the emergence of Latin American liberation theology), very few have even bothered to read Malcolm X. Black Christians may read Malcolm but they seem to hear only what he said about the hypocrisy of white churches and not what he said about "corrupt Negro preachers." Black Christians prefer to refer to Martin King when talking about themselves or about their ecumenical relations with whites. King is less offensive to their Christian sensibilities.

Racism is deeply embedded in American religion and society. We cannot get rid of it by forgetting the past and simply urging blacks and whites to develop good will toward each other. Racism is a cancer. To get rid of this deadly disease requires radical surgery that cuts deep into not only the "body politic" but also the "body of Christ," as white and black Christians like to call themselves. The best surgeon for cutting out the cancer of racism in Christian churches is Malcolm X. Malcolm's black theology is not a replacement for the Christian theology of black churches or even of white churches. Rather, it is an *indispensable corrective.* As such it can prevent black churches from becoming a mere duplication of white churches. Perhaps it can also enable white churches to discover what a truly "beloved community" without racism really is.

Black and white Christian churches (as well as other religious bodies) really need to practice and preach the gospel according to Martin and Malcolm. If they did, we would have a better America and world. They would not only declare war on racism but also on militarism, poverty, sexism, and other evils that afflict the human condition. The United States should not be allowed to continue to spend billions of dollars to build weapons of destruction. Religious bodies should register an unqualified no to death and an uncompromising yes to life.

To say yes to life is to say no not only to militarism but to poverty too. The United States should not be allowed to ignore the poor. If Martin and Malcolm teach us anything, it is that food, shelter, and quality health care are not a luxury but a human right which must be guaranteed to all.

QUALITIES AS LEADERS

Martin and Malcolm teach us the importance of courageous, intelligent, and dedicated leadership. The African-American community in particular, and poor people generally, are in dire need of such leaders. Too many of their leaders merely talk about freedom for all while gathering its benefits only for themselves and other middle-class people. It is well-known that neither Martin nor Malcolm benefited financially from the movements they led, and each paid the ultimate price — death.

Both Martin and Malcolm were best known and respected for the integrity of their leadership. They were not crowd pleasers; rather, they spoke the truth even when they stood alone. Martin's most impressive moment in this regard was his uncompromising stand against the war in Vietnam. "I am not a consensus leader," he told many people who informed him that his antiwar position was alienating many friends and supporters of the civil rights movement. "I don't care who doesn't like what I say about it." "This madness must stop."[13]

Unlike Martin, who agonized over alienating the public, Malcolm delighted in speaking the "sharp truth." Being called "irresponsible" and an "extremist" did not bother him. He accepted the descriptions as badges of truth. Malcolm did not believe that one could speak the truth about the condition of blacks in America without making whites angry. "What made Malcolm X Shabazz a great man," a Chicago doctor said, "is that he had the guts to say what nine-tenths of American Negroes would like to say but don't have the guts to say."[14]

In viewing Martin's and Malcolm's qualities as leaders it is important to observe something in addition to their courage and integrity. They were also committed to the continued development of their minds through a disciplined program of study. Martin began the development of his mind through formal education, acquiring a Ph.D. in theology by the age of twenty-six. He continued his education during his movement days by attracting committed and talented people to serve on the SCLC staff. He also organized a research committee, a New York advisory group of intellectuals and professionals. He frequently held retreats in order to debate the issues of nonviolence, civil disobedience, Black Power, and Vietnam. "We have a moral responsibility to be intelligent," he said. He criticized the black church for "reducing worship to entertainment," and was particularly critical of the black preacher who "places more emphasis on volume than on content and confuses spirituality with muscularity."

Malcolm initiated his intellectual development with a program of study in prison, copying words from the entire dictionary. After much painstaking, tedious mental work, he was able to read books with understanding. History was his favorite subject. "Of all our studies, history is best qualified to reward our research," he repeatedly said. "And when you see that you've got problems, all you have to do is to examine the historic method used all over the world by others who have problems similar to yours. Once you see how they got theirs straight, then you know how you can get yours straight."[15]

Malcolm was an avid reader, devouring books sometimes in a single evening. Like Martin, he used his knowledge to empower and to challenge African-Americans to study their past so they would know what to do in the present in order to make a new future for themselves, their children, and generations to come. Malcolm believed in *functional* education, that is, the acquisition of knowledge for the purpose of liberating African-Americans from oppression. Just because you go to college doesn't mean that you are educated, Malcolm contended. "The college and university in the American educational system are skillfully used to miseducate." He was severely critical of African-American intellectuals who used their intellects to defend the white man's value system. Malcolm's account of his well-known encounter with a Harvard professor illustrates his disdain:

> One particular university's "token-integrated" black Ph.D. associate professor I never will forget; he got me so mad I couldn't see straight. As badly as our 22 million of educationally deprived black people need the help of any brains he has, there he was looking like some fly in the buttermilk among white "colleagues" — and he was trying to *eat me up!* He was ranting about what a "divisive demagogue" and what a "reverse racist" I was. I was racking my

head, to spear that fool; finally I held up my hand, and he stopped. "Do you know what white racists call black Ph.D's?" He said something like, "I believe that I happen not to be aware of that"—you know, one of these ultraproper-talking Negroes. And I laid the word down on him, loud: "*Nigger!*"[16]

Few people loved and respected education more than Malcolm. "Without education," he said, "you are not going anywhere in this world."[17] He regretted his own lack of academic education because he realized that it hindered his ability to defend the humanity of black people. "My greatest lack has been, I believe, that I don't have the kind of academic education I wish I had been able to get—to have been a lawyer, perhaps," he said as he concluded his *Autobiography*. "I've always loved verbal battle, and challenge. You can believe me that if I had the time right now, I would not be one bit ashamed to go back into any New York City public school and start where I left off in the ninth grade, and go on through a degree."[18]

Both Malcolm and Martin realized that no people can achieve freedom as long as their leaders lack knowledge and understanding regarding how the economic and political systems of the world came into being, and how they function today. One of the chief roles of the leader is to teach the people how to organize themselves for the purpose of achieving their freedom. Organizing for freedom requires thinking about the meaning of freedom and developing strategies to implement it in the society. No leader can teach others what he or she does not know.

Today, there are many African-Americans who are vying for the leadership mantle that Martin and Malcolm left behind. But there are few who seem to possess those qualities which set Martin and Malcolm apart. Creative leadership involves much more than talking loud enough to attract the local or national news media; it involves first and foremost a sincere commitment to serve the "least of these" (to use Martin King's language)—to serve their sociopolitical and religio-cultural needs. Real leaders are not self-appointed but are chosen by the people. They are those who teach and are taught. They are best known by their solidarity, their willingness to serve, to suffer with the people, even to the point of death. That was why Malcolm said: "If you're not ready to die for it, put the word 'freedom' out of your vocabulary."[19] The bearers of Martin's and Malcolm's leadership tradition are not primarily those who invoke their names during commemorative events in their honor. They are the people who serve the poor, empowering them to fight against the inhuman conditions of poverty.

SELF-CRITICISM AND HUMILITY

Martin and Malcolm left us a legacy of self-criticism and humility, a willingness to acknowledge their mistakes and limitations.

Both Martin and Malcolm realized that their best disciples were not the "yes men" who merely repeated their views. Rather, they were those who told them about the shortcomings of their ideas and leadership. Martin and Malcolm recognized that they could provide creative and effective leadership only to the degree that they respected the views of others and encouraged their challenge and criticism.

During SCLC staff meetings and in other settings, Martin urged persons to present opposite arguments (often called the conservative and militant perspectives) against his own "middle-of-the-road" viewpoint on an issue. Largely influenced by his studies of Hegel, Martin believed that truth was found in neither of the opposites of the right or the left (thesis and antithesis) but rather in a middle position (synthesis), which itself was derived from the encounter of the two extremes. "He would always expect me to take the conservative side," Andy Young recalled, "to sorta neutralize what [James] Bevel and Hosea [Williams] were trying to do, to give him an excuse to come down the middle.... He expected me to go way to the right [laughing] on every question." Historian August Meier appropriately called Martin a "conservative militant."[20]

Unlike many of his talented disciples, Martin King was a "reluctant leader," a point that Andy Young has emphasized in several interviews. According to Young, Martin "did not ambitiously pursue leadership." In a perceptive interview, he told Howell Raines:

> I'm convinced that Martin never wanted to be a leader. I mean, everything he did, he was pushed into. He went to Montgomery in the first place because ... he wanted a nice quiet town where he could finish his doctoral dissertation and not even have the responsibility of a big church and got trapped into the Montgomery Improvement Association. They literally shamed him into gettin' involved in the Atlanta Movement. He never would get involved in the Freedom Rides. He just refused. He just did not wanna assume the leadership of the entire Southern struggle or of the entire national struggle. And it wasn't until ... the time of Birmingham that he kinda decided that he wasn't going to be able to escape that, that he was going on.[21]

Stanley Levison, one of Martin's closest advisers, made a similar observation about Martin's humility:

Martin could be described as an intensely guilt-ridden man. The most essential element in the feelings of guilt was that he didn't feel he deserved the tribute he got. He was an actor in history at a particular moment that called for a personality; he had been selected as that personality. If he had been less humble, he could have lived with this great acclaim; but as it was, he always thought of ways in which he could somehow live up to it; he talked about taking a vow of poverty; getting rid of everything he owned — including his house — so that he could at least feel that nothing material came to him from his efforts.[22]

During most of Malcolm's public career, he was a minister in the Nation of Islam, faithfully and humbly accepting Elijah Muhammad's absolute leadership, obeying the rules and regulations of the Nation of Islam to thc letter. When Muhammad suspended him, he accepted the punishment and remained silent for three months. Malcolm too was a "reluctant leader," but not quite in the same sense as Martin was. He did not wish to start a new movement and desperately tried to remain within the Nation of Islam. He believed in the religio-cultural principles of Muhammad's leadership, despite the latter's moral turpitude. It was only after Malcolm realized that his silencing would never be lifted that he decided to start his own organizations — first, the Muslim Mosque, Inc. (mainly religious), and three months later, the OAAU (primarily political). When Malcolm declared his independence, he said that "I do not pretend to be a *divine* man." He even refused to allow himself to be called "honorable." He preferred to be "known as Brother Malcolm when ... speaking in a religious capacity" and "Malcolm X when ... speaking in a political capacity."[23]

Martin's and Malcolm's humility is further seen in their willingness to confess errors in judgment, unlike many religious leaders who act as though their views are divinely inspired. In his *Autobiography,* Malcolm laid bare his life of degradation and his fanatical commitment to Elijah Muhammad. He regarded both periods of his life (as hustler and as minister in the Nation of Islam) as great mistakes. In a letter from Mecca to a friend, Malcolm denounced Elijah Muhammad as a "religious faker."

For 12 long years I lived within the narrow-minded confines of the "straightjacket world" created by my strong belief that Elijah Muhammad was a messenger direct from God Himself, and my faith in what I now see to be a pseudo-religious philosophy that he preaches. . . . I shall never rest until I have undone the harm I did to so many well-meaning, innocent Negroes who through my own evangelistic zeal now believe in him even more fanatically and more blindly than I did.[24]

Although Malcolm never retracted his strong opposition to white racism in America, he regretted his blanket condemnation of all whites and some of his most intemperate statements about them. Most notably in this regard was his infamous "I just heard some good news!" statement, referring to the plane crash, just outside of Paris, that killed 130 whites, mostly from Atlanta, Georgia. "That's one of the things I wish I had never said," he told Alex Haley. Another of these incidents involved a young white girl who came to Harlem to ask Malcolm what role she could play in the black struggle for justice. He sent her away crying as he told her that "there was nothing she could do." Malcolm later confessed: "I regret I told her that. I wish that now I knew her name, or where I could telephone her, or write to her, and tell her what I tell white people now when they present themselves as being sincere, and ask me, one way or another, the same thing she asked." He came to believe that whites should work in their communities and blacks in theirs and by "working separately, the sincere white people and sincere black people actually will be working together."[25]

Although Martin's confessions were less dramatic than Malcolm's, they were just as genuine and important. "I make mistakes tactically," he said in an address to the National Association of Television and Radio Announcers in Atlanta. He acknowledged several mistakes during the Albany and Chicago Movements, mistakes which were related to his trust of whites in the federal and city governments and his wish to accommodate their concerns.

As a theologian and a minister, Martin confessed his personal sins before God and in the presence of the people who supported the freedom movement. "I make mistakes morally and get on my knees and confess it and ask God to forgive me," he told the television and radio announcers. In sermons he frequently reminded black Christians of his moral failures. "I don't know this morning about you, but I can make a testimony. You don't need to go out this morning saying that Martin Luther King is a saint. Oh no! I want you to know . . . that I am a sinner like all of God's children. But I want to be a good man, and I want to hear a voice saying to me one day, 'I take you in and I bless you because you tried. It was well within your heart.' "[26]

Martin was slow in taking a stand against the U.S. involvement in the Vietnam War. He regretted that he allowed friends of the civil rights movement and in the government to pressure him to cease his initial criticisms.

Self-criticism and humility are rare traits among leaders in the government, churches, and freedom movements. It seems that the more recognition and status people acquire the more arrogant and certain they become of their judgment. Witness the U.S. government's attitude toward Nicaragua, or many religious and secular leaders' attitudes toward anyone who challenges their power. The leaders of the poor cannot represent their constituency well unless they remain humble and self-critical. Regarding this point, Martin and Malcolm can teach us a lot.

NONVIOLENCE AND SELF-DEFENSE

In their opposition to one another, Martin and Malcolm taught us the relationship between nonviolence and self-defense. The difference between them on this issue was a matter of emphases, contexts, and perspectives on America. Both nonviolent direct action and self-defense needed to be accented, the former in public demonstrations and the latter as a human right. There was not and is not today a need to choose between them.

Malcolm was right to insist that African-Americans should take their freedom "by any means necessary," refusing absolutely to let white exploiters shape the ethics of resistance to exploitation. "A black man has the right to do whatever is necessary to get his freedom that other human beings have done to get their freedom."[27] Malcolm felt that this point especially needed to be made to white people. What right did white people have to tell black people the methods that they should use to fight against white racism? Since whites themselves were not nonviolent when they perceived their humanity was being violated, why should they expect blacks to be nonviolent?

Martin, however, was right in his claim that nonviolent direct action is *resistance* and not passivity or cowardice. Indeed it was the only creative way that an African-American minority of 10 percent could fight for freedom and at the same time avoid genocide, the logical consequence of racism. As Malcolm spoke to the *visceral feelings* of African-Americans, Martin spoke to the *political realities* implicit in their minority status in America. Nonviolence was an effective weapon of resistance against segregation in the South.

The power of nonviolence was not only revealed in the U.S. South; it is also being used effectively today in many parts of the world. In the Philippines, China, South Africa, and Eastern Europe, the masses of people have rebelled nonviolently against their governments, often appealing to Martin King and the African-American civil rights movement as they sang "We Shall Overcome." The Marcos dictatorship in the Philippines was overthrown, and many communist governments in

Eastern Europe have been radically transformed and replaced. Instead of representing cowardice, as Malcolm sometimes claimed, King's idea of Gandhian nonviolence represents a spirit of resistance in people that has transformed the world. It seems to be the most creative moral weapon that the masses have for effecting radical change.

MILITANCY AND HUMOR

Malcolm and Martin established an effective *tone* for the freedom struggle, combining unwavering militancy with humor and irony.

Malcolm was well-known for his blunt speaking, his refusal to sugar-coat his analysis of racism in order to make it more palatable to the sensibilities of whites. His tell-it-like-it-is style earned him the title of "the angriest Negro in America."[28] He accepted the label gladly, because he believed that no people ever gained freedom until they got mad enough to do anything to get it. This was what he meant with the phrase "by any means necessary." "When a person places the proper value on freedom, there is nothing under the sun that he will not do to acquire that freedom," Malcolm proclaimed to an OAAU rally. "Whenever you hear a man saying he wants freedom, but in the next breath he is going to tell you what he won't do to get it, or what he doesn't believe in doing in order to get it, he doesn't believe in freedom. A man who believes in freedom will do anything under the sun to acquire . . . or to preserve his freedom."[29]

When Malcolm spoke to white audiences, his anger became obvious in the style of his speaking. He often spoke loudly. "Excuse me for raising my voice," he told a Harvard audience. "As long as my voice is the only thing I raise, I don't think you should become upset." To a Boston University audience, he described his speech as "raw, you don't have to interpret it, it speaks for itself." Malcolm also spoke rapidly and emphatically, freely showing his anger as he told whites what was on his mind. "Some of what we say may appear a bit blunt and frank in the ears of whites," he said as he explained the teachings of the Nation of Islam at New York's City College. "But we just don't feel that we should have to apologize for our position." Malcolm's main concern was honest communication between blacks and whites. "I would like to point something out so that we'll understand each other better," he said during his second appearance at Boston University.

I don't want you to think in the statements I make that I'm being disrespectful towards you as white people. I'm being frank. And I think that my statements will give you a better insight on the mind of a black man than most statements you get from most people who call themselves Negroes, who usually tell you what they want you to hear with the hope . . . that will make them draw closer to you and create a better possibility of getting from you some of the crumbs that you might let fall from your table. Well, I'm not looking for crumbs so I'm not trying to delude you.[30]

Many whites were not (and still are not) accustomed to engaging in conversation with an intelligent black person who spoke with Malcolm's candidness. On another occasion when he was describing how the Los Angles police killed Ronald Stokes, a fellow Muslim, his anger became so intense that he stopped the audience from applauding during his presentation. "Please! I don't want to hear that," he said. "Hand-patting has been done long enough." When whites interpreted his anger as hate, he retorted: "Don't call me antiwhite because I tell you what I think. I'm not antiwhite because I say America made a slave out of my father."[31]

Referring to white people's reaction to Malcolm, James Baldwin said: "This is the first time in the history of this country where people are forced to recognize some facts of Negro life. It's no longer possible for them to contain it and pretend it isn't true. A man like Malcolm has this utility, that he frightens people so much that finally they'd rather talk even to me than to him." Malcolm said what most blacks felt and talked about among themselves but were afraid to say publicly.

Malcolm believed that the major problem with civil rights leaders was their lack of anger. Proof was their use of nonviolence. No people would use a "turn-the-other-cheek philosophy" if they were angry. He contended that it would take anger to change the oppressed condition of African-Americans in the United States:

When [people] get angry, they aren't interested in logic, they aren't interested in odds, they aren't interested in consequences. When they get angry, they realize that the condition that they're in — that their suffering is unjust, immoral, illegal, and that anything they do to correct it or eliminate it, they're justified. When you develop that type of anger and speak in that voice, then we'll get some kind of respect and recognition, and some changes from these people who have been promising us falsely already for far too long.[32]

Civil rights leaders often accused Malcolm of being a "rabblerouser," substituting emotion for logic. When Bayard Rustin did so in a debate, Malcolm shot back:

When a man is hanging on a tree and he cries out, should he cry out unemotionally? When a man is sitting on a hot stove and he tells you how it feels to be there, is he supposed to speak without emotions? This is what you tell black people in this country when they begin to cry out against the injustices that they're suffering. As long as they describe these injustices in a way that makes you believe you have another 100 years to rectify the situation, then you don't call that emotion. But when a man is on a hot stove, he says, "I'm coming up. I'm getting up. Violently or nonviolently doesn't even enter the picture — I'm coming up, do you understand?"[33]

The injustices of whites against blacks incensed Malcolm so much that he could not hold back his rage no matter what the situation was or whom he was talking to. "Excuse me for raising my voice, but this thing, you know, gets me upset," he told a group of young African-Americans from Mississippi.

Imagine that — a country that's supposed to be a democracy, supposed to be for freedom and all that kind of stuff when they want to draft you and put you in the army and send you to Saigon to fight for them — and then you've got to turn around and all night long discuss how you're going to just get a right to register and vote without being murdered. Why, that's the most hypocritical government since the world began![34]

As Malcolm inserted militancy into the civil rights movement, Martin injected it into conservative black churches. Once militant activists against slavery and segregation, black churches after the failure of Reconstruction became primarily spiritual and social enclaves for blacks starving for recognition in a society which defined them as inferior human beings. The Montgomery bus boycott, under Martin's leadership, marked the beginning of the active participation of black churches in the modern freedom movement. The founding of the SCLC in 1957 made it nearly impossible for black preachers anywhere in the country to remain neutral. During the Birmingham Movement, for example, Martin criticized "preachers riding around in big cars, living in fine homes, but . . . not willing to take part in the fight. . . . If you can't stand up with your people, you are not fit to be a preacher!"[35]

By 1967–68, Martin's militancy had deepened to the extent of disturbing many people, not only in government and the media but in the civil rights movement itself. As David Halberstam said, Martin had begun to sound like a nonviolent Malcolm. His outspoken opposition to the war in Vietnam and his advocacy of mass civil disobedience in Washington isolated him from many former supporters. Amid much controversy and criticism, Martin held fast to his convictions and refused to compromise his fierce opposition to evil in high places.

The more Martin observed the contradictions of poverty in America's cities and the war in Vietnam, the angrier he became. On no occasions was his anger more strongly expressed than in his sermons at Ebenezer Baptist Church in Atlanta. There he laid bare all his tearing passion against America, black churches, and other groups and people who seemed indifferent to the establishment of justice and right. Like an angry prophet possessed by the righteousness of God, he proclaimed the imminent divine judgment against America. "God didn't call America to do what she's doing in the world now," he proclaimed in his famed sermon on the "Drum Major Instinct." "God didn't call America to engage in a senseless, unjust war . . . in Vietnam. And we are criminals in that war. We have committed more war crimes almost than any nation in the world, and I'm going to continue to say it. And we won't stop it because of our pride, and our arrogance as a nation." He compared the impending fate of America with the fate of wayward nations in the Bible. "But God has a way of putting nations in their place," he assured his listeners. "The God that I worship has a way of saying, 'Don't play with me.' He has a way of saying, as the God of the Old Testament used to say to the Hebrews, 'Don't play with me, Israel. Don't play with me, Babylon. Be still and know that I'm God. And if you don't stop your reckless course, I'll rise up and break the backbone of your power.' And *that* can happen to America."[36]

Malcolm and Martin taught us the value not only of anger but also of humor. So great were the moral and political contradictions that African-Americans were fighting against that humor was sometimes the only response which could keep them sane. Malcolm used humor frequently in speeches. "Pick up on that," he often said, smiling and laughing, as he pointed out the glaring contradiction of America claiming to be "the land of the free" and "the leader of the free world" while, at the same time, African-Americans were being beaten and shot by law enforcement officials, for trying to exercise their rights.

White liberal hypocrisy was Malcolm's favorite target. In a late December 1964 interview, he talked to the African-American journalist Claude Lewis about the importance of humor for keeping one's sanity in a society which says one thing but does the opposite. "Anything that's paradoxical has to have some humor in it or it'll crack you up. You know that? You put hot water in a cold glass, it'll crack. Because it's a contrast, a paradox. And America is such a paradoxical society, hypocritically paradoxical, that if you don't have some humor, you'll crack up." He burst into laughter as he talked.

Imagine Adlai Stevenson standing up in the UN and saying, "America needs no credentials for freedom"—I said, why, good God, this man is a joke, you know; and they had just turned loose twenty-one assassins in the South that had murdered three civil rights workers. They didn't murder three criminals—they murdered three civil rights workers. Naw. So that's a joke. And you have to laugh at it. You have to be able to laugh to stand up and sing, "My country 'tis of thee, sweet land of liberty." *That's* a joke. And if you don't laugh at it, it'll crack you up. I mean it's a *joke*. "Sweet land of liberty"—that's a *joke*. [Malcolm laughed again.] If you don't laugh at it you'll crack up.[37]

Martin employed humor too, though without Malcolm's heavy irony. King's sallies were directed mostly against southern bigots who inadvertently supported the African-American struggle for justice. After Bull Connor and his deputies used fire hoses and dogs against demonstrators, the following night Martin used humor to speak about the power of nonviolence. Parodying Bull Connor, Martin said, "We tried to use water on them and we soon discovered that they were used to water for they were Methodists or Episcopalians or other denominations and they had to be sprinkled. And even those who hadn't been sprinkled happened to have been Baptists and not only did they stand up to the water, they went *UNDER* the water." The audience burst into laughter. Martin also said that "I was down there going to court the other day. . . . And I looked over there and saw a tank . . . and I said, 'What is that?' Somebody said, 'Well, that's Bull Connor's tank.' And you know it's a *WHITE* tank. Now, I want to say tonight that they can bring their dogs out, they can get his white tank, and our *BLACK* faces will stand up before the *WHITE* tank." Again the audience screamed with laughter.[38]

King's staff also engaged in humor, especially Ralph Abernathy. His "doohicky" speech in Selma, during which he talked to an "antenna-like device" (which had been planted by the local police to listen secretly to a meeting), was well-known. Fréd Shuttlesworth also often spoke of how he "de-bulled ol' Bull [Connor]!"[39]

Humor served to humanize and to relax blacks in a very oppressive situation. They often laughed to keep from crying. "Segregation is a silly thing!" said Fred Shuttlesworth. Sometimes the contradictions of segregation backfired on whites, as when they were inadvertently forced to serve as chauffeurs for their maids during the Montgomery bus boycott. Mayor W. A. Gayle of Montgomery urged whites to cease the practice of using their cars as "taxi service for Negro maids and cooks who work for them" because they were "fighting to destroy our social fabric just as much as the Negro radicals who are leading them." Not intending to be funny, the Mayor said, with much seriousness, that "the Negroes are laughing at white people behind their backs. They think it's very funny and amusing that whites who are opposed to the Negro boycott will act as chauffeurs to Negroes who are boycotting the buses." It *was* funny, and blacks had a hearty laugh as they retold this and other humorous stories of the civil rights movement.[40]

Anger and humor are like the left and right arm. They complement each other. Anger empowers the poor to declare their uncompromising opposition to oppression, and humor prevents them from being consumed by their fury. Justice-loving people must never stop getting mad at oppression. Oppression is not necessary; we don't have to put up with it. And anyone who condones it should be required to experience our righteous indignation.

To fight for life is to experience the joy of life. To laugh, to have fun, is to bear witness to life against death. Freedom fighters are fun-loving people. Therefore, let us laugh, let us shout for joy, not as an indication that we are no longer angry but rather as a sign that we have just begun to fight.

SOLIDARITY WITH THE MASSES

Martin and Malcolm were not elitist leaders. They were down-to-earth leaders who respected the intelligence of ordinary black people. Both believed that freedom would be achieved only when the black masses became involved in the fight against injustice.

The Montgomery bus boycott transformed the civil rights movement into a mass movement, no longer exclusively dependent upon the slow, legal work of an elite group of officials and lawyers in the NAACP, the Urban League, and CORE. The "New Negro" who inspired Martin's leadership was not usually an intellectual or an artist, as the phrase suggested during the Harlem Renaissance of the 1920s. The "New Negro" in the South was an ordinary person—maid, cook, porter, handyman, fieldhand—whom whites had exploited and segregated for generations. Using the faith of the black churches, Martin King and other ministers inspired poor blacks to "straighten their backs up," because, as Martin often said, "nobody can ride your back unless it's bent." They concluded that the time for *their* freedom had come and that they would no longer wait for others to plead their case in the courts. Poor blacks themselves rose up against their white oppressors and demanded their God-given right to be treated as human beings.

With the black church as his base, Martin moved the black freedom struggle from the courts to the streets, from a polite discussion between the elites of two groups to a life-and-death struggle that rocked the nation. Martin often said that the court could declare rights, but it could not deliver them. Blacks themselves had to take the initiative to make sure that equal rights laws were enforced.

Although Martin was middle-class and did not experience the same need and want or the same indignity of segregation suffered by the black poor, he nevertheless had an amazing capacity to identify with them and to articulate their deepest hurts and pains. While Martin often spoke to white audiences in the sophisticated language of a university professor, almost always using a prepared text, his speech to blacks was extemporaneous and personal. Blacks could feel his solidarity with them. The passion with which Martin spoke and his courage to stand up to whites inspired them to believe that they were people of worth, just as important in God's eyes as the kings and queens of nations. As one black janitor told a northern reporter following the Montgomery bus boycott: "We got our heads up now, and we won't ever bow down again — no, sir — except before God!"[41]

In the wake of the Montgomery bus boycott emerged the sit-ins, freedom rides, March on Washington, Selma March, and many other marches and demonstrations throughout the South — all of which involved the masses of poor blacks who had been possessed by a spirit of rebellion defined by the spirituality of Martin King's nonviolent direct action. They faced head-on the violence of white policemen and other atrocities. Many were killed and wounded, as were many of their white supporters. But they refused to be intimidated into passivity and silence, and they kept on marching, singing "ain't gonna let nobody turn me 'round."

As Martin inspired the southern black masses, Malcolm inspired their counterpart in the northern ghettos. Malcolm, however, had a great advantage over Martin. He came from the underclass and thus understood better the oppressed condition of the masses and their feelings about the society that rendered them marginal. Malcolm was one of them, a "field Negro," and that enabled him to speak from *experience,* the only real authority that alienated blacks in the northern ghetto would accept. His message to them was twofold: (1) The misery in which you live is not your fault but is imposed upon you by the white liberals who support the civil rights movement. (2) Though your misery is not your fault, nevertheless it is your responsibility to free yourselves from it.

Elaborating on the first point, Malcolm identified the enemy as white society, and the black masses responded to what they heard as if he were a jazz man, playing and singing their favorite song of trouble. He understood them and thus could express their feelings of hurt in a language which they had created. Malcolm knew how they felt, and they loved him for having the audacity to "talk bad" to the white man. Just listening to Malcolm "sock it to the Man" was a liberating experience. It was also empowering to know that the poor themselves were not responsible for their miserable condition.

Malcolm's solidarity with the masses was also expressed in his critical comments about them. He told them that if their wretched condition was going to change, they could not depend upon the whites—the very ones who created the situation—to change it. On the contrary, the poor blacks themselves must do it. Malcolm was unmercifully critical of poor blacks for their lack of initiative in doing something about their "miserable plight." He referred to them as "this poor, dumb, deaf, and blind, ignorant, brainwashed, so-called Negro" — "walking zombies." Malcolm called them "lost sheep," "dry bones," and "dead people cut off from their cultural history." He used the Bible to make his point: "You're the one that the book [Bible] is talking about who is dead: dead to the knowledge of yourself, dead to the knowledge of your own people, dead to the knowledge of your own God, dead to the knowledge of the devil." This was bitter medicine for blacks to take. But Malcolm would not let up. "Why, you don't even know who the devil is," he continued. "You think the devil is someone inside the ground that's going to burn you after you're dead. The devil is right here on top of this earth. He's got blue eyes, brown hair, white skin, and he's giving you hell every day. And you're too dead to see it."[42]

Only someone who shared their lot could have said to the black masses what Malcolm did. They knew he loved them and would die for them. When blacks heard Malcolm, they began to see themselves in a new light, more possessed of an inner freedom than ever before.

Solidarity with the poor is the only genuine way to liberate them and ourselves. We must share their lot, not because we feel sorry for them and want to help them but because they are a part of us and we are a part of them. There can be no "us" and "them." "Them is us," to use the language of the street. We are bound together. When we help another we help ourselves. This is the way the world is made. No lives demonstrate this ethical principle more than those of Martin and Malcolm. And today more than at any other time in history we need this principle of mutuality applied in human relations.

LINK WITH OTHER LIBERATION MOVEMENTS

Martin and Malcolm left us a legacy of linking the African-American freedom struggle in the United States with the liberation movements of the poor in the Third World. Like Du Bois and Garvey before them,

Martin and Malcolm realized that the African-American struggle was not just a domestic affair but was also an international issue. Early in the Montgomery bus boycott, Martin made the connection. Explaining the significance of the boycott at a Chicago press conference, he said: "It's part of something that's happening all over the world. . . . The oppressed peoples of the world are rising up. They are revolting against colonialism, imperialism and other systems of oppression."[43] He referred to the worldwide struggle for freedom as the *Zeitgeist,* the cosmic, divine spirit realizing itself in history.

Martin attended Ghana's independence celebration in 1957 and Nigeria's in 1960. He also made a month-long visit to India in 1959 in order to deepen his understanding of nonviolence as taught by "the little brown saint," as he sometimes called Gandhi. His travels and discussions with many persons in the Third World reinforced his belief that the "Negro revolution," as he called it, in the United States was part of a worldwide revolt of oppressed peoples. The same theme was emphasized in his Nobel Lecture in Oslo, and it occupied a central place in his opposition to the Vietnam War.[44]

Malcolm expressed an even closer connection between blacks in the United States and Third World peoples. As a black nationalist, he emphasized that *all* non-European peoples of the world were a part of one family who together constituted the majority of humankind. Black Muslims defined themselves as people of the East with Asian origins. In 1959 he urged Elijah Muhammad to go to Mecca in order to link the Nation of Islam with worldwide Islam.

Malcolm frequently referred to the 1955 Bandung conference of Third World nations as a model of unity that blacks in the United States should emulate. Although his best-known reference to the conference was made in his "Grass Roots" speech, he called for a "Bandung Conference of Negro Leaders" as early as April 1959 at a Harlem rally. Speaking directly to the Harlem leaders who shared the platform with him at the rally, Malcolm said: "Let us put aside all petty differences of religion and politics and hold a Bandung Conference in Harlem." Like the nations of the Third World, "We must come together and . . . unite before we can effectively face our enemy, and the enemy must be recognized by all of us as a common enemy to all of us before we can put forth a united effort against him for the welfare of all our downtrodden people."[45]

As the number two man in the Nation of Islam and the head of Temple Number Seven in New York, Malcolm frequently invited African and Asian representatives of the United Nations to attend Muslim activities. During Fidel Castro's visit to the United Nations, Malcolm met with him, on 20 September 1960, for approximately thirty minutes at the Hotel Theresa in Harlem, the place Castro chose to stay while in New York.[46]

Perhaps the most important indication of the significance of the Third World for Malcolm was his travel to the Middle East and Africa following his break with the Black Muslim movement. He believed that "the same rebellion, the same impatience, the same anger that exists in the hearts of the dark people in Africa and Asia is existing in the hearts and minds of 20 million black people in this country who have been just as thoroughly colonized as the people in Africa and Asia."[47]

During his first trip abroad (13 April to 21 May 1964), Malcolm visited Arabia, Lebanon, Egypt, and countries in Africa. In Nigeria he spoke to an assembly of students at Ibadan University where they gave him a new name, Omowale, "the son who has come home." He also went to Ghana and met with Prime Minister Kwame Nkrumah and addressed the members of the Ghanaian Parliament and university students. When Malcolm returned to the United States, every speech and interview he gave emphasized the linkage between the African-American freedom struggle and Third World liberation movements. "The only way we'll get freedom for ourselves is to identify ourselves with every oppressed people in the world," he told blacks. "We are blood brothers to the people of Brazil, Venezuela, Haiti, . . . Cuba—yes Cuba too."[48]

During his second trip abroad (9 July to 24 November 1964), Malcolm visited no less than eighteen countries. They were Egypt, Arabia, Kuwait, Lebanon, Khartoum, Ethiopia, Kenya, Zanzibar and Tanganyika (now Tanzania), Nigeria, Ghana, Liberia, Guinea, Senegal, Algeria, Switzerland, France, and Britain. He attended the second Organization of African Unity meeting in Cairo, gave many talks and lectures, and held private conferences with African heads of state and leaders of liberation movements in many lands. He also visited the embassies of Third World nations, including China and Cuba. "My main theme, while traveling with our brothers abroad, on the African continent," he said at an OAAU homecoming rally, "was to try and impress upon them that 22 million of our people here in America consider ourselves inseparably linked with them, that our origin is the same and our destiny is the same, and that we have been kept apart for too long." To African-American leaders, he said: "There is no kind of action in this country ever going to bear fruit unless that action is tied in with the overall international struggle."[49]

By linking the black struggle in the United States with a worldwide revolution among Third World nations, Malcolm was able to challenge the typical assumption of the civil rights movement: Since blacks were a minority, they had no other option than to negotiate their freedom through nonviolence. "I don't believe in this outnumbered business,"

Malcolm said during the question and answer period following a lecture entitled "The African Revolution and Its Effect on the Afro-American." "You're only outnumbered when you think you're in Mississippi and New York and that's it." But "when . . . black Americans see that our problem is the same as the problem of the people who are being oppressed in South Vietnam and the Congo and Latin America," he said in a radio interview, "then—the oppressed people of this earth make up a majority, not a minority—then we approach our problem as a majority that can *demand,* not as a minority that has to beg."[50]

No theme defined Malcolm's activities and speeches, during the last year of his life, more than the link between the African revolution and the "Afro-American revolution," as he called it, in the United States, Latin America, and the Caribbean. He frequently concretized this point in a manner that everyone could understand: "You can't understand what is going on in Mississippi, if you don't know what is going on in the Congo. . . . They're both the same. The same interests are at stake. The same sides are drawn up, the same schemes are at work in the Congo that are at work in Mississippi."[51]

Besides Malcolm's and Martin's accent on politics and culture, their *internationalism* was their most important contribution to the African-American struggle for freedom in the United States. Martin's greatest hour in this regard was his uncompromising stand against the war in Vietnam. He saw more clearly than anyone in the civil rights movement the link between the freedom of blacks in America and the self-determination of people in Vietnam. Martin really believed that the people of the world are one. It is appropriate, therefore, for his name to serve as a symbol of the oneness of humanity not only in the United States but around the world.

Malcolm's influence outside the United States has been less than Martin's. But his international perspective is just as important. As powerfully as W. E. B. Du Bois's Pan-Africanism and Marcus Garvey's back to Africa movement, Malcolm's work influenced the political consciousness of both Africans and African-Americans in regard to their link to each other. Malcolm helped "so-called Negroes" in the United States to realize that they are an *African* people, and he helped Africans on the continent to realize that they have brothers and sisters in the United States and around the world. Malcolm, however, extended his idea of unity beyond race. "Humanity" became the key word that described his vision.

Because of both Martin and Malcolm, African-Americans have become much more internationally minded, supporting the antiapartheid struggle in South Africa and the struggles of the poor against the rich around the world. Freedom fighters everywhere should join hands as one people and declare war on injustice. Martin was right: "Injustice anywhere is a threat to justice everywhere."

12

CONCLUSION

If physical death is the price I must pay to free my white brothers and sisters from the permanent death of the spirit, then nothing could be more redemptive.

Martin Luther King, Jr.
St. Augustine, Florida
5 June 1964

It is a time for martyrs now, and if I am to be one, it will be for the cause of brotherhood. That's the only thing that can save this country.

Malcolm X
New York City
19 February 1965

People frequently ask: "Who are the Martin King and Malcolm X of our time? The Reverend Jesse Jackson and Minister Louis Farrakhan?" In desperate situations, people look for messiahs to deliver them out of their misery. Because the socioeconomic condition of poor African-Americans is worse today than during Martin's and Malcolm's time, many hope for charismatic leaders with spiritual power and intellectual insights which transcend capabilities of ordinary human beings.

Charismatic leaders, however, cannot liberate black people from their misery. They may even hinder the process. Thus, it is important to emphasize that Martin and Malcolm, despite the excessive adoration their followers often bestow upon them, were not messiahs. Both were *ordinary* human beings who gave their lives for the freedom of their people. They show us what ordinary people can accomplish through intelligence and sincere commitment to the cause of justice and freedom. There is no need to look for messiahs to save the poor. Human beings can and must do it themselves.

Martin and Malcolm are important because they symbolize two necessary ingredients in the African-American struggle for justice in the United States. We should never pit them against each other. Anyone, therefore, who claims to be for one and not the other does not understand their significance for the black community, for America, or for the world. We need both of them and we need them *together*. Malcolm keeps Martin from being turned into a harmless American hero. Martin keeps Malcolm from being an ostracized black hero. Both leaders make important contributions to the identity of African-Americans and also, and just as importantly, to white America and Americans in general.

Racial justice was the area in which Martin and Malcolm made their mark. They gave their lives for America's salvation; but America is not redeemed. Racism is still alive and well, operating in every segment of American society. The main difference between racism in their time and today is its refinement and more subtle manifestation. America, North and South, advocates a liberal approach to the race issue. It speaks the language of equality, justice, and integration, but the black masses remain trapped in a world of poverty and death. Only a small number of middle-class blacks are experiencing the American dream. These include some students and teachers at the nation's privileged educational institutions, mayors of several major cities, administrators for city, state, and federal agencies, and legal counselors, especially those of multinational corporations. A few African-American pastors are living well, as are most of the more than seven thousand blacks who hold elective office. In Virginia, one is serving as the nation's first African-American governor. Another made a good bid for the highest office in the land. Several astute observers of American politics say that the election of an African-American as president is not too far in the future. Often willing to place black identity in the background in order to placate white fears, America's black middle class is highly visible in most segments of the society. This group has come a long way since the days of Jim Crow. But despite all the window dressing, very little has changed to uplift the quality of life for the black underclass, the people Malcolm described as living "at the bottom of the social heap" in an "extremely wretched condition." They are the nation's "truly disadvantaged." Unemployed and underemployed, their children are having babies who will be locked in the same cycle of poverty as their parents. Fifty percent of black babies are born in poverty! Where is the American dream for them?

America is a nightmare for the poor of every race. In this land of plenty, there are nearly 40 million poor people who are trying to survive with little or no resources for their emotional and physical well-being. The Washington-based Community for Creative Nonviolence has estimated that as many as 19 million Americans might be homeless in less than fifteen years. One does not need a graduate degree in religion, ethics, or philosophy to know that America's national and international policies are morally bankrupt. Its priorities are screwed up. This nation can find the scientific, technological, and financial resources to build spaceships to explore other planets, but it cannot provide food and shelter for its poor citizens.

Eight years of Ronald Reagan struck a devastating blow to the cause of justice, especially in the area of civil rights. African-Americans, Indians, and Latinos are getting two to three times their share of the ugly side of America. The women of these groups have to deal with the added burden of sexism in the society at large and in their own communities. To be a poor woman of color means being regarded as unimportant by makers of public policy in America. It means going without basic health care for yourself and your family. Most of the time, day-to-day survival, finding bread to eat and a place to lay one's head, is the sole preoccupation.

It is not easy to survive in a society that says you do not count. Many do not survive. With the absence of black pride, that "I am somebody" feeling, many young African-Americans have no respect for themselves or for anybody else. They are dropping out of secondary schools at an alarming rate. They are joining gangs, selling and using drugs, and going to prisons. Black teenagers have begun to kill each other with a frequency that boggles the human imagination. More than 480 persons were killed in the nation's capital in 1989, and the number is steadily climbing each year. If something radical is not done soon to put an end to this madness, the African-American community will soon commit genocide against itself.

Malcolm X is the best medicine against genocide. He showed us by example and prophetic preaching that one does not have to stay in the mud. We can wake up; we can stand up; and we can take that long walk toward freedom. Freedom is first and foremost an inner recognition of self-respect, a knowledge that one was not put on this earth to be a nobody. Using drugs and killing each other are the worst forms of nobodyness. Our foreparents fought against great odds (slavery, lynchings, and segregation), but they did not self-destruct. Some died fighting, and others, inspired by their example, kept moving toward the promised land of freedom, singing "we ain't gonna let nobody turn us around." African-Americans can do the same today. We can fight for our dignity and self-respect. To be proud to be black does not mean being against white people, unless whites are against respecting the humanity of blacks. Malcolm was not against whites; he was for blacks and against their exploitation.

As Americans we (blacks, whites, Latinos, Asians, and Indians) should create a society which contributes to the well-being of all citizens, not just to the well-being of some. Black teenagers are not responsible for being born in the violence-prone conditions of the urban ghetto. Unless we give them hope in themselves and in this nation, they will be lost. The same is true for all races of people.

Martin King was right: "The hour is late" and "the clock of destiny is ticking out." We must declare where we stand on the great issues of our time. Racism is one of them. Poverty is another. Sexism another. Class exploitation another. Imperialism another. We must break the cycle of violence in America and around the world. Human beings are meant for life and not death. They are meant for freedom and not slavery. They were created for each other and not against each other. We must, therefore, break down the barriers that separate people from one another. For Malcolm and Martin, for America and the world, and for all who have given their lives in the struggle for justice, let us direct our fight toward one goal—the beloved community of humankind.

ABBREVIATIONS

AA	*Afro-American* (Baltimore)
AC	*Atlanta Constitution*
AME	African Methodist Episcopal (Church)
AMEZ	African Methodist Episcopal Zion (Church)
BG	*Boston Globe*
BN	*Birmingham News*
BU	Boston University
CD	*Chicago Defender*
CDS	*Columbia Daily Spectator*
CEP	Citizenship Education Program
CM	*Chicago Maroon*
CORE	Congress of Racial Equality
CP	*Courier-Post* (Camden, New Jersey)
CSM	*Christian Science Monitor*
DC	*Democrat & Chronicle* (Rochester, New York)
DG	*Daily Graphic* (Accra, Ghana)
DN	*Detroit News*
DP	*Denver Post*
EG	*Egyptian Gazette* (Cairo, Egypt)
ES	*Evening Star* (Washington, D.C.)
GOAL	Group On Advanced Leadership
GPR	*Grand Rapids Press*
GT	*Ghanian Times* (Accra, Ghana)
IR	*Indianapolis Recorder*
JA	*Journal American* (New York)
J&G	*Journal and Guide* (Norfolk, Virginia)
KCA	Martin Luther King, Jr., Papers, Martin Luther King, Jr., Center for Nonviolent Social Change, Atlanta, Georgia
LAHD	*Los Angeles Herald Dispatch*
LAHE	*Los Angeles Herald Examiner*
LAT	*Los Angeles Times*
LT	*London Times*
MA	*Montgomery Advertiser*
MC	*Michigan Chronicle*
MH	*Miami Herald*
MLK/BU	Martin Luther King, Jr., Collection, Mugar Memorial Library, Boston University

MMI	Muslim Mosque, Inc.
MS	*Mohammad Speaks*
NAACP	National Association for the Advancement of Colored People
NC	*New Crusader* (Chicago)
NCC	National Council of Churches
ND	*Newsday* (New York)
NG	*National Guardian*
NJHN	*New Jersey Herald News*
NOI	Nation of Islam
NYAN	*Amsterdam News* (New York)
NYDN	*Daily News* (New York)
NYHT	*New York Herald Tribune*
NYM	*NewYork Mirror*
NYP	*New York Post*
NYT	*New York Times*
OAAU	Organization of Afro-American Unity
OW	*Omaha World*
PC	*Pittsburgh Courier*
PT	*Philadelphia Tribune*
SCLC	Southern Christian Leadership Conference
SJ	*State Journal* (Lansing, Mich.)
SLA	*St. Louis Argus*
SNCC	Student Nonviolent Coordinating Committee
UNIA	Universal Negro Improvement Association
WAA	*Washington Afro-American* (Washington, D.C.)
WO	*Westchester Observer*
WP	*Washington Post*
WS	*Washington Star*
YDN	*Yale Daily News*

NOTES

INTRODUCTION. AMERICA: A DREAM OR A NIGHTMARE?

1. NYAN, 28 March 1964, p. 50; WP, 27 March 1964, pp. 4, 6; NYT, 27 March 1964, p. 10; "Integration: Long Day," *Newsweek,* 6 April 1964, p. 22; Peter Goldman, *The Death and Life of Malcolm X,* 2d ed. (Urbana: University of Illinois Press, 1979), p. 95; "The Time Has Come, 1964–66," pt. 2 of *Eyes on the Prize,* Channel 13, New York, 15 January 1990.

2. WP, 27 March 1964, p. 6; NYT, 27 March 1964, p. 10.

3. W. E. B. Du Bois, *The Souls of Black Folk* (1903; reprint, New York: Fawcett Premier Book, 1968), pp. 16, 17; idem, "The Conservation of Races" (1897), in Julius Lester, ed., *The Seventh Son: The Thought and Writings of W. E. B. Du Bois* (New York: Vintage Book, 1971), vol. 1, p. 182.

4. Philip S. Foner, ed., *Frederick Douglass: Selections from His Writings* (New York: International Publishers, 1964), p. 57.

5. Ibid., pp. 52–53.

6. Cited in Lerone Bennett, Jr., *Pioneers in Protest* (Chicago: Johnson Publishing Co., 1968), pp. 208–9.

7. Foner, ed., *Frederick Douglass,* p. 44.

8. Cited in Peter J. Paris, *The Social Teaching of the Black Churches* (Philadelphia: Fortress Press, 1985), p. 25, n. 26.

9. Henry Highland Garnet, *An Address to the Slaves of the United States of America* (1843), reprinted with David Walker's *Appeal* (1829), in *Walker's Appeal & Garnet's Address to the Slaves of the United States of America* (New York: Arno Press/New York Times, 1969), p. 93.

10. Adam Clayton Powell, Jr., *Marching Blacks,* rev. ed. (New York: Dial Press, 1973), p. 194.

11. Kenneth B. Clark, "The Civil Rights Movement: Momentum and Organization," *Daedalus,* 95 (Winter 1966), p. 245.

12. Cited in Theodore Draper, *The Rediscovery of Black Nationalism* (New York: Viking Press, 1970), p. 22; for an interpretation of the origin of black nationalism, see August Meier, "The Emergence of Negro Nationalism," Parts I and II, *Midwest Journal,* vol. 45, Winter 1951 and Summer 1953, pp. 96–104 and 95–111.

13. *Walker's Appeal and Garnet's Address,* pp. 71, 73, 27–28; see also Sterling Stuckey, *The Ideological Origins of Black Nationalism* (Boston: Beacon Press, 1972), pp. 97, 99, 55–56.

14. Carter G. Woodson, ed., *The Mind of the Negro as Reflected in Letters*

Written during the Crisis, 1800–1860 (1926; reprint, New York: Russell & Russell, 1969), p. 293.

15. Martin Robison Delany, *The Condition, Elevation, Emigration, and Destiny of the Colored People of the United States* (1855; reprint, New York: Arno Press/New York Times, 1969), p. 209; see also John H. Bracey, Jr., August Meier, and Elliott Rudwick, eds., *Black Nationalism in America* (Indianapolis: Bobbs-Merrill Co., 1970), p. 89.

16. Henry McNeal Turner, "The Barbarous Decision of the Supreme Court" (1883), in Edwin S. Redkey, ed., *Respect Black: The Writings and Speeches of Henry McNeal Turner* (New York: Arno Press/New York Times, 1971), p. 63.

17. Ibid., p. 165; Edwin S. Redkey, *Black Exodus: Black Nationalist and Back-to-Africa Movements, 1890–1910* (New Haven: Yale University Press, 1969), p. 29.

18. Henry McNeal Turner, "God Is a Negro" (1898), in Redkey, ed., *Respect Black,* pp. 176–77.

19. Amy Jacques Garvey, ed., *Philosophy and Opinions of Marcus Garvey* (New York: Arno Press/New York Times, 1969), vol. 2, p. 126.

20. Ibid., pp. 325–26.

21. Ibid., vol. 1, pp. 5, 2.

22. Cited in E. David Cronon, *Black Moses: The Story of Marcus Garvey and the Negro Improvement Association* (Madison: University of Wisconsin Press, 1955), p. 173.

23. Garvey, ed., *Philosophy and Opinions,* vol. 2, p. 326.

24. Cited in Louis E. Lomax, *When the Word Is Given . . .* (New York: Signet Book, 1964), p. 56. The classic study on the Nation of Islam is C. Eric Lincoln, *The Black Muslims in America* (Boston: Beacon Press, 1961, Rev. ed., 1973). See also E. U. Essien-Udom, *Black Nationalism: The Search for an Identity in America* (Chicago: University of Chicago Press, 1962); James Baldwin, *The Fire Next Time* (New York: Dell, 1962). An early significant study is Erdmann Doane Beynon, "The Voodoo Cult Among Negro Migrants in Detroit," *American Journal of Sociology,* May 1938, pp. 894–907. See also Monroe Berger, "The Black Muslims," *Horizon,* Winter, 1964, pp. 48–65. The best source for the teaching of Elijah Muhammad is his *The Supreme Wisdom: The Solution to the So-Called Negroes' Problem* (Chicago: University of Islam, 1957); also his *Message to the Blackman* (Chicago: Muhammad's Temple No. 2).

25. Vincent Harding, *There Is a River: The Black Struggle for Freedom in America* (New York: Harcourt Brace Jovanovich, 1981), p. 83.

1. THE MAKING OF A DREAMER (1929–55)

1. Martin Luther King, Sr., *Daddy King: An Autobiography,* with Clayton Riley (New York: William Morrow, 1980), pp. 109–10; Coretta Scott King, *My Life with Martin Luther King, Jr.* (New York: Holt, Rinehart and Winston, 1969), p. 77.

2. King, Sr., *Daddy King,* p. 131; Lerone Bennett, Jr., *What Manner of Man: A Biography of Martin Luther King, Jr.* (Chicago: Johnson Publishing Co., 1964), p. 18.

3. Martin Luther King, Jr., "Autobiography of Religious Development," a fifteen-page, handwritten essay for a course at Crozer Theological Seminary, taught by George Davis, in MLK/BU (also in Mervyn A. Warren, "A Rhetorical Study of the Preaching of Doctor Martin Luther King, Jr., Pastor and Pulpit Orator" [Ph.D. diss., Michigan State University, 1966], pp. 269–84); Martin Luther King, Jr., *Stride toward Freedom* (New York: Harper & Row, 1958), pp. 18–19; Ted Poston, "Fighting Pastor: Martin Luther King," NYP, 8 April 1957, p. 42, article 1 of a series of 6; Bennett, *What Manner of Man,* p. 19; Hugh Burnett, *Face to Face* (New York: Stein & Day, 1965), p. 78.

4. King, "Autobiography."

5. King, *Stride toward Freedom,* pp. 19, 20; L. D. Reddick, *Crusader without Violence: A Biography of Martin Luther King, Jr.* (New York: Harper, 1959), p. 57; C. King, *My Life,* pp. 82, 83; Jerry Tallmer, "Martin Luther King, Jr.: His Life and Times," *Post Daily Magazine* of the NYP, 9 April 1968, p. 1, article 2 of a series of 6.

6. King, *Stride toward Freedom,* p. 19; C. King, *My Life,* p. 83; Poston, NYP, 8 April 1957, article 1 of series; Reddick, *Crusader without Violence,* p. 57; King, Sr., *Daddy King,* pp. 107–9.

7. Burnett, *Face to Face,* p. 78; King, *Stride toward Freedom,* p. 37.

8. Reddick, *Crusader without Violence,* pp. 59–60; Burnett, *Face to Face,* p. 78; "The South: Attack on the Conscience," *Time,* 18 February 1957, p. 17.

9. "Man of the Year: Never Again Where He Was," *Time,* 3 January 1964, p. 14; Tallmer, *Post Daily Magazine* of the NYP, 9 April 1968, p. 1, article 2 of series.

10. King, "Autobiography."

11. Cited in Tallmer, *Post Daily Magazine* of the NYP, 8 April 1968, p. 1, article 1 of series.

12. Poston, NYP, 8 April 1957, p. 1, article 1 of series; C. King, *My Life,* p. 80.

13. King, "Autobiography"; Poston, NYP, 10 April 1957, p. 65, article 3 of series; "The South: Attack on the Conscience," *Time,* 18 February 1957, p. 18; Stephen B. Oates, *Let the Trumpet Sound: The Life of Martin Luther King, Jr.* (New York: Mentor Books, 1985 [reprint]), pp. 17–20.

14. Cited in Poston, NYP, 10 April 1957, p. 65, article 3 of series; C. King, *My Life,* p. 85.

15. "The South: Attack on the Conscience," p. 18; "Man of the Year: Never Again Where He Was," p. 14; William Peters, "The Man Who Fights Hate with Love," *Redbook* (September 1961), p. 94; Poston, NYP, 10 April 1957, p. 1, article 3 of series.

16. King, "Autobiography"; see his 7 August 1957 statement for the American Baptist Convention, in MLK/BU.

17. Bennett, *What Manner of Man,* p. 34.

18. Cited in Peters, "The Man Who Fights Hate with Love," p. 94.

19. King, *Stride toward Freedom,* p. 91.

20. See King's letter to George Davis, 1 December 1953, in MLK/BU.

21. King, *Stride toward Freedom,* p. 100.

22. Ibid., p. 99; see his graduate essays, "Reinhold Niebuhr's Ethical Dualism" and "Reinhold Niebuhr," in MLK/BU; see also especially David Garrow, "The Intellectual Development of Martin Luther King, Jr.: Influences and Commentaries," *Union Seminary Quarterly Review* 40, no. 4 (1986), pp. 5–20.

23. King, "Pilgrimage to Nonviolence," *The Christian Century,* 13 April 1960, p. 439. King wrote three versions of this essay — see *Stride toward Freedom,* chap. 6; *Strength To Love* (1963; reprint, Philadelphia: Fortress, 1981), chap. 15.

24. See James H. Cone, "The Theology of Martin Luther King, Jr.," *Union Seminary Quarterly Review* 40, no. 4 (1986), pp. 21–39; idem, "Martin Luther King, Jr., Black Theology — Black Church," *Theology Today* 40, no. 4 (January 1984), pp. 409–20.

25. King, "What a Mother Should Tell Her Child," a sermon preached 12 May 1963 at Ebenezer Baptist Church, in KCA.

26. King, *Stride toward Freedom,* p. 21; C. King, *My Life,* pp. 94–95.

27. Oates, *Let the Trumpet Sound,* pp. 45–46.

28. King, *Stride toward Freedom,* p. 25.

29. Ibid., p. 15.

30. See Ralph D. Abernathy, *And the Walls Came Tumbling Down* (New York: Harper & Row, 1989), pp. 122ff.; Taylor Branch, *Parting the Waters: America in the King Years, 1954–63* (New York: Simon and Schuster, 1988), chap. 4.

31. King, "Recommendations to the Dexter Avenue Baptist Church for the Fiscal Year 1954–1955," in KCA.

32. Ibid.

33. Cited in Oates, *Let the Trumpet Sound,* p. 53.

34. Cited in ibid., p. 57.

35. King, *Stride toward Freedom,* pp. 28, 40.

36. Ibid., p. 41.

37. Ibid., p. 33.

2. THE MAKING OF A "BAD NIGGER" (1925–52)

1. Cited in Peter Goldman, *The Death and Life of Malcolm X,* 2d ed. (Urbana: University of Illinois Press, 1979), p. 6.

2. NYAN, 7 September 1963, p. 6.

3. YDN, 17 October 1960, p. 1; see Eliot Freemont-Smith's review of *The Autobiography of Malcolm X,* in NYT, 5 November 1965, p. 35.

4. WP, 23 February 1965, p. 16.

5. "Death of a Desperado," *Newsweek,* 8 March 1965, p. 24.

6. "Death and Transfiguration," *Time,* 5 March 1965, p. 23.

7. NYT, 14 March 1964, p. 22; NYT, 22 February 1965, p. 20.

8. NYHT, 23 February 1965, p. 26.

9. Walter Winchell, JA, 28 February 1965, p. 29–I.

10. "Malcolm X," *Nation,* 8 March 1965, p. 239.

11. "The Lessons of Malcolm X," *Saturday Evening Post,* 12 September 1964, p. 84.

12. Pierre Berton, ed., *Voices from the Sixties* (Garden City, N.Y.: Doubleday, 1967), p. 31.

13. Videotape and transcript of "Oxford Debate," on Gil Noble, "Like It Is," aired 20 February 1977, author's library.

14. LT, 23 February 1965, p. 13; NYT, 28 February 1965, p. 74.

15. WAA, 3 May 1963, p. 3; MS, 3 July 1964, p. 9.

16. MS, 4 December 1964, p. 11. We should note that Minister Louis Farrakhan has radically changed his views about Malcolm X and now regards him as a leader worthy of respect and admiration for his contributions to the African-American struggle for justice. However, he does not place him on the par with Elijah Muhammad. See especially his interview in *Emerge*, August 1990, pp. 28–37, "The Remaking of Louis Farrakhan" by George E. Curry.

17. *Call,* 26 February 1965, p. 17.

18. MC, 6 March 1965, p. 6.

19. NYT, 26 February 1965, p. 15; Walter Seraile, "The Assassination of Malcolm X: The View from Home and Abroad," *The Afro-American in New York Life and History* (January 1981), p. 45. For examples of the African media on Malcolm X, see especially the editorial, "Malcolm Will Live On" in GT, 23 February 1965, p. 6; Julian Mayfield, "Malcolm X: A Tragic Loss" in GT, 24 February 1965, p. 6; "Malcolm X Stood for Racial Equality Says—KWAME" (Nkrumah), GT, 25 February 1965, p. 1; see also DG, 23 February 1965, p. 5; DG, 25 February, p. 1, 2.

20. IR, 27 February 1965, p. 10.

21. BG, 25 March 1961; BH, 25 March 1961, p. 5; NJHN, 1 April 1961, FBI files 105-8999-2242 (Nation of Islam); PC, 14 July 1962, p. 7; CD, 14–20 July 1962, p. 5; *Playboy* interview (May 1963), p. 56; Goldman, *Death and Life of Malcolm X,* p. 142; Tom Kahn and Bayard Rustin, "The Ambiguous Legacy of Malcolm X," *Dissent* (Spring 1965), p. 190.

22. "Rediscovering Malcolm X," *Newsweek,* 26 February 1990, p. 69.

23. Malcolm X, *The Autobiography of Malcolm X,* with Alex Haley (reprint, New York: Ballantine Books, 1973), pp. 1, 6; Ted Vincent, "The Garveyite Parents of Malcolm X," *Black Scholar* (March/April 1989), pp. 10–13; Yael Lotan, " 'No Peaceful Solution to Racism': An Exclusive Interview With Malcolm X," *Sunday Gleaner Magazine,* 12 July 1964, pp. 5–6; Kenneth B. Clark, *King, Malcolm, Baldwin: Three Interviews,* rev. ed. (Middletown, Conn.: Wesleyan University Press, 1985), pp. 33–48.

24. Malcolm X, *Autobiography,* p. 282.

25. Ibid., p. 3.

26. Ibid., pp. 4, 7.

27. Ibid., pp. 7, 8.

28. Ibid., pp. 9–10; SJ, 24 January 1963, pp. 3–6; *Playboy* interview, p. 60; Clark, *King, Malcolm, Baldwin,* p. 36; *Sunday Gleaner Magazine,* 12 July 1964, p. 5; OW, 1 July 1964, p. 1.

29. Malcolm X, *Autobiography,* pp. 16, 13.

30. Ibid., p. 21.

31. King, "Autobiography of Religious Development," a fifteen-page, hand-

written essay for a course at Crozer Theological Seminary, taught by George Davis, in MLK/BU (also in Mervyn A. Warren, "A Rhetorical Study of the Preaching of Doctor Martin Luther King, Jr., Pastor and Pulpit Orator" [Ph.D. diss., Michigan State University, 1966], pp. 269–84).

32. Clark, *King, Malcolm, Baldwin,* p. 36.
33. Malcolm X, *Autobiography,* pp. 34, 35.
34. Ibid., pp. 36, 37.
35. Ibid., pp. 36, 37, 38.
36. Ibid., pp. 40, 41, 42, 43.
37. Ibid., pp. 47, 54.
38. Ibid., pp. 72, 76, 77, 78.
39. Ibid., pp. 75, 83, 108.
40. Ibid., chap. 9.
41. Ibid., pp. 153, 154.
42. Ibid., pp. 155, 156.
43. Ibid., p. 154.
44. King, "Autobiography."
45. Malcolm X, *Autobiography,* pp. 161, 163, 164.
46. Ibid., p. 161.
47. Ibid., pp. 170, 171, 178, 179, 173, 174.
48. Ibid., p. 22.
49. Ibid., p. 159.
50. Ibid., pp. 201, 202.
51. Ibid., pp. 87, 389.

3. "I HAVE A DREAM" (1955–64)

1. Martin Luther King, Jr., "Address to the Initial Mass Meeting of the Montgomery Improvement Association," delivered 5 December 1955 at the Holt Street Baptist Church, in KCA. Compare the tape and printed copy of this address with King's later account in *Stride toward Freedom* (New York: Harper & Row, 1958), p. 62. King reported in the latter: "I urged the people not to force anybody to refrain from riding the buses. 'Our method will be that of persuasion, not coercion. . . .' Emphasizing the Christian doctrine of love, 'our actions must be guided by the deepest principles of our Christian faith. Love must be our regulating ideal. Once again we must hear the words of Jesus echoing across the centuries: "Love your enemies, bless them that curse you, and pray for them that despitefully use you." . . . In spite of the mistreatment that we have confronted we must not become bitter, and end up by hating our white brothers. As Booker T. Washington said, "Let no man pull you so low as to make you hate him." ' " There is nothing like this in the original address. There is no reference to Booker T. Washington.

2. Cited in David J. Garrow, *Bearing the Cross: Martin Luther King, Jr., and the Southern Christian Leadership Conference* (New York: William Morrow, 1986), p. 24. For an eyewitness account of the origins of the boycott, see especially Jo Ann Gibson Robinson, *The Montgomery Bus Boycott and the Women*

Who Started It, ed. David J. Garrow (Knoxville: University of Tennessee Press, 1987); also an important essay by Mary Fair Burks, "Trailblazers: Women in the Montgomery Bus Boycott," in Vicki Crawford et al., eds., *Women in the Civil Rights Movement: Trailblazers and Torchbearers, 1941–1965* (Brooklyn: Carlson Publishing, 1990), pp. 71–83.

3. MA, 19 January 1956, p. 4–A; NYT, 21 March 1956, p. 28.

4. MA, 19 January 1956, p. 4–A.

5. NYT, 24 February 1956, p. 8; "The South: City on Trial," *Time,* 5 March 1956, p. 21.

6. NYT, 27 February 1956, p. 17.

7. See essays by Martin King and Grover C. Hall, Jr. (of the *Montgomery Advertiser*), "Pro and Con, Alabama's Bus Boycott: What's It All About?" *U.S. News & World Report,* 3 August 1956, pp. 82–87.

8. *Nation,* 3 March 1956, p. 169.

9. Malcolm X, *The Autobiography of Malcolm X,* with Alex Haley (reprint, New York: Ballantine Books, 1973), p. 269.

10. These "American Dream" addresses were given several times on different occasions: Charlotte, N.C. (25 September 1960); Savannah, Ga. (1 January 1961); Lynchburg, Va. (12 March 1961); Lincoln University (6 June 1961); Brooklyn, N.Y. (10 February 1963), in KCA.

11. King, "The American Dream" (6 June 1961) (also in *Negro History Bulletin* [May 1968], p. 10).

12. King, "Message Delivered at the Prayer Pilgrimage" (hereafter "Prayer Pilgrimage"), given on 17 May 1957 at the Lincoln Memorial, Washington, D.C., in KCA.

13. See the "Prepared Statement for Conference with President Eisenhower," 23 June 1958, and "A Statement to the South and Nation Issued by the Southern Leaders Conference on Transportation and Nonviolent Integration," in KCA.

14. See King's essays in *Nation,* 4 February 1961, pp. 91–95; and 3 March 1962, pp. 190–93.

15. "Boycotts Will Be Used," interview in *U.S. News & World Report,* 24 February 1964, p. 61.

16. King, "The American Dream" (12 March 1961) (also in author's library).

17. Quoted in Loudon Wainwright, "Martyr of the Sit-ins," *Life,* 7 November 1960, pp. 123–24.

18. See King, "The American Dream" (25 September 1960 and 1 January 1961).

19. See King's address "Some Things We Must Do," given 5 December 1957 on the second anniversary of the Montgomery bus boycott; see also his address given on 23 September 1959 at the Southern Christian Ministers Conference of Mississippi (hereafter "Southern Ministers"), in KCA.

20. King, "Southern Ministers."

21. King, "Some Things," and "Southern Ministers."

22. Malcolm X, *By Any Means Necessary,* ed. George Breitman (New York: Pathfinder Press, 1970), p. 124.

23. See King, "The American Dream" (6 June 1961); idem, "Some Things"; idem, "Demonstrating Our Unity," speech given 15 December 1963 at a civil rights rally, Hurt Park, Atlanta, in KCA.

24. King, "Prayer Pilgrimage."

25. King, "Letter from Birmingham City Jail," *New Leader,* 24 June 1963, p. 8; idem, "Some Things."

26. King, "Answer to a Perplexing Question," sermon given 3 March 1963 at Ebenezer Baptist Church, in KCA.

27. King, "Address at March in Detroit," given 23 June 1963 at Cobo Hall, in KCA; PC, 29 August 1959, p. 6; PC, 2 May 1959, p. 2.

28. Transcript of "For Freedom Now," a National Educational TV Presentation that included Martin Luther King, Jr., James Farmer, Roy Wilkins, Kenneth Clark, Whitney Young, and James Forman, in KCA.

29. King, *Stride toward Freedom,* p. 85. For George Kelsey's influence, see his letter to King, 4 April 1958, and his suggestion of the statement in the margin of King's typewritten manuscript, in MLK/BU.

30. King, "The American Dream" (12 March 1961).

31. A tape of King's talk given 3 May 1963 in Birmingham, author's library (printed copy in Charles V. Hamilton, *The Black Experience in American Politics* [New York: G. P. Putnam's Sons, 1973], pp. 160–64).

32. King, "Nonviolence and Racial Justice," *Christian Century,* 6 February 1957, p. 166.

33. King, "Desegregation and the Future," address given 1 December 1956 at the National Committee for Rural Schools, New York, in KCA.

34. King, "The American Dream" (12 March 1961).

35. *Playboy* interview (January 1965), p. 74.

36. King, "The American Dream" (6 June 1961).

37. Ibid.

38. Pat Waters, *Down to Now: Reflections on the Southern Civil Rights Movement* (New York: Pantheon Books, 1971), pp. 11–15; Howard Raines, *My Soul Is Rested: The Story of the Civil Rights Movement in the Deep South* (New York: Penguin Books, 1983), p. 425; Reese Cleghorn, "Martin Luther King, Jr.: Apostle of Crisis," *Saturday Evening Post,* 15 June 1963, p. 18.

39. Raines, *My Soul Is Rested,* pp. 361–62.

40. See Raines, *My Soul Is Rested,* p. 362; Garrow, *Bearing The Cross,* pp. 204, 664, n. 30.

41. Wyatt Tee Walker, "Albany, Failure or First Step?" *New South* (June 1963), pp. 3, 5. For King's reflections on his "mistakes in Albany," see his *Playboy* interview, p. 66.

42. For the transcript of the president's address, see NYT, 12 June 1963, p. 20.

43. Transcript of "American Experience," WNEW-TV, Channel 5, with Richard Heffner, Malcolm X, James Farmer, Wyatt T. Walker, and Alan Morrison, aired Sunday, June 16, 1963, in KCA; King, *Why We Can't Wait* (New York: Harper & Row, 1963), pp. 158–59.

44. NYAN, 29 June 1963, p. 6.

45. *Time,* 30 August 1963, p. 11.

46. King, "I Have A Dream," speech given 28 August 1963 at the March on Washington, in KCA.

47. NYT, 1 September 1963, p. 44.

48. King, "Eulogy for the Martyred Children," in James M. Washington, ed., *The Testament of Hope: The Essential Writings of Martin Luther King, Jr.* (San Francisco: Harper & Row, 1986), pp. 221, 222.

49. Ibid., p. 222.

50. NYT, 25 September 1963, p. 33; Garrow, *Bearing the Cross,* pp. 291f.

51. NYT, 11 December 1964, pp. 1, 32; NYT, 7 December 1964, pp. 1, 6.

52. NYT, 18 December 1964, p. 37; NYT, 29 December 1964, p. 1; NYT, 24 January 1965, p. 39; NYT, 28 January 1965, p. 15; J&G, 6 February 1965, p. 1.

53. NYT, 18 December 1964, p. 37; NYT, 24 December 1964, p. 17.

54. NYT, 11 December 1964, p. 33.

55. Raines, *My Soul Is Rested,* p. 427.

56. NYT, 15 October 1964, p. 14.

4. "I SEE A NIGHTMARE" (1952–63)

1. Louis Lomax, *When the Word Is Given . . .* (New York: Signet Books, 1964), p. 81.

2. Malcolm X, *The Autobiography of Malcolm X,* with Alex Haley (reprint, New York: Ballantine Books, 1973), p. 295.

3. Ibid., pp. 252, 198, 199, 288.

4. See Peter Goldman, *The Death and Life of Malcolm X,* 2d ed. (Urbana: University of Illinois Press, 1979), p. 48; NYAN, 20 April 1957, p. 4; Malcolm X, *Autobiography,* p. 146.

5. Malcolm X: FBI Surveillance File, A Microfilm Project by Scholarly Resources, 1978, Wilmington, Delaware, Reel #1.

6. NYAN, 4 May 1957, p. 1; Alfred Balk and Alex Haley, "Black Merchants of Hate," *Saturday Evening Post,* 26 January 1963, p. 68.

7. Malcolm X, "Unity Rally" speech, given 10 August 1963 in Harlem, New York, audiotape, author's library; *Playboy* interview (May 1963), p. 62; video interview, University of California at Berkeley, October 1963, in author's library; videotape and transcript of "The Early Years of Malcolm X," on Gil Noble, "Like It Is," aired 16 February 1986, author's library; audiotape of Malcolm's lecture at University of California at Berkeley, 11 October 1963, author's library.

8. Malcolm X, "Unity Rally"; FBI files, Reel #1; CP, 1 July 1963, p. 17.

9. Malcolm X, *The End of White World Supremacy,* ed. Benjamin Goodman (New York: Merlin House, 1971), p. 70; Louis Lomax, *To Kill a Black Man* (Los Angeles: Holloway House, 1968), p. 35; Malcolm X, *Autobiography,* pp. 175, 212.

10. Elijah Muhammad's letter to King, 19 March 1958; Malcolm's letter to King, 21 July 1960; letter of King's secretary (Maude L. W. Ballou) to Malcolm, 10 August 1960, all in MLK/BU.

11. Malcolm X, "Unity Rally"; video interview at Berkeley; Malcolm X, *Autobiography,* p. 243.

12. Malcolm X, FBI files, Reel #2.

13. Malcolm X, *Autobiography,* pp. 403, 283; WAA, 3 May 1963, p. 3.

14. Helen Dubar, "The Muslims and Black Nationalism," NYP, 10 April 1964, p. 69, article 5 of a series of 6. Malcolm X, *Autobiography,* p. 403.

15. CSM, 29 August 1959, p. 14; CSM, 16 May 1960, p. 10; DP, 13 August 1959, p. 26; Malcolm X, speech given 24 May 1960 at Boston University, audiotape, author's library; idem, *Autobiography,* p. 366.

16. *Playboy* interview, p. 56.

17. My thanks to Professor Lewis Baldwin of Vanderbilt University for providing me with a copy of Dora McDonald's letter to Frank Clark, 26 November 1962, and of Frank Clark's letter to Martin King, 26 December 1962; transcript of "American Experience: Race Relations in Crisis," WNEW-TV, Channel 5, aired 16 June 1963.

18. NYAN, 6 April 1963, p. 13. For examples of Malcolm's debating skills, see "Malcolm X Debates Four Scholars," "Open Mind," NBC-TV program on "The Black Muslims in America," C. Eric Lincoln, James Baldwin, Eric Goldman, professor of history at Princeton (moderator), and George Schuyler of *Pittsburgh Courier,* 23 April 1961, audiotape in Schomburg Center Oral History Tapes Collection; "Malcolm X Debates Bayard Rustin," 7 November 1960, audiotape, author's library; "Malcolm Debates with James Baldwin and LeVern McCumming," ND, about 1962, audiotape, author's library. "Where is the Negro Headed?" "Open Mind," NBC-TV, Eric Goldman, Malcolm X, Constance Baker Motley of the Legal Defense Fund of the NAACP, Richard Haley of CORE, Monroe Berger, Associate Professor of Sociology at Princeton University, and Kenneth Clark, Professor of Psychology at CCNY, 15 October 1961, transcript printed in John H. Clarke (ed.), *Malcolm X: The Man and His Times* (New York: Collier Books, 1969), pp. 149–67.

19. Malcolm X, *Autobiography,* pp. 282–83; Lomax, *When the Word,* pp. 156, 173; *Playboy* interview, p. 56.

20. Malcolm X, *Autobiography,* p. 266; Alex Haley, "Alex Haley Remembers Malcolm X," *Essence* (November 1983), p. 54; Goldman, *Death and Life,* pp. 67, 69. In a discussion with Bob Hunter, Malcolm elaborated on his claim that "the white race is a race of devils." "What a white person should do if he is not a devil is to prove it. . . . But I have never heard any white man yet come up with a history of angelic deeds towards nonwhite people. This history as we know it has been a history of oppression, exploitation, and colonialization. . . . If the white race doesn't want to be classified as devils, all I say, sir, is that they change their attitude towards the black people in this country." Malcolm X, FBI Files, Reel #1, transcript of the Bob Hunter Show, Los Angeles, 29, 30 March 1963.

21. Malcolm X, "Unity Rally"; FBI files, Reel #1; Kenneth B. Clark, *King, Malcolm, Baldwin: Three Interviews,* rev. ed. (Middletown, Conn.: Wesleyan University Press, 1985), pp. 29, 28.

22. Malcolm X, FBI files, Reel #1; Malcolm X, "We Arose from the Dead," *Moslem World and the U.S.A.*, August–September, 1956, p. 25; NYAN, 17 November 1962, pp. 1–2.

23. See " 'Negro an African' Malcolm X Says," LAHD, 10 April 1958, FBI files 25–330971 (Nation of Islam); "The Word Negro Means a Walking Dead Man," LAHD, 24 December 1959, FBI files 25–330971 (Nation of Islam).

24. Malcolm X, FBI files, Reel #1.

25. Malcolm X, "God's Angry Men," LAHD, 18 May 1957; idem, speech given 23 January 1963 at Michigan State University (hereafter "MSU" speech), audiotape, author's library; idem, speech given 24 May 1960 at Boston University, audiotape, author's library.

26. Malcolm X, speech given 15 February 1960 at Boston University, audiotape, author's library.

27. NYHT, 28 August 1961, p. 5; Helen Dubar, "The Muslims and Black Nationalism," NYP, 7 April, 1964, p. 29, article 2 of a series of 6; Clark, *King, Malcolm, Baldwin*, p. 42.

28. Cited by Robert G. Spivack, "Murder of Angry Man," in J&G, 13 March 1965, p. 8.

29. Clark, *King, Malcolm, Baldwin*, pp. 42–43.

30. LAHD, 24 October 1957, FBI files 25–330971 (Nation of Islam); LAHD, 14 November 1957, FBI files 25–330971 (Nation of Islam); Malcolm X, FBI files, Reel #1; "MSU," speech; idem, speech given 12 May 1963 at Boston University, audiotape, author's library.

31. Malcolm X, "Unity Rally."

32. "Malcolm X on 'Unity,' " in Lomax, *When the Word*, p. 135.

33. King, "Desegregation and the Future," address given 1 December 1956 to the National Committee of Rural Schools, New York City, in KCA.

34. Transcript of the TV show, "At Random," Carter Davidson host, 3 March 1963, FBI files 105–8999-3434 (Nation of Islam); Gertrude Samuels, "Two Ways: Black Muslim and N.A.A.C.P.," *New York Times Magazine*, 12 May 1963, pp. 26–27, 86–87. NYAN, 1 July 1961, p. 37.

35. See "Muslim Minister Rips 'Token Integration': Cites Differences between Segregation, Separation," MS, 15 September 1962, p. 14; Malcolm X, "The American Negro: Problems and Solutions" (24 March 1961), the first of three speeches given at Harvard, in Archie Epps, ed., *The Speeches of Malcolm X at Harvard* (New York: Morrow, 1968), p. 127; "James Farmer and Malcolm X: Separation or Integration," a debate at Cornell University on 7 March 1962, in James Golden and Richard Rieke, eds., *The Rhetoric of Black Americans* (Columbus, Ohio: Charles Merrill, 1971), pp. 438–39.

36. MS, 15 September 1962, p. 14; Malcolm X, *Autobiography*, p. 246.

37. WS, 13 May 1963, p. 1–B; NYT, 11 May 1963, p. 9.

38. NYT, 17 May 1963, p. 14; WS, 17 May 1963, p. 1; NYT, 30 June 1963, p. 45.

39. MH, 19 September 1963; NYAN, 7 September 1963, p. 6; NYAN, 19 October 1963, p. 7.

40. "Talk Is of a Revolution—Complete with Mixed Blood," *Jet*, 28 November 1963, p. 14; MC, 16 November 1963, p. 4; PC, 9 November 1963, p. 1.

41. See Goldman, *Death and Life*, pp. 117–18; *NOW!* (March/April 1966), p. 14; "Message to the Grass Roots" is the most widely distributed of all of Mal-

colm X's speeches. A printed version is found in George Breitman, ed., *Malcolm X Speaks* (New York: Grove Press, 1966), pp. 4–17.

42. See "Malcolm X Calls for Bandung Conference of Negro Leaders," LAHD, 23 April 1959, FBI files 25–330971 (Nation of Islam); LAHD, 14 May 1959, FBI files 25–330971 (Nation of Islam); *The Worker*, 31 March 1963, p. 12.

43. See transcript of Gil Noble, "Like It Is," WABC-TV, aired 18 September 1977.

44. PT, 19 November 1963, p. 4.

45. See "God's Judgment of White America," in Malcolm X, *End of White World Supremacy*, p. 146.

46. Malcolm X, *Autobiography*, p. 395; GRP, 18 February 1962, p. 8.

47. See Malcolm X, speech delivered 24 May 1960 at Boston University; idem, *Autobiography*, p. 394.

5. "WE MUST LOVE OUR WHITE BROTHERS"

1. An account of King's kitchen experience is found in PC, 9 February 1957, p. 2; see also King, *Stride toward Freedom* (Harper & Row, 1958), pp. 134f.; idem, *Strength To Love* (reprint, Philadelphia: Fortress, 1981), pp. 113f.; and idem, "Thou Fool," sermon given 27 August 1967 at Mt. Pisgah Baptist Church, Chicago, in KCA. David J. Garrow, in *Bearing the Cross: Martin Luther King, Jr., and the Southern Christian Leadership Conference* (New York: William Morrow, 1986), appropriately uses this experience as the chief principle for interpreting King's life.

2. PC, 9 February 1957, p. 2; Jerry Tallmer, "Martin Luther King, Jr.: His Life and Times," *Post Daily Magazine* of the NYP, 10 April 1968, article 3 of a series of 6; King, *Strength To Love*, p. 114; *Stride toward Freedom*, pp. 135f.

3. See PC, 9 February 1957, p. 2; Tallmer, *Post Daily Magazine* of the NYP, 8 April 1968, p. 1, article 1 of series.

4. King, *Strength To Love*, pp. 65, 114.

5. King, "Discerning the Signs of History," sermon given 15 November 1964 at Ebenezer Baptist Church, in KCA.

6. King, "A Walk through the Holy Land," sermon given 29 March 1959 at Dexter Baptist Church, in KCA.

7. King, "Revolution and Redemption," address given 16 August 1964 to the European Baptist Assembly, Amsterdam, Holland, in KCA.

8. See King's letter of 26 October 1960 to his wife while he was in the state prison in Reidsville, Georgia; King, speech at staff retreat, 29–31 May 1967, Frogmore, South Carolina, in KCA.

9. King, "Revolution and Redemption"; idem, "A Challenge to the Churches and Synagogues," address given 17 January 1963 to the National Conference on Religion and Race, Chicago, in Mathew Ahmann, ed., *Race: Challenge to Religion* (Chicago: Henry Regnery, 1963), pp. 168–69; idem, "The Christian Way in Human Relations," address given 4 December 1957 to the National Council of Churches, in *Presbyterian Life* (8 February 1958).

10. King, "My Trip to the Land of Gandhi," *Ebony* (July 1959), p. 88.

11. See especially, King, "Nonviolence and Racial Justice," *Christian Century*, 6 February 1957, p. 166; Taylor Branch, *Parting the Waters: America in the King Years 1954–63* (New York: Simon & Schuster, 1988), pp. 773–774. Malcolm X, "Unity Rally" speech given 10 August 1963 in Harlem, New York, audiotape, author's library.

12. King, address given 3 December 1956 to the First Annual Institute on Nonviolence and Social Change, at Holt Street Baptist Church, Montgomery, Alabama, in KCA (published in *Phylon* [April 1957], p. 25).

13. Ibid.

14. Ibid.

15. King, "Letter from Birmingham City Jail," *New Leader,* 24 June 1963, p. 8.

16. King, *Strength To Love,* p. 154; idem, *Stride toward Freedom,* p. 44; Coretta Scott King, *My Life with Martin Luther King, Jr.* (New York: Holt, Rinehart and Winston, 1969), p. 183; NYT, 11 December 1964, p. 33.

17. King, "Quest for Peace and Justice," Nobel Lecture given 11 December 1964 in the Aula of the University, Oslo, Norway, in KCA.

18. King, *Stride toward Freedom,* pp. 116–17.

19. King, "The Role of the Church in Facing the Nation's Chief Moral Dilemma," address to Conference on Christian Faith and Human Relations, 23–25 April 1957, Nashville, Tenn.; idem, "The Church on the Frontier of Racial Tension," address given 19 April 1961 at Southern Baptist Theological Seminary, Louisville, Kentucky, in KCA.

20. King, "Role of the Church."

21. King, "Who Is Their God?" *Nation,* 13 October 1962, p. 210.

22. For the white clergy's statement, see "Letter to Dr. King," reprinted in *New Leader,* 24 June 1963, p. 5; see also "White Clergymen Urge Local Negroes to withdraw from Demonstrations," BN, 13 April 1963, p. 2.

23. King's "Letter from Birmingham City Jail" is widely reprinted—see *New Leader,* 24 June 1963, pp. 3–11; King, *Why We Can't Wait* (New York: Harper, 1963), pp. 77–100. King's sermon entitled "Paul's Letter to American Christians," given 4 November 1956, is in KCA, and is also included in *Strength To Love,* pp. 138–46.

24. "An Appeal to the Conscience of the American People" and the major addresses of the National Conference on Religion and Race are found in Ahmann, ed., *Race.* See also John F. Cronin, "Religion and Race," *Extension* (April 1963), pp. 12, 13, 35; *Ebony* (April 1963), pp. 43, 44, 50. For King's reflections on the conference, see "Segregation and the Church," NYAN, 2 February 1963, p. 8. For an account of how southern white churches faced the question of racial segregation, see the important series of four articles in the NYT by John Wickein: "Churches of South Beset by Segregation Dilemma" (5 July 1959, pp. 1, 40); "Atlanta Leading in Negroes' Gains: City's Clerics Most Moderate in Area of Segregation" (6 July 1959, pp. 1, 14); "Birmingham Resists Church Integration: Citizens' Groups Harass Liberals" (7 July 1959, p. 30); "Catholic Archbishop Backs New Orleans Integration" (8 July 1959, p. 20). See also Samuel Southard, "Are Southern Churches Silent?" *Christian Century,* 20

November 1963, pp. 1429–32; Charles Teel, Jr., "Martin Luther King's Protesting Pastors," *Worldview*, June 1978, pp. 38–43.

25. NYT, 8 June 1963, p. 11.

26. "Boycotts Will Be Used," *U.S. News & World Report,* 24 February 1964, p. 60.

27. King, "Man in a Revolutionary World," in *Minutes* of the Fifth General Synod of the United Church of Christ, Chicago, 1–7 July 1965, p. 244. For an interpretation of King's impact on white churches, see Ardis Whitman, "How the Civil Rights Struggle Challenges Our Churches," *Redbook* (August 1965), pp. 56–57, 131–34, 141; Kyle Haselden, "11 A.M. Sunday Is Our Most Segregated Hour," *NYT Magazine,* 12 August 1964, pp. 9, 25, 27.

28. PC, 31 May 1958, p. 3.

29. King, *Strength To Love,* pp. 62, 63.

30. See King's address "Some Things We Must Do," given 5 December 1957 on the second anniversary of the Montgomery bus boycott; King, *Strength To Love,* pp. 131–32; idem, address given 11 May 1959 to a conference of religious leaders, Washington, D.C., in KCA.

31. King, "Remember Who You Are," sermon given 7 July 1963 at Ebenezer Baptist Church, in KCA.

32. King, *Strength To Love,* p. 63.

33. King, *Playboy* interview (January 1965), p. 67.

34. Ibid.

6. "WHITE MAN'S HEAVEN IS A BLACK MAN'S HELL"

1. Malcolm X, *The Autobiography of Malcolm X,* with Alex Haley (reprint, New York: Ballantine Books, 1973), p. 5.

2. Ibid., pp. 27, 26.

3. Ibid., pp. 6–7.

4. Ibid., pp. 5, 150, 134, 108.

5. *Playboy* interview (May 1963), p. 60; Malcolm X, *Autobiography,* pp. 183, 162, 185; Elijah Muhammad, *The Supreme Wisdom: Solution to the So-called Negroes' Problem* (Chicago: The University of Islam, 1957), p. 33. FBI files 105-8999-3438 (Nation of Islam), transcript of Malcolm's appearance on "City Desk," NBC-TV, Chicago, 17 March 1963.

6. Malcolm X, "God's Angry Men," LAHD, 28 August 1958, FBI files 25–330971 (Nation of Islam). Audiotape of Malcolm X at Temple No. Seven, ND (approximately 1960) author's library; Malcolm X, "We Have Risen from the Dead," PC, 22 December 1956, magazine section, p. 6.

7. *Playboy* interview, p. 54; Malcolm X: FBI Surveillance File, A Microfilm Project by Scholarly Resources, 1978, Wilmington, Delaware, Reel #1.

8. Malcolm X, *Autobiography,* pp. 169–70.

9. Malcolm X, "God's Angry Men," LAHD, 28 March 1958, FBI files 25–330971 (Nation of Islam).

10. *Playboy* interview, p. 60.

11. Malcolm X, *Autobiography,* p. 287.

12. Malcolm's report on the incident is on the video tape entitled "Vintage Malcolm X," Los Angeles, 1962; and the audiotape of "Crisis of Racism," a panel discussion held in New York on 1 May 1962 among Malcolm X, Murray Kempton (moderator), James Farmer, and William Worthy, author's library; for the media report on Malcolm's statement, see LAHD, 17 May 1962, 10 May 1962, New York file 100–8999 (Malcolm X Little); also see FBI files, Reel #1; C. Eric Lincoln, "Extremist Attitudes in the Black Black Muslim Movement," in his *Sounds of the Struggle* (New York: Morrow, 1967), pp. 62–75. Malcolm later expressed regrets for having made the statement. See Alex Haley's "Epilogue" in Malcolm's *Autobiography,* p. 394; NYM, 20 June 1962, p. 22; LAT, 7 June 1962, part 2, p. 1; LAHE, 6 June 1962, section E, p. 1.

13. For Malcolm's account of the Yacob myth, see "Black Man's History," in Malcolm X, *The End of White World Supremacy,* ed. Benjamin Goodman (New York: Merlin House, 1971), pp. 23–66.

14. Malcolm X, "God's Judgment on White America," in *End of White World Supremacy,* p. 125.

15. Ibid., pp. 124, 127, 130.

16. Ibid., pp. 121, 124–25.

17. Ibid., p. 131.

18. Malcolm X, "God's Angry Men," LAHD, 25 July 1957; idem, "Unity Rally" speech given 10 August 1963 in Harlem, New York, audiotape, author's library.

19. Malcolm X, speech given 15 February 1960 at Boston University, audiotape, author's library; NYAN, 24 November 1962, p. 39.

20. Malcolm X, FBI files, Reel #1.

21. PT, 21 July 1962, p. 1; CD, 3 October 1959, p. 12; CM, 14 February 1962, p. 1; LAHD, 6 February 1958; LAHD, 27 February 1958, FBI files, Reel #1; FBI files 25–330971 (Nation of Islam); PC, 12 November 1960, p. 2.

22. Malcolm X, "Mr. Muhammad Speaks," audiotape, n.d. (probably 1960), author's library.

23. Malcolm X, "God's Angry Men," LAHD, 27 March 1958, FBI files 25–330971 (Nation of Islam).

24. Malcolm X, "God's Angry Men," LAHD, 3 October 1957, FBI files 25–330971 (Nation of Islam); idem, *Autobiography,* pp. 241–42; SFE, 8 May 1961.

25. Malcolm X, "Unity Rally"; CM, 16 February 1962, p. 1.

26. Malcolm X's speech given 24 May 1960 at Boston University, audiotape, author's library; Malcolm X, *End of White World Supremacy,* pp. 16, 148; transcript of a show on 30 March 1960, on Radio-WMAC, New York; in the transcript Malcolm discusses "Negro Racism" with William Kunstler and Rev. William James of Metropolitan Methodist Church, FBI files 1–105–8999–1702 (Nation of Islam). "Malcolm X Debates Bayard Rustin," 7 November 1960, audiotape, author's library.

27. Malcolm X, speech given 24 May 1960 at Boston University; DC, 29 January 1963, p. 15.

28. In a study sponsored by the Fund for Theological Education, Charles Shelby Rooks found that forty African-Americans were awarded doctorate

degrees by schools accredited by the Association of Theological Schools (ATS) between the years of 1953–68. Eighteen of the forty — nearly half — were received from Boston University School of Theology. See Rooks, *Revolution in Zion: Reshaping African American Ministry, 1960–1974* (New York: Pilgrim Press, 1990).

29. PT, 2 July 1963, p. 3; NYAN, 20 April 1957, p. 4; Malcolm X, FBI files, Reel #2.

30. Malcolm X, *End of White World Supremacy,* p. 25; *Playboy* interview, p. 62; Malcolm X, FBI files, Reel #1.

31. Malcolm X, FBI files, Reel #1. Malcolm X, "We Are Rising from the Dead Since We Heard Messenger Muhammed Speak," PC, magazine section, 15 December 1956, p. 6.

32. Malcolm X, *End of White World Supremacy,* pp. 71, 25; *Autobiography,* 156.

33. Malcolm X, *Autobiography,* pp. 218, 219.

34. Ibid., pp. 218, 219, 220–21; Malcolm X, FBI files, Reel #1; idem, "God's Angry Men," LAHD, 24 July 1958, Chicago, FBI files 25–20607 (Nation of Islam).

35. Malcolm X, FBI files, Reel #1; idem, "God's Angry Men," LAHD, 27 March 1958.

36. SLA, 30 January 1959, p. 5.

37. Malcolm X, "God's Angry Men," LAHD, 1 August 1957; LAHD, 24 October 1957, FBI files, Reel #1; idem, "The American Negro: Problems and Solutions" (24 March 1961), the first of three speeches given at Harvard, in Archie Epps, ed., *The Speeches of Malcolm X at Harvard,* (New York: Morrow, 1968), p. 116.

38. Malcolm X, "The Black Revolution," speech given June 1963 at the Abyssinian Baptist Church, Harlem, New York, audiotape, author's library (for a printed copy, see Malcolm X, *End of White World Supremacy,* p. 70).

39. Cited in William Worthy, "The Angriest Negroes," *Esquire* (February 1961), p. 104.

40. *Life,* 31 May 1963, p. 30.

41. Malcolm X, "God's Angry Men," LAHD, 27 March 1958; LAHD, 27 April 1957, FBI files 25–330971 (Nation of Islam).

42. FBI files 105–8999–2156 (Nation of Islam).

43. NC, 31 December 1960, p. 10; PC, 10 February 1961, p. 10; NJHN, 17 December 1960, FBI files 105–8999–2095; NJHN 31 December 1960, FBI files 105–8999–2106; NJHN, 7 January 1961, FBI files 105–8999–2123 (Nation of Islam).

44. NC, 31 December 1960, p. 10.

45. FBI files, Reels #1 and #2; transcript of "Focus," radio station MUST, Washington, D.C., aired 12 May 1963; *Playboy* interview, pp. 54, 56.

46. PC, 2 August 1958, p. 7.

47. LAHD, 17 April 1958; LAHD, 3 April 1958; LAHD, 17 April 1958; LAHD, 24 July 1958, FBI files 25–330971 (Nation of Islam); PC, 12 April 1958, p. 8; PC, 16 August 1958, p. 6; PC, 2 August 1958, p. 7; NYAN, 26 April 1958, p. 1; NC, 31 December 1960, p. 10.

48. NYAN, 15 June 1957, p. 25; NYAN, 9 December 1961, p. 9; NYAN, 14 April 1962, p. 18; NYAN, 28 April 1962, p. 30; NYAN, 10 February 1962, p. 19; LAHD, 27 March 1958; NC, 3 February 1962, p. 3; NC, 10 February 1962, p. 9; "American Experience," WNEW-TV, Channel 5, aired 16 June 1963; William James appeared with Malcolm on the WMCA radio program "Pro and Con," moderated by William Kunstler, 3 March 1960, in KCA.

49. PC, 2 August 1958, p. 7; WO, 26 May 1957, FBI files 105–8999–449.

50. Malcolm X, "God's Angry Men," LAHD, 5 December 1957, FBI files 25–330971 (Nation of Islam).

7. "CHICKENS COMING HOME TO ROOST" (1964–65)

1. Malcolm X, video interview, University of California at Berkeley, October 1963, in author's library.

2. "Malcolm X on 'Unity,' " in Louis Lomax, *When the Word Is Given . . .* (New York: Signet Books, 1964), p. 135.

3. Malcolm X, "God's Judgment of White America," in Malcolm X, *The End of White World Supremacy,* ed. Benjamin Goodman (New York: Merlin House, 1971), p. 148.

4. Ibid., pp. 124, 131.

5. Ibid., p. 131.

6. Malcolm X, "The Black Revolution," speech given 8 April 1964 at the Militant Labor Forum, New York, audiotape, author's library (for a printed version see George Breitman, ed., *Malcolm X Speaks* [New York: Grove Press, 1963], p. 46).

7. Malcolm X, *The Autobiography of Malcolm X,* with Alex Haley (reprint, New York: Ballantine Books, 1973), pp. 293–94.

8. Ibid., p. 301.

9. NYT, 2 December 1963, p. 21; Pierre Berton, ed., *Voices from the Sixties* (Garden City, N.Y.: Doubleday, 1967), p. 33.

10. Malcolm X, *Autobiography,* pp. 300–302; PC, 28 December 1963, p. 3; PT, 7 December 1963, p. 5; NYAN 7 December 1963, pp. 1, 2; WP, 5 December 1963, p. 4.

11. Malcolm X, *Autobiography,* pp. 300–302.

12. Ibid.; "Will Scandal Destroy the Black Muslims?" *Sepia* 13, no. 9 (September 1964), p. 67; PT, 10 March, 1964, pp. 1, 2; PT, 22 February 1965, p. 3; PC, 14 December 1963, pp. 1, 4; IR, 27 February, 1965, p. 2; NYP, 5 December 1963, p. 2; see also the account of Louis Farrakhan (Louis X), *The Honorable Louis Farrakhan: A Minister for Progress* (New York: Practice Press, 1985), pp. 10–26.

13. NYT, 8 November 1964, p. 48. See also Malcolm's second speech at Harvard, following his break, 18 March 1964, in Archie Epps, ed., *The Speeches of Malcolm X at Harvard* (New York: Morrow, 1968) p. 140.

14. Malcolm X, *Autobiography,* 289; Lomax, *When the Word,* p. 179. Following Malcolm's break, he identified his accent on political action as the major difference between himself and Muhammad. "The only difference probably is that

the Nation of Islam ... doesn't involve itself in politics in any form. ... But because of its failure to become actively involved in the struggle ..., many persons ... have drifted away from it and are now becoming involved with us in an active effort toward solving the political, social, and economic evils that afflict our people." Transcript of "Dateline Chicago," Channel 5, WMBQ-TV, Chicago, 31 May 1964, "Black Muslims at the Crossroads."

15. Malcolm X, *By Any Means Necessary,* ed. George Breitman (New York: Pathfinder Press, 1970), p. 140.

16. Malcolm X, *Autobiography,* p. 289.

17. Ibid., pp. 288–289, 294.

18. Ibid., p. 295.

19. Ibid., p. 296; Malcolm claimed that Wallace D. Muhammad told him about Elijah's infidelity, but Wallace denies that he told Malcolm and claimed that Malcolm told him. See transcript of "An Interview with Iman Warith D. Muhammad," Gil Noble, "Like It Is," WABC, aired 18 May 1986, pp. 13f.

20. Malcolm X, *Autobiography,* p. 297.

21. Malcolm X, "Black Man's History," lecture given 23 December 1962 at Temple Number Seven, New York, audiotape, author's library (printed version in Malcolm X, *End of White World Supremacy,* p. 51); Malcolm X, *Autobiography,* p. 296.

22. Malcolm X, *Autobiography,* p. 297.

23. Ibid., pp. 297, 298–99.

24. Ibid., p. 299.

25. Berton, ed., *Voices,* p. 34; Lawrence H. Mamiya, "From Black Muslim to Bilalian," *Journal for the Scientific Study of Religion* 21, no. 2 (June 1982), pp. 140f.

26. Malcolm X, *Autobiography,* pp. 309, 305; NYAN, 21 March 1964, p. 50.

27. Ibid., pp. 304, 303.

28. MC, 6 March 1965, pp. 1, 4; Malcolm X, *Autobiography,* pp. 305, 306. See also Malcolm's comments about Muhammad during his appearance on "Kup's Show," WBKB–TV, Chicago, 31 January 1965, FBI files, Reel #2.

29. NYAN, 14 March 1964, p. 1; NYT, 9 March 1964, p. 1; NYHT, 9 March 1964, p. 1; NYT, 10 March 1964, p. 22; NYP, 9 March 1964, p. 4; WP, 9 March 1964, p. 6.

30. For the text of Malcolm X's statement on 12 March 1964, see the *Militant,* 23 March 1964 (also in Breitman, ed., *Malcolm X Speaks,* pp. 20–22). "Why Malcolm X Quit the Black Muslims," *SEPIA,* May 1964, pp. 58–61.

31. Ibid.

32. Ibid.; NYHT, 13 March 1964, p. 19; NYAN, 14 March 1964, p. 1; "Malcolm's Brand X," *Newsweek,* 23 March 1964, p. 32; WP, 9 March 1964, p. 6; Marc Crawford, "The Ominous Malcolm X Exits from the Muslims," *Life,* 20 March 1964, pp. 40–40A.

33. See NYT, 23 March 1964, p. 18; NYP, 23 March 1964, p. 10; NYP, 30 March 1964; NYAN, 28 March 1964, p. 35. A printed copy of the Cleveland version of "The Ballot or the Bullet," given 3 April 1964, is found in Breitman, ed., *Malcolm X Speaks,* pp. 23–44; a recording of the Detroit speech, given 12

April 1964, was released by First Amendment Records; an audiotape of both the Cleveland and Detroit versions of the speech is found at the Schomburg Center Oral History Collection. See also Malcolm's discussion of "the ballot or the bullet" theme on the recording "Malcolm X Speaks Again," Grand Records, 1964.

34. Malcolm X, "Ballot or Bullet," Cleveland and Detroit speeches.

35. Ibid.

36. Ibid.; NYT, 13 March 1964, p. 20; *Militant,* 23 March 1964, p. 6; Breitman, ed., *Malcolm X Speaks,* pp. 22, 31.

37. *Militant,* 23 March 1964, p. 6; NYT, 13 March 1964, p. 20; Breitman, ed., *Malcolm X Speaks,* p. 22; BH, 19 March 1964, p. 12.

38. "Brother Malcolm: His Theme Now Is Violence," *U.S. News & World Report,* 23 March 1964, p. 19; and "Now It's a Negro Drive for Segregation," *U.S. News and World Report,* 30 March 1964, pp. 38–39; CD, 14–20 March 1964, p. 1; NYAN, 14 March 1964, p. 12; NYAN, 28 March 1964, p. 35; NYT, 13 March 1964, p. 20; NYT, 14 March 1964, p. 22; "Malcolm's Brand X," p. 32; NYHT, 13 March 1964, p. 19; FBI, MMI; MC, 25 April 1964, p. 1; NYAN, 28 March 1964, p. 35.

39. Malcolm X, "The African Revolution and Its Impact on the American Negro," speech given 16 December 1964 at the Harvard Law School Forum, audiotape, in Schomburg Center Oral History Collection (also in Archie Epps, ed., *The Speeches of Malcolm X at Harvard* [New York: Morrow, 1968], p. 171); WS, 14 June 1964, p. 1; Breitman, ed., *Malcolm X Speaks,* pp. 197–98.

40. Malcolm X, "Ballot or Bullet," Cleveland and Detroit speeches (see Breitman, ed., *Malcolm X Speaks,* for the Cleveland speech).

41. Ibid.

42. Ibid.

43. Cited in Peter Goldman, *The Death and Life of Malcolm X,* 2d ed. (Urbana: University of Illinois Press, 1979), p. 157.

44. Malcolm X, "Ballot or Bullet," Cleveland and Detroit speeches (see Breitman, ed., *Malcolm X Speaks*).

45. Ibid.

46. Ibid.

47. NYT, 3 April 1964; Malcolm X, "Ballot or Bullet," Detroit.

48. Malcolm X, "Ballot or Bullet," Detroit.

49. NYT, 15 March 1964, p. 46. See also Gertrude Samuels, "Feud within the Black Muslims," *New York Times Magazine,* 22 March 1964, pp. 17, 104–105.

50. NYT, 16 March 1964, p. 1; NYT, 17 March 1964, p. 25; NYT, 22 March 1964, p. 4–E; NG, 21 March 1964, p. 4; DN, 19 March 1964, p. 3–A.

51. NYT, 16 March 1964, p. 1; NYT, 18 March 1964, p. 25; NYT, 24 March 1964, p. 22; NYAN, 28 March 1964, p. 35.

52. "Gloria Richardson: Lady General of Civil Rights," *Ebony* (July 1964), p. 28.

53. AA, 28 March 1964, p. 13. NYHT, 13 March 1964, p. 19; NYHT, 15 March 1964; "Malcolm's Brand X," p. 32.

54. NG, 21 March 1964, p. 4; NYT, 15 March 1964, p. 46; "Gloria Richardson," p. 23.

55. CD, 21–27 March 1964, pp. 1, 2; NYT, 17 April 1964, p. 18; "Gloria Richardson," p. 28. Transcript of Malcolm's appearance on the Joe Rainey Show, Listening Post, radio station WDAS, Philadelphia, 20 March 1964.

56. NYT, 3 April 1964, p. 23.

57. NYT, 7 April 1964, p. 24.

58. NYT, 23 March 1964, p. 18; NYAN, 18 April 1964, p. 2.

59. NYT, 15 March 1964, p. 46; NYAN, 18 April 1964, p. 2.

60. NYT, 15 March 1964, p. 46; NG, 21 March 1964, p. 3.

61. AA, 28 March 1964, p. 13; DN, January 1965, p. 20–E; NYT, 15 March 1964, p. 46.

62. NYT, 15 March 1964, p. 46; Marc Crawford, "The Ominous Malcolm X Exits from the Muslims," *Life*, 20 March 1964, p. 40A; NYAN, 28 March 1964, p. 35.

63. NYT, 15 March 1964, p. 46.

64. Personal interview with Wyatt Tee Walker, 20 July 1988, Atlanta, Ga.

65. Malcolm X, *Autobiography*, pp. 340, 378, 339; Breitman, ed., *Malcolm X Speaks*, p. 59. "The Real Reason Why Malcolm X Went to Africa," SEPIA, October 1964, pp. 142–46.

66. Malcolm X, "Audubon" speech, given 15 February 1965, audiotape, author's library (printed version in Bruce Perry, ed., *Malcolm X: The Last Speeches* [New York: Pathfinder, 1989], p. 116).

67. Breitman, ed., *Malcolm X Speaks*, p. 212. See Malcolm's lecture at the University of Ghana in Ed Smith, *Where To, Black Man?* (New York: Quadrangle Books, 1967), pp. 211–220.

68. Malcolm X, *Autobiography*, pp. 340, 339.

69. DG, 13 May 1964, p. 1; DG, 15 May 1964, p. 7; Malcolm X, interview on 18 January 1965 with Jack Barnes and Barry Sheppard of the Young Socialist Alliance, in Malcolm X, *By Any Means*, p. 158. Hans J. Massaquoi, "Mystery of Malcolm X," *Ebony*, September 1964, pp. 39, 42, 46; "Interview with Malcolm X and Harry Rings of WBAI," 28 January 1965, audiotape in Schomburg Center Oral History Collection; NYAN, 30 May 1964, pp. 1, 32; EG, 25 August 1964; also in John H. Clarke, ed., *Malcolm X: The Man and His Times* (New York: Collier Books, 1969), pp. 302–306.

70. Malcolm X Little: FBI files 105–8999–1–25a, 27 June 1964 (telephone log).

71. NYT, 29 July 1964, p. 40.

72. See Malcolm X, "An Appeal to African Heads of State," address given 17 July 1964, in Breitman, ed., *Malcolm X Speaks*, pp. 72–77.

73. Malcolm X, *By Any Means*, pp. 133–56; videotape and transcript of "Oxford Debate," on Gil Noble, "Like It Is," aired 20 February 1977, author's library; NYT, 7 December 1964, pp. 1, 6; *Manchester Guardian Weekly*, 10 December 1964, p. 6.

74. *Liberator* (January 1965); Malcolm X, "African Revolution and Its Effects on the Afro-American," speech given 12 December 1964 in New York to the

Domestic Peace Corps, in John H. Clarke, ed., *Malcolm X: The Man and His Times* (New York: Collier, 1969), p. 316.

75. "Malcolm Seemed Sincere about Helping Cause: Mrs. King," *Jet*, 11 March 1965, p. 30.

76. Malcolm X, "Selma" speech, given 4 February 1965, audiotape, author's library; "Malcolm Seemed Sincere," p. 30; MC, 13 February 1965, pp. 1, 3; Malcolm X, *By Any Means*, pp. 183–84; *Liberator* (June 1965), p. 12; transcript of "Like It Is," WABC-TV, aired 22 March 1975, pp. 35–38.

77. NYHT, 22 February 1965, p. 3; Coretta Scott King, *My Life with Martin Luther King, Jr.* (New York: Holt, Rinehart and Winston, 1969), p. 256; "Malcolm Seemed Sincere," pp. 28–30; NYT, 5 February 1965, p. 1.

78. J&G, 20 February 1965, p. 2; "Malcolm at the London School of Economics," audiotape in Schomburg Center Oral History Collection; NYT, 10 February 1965, p. 3; NYT, 14 February 1965, p. 24; NYT, 15 February 1965, pp. 1, 21; NYT, 16 February 1965, p. 18; NYT, 17 February 1965, p. 34; Malcolm X, "Last Message," given 14 February 1965, audiotape, author's library (printed under the title "After the Bombing," in Breitman, ed., *Malcolm X Speaks*, pp. 157–77); Malcolm X, "Audubon" speech, given 15 February 1965, and address at Corn Hill Methodist Church, given 16 February 1965, audiotapes, author's library (printed in Perry, ed., *Malcolm X: The Last Speeches*, pp. 111–81); *Columbia Daily Spectator*, 19 February 1965, p. 3; Gordon Parks, "I Was a Zombie," *Life*, 5 March 1965, pp. 28–30; Marlene Nadle, "Malcolm X: The Complexity of a Man in the Jungle," *Village Voice*, 25 February 1965, pp. 1, 6, 9; Theodore Jones, "Malcolm Knew He Was a 'Marked Man,'" NYT, 22 February 1965, pp. 1, 11.

79. Malcolm X, interview with Barnes and Sheppard, in Malcolm X, *By Any Means*, pp. 159–60; ND, 4 June 1964, p. 29.

80. Malcolm X, *Autobiography*, p. 378.

8. "SHATTERED DREAMS" (1965–68)

1. NYT, 21 March 1956, p. 28; 24 December 1956, p. 6.

2. King, "Address at March in Detroit," given 23 June 1963, in KCA.

3. King, "How Long? Not Long!" address given 25 March 1965 at the end of the Selma-to-Montgomery March, steps of the Capitol, Montgomery; idem, "Message Delivered at the Prayer Pilgrimage" (hereafter "Prayer Pilgrimage"), given on 17 May 1957 at the Lincoln Memorial, Washington, D.C., in KCA.

4. King, "To Minister to the Valley," address given 23 February 1968 at the Ministers Leadership Training Program, Miami, in KCA.

5. King, "How Long? Not Long!"

6. King, "Prayer Pilgrimage."

7. King, "How Long? Not Long!"

8. Ibid.

9. NYT, 24 March, 1965, p. 32; NYT, 15 August 1965, p. 73; AC, 13 August 1965, p. 2.

10. Milton Viorst, *Fire in the Streets: America in the 1960's* (New York: Touchstone Book, 1981), pp. 331, 325, 321.

11. King, "Next Stop: The North," *Saturday Review,* 13 November 1965; idem, *Where Do We Go from Here: Chaos or Community?* (Boston: Beacon Press, 1967), p. 112; Viorst, *Fire in the Streets,* p. 321.

12. King, "Two Sides of America," address given 16 March 1968 at the luncheon of the California Democratic Council Convention, in KCA; Rustin is cited in David J. Garrow, *Bearing the Cross: Martin Luther King, Jr., and the Southern Christian Leadership Conference* (New York: William Morrow, 1986), p. 439.

13. Cited in Garrow, *Bearing the Cross,* p. 439.

14. "The Chicago Plan," a seven-page, typewritten press release given by Martin Luther King, Jr., on 7 January 1966; "Chicago Freedom Festival" address, given 12 March 1966, in KCA; NYT, 11 August 1966, p. 23.

15. See especially David J. Garrow, *The FBI and Martin Luther King, Jr.* (New York: Norton, 1981).

16. King, audiotape of an address given 17 February 1968 to a mass meeting in Montgomery during the pre-Washington Campaign, in KCA; idem, *Where Do We Go From Here,* p. 133; cited in Stephen B. Oates, *Let the Trumpet Sound: The Life of Martin Luther King, Jr.* (New York: Mentor Books, 1985 [reprint]), pp. 375–76.

17. King, "President's Address," given 16 August 1967 to the Tenth Anniversary Convention of the SCLC, Atlanta; see also his addresses at staff retreats, 14 November 1966 and 29–31 May 1967, Frogmore, South Carolina, in KCA.

18. King, *Where Do We Go from Here,* p. 167.

19. NYT, 21 June 1966, p. 30; NYT, 22 June 1966, p. 25; NYT, 12 September 1966, p. 49; NYT, 28 June 1966, p. 29; King, "Which Ways Its Soul Shall Go?" address given 2 August 1967 at voter registration rally, Louisville, Kentucky, in KCA; idem, *Where Do We Go From Here,* p. 63; "Showdown for Non-violence," *Look,* 16 April 1968, p. 25.

20. King, "Which Ways Its Soul Shall Go?"

21. NYT, 16 January 1967, p. 22.

22. James R. McGraw, "An Interview with Andrew J. Young," *Christianity and Crisis,* 22 January 1968, p. 326.

23. NG, 25 June 1966, p. 1; King, address to staff retreat, 14 November 1966, in KCA; NYT, 7 July 1966, p. 23.

24. NYT, 6 July 1966, p. 8; NYT, 10 July 1966, sec. 4, p. 1.

25. Garrow, *Bearing the Cross,* p. 707, n.9.

26. NYT, 2 July 1966, p. 24.

27. NYT, 28 June 1966, p. 23. Several headlines in the *New York Times* on Black Power accented the differences among black leaders: "Dr. King Deplores 'Black Power' Bid," 21 June 1966, p. 30; "Dr. King Disputed on 'Black Power,' " 22 June 1966, p. 24; "Rights March Disunity: Campaign in Mississippi Emphasized a New 'Black Consciousness' Force," 28 June 1966, p. 23; "CORE Hears Cries of 'Black Power,' " 2 July 1966, p. 24; "Wilkins Says Black Power Leads Only to Black Death," 6 July 1966, p. 1; "Dr. King Declares Rights Movement Is 'Close' to a Split," 9 July 1966, p. 1; "Black Power: Negro Leaders Split over Policy," 10 July 1966, sec. 4, p. 1; "Dr. King and CORE Chief Act to Heal

Rights Breach," 11 July 1966, p. 1; "Dr. King on the Middle Ground," 17 July 1966, sec. 5, p. 1; "6 Rights Leaders Clash on Tactics in Equality Drive," 22 August 1966, p. 1; "Dr. King Weighing Plan to Repudiate 'Black Power' Bloc," 10 October 1966, p. 1.

28. NYT, 17 July 1966, sec. 4, p. 5; NYT, 1 October 1966, p. 14; NYT, 11 July 1966, p. 1; NYT, 19 August 1967, p. 12; King, *Where Do We Go from Here,* p. 48.

29. NYT, 9 July 1966, p. 8; NYT, 19 August 1967, p. 12; King, address at staff retreat, 14 November 1966, in KCA.

30. *Playboy* interview, p. 77; King, address given 19 March 1968 at rally, Clarksdale, Mississippi, in KCA.

31. King, "Advice for Living," *Ebony* (October 1957), p. 53; idem, "To Minister to the Valley."

32. Viorst, *Fire in the Streets,* p. 372.

33. NYT, 17 October 1966, p. 42; NYT, 10 October 1966, pp. 1, 33; NYT, 26 July 1966, p. 23.

34. *Playboy* interview; King, address given 10 August 1967 to the National Association of Real Estate Brokers, San Francisco, in KCA.

35. King, "Sickness of America," audiotape of address given 16 March 1968 in Los Angeles, in KCA; NYT, 9 July 1966, p. 8; King, "Which Ways Its Soul Shall Go?"; idem, address given 17 January 1968 at staff retreat at Ebenezer Baptist Church, in KCA; idem, "In Search of New Direction," speech delivered 7 February 1968 at the Vermont Avenue Baptist Church, Washington, D.C., in KCA.

36. King, address given 19 March 1968 at pre-Washington Campaign, Laurel, Mississippi, in KCA.

37. "Conversation With Martin Luther King," *Conservative Judaism* (Spring 1968), pp. 8, 9.

38. King, "The Three Dimensions of a Complete Life," a sermon given 9 April 1967 in Chicago, in KCA.

39. Ibid.

40. King, address at staff retreat, 29–31 May 1967, in KCA; the article was in *Ramparts* (January 1967).

41. King, address at staff retreat, 29–31 May 1967, in KCA.

42. King, "Beyond Vietnam," address given 4 April 1967 at Riverside Church, New York City, sponsored by Clergy and Laymen Concerned about Vietnam, in KCA.

43. King's "Drum Major Instinct" is found in James M. Washington, ed., *The Testament of Hope: The Essential Writings of Martin Luther King, Jr.* (San Francisco: Harper & Row, 1986), pp. 259–67; the others are found in KCA.

44. King, "Why I Am Opposed to the War in Vietnam," address given 30 April 1967 at Ebenezer Baptist Church, Atlanta, in KCA.

45. King, "A Testament of Hope," *Playboy* (January 1969), reprint, p. 4; idem, "Why I Am Opposed."

46. David Halberstam, "The Second Coming of Martin Luther King," *Harper's Magazine* (August 1967), p. 49.

47. King, "Who Are We," address given 5 February 1966 at Ebenezer Baptist Church, Atlanta, in KCA.

48. King, "Why I Am Opposed."

49. King, "Standing by the Best in an Evil Time," address given 6 August 1967 at Ebenezer Baptist Church, Atlanta; idem, "To Minister to the Valley."

50. King, "Beyond Vietnam"; idem, address given 22 March 1968 during a pre-Washington Campaign, Albany, Georgia, in KCA; idem, "Which Ways Its Soul Shall Go?" in KCA.

51. King, "Two Sides of America," address given 16 March 1968 at a luncheon of the California Democratic Council Convention, in KCA; idem, "A Christmas Sermon on Peace," in *The Trumpet of Conscience* (New York: Harper, 1967), p. 76.

52. King, "The Other America," address given 10 March 1968 at Local 1199, Hunter College, New York, in KCA.

53. King, "Guidelines for a Constructive Church," sermon given 5 June 1966 at Ebenezer Baptist Church, Atlanta, in KCA.

54. Cited in Adam Fairclough, *To Redeem the Soul of America: The Southern Christian Leadership Conference and Martin Luther King, Jr.* (Athens: University of Georgia Press, 1987), p. 337.

55. King, "Standing by the Best."

9. TWO ROADS TO FREEDOM

1. Transcript of Malcolm X, with Louis Lomax, on Cleveland television station KYW, aired 4 April 1964, FBI, MMI, 100–26888; Malcolm X, address given 28 June 1964 to the Organization of Afro-American Unity Founding Rally, in Malcolm X, *By Any Means Necessary,* ed. George Breitman (New York: Pathfinder Press, 1970), p. 56.

2. Malcolm X, "The Ballot or the Bullet," speech given 12 April 1964, Detroit (a recording of the Detroit speech was released by First Amendment Records; an audiotape of both the Cleveland and Detroit versions of speech is found at the Schomburg Center Oral History Collection); transcript of "Kup's Show," Channel 7, TV, Chicago, aired 23 May 1964, FBI, MMI, 100–41040.

3. MA, 29 March 1956.

4. King, "Our Struggle," *Liberation* (April 1956), p. 5.

5. Cited in Howard Raines, *My Soul Is Rested: The Story of the Civil Rights Movement in the Deep South* (New York: Penguin Books, 1983), pp. 57, 56.

6. Cited in ibid., p. 57.

7. King, "Thou Fool," sermon given 27 August 1967 at Mt. Pisgah Baptist Church, Chicago, in KCA.

8. Alfred Duckett, "Death in the Family: A Memory of Malcolm," *Steppingstones* (Winter 1983), pp. 42, 43, 44.

9. Peter Goldman, "Malcolm X: Witness for the Prosecution," in John Hope Franklin and August Meier, eds., *Black Leaders of the Twentieth Century* (Urbana: University of Illinois Press, 1982), pp. 305–30.

10. Duckett, "Death in the Family," p. 43; Malcolm X, "Last Message,"

given 14 February 1965, audiotape, author's library (published as "After the Bombing," in George Breitman, ed., *Malcolm X Speaks* [New York: Grove Press, 1966], pp. 157–77). Malcolm used the root/tree analogy in his international travels also. He began his lecture in Paris with the statement: "If you hate the roots, you will hate the tree. If you love the roots, you will love the tree also." See Malcolm X, "The Black Struggle in the United States," *Présence Africaine*, second quarter, 1965, p. 8.

11. "Malcolm X on Afro-American History," address given 24 January 1965 at the Audubon, at a meeting of the OAAU, audiotape in the Schomburg Center Oral History Collection; see also *Malcolm X on Afro-American History* (New York: Pathfinder, 1970), p. 16; Malcolm X, "Message to the Grass Roots," in Breitman, ed., *Malcolm X Speaks*, p. 11.

12. Malcolm X, *The Autobiography of Malcolm X*, with Alex Haley (reprint, New York: Ballantine Books, 1973), p. 271.

13. Ibid., p. 272.

14. Ibid., pp. 271, 272.

15. Malcolm X, "Prospects for Freedom," address sponsored by the Militant Labor Forum, held at Palm Gardens in New York (a selection is in Breitman, ed., *Malcolm X Speaks*, pp. 147–56).

16. Malcolm X, *By Any Means*, pp. 91–92, 92.

17. "Malcolm X with Fannie Lou Hamer," interview on 20 December 1964, audiotape, author's library (printed in Breitman, ed., *Malcolm X Speaks*, pp. 103–36).

18. Malcolm X, "An Appeal to African Heads of State," address given 17 July 1964 (printed in Breitman, ed., *Malcolm X Speaks*, p. 75).

19. George Plimpton, "Miami Notebook: Cassius Clay and Malcolm X," *Harper's Magazine* (June 1964), p. 57; Carlos E. Russell, "Exclusive Interview with Brother Malcolm X," *Liberator* (May 1964), p. 12.

20. Transcript of "Andrew Young Remembers Martin Luther King," on "Bill Moyers' Journal," WNET, Channel 13, aired 2 April 1979.

21. Cited in Nat Henthoff, *The New Equality* (New York: Viking, 1964), pp. 47–48.

22. David Halberstam, "The Second Coming of Martin Luther King," *Harper's Magazine* (August 1967), p. 47; King, press conference, 24 February 1965, Los Angeles, in KCA.

23. Cited in Halberstam, "Second Coming of Martin Luther King," pp. 47, 48.

24. King, "Rally Speech," pre-Washington Campaign, Clarksdale, Mississippi, in KCA.

25. Halberstam, "Second Coming of Martin Luther King," pp. 47, 48.

26. WP, 25 July 1966, p. 8–A; NYT, 29 May 1964, p. 10.

27. *Manchester Guardian Weekly*, 10 December 1964.

28. King, telegram to Mrs. Malcolm X, 26 February 1965, in KCA. According to Betty Shabazz, she never received the telegram or any word from Martin King regarding her husband's death.

29. "The Black Scholar Interviews: Alex Haley," *Black Scholar* (September

1976), p. 38; Alex Haley, "Alex Haley Remembers Malcolm," *Essence* (November 1983), p. 122.

30. Carlos Russell, "Exclusive Interview with Brother Malcolm X," p. 12.

31. R. E. Burns, *The Critic* (March–April 1973), p. 72; Lisa C. Jones, "Talking Book: Oral History of a Movement," *Village Voice*, 26 February 1985, p. 20.

32. NYT, 29 July 1964, p. 40.

33. James Baldwin, "Martin and Malcolm," *Esquire* (April 1972), p. 201.

34. Martin Luther King, Jr., *Stride toward Freedom* (New York: Harper & Row, 1958), p. 217.

35. Malcolm X, FBI files, Reel #2; idem, "Ballot or Bullet," Detroit.

36. Malcolm X, address given 5 July 1964 at the Second Rally of the OAAU (printed in Malcolm X, *By Any Means*, p. 84).

37. "Malcolm X with Fannie Lou Hamer"; NYDN, 13 April 1964, p. 6; NYT, 21 December 1964, p. 20; Breitman, ed., *Malcolm X Speaks*, p. 106; A. Philip Randolph's letter to Martin King, 7 April 1964, in KCA.

38. Kenneth Clark, "The New Negro in the North," in M. H. Ahmann, ed., *The New Negro* (Notre Dame, Ind.: Fides Publishers, 1961), pp. 36–37.

39. Ibid., p. 37.

40. Kenneth B. Clark, *King, Malcolm, Baldwin: Three Interviews*, rev. ed. (Middletown, Conn.: Wesleyan University Press, 1985), p. 61.

41. Ibid., pp. 59–60.

42. WS, 13 May 1963, section B, p. 1.

43. NYT, 5 June 1963, p. 29; NYT, 25 June 1963, p. 13; Clark, *King, Malcolm, Baldwin*, pp. 26–27.

44. NYT, 23 April 1963, p. 20.

45. NYT, 19 May 1963, p. 10E.

46. NYT, 15 May 1963, p. 26.

47. NYT, 6 May 1963, p. 59.

48. Julius Lester, "The Angry Children of Malcolm X," in A. Meier, E. Rudwick, and F. L. Broderick, eds., *Black Protest Thought in the Twentieth Century*, 2d ed., (Indianapolis: Bobbs-Merrill, 1980), pp. 469–84.

49. Malcolm X, "Unity Rally" speech, given 10 August 1963 in Harlem, New York, audiotape, author's library.

50. King, *Playboy* interview (January 1965), p. 73.

51. See the telegram Malcolm sent to Martin in St. Augustine, Florida, 30 June 1964, in KCA.

52. Clark, *King, Malcolm, Baldwin*, pp. 12–13.

53. Malcolm X, *Autobiography*, pp. 374–75.

54. David Halberstam, "Second Coming of Martin Luther King," p. 51; see also "Andrew Young Remembers Martin Luther King" and King's comments about his "personal respect" for Malcolm despite their philosophical differences, in his federal court testimony at the Selma trial, "Transcript of Testimony," in William v. Wallace, pp. 74–75, in KCA.

55. FBI, MMI; James Farmer, *Freedom—When?* (New York: Random House, 1965), p. 96; Wyatt Tee Walker, "Nothing but a Man," *Negro Digest* (August 1965), pp. 30–31.

56. Cited in Peter Goldman, *The Death and Life of Malcolm X,* 2d ed. (Urbana: University of Illinois Press, 1979), p. 232.

57. Malcolm X, "Homecoming" speech, given 29 November 1964, in Malcolm X, *By Any Means,* p. 140.

58. King, speech at staff retreat, 14 November 1966, in KCA.

59. Ibid.

10. NOTHING BUT MEN

1. L. D. Reddick, *Crusader without Violence: A Biography of Martin Luther King, Jr.* (New York: Harper, 1959), p. 5; Coretta Scott King, *My Life with Martin Luther King, Jr.* (New York: Holt, Rinehart and Winston, 1969), pp. 60, 91.

2. Malcolm X, *The Autobiography of Malcolm X,* with Alex Haley (reprint, New York: Ballantine Books, 1973), p. 226.

3. Ibid., pp. 226, 225.

4. Malcolm X: FBI Surveillance File, A Microfilm Project by Scholarly Resources, 1978, Wilmington, Delaware, Reel #1.

5. Ibid.

6. Ralph D. Abernathy, *And the Walls Came Tumbling Down* (New York: Harper & Row, 1989), pp. 434f.

7. Daniel P. Moynihan, *The Negro Family: The Case for National Action* (Washington, D.C.: U.S. Government Printing Office, 1965).

8. King, speech given in March 1966 during European Tour; transcript of interview on "Face the Nation," 29 August 1965, in KCA.

9. "Rev. M. L. King's Diary in Jail," *Jet,* 23 August 1962, p. 14; June Jordan, "How Shall We Know His Name?" *Christianity and Crisis,* 18 May 1987, p. 193; Jo Ann Gibson Robinson, *The Montgomery Bus Boycott and the Women Who Started It,* ed. David J. Garrow (Knoxville: University of Tennessee Press, 1987). See also the important essay by Mary Fair Burks, "Trailblazers: Women in the Montgomery Bus Boycott," in Vicki Crawford, et al., eds., *Women in the Civil Rights Movement: Trailblazers and Torchbearers, 1941–1965* (Brooklyn: Carlson Publishing, 1990), pp. 71–83.

10. Howard Raines, *My Soul Is Rested: The Story of the Civil Rights Movement in the Deep South* (New York: Penguin Books, 1983), pp. 432, 433. For an introduction to the role of women in the Civil Rights Movement and additional primary and secondary references, see Vicki Crawford, et al., *Women in the Civil Rights Movement* and Paula Giddings, *When and Where I Enter: The Import of Black Women on Race and Sex in America* (New York: William Morrow, 1984).

11. Malcolm X, "Paris Interview," November 1964, in Malcolm X, *By Any Means Necessary,* ed. George Breitman (New York: Pathfinder Press, 1970), p. 179.

12. Malcolm X, "At the Audubon," address given 20 December 1964, in George Breitman, ed., *Malcolm X Speaks* (New York: Grove Press, 1965), p. 135. Malik Shabazz (Malcolm X), "Roots and Islam in Slave America," reprinted by the Muslim Students' Association, Indiana University, Blooming-

ton, Indiana; Betty Shabazz, "The Legacy of My Husband Malcolm X," *Ebony*, June 1969, pp. 172–82.

13. See Maya Angelou, *All God's Children Need Traveling Shoes* (New York: Random House, 1986), pp. 193f.; Earl Grant, "The Last Days of Malcolm X," in John H. Clarke, *Malcolm X: The Man and His Times* (New York: Collier Books, 1969), p. 90; Peter Goldman, *The Death and Life of Malcolm X,* 2d ed. (Urbana: University of Illinois Press, 1979), p. 245.

14. Raines, *My Soul Is Rested,* p. 433. See also Betty Shabazz, "Malcolm X as Husband and Father," in John H. Clarke, *Malcolm X*, pp. 132–43.

15. *Jet*, 3 September 1964, p. 30.

16. King, *Strength To Love* (1963; reprint, Philadelphia: Fortress, 1981), pp. 96, 97, 98; see also King's letter of 1 May 1964 to Rev. Charles R. Ehrhardt of Phoenix, Arizona, who was "concerned about the question of Communist infiltration in the civil rights movement," in KCA.

17. NG, 21 March 1964, p. 4.

18. Malcolm X, *By Any Means*, p. 20.

19. Breitman, ed., *Malcolm X Speaks*, pp. 68–69; Malcolm gave the same analogy on several occasions, see *By Any Means*, p. 116.

20. Malcolm X, "Young Socialist Interview," in *By Any Means*, pp. 165–66.

21. Leslie Alexander Lacy, "African Responses to Malcolm X," in LeRoi Jones and Larry Neal, eds., *Black Fire* (New York: William Morrow, 1968), p. 31.

22. Breitman, ed., *Malcolm X Speaks*, p. 69.

23. Malcolm X, *By Any Means*, p. 181.

24. Malcolm X, *By Any Means*, pp. 13, 7; transcript of "Kup's Show," Channel 7, TV, Chicago, aired 23 May 1964; Breitman, ed., *Malcolm X Speaks*, p. 136.

25. King, *Stride toward Freedom*, p. 92; idem, *Strength To Love*, p. 100; idem, address to staff at retreat, 14 November 1966, in KCA.

26. King, "Showdown for Nonviolence," *Look*, 16 April 1968, p. 25; idem, Gandhi Memorial Lecture, delivered 6 November 1966 at Howard University, Washington, D.C.; idem, address at staff retreat, 14 November 1966, in KCA.

11. MAKING THEIR MARK: LEGACIES

1. WP, 27 August 1983, pp. A11, A14.

2. Kenneth B. Clark, *King, Malcolm, Baldwin: Three Interviews*, rev. ed. (Middletown, Conn.: Wesleyan University Press, 1985), p. 59.

3. Malcolm X, "Last Message," given 14 February 1965, audiotape, author's library (printed under the title "After the Bombing," in George Breitman, ed., *Malcolm X Speaks* [New York: Grove Press, 1966], p. 169).

4. Malcolm X, "God's Angry Men," WO, 31 May 1958 (FBI files 105–8999-788). Regarding Malcolm's cultural legacy, see M. Ron Karenga, "The Socio-Political Philosophy of Malcolm X," *Western Journal of Black Studies*, Winter 1976, pp. 251–62.

5. Maya Angelou, *All God's Children Need Traveling Shoes* (New York: Random House, 1986), p. 136.

6. DN, 7 March 1965, p. 2–F.

7. Marlene Nadle, "Burying Malcolm X," *Village Voice,* 4 March 1965, p. 10.

8. King, "Some Things We Must Do," address given April 1967 in Cleveland, audiotape, author's library; see also idem, "The Three Dimensions of a Complete Life," a sermon given 9 April 1967 in Chicago, in KCA.

9. Coretta Scott King, *My Life with Martin Luther King, Jr.* (New York: Holt, Rinehart and Winston, 1969), p. 294.

10. CDS, 19 February 1965, p. 3.

11. Cited in David Halberstam, "The Second Coming of Martin Luther King," *Harper's Magazine* (August 1967), p. 47.

12. Gordon Parks, *To Smile in Autumn: A Memoir* (New York: Norton, 1979), p. 144.

13. King, "Standing by the Best in an Evil Time," address given 6 August 1967 at Ebenezer Baptist Church, Atlanta.

14. *Militant,* 19 April 1965, p. 2.

15. Malcolm X, "Message to the Grass Roots," in Breitman, ed., *Malcolm X Speaks,* p. 8.

16. Malcolm X, *By Any Means Necessary,* ed. George Breitman (New York: Pathfinder Press, 1970), pp. 160–61; Malcolm X, *The Autobiography of Malcolm X,* with Alex Haley (reprint, New York: Ballantine Books, 1973), p. 284.

17. Malcolm X, speech given 29 May 1964 at the Militant Labor Forum, New York, in *By Any Means,* p. 178.

18. Malcolm X, *Autobiography,* pp. 379–80.

19. CD, 28 November 1962, p. 8.

20. Howard Raines, *My Soul Is Rested: The Story of the Civil Rights Movement in the Deep South* (New York: Penguin Books, 1983), p. 426; August Meier, "On the Role of Martin Luther King," *New Politics* 4 (Winter 1965), p. 53.

21. Raines, *My Soul Is Rested,* pp. 425–26.

22. Jean Stein with George Plimpton, *American Journey: The Times of Robert Kennedy* (New York: Harcourt Brace Jovanovich, 1970), p. 108.

23. Malcolm X, "Declaration of Independence," in Breitman, ed., *Malcolm X Speaks,* p. 20 (emphasis added); interview with Bernice Bass, 27 December 1964, audiotape, author's library (printed version in Bruce Perry, ed., *Malcolm X: The Last Speeches* [New York: Pathfinder, 1989], p. 95); Harvard University speech, delivered 16 December 1964, author's library (printed version in Archie Epps, ed., *The Speeches of Malcolm X at Harvard* [New York: Morrow, 1968], p. 161).

24. NYT, 4 October 1964, p. 59.

25. Malcolm X, *Autobiography,* pp. 394, 376, 377; Gordon Parks, "I Was a Zombie," *Life,* 5 March 1965, p. 29.

26. King, "Transforming a Neighborhood into a Brotherhood," address given 11 August 1967 to the National Association of Television and Radio Announcers, Atlanta; idem, "Unfulfilled Dreams," sermon given 3 March 1968 at Ebenezer Baptist Church, Atlanta, in KCA.

27. Malcolm X, speech given 20 December 1964 with Fannie Lou Hamer, in Breitman, ed., *Malcolm X Speaks,* p. 113.

28. Malcolm X, *Autobiography,* p. 366.

29. Malcolm X, "Homecoming" speech, given 29 November 1964, in *By Any Means,* p. 141.

30. Malcolm X, "The African Revolution and Its Impact on the American Negro," speech given 16 December 1964 at the Harvard Law School Forum, audiotape, in Schomburg Center Oral History Collection (also in Archie Epps, ed., *The Speeches of Malcolm X at Harvard* [New York: Morrow, 1968], p. 170); Malcolm X, speech given 7 November 1963 at CCNY, audiotape, author's library; Malcolm X, speech given 24 May 1960 at Boston University, audiotape, author's library.

31. "Crisis of Racism," a panel discussion held in New York on 1 May 1962 among Malcolm X, Murray Kempton (moderator), James Farmer, and William Worthy, audiotape, author's library; Malcolm X, speech given 24 May 1960 at Boston University, audiotape, author's library.

32. Malcolm X, speech given 20 December 1964 with Fannie Lou Hamer, in Breitman, ed., *Malcolm X Speaks,* pp. 107–8.

33. Cited in Peter Goldman, "Malcolm X: Witness for the Prosecution," in John Hope Franklin and August Meier, eds., *Black Leaders of the Twentieth Century* (Urbana: University of Illinois Press, 1982), p. 315. Malcolm made the same point in a speech at the Uline Arena, Washington, D.C., 25 June 1961, Muhammad's Mosque No. Four: "They say he [Mr. Muhammad] deals with the emotions of the people. No! When you tell a man that he is JIM-CROWED, you don't deal with his emotions. You tell him the truth. What you talking about? Hold it! You tell a black man that his neck is being broken on the tree day in and out, that he is segregated, JIM-CROWED, spit on, deprived of civil rights and equal rights, deprived of first-class citizenship—that's not playing on a man's emotions. That's playing on a man's intelligence." FBI files 105-89999-2467 (Nation of Islam).

34. "Malcolm X Talks to Young People," speech given 31 December 1964 in New York, audiotape, author's library (printed version in Breitman, ed., *Malcolm X Speaks,* p. 144).

35. Cited in Adam Fairclough, *To Redeem the Soul of America: The Southern Christian Leadership Conference and Martin Luther King, Jr.* (Athens: University of Georgia Press, 1987), p. 119.

36. King, "Drum Major Instinct," in James M. Washington, ed., *The Testament of Hope: The Essential Writings of Martin Luther King, Jr.* (San Francisco: Harper & Row, 1986).

37. Cited in Peter Goldman, *The Death and Life of Malcolm X,* 2d ed. (Urbana: University of Illinois Press, 1979), pp. 24–25.

38. King, address given 3 May 1963 at Sixteenth Baptist Church, Birmingham, Alabama, audiotape, author's library (printed text in Charles V. Hamilton, ed., *The Black Experience in American Politics* [New York: Capricorn Books, 1973], pp. 160–64).

39. Charles E. Fager, *Selma, 1965* (New York: Charles Scribner's Sons, 1974), pp. 45–46; Taylor Branch, *Parting the Waters: America in the King Years, 1954–63* (New York: Simon and Schuster, 1988), p. 802.

40. Branch, *Parting the Waters,* p. 751; MA, 25 January 1956, p. 1; "Negroes Laughing," *Time,* 6 February 1956, p. 21.

41. King, *Stride toward Freedom* (New York: Harper & Row, 1958), p. 187.

42. Malcolm X, *Malcolm X on Afro-American History* (New York: Pathfinder Press, 1970), p. 17; Malcolm X, "Unity Rally" speech, given 10 August 1963 in Harlem, New York, audiotape, author's library.

43. MA, 15 February 1956, p. 1.

44. For an important discussion of King's linkage with Africa, see *King's Legacy: Unfinished Business,* the entire edition of *African Commentary* (March 1990); note especially the "cover story," by Lewis V. Baldwin, "Toward the Dawn of Freedom: Martin Luther King, Jr.'s Vision of an Independent Africa," pp. 6–8.

45. Malcolm X, FBI files, Reel #1.

46. PC, 1 October 1960, p. 3.

47. Malcolm X, "Separation or Integration," speech given 7 March 1962, in James L. Golden and Richard D. Rieke, eds., *The Rhetoric of Black Americans* (Columbus, Ohio: Charles Merrill, 1971), p. 431.

48. *Militant,* 10 June 1964, p. 3.

49. Malcolm X, *By Any Means,* pp. 145, 153.

50. Malcolm X, question and answer period following "African Revolution and Its Effects on the Afro-American," speech given 12 December 1964 in New York to the Domestic Peace Corps (the speech is in John H. Clarke, ed., *Malcolm X: The Man and His Times* [New York: Collier, 1969], pp. 307–20); Breitman, ed., *Malcolm X Speaks,* p. 218.

51. Malcolm X, *By Any Means,* p. 161; CDS, 19 February 1965, p. 3; Breitman, ed., *Malcolm X Speaks,* p. 125.

Index